With Charity
for All

With Charity for All

Lincoln and the Restoration of the Union

WILLIAM C. HARRIS

THE UNIVERSITY PRESS OF KENTUCKY

Publication of this volume was made possible in part
by a grant from the National Endowment for the Humanities.

Scholarly publisher for the Commonwealth,
serving Bellarmine College, Berea College, Centre
College of Kentucky, Eastern Kentucky University,
The Filson Club Historical Society, Georgetown College,
Kentucky Historical Society, Kentucky State University,
Morehead State University, Murray State University,
Northern Kentucky University, Transylvania University,
University of Kentucky, University of Louisville,
and Western Kentucky University.

Editorial and Sales Offices: The University Press of Kentucky
663 South Limestone Street, Lexington, Kentucky 40508-4008

01 00 99 98 97   5 4 3 2 1

Frontispiece: Abraham Lincoln, photographed by Alexander Gardner
four weeks before Lincoln issued his Proclamation of Amnesty and
Reconstruction (courtesy of the Lincoln Museum, Fort Wayne, Ind.).

Library of Congress Cataloging-in-Publication Data

Harris, William C. (William Charles), 1933-
    With charity for all : Lincoln and the restoration of the Union /
William C. Harris.
        p.   cm.
    Includes bibliographical references and index.
    ISBN 0-8131-2007-1 (cloth : alk. paper); ISBN 0-8131-0971-x (paper: alk. paper)
    1. Reconstruction.   2. Lincoln, Abraham, 1809-1865.   3. United
States—Politics and government—1861-1865.   I. Title.
E668.H37   1997
973.7'092—dc20   96-35903

To Thomas B. Alexander,
mentor, friend, and scholar

Contents

Illustrations

Acknowledgments

Many people have contributed to the preparation of this book. I owe a special debt to Ann Baker Ward and her staff of the Interlibrary Loan section, D.H. Hill Library, North Carolina State University, for their persistence in obtaining source materials for me. A number of librarians, archivists, and curators of manuscript collections have also assisted in the research. I am thankful for the aid of William H. Richter of the Eugene C. Barker Texas History Center, Christie L. Chappell of the Department of Rare Books and Special Collections, University of Rochester Library, Harold M. Forbes of the West Virginia Regional History Collection, West Virginia University, Louise T. Jones of the Historical Society of Pennsylvania, Mary F. Bell of the Buffalo and Erie County Historical Society, Theresa Hambrick of the Tennessee State Library and Archives, Michael P. Musick of the Military Reference Branch, National Archives, John H. Ferguson of the Arkansas History Commission, Minor Weisiger and Jane Pairo of the Virginia State Library and Archives, and Hilary Shore of the Department of Special Collections and University Archives, the Stanford University Libraries. In addition, the staffs of the Manuscript Division, Library of Congress, the North Carolina Division of Archives and History, the Southern Historical Collection, University of North Carolina Library, the Perkins Library, Duke University, the University of Tennessee Library, and the Norfolk Public Library have provided valuable assistance.

Several historians and friends have provided insights on Lincoln and wartime reconstruction and have read parts or all of the manuscript. I am especially grateful to my colleagues John David Smith and Alexander J. De Grand of North Carolina State University for reading the entire manuscript and suggesting important improvements in it. Professor Smith also provided other valuable assistance in preparation of the book. In addition, David Zonderman, another colleague, read parts of the manuscript and made useful suggestions. In the beginning of the study, Mark E. Neely Jr., in a long letter, shared his thoughts about Lincoln and northern views of southern loyalty during the Civil War. Joe A. Mobley, editor and administrator of the Historical Publications Section, North Carolina Division of Archives and History, has generously extended advice and assistance in the completion of this work. Joe specifically identified or contacted several libraries regarding photographs for the book. As a result of Joe's assistance, David Ware of the West Virginia and Regional History Collection, West Virginia University, Michael J. Winey of the U.S. Army Military History Institute, Carlisle Barracks, Virginia R. Smith of the State Library of Louisiana, and Lynn Ewbank of the Arkansas History Commission supplied photographs. Joe himself sent me two prints from his own office files. James E. Eber of the Lincoln Museum, Fort Wayne, provided the fine photograph of Lincoln made by Alexander Gardner in November 1863. I am grateful for the assistance of all of these professionals.

I am indebted to North Carolina State University for research support and a semester's leave to pursue this study. Former Dean William B. Toole gave encouragement not only for my scholarly efforts but also to those of other faculty members in the humanities at N.C. State University. Graduate assistants Lee Bumgarner, Craig McConnell, Kelly Lawton, Deborah Blackwell, Steve Lisk, Gary Gilbody, and Joanna Grant, at different times, aided in the research for this book. My daughter Sehoya drew the draft of the map. I am enormously grateful to June Bowles and Norene Miller for typing the manuscript. Mrs. Miller typed most of it, as well as the revisions, and performed numerous other tasks associated with the study. When I was department chair, Janice Mitchell, my administrative secretary, relieved me of many chores while I worked on the book.

As always, my wife, Betty, provided encouragement and assistance in the study. Finally, I want to express my deep appreciation to Thomas B. Alexander, who more than three decades ago pointed me in the direction of Civil War–Reconstruction history and patiently worked with me as I stumbled to become a historian. Professor Alexander continues to be a source of inspiration to me.

Introduction

Reconstruction usually is associated with the period after the Civil War. Actually it began in 1861, when Abraham Lincoln, in his inaugural address, announced his intention to preserve the Union and, by implication, to restore the seceded states to the Union. The reconstruction of these states—or, as he preferred, restoration—was his duty under the Constitution by virtue of his elevation to the presidency. Lincoln never recognized the secession of the Southern states or the legitimacy of the Confederate States government. He reasoned that individuals, not states, had rebelled and thereby had overturned republican forms of government in the South. Lincoln believed that it was the supreme constitutional responsibility of the president as commander-in-chief of American military forces to suppress the rebellion and restore legitimate, loyal governments in the Southern states.

Lincoln never wavered from this theory. In his mind, the states were indestructible and their prewar constitutions and laws remained unchanged unless amended or replaced through the normal state processes. His aim, he insisted, was to return the Southern states to their "proper practical relation with the Union." Even Lincoln's emancipation policy, which emerged in 1862 and 1863 and eventually became an essential part of his reconstruction plan, was designed to win the war and achieve the overarching purpose of restoring the Union. Clearly Lincoln opposed slavery for moral and humane reasons, but these concerns were secondary and not primary in his justification for the Emancipation Proclamation. He justified his actions against slavery on the constitutional ground of military necessity to suppress the Southern rebellion.

Most historians usually have ignored or given short shrift to political efforts during the war to restore the Southern states to the Union. General accounts of the Civil War era mention Lincoln's 1863 Proclamation of Amnesty and Reconstruction outlining his Ten Percent Plan for Southern restoration, but they conclude that his effort was premature and of no lasting significance. Eric Foner, in his *Reconstruction: America's Unfinished Revolution, 1863-1877* (1988), advances the interpretation that "rather than as a design for a reconstructed South," Lincoln's Ten Percent Plan "might better be viewed as a device to shorten the war and solidify white support for emancipation." David Donald, in his recent magisterial biography of Lincoln, agrees with Foner when he writes that the president in developing his reconstruction policy "was thinking less of the status of the South after the war than of means to stop the fighting."[1] My contention is that Lincoln, though anxious to use any means to shorten the conflict and, after January 1, 1863, to undermine slavery, did not think of reconstruction policy primarily as an instrument for winning the war or securing white support for black freedom. For Lincoln, wartime reconstruction was designed to initiate the restoration of civil self-government in the South, a process that had a high and immediate priority for him, though it need not be completed until after the war. Lincoln believed that once the local governments were firmly in power only a minimum exercise of federal authority would be required to protect them. According to the president, the pace of reconstruction would vary with the military and political circumstances in each state; he did not believe that a rigid rule should or could be applied for the South as a whole, a point that Lincoln made both in his Proclamation of Amnesty and Reconstruction and in his April 11, 1865, address on reconstruction, delivered three days before his assassination.

A few scholars have undertaken specific studies of wartime reconstruction, or some aspect of it. In 1960 William B. Hesseltine wrote a brief treatment of the subject. Entitled *Lincoln's Plan of Reconstruction,* this book, originally prepared as a series of lectures, argues that Lincoln's purpose in the war was to reorder the Southern political structure and reshape the country, destroying the Union of state's rights and creating a real nation. Hesseltine concludes that Lincoln failed in his reconstruction plan for the South but succeeded in the reconstruction of the nation. In winning the war "he had destroyed the rights and powers of the states and had concentrated power in the hands of the national government."[2] Later historians have rejected—correctly, I believe—any such Bismarkian or centralizing designs on Lincoln's part.

Writing a few years after Hesseltine, Kenneth M. Stampp found a narrower political purpose in Lincoln's reconstruction plan. According to Stampp in *The Era of Reconstruction, 1865-1877,* Lincoln adopted a lenient policy toward the South for the purpose of bringing prewar Southern

Whigs into a national conservative coalition with the Republican party, one that would dominate the nation's politics after the war. Lincoln, Stampp suggests, understood that a stringent policy requiring extensive federal intervention in the South, as the Radicals of his party desired, would alienate antebellum Whigs and, to the detriment of the Republican party, continue political divisions along sectional lines.[3] I have found no evidence that Lincoln approached reconstruction with any such partisan intent. Consumed by the war and a determination to restore as soon as possible the South to the Union, Lincoln ignored past political affiliations in seeking loyal support for his efforts. His thoughts did not extend to postwar political-party building in the South. Though historians have demonstrated that former Whigs were more likely to support the Union than former Democrats, Lincoln had good cause to ignore prewar political alignments. After all, some of the South's leading Unionists and supporters of his administration were old Democrats like Andrew Johnson of Tennessee, Michael Hahn of Louisiana, and Andrew Jackson Hamilton of Texas. These former Democrats, as well as other Southern Unionists who had followed the political standard of Andrew Jackson before the war, could not be expected to aid in the restoration of a conservative Whig party as Stampp suggests in his study.

Other historians in writing about wartime reconstruction have reflected the intense interest in race relations and civil rights among late-twentieth-century scholars. Herman Belz, Hans L. Trefousse, Michael Les Benedict, Peyton McCrary, and LaWanda Cox maintain that Lincoln, after a conservative start in his Southern policy, moved toward a radical position, making black rights an integral part of his reconstruction plan. By the end of the war, Lincoln and the Republican majority in Congress were close to agreement on black suffrage as a requirement for Southern restoration to the Union.[4] These historians focus on different aspects of wartime reconstruction: Belz on congressional action and constitutional theory; Trefousse on Radical Republicans in Congress and their relationship with Lincoln; Benedict on congressional Republicans during and after the war; and McCrary and Cox on Louisiana and the struggle to insure black freedom and rights in that state. Some historians have suggested that after 1862 a partnership in revolution developed between Lincoln and congressional Radicals. The purpose of this alliance, they claim, was "to overturn the Southern social order as a means of reconstructing the Union."[5] Harold M. Hyman contends that by the end of the war Lincoln had advanced to "Radical heights" when, on April 11, 1865, he announced publicly his support for black suffrage, making it a "firm, open policy for Louisiana" and "for all the crumpled Confederate states."[6]

I challenge the view of these historians that late in the war Lincoln changed his reconstruction policy to accommodate to the Radicals' demand for black suffrage and for other revolutionary changes in Southern society. It is my contention that Lincoln did not desire to use the war or reconstruction policy "to overturn the Southern social order." Rather, he sought to restore the South as it existed before the conflict, shorn, however, of the spirit of disunion and the institution of slavery that, as he said, "somehow [was] the cause of the war."[7] These objectives, Lincoln believed, could be achieved without a significant change in the Southern states' constitutional and political structures.

Though concerned for blacks in freedom, Lincoln pursued a nonintervention policy regarding African-American rights in the reorganized states. He assumed that once Southern Unionists had gained firm control they would extend fundamental rights to blacks, perhaps along the lines of those in his home state of Illinois. However, this does not mean that had Lincoln survived the war to face the hard postwar realities of sustaining black freedom he would have sat idly by while returning Confederates, in league with conservative Unionists, advanced black codes with the object of maintaining a form of slavery. Lincoln, still without the use of direct federal power, probably would have pressed his loyal governments to reject such discriminatory laws and provide at least basic rights for blacks.

This book thus fills a void in Lincoln and Civil War–Reconstruction historiography. It provides the first comprehensive account of Lincoln's effort to restore the seceded states to the Union, focusing both on Lincoln and on Southern white Unionists and military officers who implemented his policies in the South. The course of the war, emancipation, and local and national political developments greatly influenced the history of wartime reconstruction, producing, as Lincoln understood, complications that varied by states and regions within states. Lincoln's theory that the states had never really left the Union and needed only to be restored to loyal control further complicated reconstruction, creating serious obstacles to the implementation of a uniform policy for the South. Though he developed general policies for restoring the South—first with the appointment of military governors in 1862 and later, in 1863, with his Ten Percent Plan—Lincoln viewed the pace of civil restoration and its substance as a matter for Southern white Unionists to determine based on the particular circumstances in their states.[8] Because of Lincoln's commitment to self-reconstruction controlled by local Unionists and subject only to a minimum of federal oversight, a state-by-state study provides the best method for understanding the history of reconstruction during the war and the direction that it might have taken had Lincoln survived John Wilkes Booth's bullet. This book offers a window on reconstruction at the grassroots level while the armed struggle over secession raged. Though I disagree with some of the findings and interpretations of Professors Stampp, Belz, Cox, McCrary, and others, my study is in no way an attack upon their fine scholarship. My goal is to build upon their important work and to expand our knowledge of wartime reconstruction and Lincoln's role in it.

First, an explanation regarding terms is in order. The word *reconstruction* typically was a misnomer when used during the Civil War. It usually meant the restoration of relations between the secessionist states and the federal government, not a reconstruction of society and government, as the term suggests today. Reconstruction, according to this definition, included the reorganization of state and local governments by Southern white Unionists largely along prewar lines and the acceptance of Southern senators and representatives by Congress. Though Northerners disagreed on what guarantees of future loyalty should be required of the South, most expected few changes in the fundamental laws of the states or the political rights of rank-and-file Confederates. As the war progressed, an important exception to Northern expectations regarding reconstruction, particularly among Lincoln and Republicans, was the abolition of slavery in the Southern states. Lincoln, nonetheless, intended the word *reconstruction* to mean political restoration, not the revamping of Southern governmental structures or the placing of "the bottom rail on top."

The words *radical, moderate,* and *conservative* in referring to individuals and factions in the reconstruction drama do not lend themselves to easy and consistent definitions. Contemporaries did not usually apply the word *moderate* to a Northern political faction, as historians have done. On occasion, I have found it appropriate to use the term, particularly when referring to individuals like Republican Henry J. Raymond of the *New York Times* who defy labeling as conservative or radical. Northern Radicals, on the other hand, belonged to a specific faction in the Republican party that, particularly as the war progressed, saw the need for a more thorough reconstruction program than Lincoln advocated. They supported policies that most contemporaries and later historians have considered radical for the period. Though not always consistent, Northern Radicals, whose leading spokesmen in Congress were Benjamin F. Wade, Charles Sumner, and Henry Winter Davis, advocated strong federal action to end slavery, a vigorous prosecution of the war, the confiscation of rebel property, and the political proscription of insurgent leaders. They were vague as to whether rank-and-file insurgents should lose their property and also what disposition should be made of confiscated estates. Many congressional Radicals preferred that confiscated property should be sold by the government to pay for the war; others thought that it should be distributed to blacks and white Unionists. By the end of the war, Radicals favored a reconstruction policy that also included black political and civil equality as a protection for freedom and loyalty in the South. Lincoln's rejection of a stringent Southern policy, dictated from Washington, caused Radicals to seek congressional control of reconstruction.

Radicals, a vocal minority in Congress and in the North, were not of one mind on what reconstruction theory should be applied to the South. Some of them asserted that the states had committed state suicide when they seceded. As early as 1862, these Radicals wanted Congress to return the rebel states to a territorial status, preparatory to the framing of new constitutions that would meet congressional requirements before they could be restored to the Union. Others preferred to act under the clause in the U.S. Constitution guaranteeing to each state a republican form of government. Such an approach retained the theory, shared with Lincoln and conservatives, that the states had never actually left the Union. Contrary to Lincoln's position, however, Radicals believed that the Constitution gave authority to Congress, not the president, to determine what constituted a republican form of government and the extent to which federal intervention should occur to restore republican or loyal governments in the South. Still, Radicals were not always at loggerheads with Lincoln and conservatives in their party. All Republicans united behind a no-compromise policy on the suppression of the rebellion and, ultimately, on emancipation, though conservatives wavered on black freedom when the Union cause faltered and defeat loomed at the polls (for example, during the summer of 1864). Most Radicals, despite their convictions, also were realists who sought to cooperate with Lincoln and conservative Republicans when their political position in the North was weak.

Because of their identification as a faction in the Republican party, I have chosen, like historians before me, to use the uppercase spelling when referring to Northern Radicals. On the other hand, Southern radicals like Andrew Johnson of Tennessee, though viewed as extremists at home, did not normally identify with the Radical faction in Congress, despite their passionate hatred of rebels and their desire to see the Confederate leadership punished and rank-and-file rebels disfranchised. Unlike congressional Radicals, few Southern radicals ever supported black rights or the reconstruction theory that the seceding states had reverted to a territorial status under congressional control. Because they belonged to no specific national faction (with some exceptions, particularly those in Louisiana), I have chosen to use the lowercase when referring to Southern radicals.[9]

Northern and border-state conservatives, including many nonaffiliated former Whigs, like Lincoln fundamentally favored a reconstruction policy that would restore republican (Union) governments in the South as soon as possible and with minimum federal intervention. Along with staunch Southern Unionists, Northern conservatives generally, but not always, demanded punishment for high-ranking Confederate leaders. They expected political and even social and racial changes to occur in the wake of emancipation and Confederate defeat, but insisted that Southern Unionists acting in state conventions and legislative bodies should determine these changes, not federal authorities. Most conservatives, including Lincoln, opposed the national confiscation of rebel property on constitutional grounds. Conservatives also objected to any expansion of federal power except when necessary to suppress the rebellion in the South and its aiders and abettors in the North.

Some conservatives, whom I shall call *ultraconservatives,* consistently opposed emancipation and what they perceived to be a determination on the part of Lincoln and dominant Republicans to subjugate the South and suppress individual liberties in the Union states. Though in most cases loyal to the Union, ultraconservatives, lodged mainly in the Democratic party but including a number of nonaffiliated border-state members of Congress, clamored for negotiations with the Confederacy to restore the Union on the basis of the status quo antebellum and, until the closing months of the war, charged that as long as an antislavery party remained in power the restoration of the Union could not be achieved. Loosely referred to by their opponents as Copperheads, ultraconservatives labeled all Republicans, including Lincoln, as Radicals bent upon destroying the Union and undermining the Constitution.

In this study the terms *Unionist* or *loyalist* will be used to designate white Southerners who opposed the rebellion for most or all of the war.[10] The majority of the Unionists never wavered—or reputedly never wavered—in their loyalty to the old government. Some who have been identified as Unionists briefly supported secession but resumed their allegiance to the Union after becoming disillusioned with the rebellion. The extent of loyalist resistance to Confederate authority varied with individuals and local circumstances. My account describes conditions that influenced many Southerners, including many who were not staunch loyalists, to seek an early restoration of Union authority in their communities and states. Historians Frank W. Klingberg, Carl N. Degler, and most recently Richard N. Current have demonstrated that Unionists—though a distinct minority, except in a few enclaves like East Tennessee, where they were a majority—were more numerous than has been previously recognized. As many as seventy thousand served in the Federal army at sometime during the war. Perhaps most surprising is the fact that Unionism cut across class lines. Many loyalists, for example, were ex-Whig slaveholding planters and pillars of their communities before the war.[11]

Like Lincoln, Southern Unionists were the products of a rural culture that was fundamentally conservative and individualistic. Many viewed the rebellion as immoral and a violation of the principle of self-government, leading to the destruction of republican institutions as they existed in America. Also like Lincoln, they downplayed the war as primarily a sectional conflict, finding "traitors" on both sides of the Mason-Dixon line. Unlike the president, however, they supported slavery and believed that antislavery forces were as responsible for the war as secessionists. After Lincoln issued the Emancipation Proclamation, most loyalists accepted the end of slavery as a necessary measure to suppress the rebellion and restore a harmonious Union. Others, who often styled themselves *conservative Unionists,* though generally supportive of Lincoln and his reconstruction policies, continued to view emancipation with misgivings if not opposition and sought to retain as much control over blacks as possible.[12] These Unionists also feared the control of their states and communities by radicals like Andrew Johnson in Tennessee and Thomas J. Durant in Louisiana. They believed that the radicals, backed by military power and perhaps blacks votes, would use state authority to take revenge on their political enemies, disfranchise rank-and-file Southerners, and suppress civil liberties. Their fears of a radical political and racial transformation, though exaggerated, caused many conservative Unionists to support an early restoration of the rights of former rebels as provided for in Lincoln's plan. However, like their counterparts in the North some Southern Unionists, such as Michael Hahn of Louisiana, do not fit neatly into a radical-conservative political mode.

Lincoln had great faith in the "good sense" of the Southern people and expected them to desire an early return to the Union. He consistently overestimated the strength of Southern Unionism and, conversely, underestimated the support of the Southern people for the rebellion. A large majority in the seceded states had joined the rebellion believing that Lincoln and his party were bent upon the destruction of slavery and their constitutional rights. When Southerners took no action toward reunion, Lincoln assumed that military coercion by rebel leaders prevented them from doing so. The president indicated that, after Federal military forces had occupied an area and provided security for local Unionists, he would accept a loyal nucleus as the body politic to launch the reorganization process in the state. As the Union army occupied more areas, an increasing number of Southerners, he believed, would take the oath of allegiance and participate in their state and local governments.

Lincoln favored a large measure of self-reconstruction, a position that owed a great deal to the nineteenth-century American commitment to local self-government as the cornerstone of republicanism and the nation's federal system of government. Such a reconstruction policy would reassure Southerners of his limited purposes in the war and underscore Lincoln's intention of restoring as soon as possible self-government in the South. In addition, this policy would aid in bringing the rebellion to an early end. To preserve self-government and avoid the appearance of federal dictation, the president was frequently vague and unhelpful in his instructions to military governors and others whom he entrusted with reconstruction, which often created confusion in the execution of his policies. The uniqueness of the Southern rebellion in the American experience and the political sensitivity of the reconstruction issue also contributed to Lincoln's unwillingness to be more forthright in the reorganization of the Southern states. He assumed that the loyal people and military authorities on the scene would know what needed to be done because they would be in a better position than remote authorities in Washington to understand the political peculiarities of their state and area. Having committed himself to a policy of self-reconstruction, Lincoln, when the reorganization effort faltered, could not consistently or in good faith to Southern Unionists change the rules and repudiate the work that had been done. Lincoln's commitment to Southern Unionists and to the principle of self-reconstruction thus significantly restricted his vaunted flexibility as president.

After he issued his Proclamation of Amnesty and Reconstruction in December 1863, Lincoln took a more active role in the Southern restoration effort. Even though his new plan was more broadly conceived, it retained Lincoln's reluctance to require more than minimum guarantees for the restoration of the states to the Union. The president's purpose, as it had been from the beginning of the war, was not to impose a new political system on the South. Rather Lincoln sought to replace in power those disloyal Southerners who had usurped constitutional authority with loyal Southerners who would restore legitimate governments in their states. In addition to a pledge of loyalty, in his 1863 plan Lincoln insisted only that Southerners abolish slavery and provide for the education of young blacks. Such a change, though radical on the surface, could hardly be revolutionary as long as white supremacy was not threatened by a reconstruction settlement. Neither in his emancipation policy nor in his reconstruction plan did Lincoln seek to challenge Southern white control. This is not to suggest that Lincoln designed his Southern policy to insure white supremacy. The question of race control in the restored states was not an issue with Lincoln, though Northern Copperheads and others repeatedly charged that he schemed to establish "social equality" between the races. Like many Northerners, Lincoln assumed that Southern whites, albeit Unionists, would continue after the war to control their states and communities and provide protection for the fruits of Union victory, including black freedom. Lincoln's wartime aim was to restore loyalty and civil government in the South as soon as possible and thereby check the forces of disorder leading to anarchy, which he believed had been unleashed by the rebellion to threaten the republic of the Founding Fathers.

Late in the war, the president signed the Freedmen's Bureau Act, creating a federal agency to aid displaced black and white Southerners, and in his last public speech he indicated his preference for qualified black suffrage in Louisiana. But the establishment of the Freedmen's Bureau, whose existence would be temporary and without real authority to confiscate rebel estates or make political changes, did not threaten white supremacy in the defeated South. Neither did Lincoln's announced preference for limited black suffrage.

Lincoln remained committed to the principle of self-reconstruction controlled by Southern white Unionists. Though the president rejected a policy of federal dictation, throughout the war he maintained a keen interest in the process of Southern reorganization. Lincoln repeatedly reminded Unionists and military commanders of his desire for an early restoration of civil government, followed soon by the return of the states to the Union with the seating of their representatives in Congress. After 1863 Lincoln also repeatedly reminded Unionists of the great need as a war measure to abolish slavery in their states. Only then could the root cause of the Civil War be eradicated, republican or loyal governments be secured, and a just and lasting peace be achieved.

Part 1

First Phase

1

1861:
An Early Start

Under the most unfavorable circumstances in American history, on March 4, 1861, Abraham Lincoln took the oath of office as president. Having secretly slipped into Washington ten days earlier, Lincoln delivered his long-awaited inaugural address before an anxious crowd that was protected by several hundred United States troops. In his address the new president firmly announced his intention to preserve the Union, which, he insisted, was his constitutional duty as the nation's chief executive. "I hold," Lincoln declared, "that in contemplation of universal law, and of the Constitution, the Union of these States is perpetual. . . . No State, upon its own mere motion, can lawfully get out of the Union." The success of the Southern disunionists would mean that America was imperfect, "having lost the vital element of perpetuity." "The central idea of secession," Lincoln asserted, was "the essence of anarchy" because it rested on the destructive principle that a minority might secede whenever it disapproved of the will of the majority as had occurred after his election, when the lower Southern states had presumed to leave the Union. "A majority, held in restraint by constitutional checks, and limitations, . . . is the only true sovereign of a free people. Whoever rejects it, does, of necessity, fly to anarchy or to despotism."[1]

Most Americans, including Southerners, held the same view of the Union. The idea of Union transcended ordinary political matters. The Union of the states had been created by the Founding Fathers as a model for the world, a constitutional republic based on the principles of

Andrew Johnson, U. S. Senator, 1857-1862, Union military governor of
Tennessee, 1862-1865; vice president, 1865; and president, 1865-1869
(courtesy of the North Carolina Division of Archives and History).

self-government, limited central power, and individual liberty. It embodied the spirit of progress in every aspect of life—political, social, economic, cultural, and religious. If the Union were broken, most Americans, including Lincoln, assumed that progress would cease and America would become no better than the decadent and oppressive nations of Europe. Not all Americans, however, could agree on how the Union should be maintained, or even whether federal power, particularly in the hands of the antislavery Republican party, should be used to force Southern states to remain in the nation. Despite affection for the old Union, most Southerners in the seceded states, after years of sectional conflict over slavery, believed that the mere election of Lincoln meant that the Northern people had broken the bond of Union and would be willing accomplices to an antislavery effort to destroy their rights and the security of their communities. But many Southerners at the time of Lincoln's inaugural, including a majority in the upper South and the border slave states, still clung to the notion that the Union should and could be preserved.[2] It was to these Southerners, and also to many in the lower South whom Lincoln believed had been driven by momentary passion and against their better judgment to abandon the Union of their fathers, that the new president directed his inaugural remarks.

Lincoln reassured Southerners that he had no intention of interfering with slavery where it existed, and he even reminded them that he had a constitutional obligation to uphold the Fugitive Slave law, a statute that was vehemently opposed by Northern antislavery groups. He would "press upon [Southern] attention the most conclusive evidence of which the case is susceptible, that the property, peace and security of no section are to be in anywise endangered" by his administration. The new president declared that he did not plan to violate any Southern rights under the constitution. Lincoln insisted that he took the oath "with no mental reservations, and with no purpose to construe the Constitution or laws, by any hypercritical rules."[3]

Having firmly announced his intention to preserve the Union, Lincoln advanced what essentially was a peaceful plan of reconstruction—a policy that was also designed to hold the upper South in the Union. Though he would perform his "simple duty" to enforce the laws of the Union in all the states "so far as practicable," the new president declared that he would not force the issue. "The power confided to me," Lincoln told Southerners, would be used "to hold, occupy, and possess the property and places belonging to the government, and to collect the duties and imports; but beyond what may be necessary for these objects, there will be no invasion—no using of force against, or among the people anywhere."

Furthermore, he would not appoint "obnoxious strangers" to federal offices in the South but would seek "competent resident citizens" for these posts. Lincoln assured Americans that, though circumstances may cause him to modify the particulars of his policy, he would continue to seek "a peaceful solution of the national troubles, and the restoration of fraternal sympathies and affections." As one possible mode of restoration, he would support the assembling of a national convention to amend the Constitution, and would not object to an amendment forever prohibiting federal interference with slavery in the South.[4]

Lincoln admonished "dissatisfied" Southerners to "think calmly and *well,* upon this whole subject." The federal government "will not assail you," and you will "still have the old Constitution unimpaired," including provisions protecting slavery. He closed his inaugural address by appealing to the spirit of American patriotism among disaffected Southerners. "We are not enemies, but friends. We must not be enemies. Though passion may have strained, it must not break our bonds of affection. The mystic chords of memory, streching [sic] from every battle-field, and patriot grave, to every living heart and hearth-stone, all over this broad land, will yet swell the chorus of the Union, when again touched, as surely they will be, by the better angels of our nature."[5]

In a concrete effort to show his good will toward the South, Lincoln sought to appoint prominent upper southern and border-state Unionists to his Cabinet. As president-elect, Lincoln offered John A. Gilmer, an able congressman and large North Carolina slaveholder, an unnamed position in his Cabinet, but Gilmer, who opposed the antislavery platform of the Republican party, refused the appointment. Lincoln then selected Montgomery Blair of the border state of Maryland as postmaster general. He had already revealed his intention to appoint Edward Bates of Missouri, another border-state Unionist, as attorney general.[6] However, neither Lincoln's conciliatory inaugural address nor his patronage policy changed opinions of him in the greater South or reversed secession in the "dissatisfied" states.

A few weeks after Lincoln's inauguration, hostilities in Charleston Harbor, where the new president sought to maintain a symbol of Union authority in the seceded states, shattered hopes for a peaceful restoration of the Union. One day after the American flag came down over Fort Sumter, Lincoln issued a proclamation calling for seventy-five thousand troops to put down rebellious "combinations too powerful to be suppressed by the ordinary course of judicial proceedings." Clearly he believed that individuals acting in combinations, not the states, were in rebellion against the United States. Lincoln announced that "the utmost care will be observed," consistent with the restoration of federal control over its forts and property, "to avoid any devastation, any destruction of, or interference with, property, or any disturbance of peaceful citizens in any part of the country." The new president also summoned Congress to meet in special session on July 4 to deal with the crisis.[7]

Meanwhile, the fighting at Fort Sumter and Lincoln's proclamation had caused four upper Southern states to leave the Union and join the Confederate States of America. The secessionist fever also threatened to overwhelm the border slave states of Maryland, Kentucky, and Missouri.[8] Because of their strategic location and their human and material resources, Lincoln knew that if these states fell to the "rebels," "the whole game" would be lost. Accordingly, he pursued a cautious though firm policy toward the borderland, believing that as president he had a constitutional responsibility to preserve loyal governments in those states and to suppress individuals who sought, through violence, to overthrow the Constitution of the United States. In his management of the border crisis, Lincoln displayed the deft leadership that historians later would associate with him.

Maryland offered an immediate and critical test of the president's authority to check the forces of secession in the border states. Lincoln courted and ultimately obtained the support of powerful anti-Republican Unionists like Governor Thomas H. Hicks and Senator Reverdy Johnson, both of whom early in the war sought a neutral status for Maryland. Soon after Fort Sumter, an attack on Massachusetts troops in Baltimore and the destruction of railroad bridges by pro-Confederates elsewhere in Maryland created the possibility that secessionists would seize control of the state and isolate Washington. At first Lincoln hesitated to intervene in Maryland because of his reluctance to violate state rights and the civil liberties of the people. Finally, however, aware of "the extremest necessity" for federal action, the president moved to insure the loyalty of the state and the security of the national capital. He authorized the suspension of the writ of habeas corpus in portions of Maryland; sanctioned the arrest of suspected rebels; and approved the purge of secessionists in the legislature. Partly because of these actions, Maryland remained in the Union.[9]

Reacting to sharp criticism of his suspension of the writ in Maryland, Lincoln in his July 4, 1861, message to the special session of Congress vigorously defended his action. He asserted that under the provision in the Constitution authorizing the suspension of the writ "in cases of rebellion, or invasion" the president could act without congressional approval when "a dangerous emergency" existed and Congress could not be called into immediate session. Lincoln said that an emergency situation existed in 1861, and his measures had been designed solely to prevent the overthrow of the government. "Are all the laws, *but one* [the right of habeas corpus], to go unexecuted, and the government itself go to pieces, lest that one be violated," he asked?[10]

In Missouri and Kentucky, Lincoln allowed events in 1861 to take their course. However, he permitted military arms and equipment to be shipped into both states to aid the Union cause. In Missouri, pro-Confederate Governor Claiborne F. Jackson on January 5, 1861, told the citizens that the state should make "a timely declaration of her determination to stand by her sister slave-holding States." A state convention called to consider the issue, however, refused to take Missouri out of the Union. Undeterred by this rebuff, Jackson moved to secure military control of the state. Ardent Unionists in St. Louis, mainly German-Americans led by Captain Nathaniel Lyon, commander of the U.S. arsenal in the city, proceeded to drive the governor's forces to the southwestern corner of the state. The state convention reassembled in July and elected a new governor and other state officers, all of whom were loyal to the Union. Fighting, especially of the guerrilla variety, continued in Missouri, though after 1861 Unionist control of the state was not seriously threatened.[11] Lincoln's primary task in Missouri for the rest of the war was to maintain the political peace between radicals, who wanted to adopt a state constitution abolishing slavery and enact draconian provisions against Confederate sympathizers, and conservative Unionists who opposed such measures. In the end, the radicals won control of the state.

Kentucky, more evenly divided over the war than Maryland and Missouri, proclaimed its neutrality while remaining in the Union. Although Lincoln told Congress that "armed neutrality" was "treason in effect" because it aided secessionists, he exercised restraint in his dealings with the people of his native state. The president, like pragmatic Unionists in Kentucky, realized that neutrality was all that could be expected in the beginning of the war. He could not take a chance in 1861 on the state leaving the Union. Lincoln probably was correct when he wrote that with "Kentucky gone, we can not hold Missouri, nor, as I think, Maryland. These all against us, and the job on our hands is too large for us." The president assured Kentuckians that he would respect their neutrality and would do nothing to disturb the slave institution. In September, Lincoln demonstrated his goodwill toward Kentucky Unionists as well as other loyal Southern whites when he countermanded General John C. Frémont's order freeing slaves of rebel owners in Missouri. He also dispatched loyal Kentucky officers to recruit and arm Federal units in the state.[12]

The president's policy toward Kentucky paid off. Unionist sentiment there soared during the summer, and when Confederate forces seized Columbus, Kentucky, the legislature abandoned its neutral pose and sought Federal military intervention to expel the invaders. As in Missouri, pro-Confederates fled southward, carrying with them a number of prominent Kentuckians, including a former U.S. vice president, John C. Breckinridge, to serve in the Confederate army.

Unionist success in the border region persuaded Lincoln that similar results could be achieved in the seceded states, except perhaps in South Carolina, where the fire-eaters had long held forth and secession sentiment was overwhelming. Lincoln in 1861 believed that in the rebel-controlled states secessionist leaders had seized control by temporarily deceiving the people into believing that their rights in the Union were jeopardized by a Republican administration and that they had the constitutional right to leave the Union. He reported to Congress on July 4, 1861, that in at least two states, Tennessee and Virginia, "military coercion" at the polls had been employed by the rebels to win control. In making his case for Southern Unionism, Lincoln insisted that the Southern people possessed "as much of moral sense, as much of devotion to law and order, and as much pride in, and reverence for, the history, and government, of their common country, as any other civilized, and patriotic people." He asserted that "there is much reason to believe that the Union men are [today] the majority in many, if not every other one [except South Carolina], of the so-called seceded States."[13]

It was his task, Lincoln told Congress, to nurture the latent Unionism in the South and "call out the war power" to resist the rebellion and preserve the government. The president cited the provision in the Constitution that "the United States shall guarantee to every State in this Union a republican form of government" as the legal justification—in fact, duty—for him to put down the rebellion and restore self-government. He reassured Southerners that despite the use of military force to suppress the rebels, he would not disturb their institutions and laws, which meant that he would not interfere with slavery.[14] As he later told Congress, Lincoln did not want to see the war "degenerate into a violent and remorseless revolutionary struggle." Any radical or extreme measures by the administration, the president declared, would "reach the loyal as well as the disloyal," depriving Unionists of their constitutional rights and making it more difficult for them to cooperate in the restoration of loyal governments in the South.[15]

Although Union sentiment had been temporarily suppressed in the seceded states, Lincoln believed that as areas were liberated Unionists would take the initiative in forming state and local governments. Initially only a minority needed to participate in these governments. This minority would serve as a nucleus around which otherwise timid Unionists and disenchanted rebels could rally and rapidly restore civil authority in their states. He recognized, however, that Congress might prevent the completion of the process by rejecting representatives elected by the restored governments. In the beginning, with his party in control of Congress and inclined to follow his lead, Lincoln did not expect any trouble on the admission of Union representatives from the South.

Congress soon gave Lincoln good reason to believe that it would cooperate with him in his plan to suppress the rebellion and restore loyal governments in the South. When Congress met in July 1861, it approved the war initiatives that Lincoln had taken following Fort Sumter, retroactively providing for troops and money to put down the rebellion. Congress overwhelmingly passed the Crittenden-Johnson resolutions affirming Lincoln's purpose that the war was fought, not to interfere with the institutions of the South, but "to defend and maintain the supremacy of the Constitution and to preserve the Union, with all the dignity, equality, and rights of the several States unimpaired."[16] Finally, Congress recognized Lincoln's "Restored Government of Virginia" as the legitimate government of that state.

The effort to establish a Union government in Virginia was Lincoln's first step toward wartime reconstruction. It began immediately after the state convention, meeting in Richmond, voted on April 17, 1861, to take Virginia out of the Union. On April 20 John S. Carlile, the leading spokesman of western Virginia Unionists in the convention, visited Lincoln in Washington. Carlile was no antislavery zealot from the mountains of western Virginia. In the state convention, he had defended slavery as "a social, political and religious blessing" that was (paradoxically) "essential to the preservation of our liberties." But, he told Virginians, the institution would not exist five years after the state's separation from the nonslaveholding states. Carlile, himself a slaveholder of Clarksburg, explained that "the whole civilized world is arrayed against the institution of slavery, and it is nothing but the prestige and the power of the General Government now that guarantees to the slaveholder his right." He reminded Virginians that Lincoln as president was bound to protect the institution. Like other Southern Unionists who desperately wanted to avoid secession, Carlile, a conservative Whig, predicted anarchy and ruin if Virginia left the Union. "Dissolve the Union, and a military despotism, the licentiousness of the camp and ragged poverty will be substituted in its place."[17] Eastern Virginians were deaf to Carlile's arguments, and they voted overwhelmingly in May to ratify the state's secession ordinance.

When Carlile met with Lincoln on April 20, the president encouraged him to go home and rally western Virginia opposition to secession.

Two days later at a large meeting of Unionists in Clarksburg, Carlile secured the call for a convention to meet at Wheeling on May 13 to consider what action "the people of Northwestern Virginia should take in the present fearful emergency."[18]

In Carlile's meeting with the president, the question of the separation of the western counties from Virginia probably was not considered. Lincoln at this time opposed the dismemberment of any Southern state because he believed such an action would violate the Constitution and contradict his purpose of preserving the sanctity of the states, in this case Virginia. His endorsement of a division also would undermine moderate or conservative support for his war policies in the North and the border South.[19] Carlile probably was aware of the president's objections to separation, but on his return home, he found strong support for western Virginia statehood. Pressured by local Unionists and inflamed by the treatment westerners had received in Richmond, Carlile immediately assumed leadership of the movement for a "New Virginia."

Delegates to the Wheeling convention met as scheduled on May 13. Before deciding on a course of action for the western counties, however, they adjourned to await the results of the ratification election on Virginia's secession ordinance.[20] After the ordinance was approved, Unionists in thirty-two northwestern and two Potomac counties, Fairfax and Alexandria, sent representatives to a second Wheeling convention. The counties represented at this convention, which met on June 11, contained more than one fourth of Virginia's white population and was largely nonslaveholding, but not antislavery. This area, except for the Potomac counties, had long bristled at eastern domination of the state government at the expense of the transmontane region.

The convention, despite Carlile's vigorous efforts on behalf of statehood, rejected immediate separation from Virginia. Like Lincoln, the majority of the delegates, though not directly influenced by the president, took a strict constructionist view of the Constitution, opposing dismemberment without the required approval of the legislature of the mother state. To appease the Carlile faction, a compromise was arranged. The convention created the "Restored Government of Virginia," a move that satisfied both the Carlile forces and those who opposed immediate statehood. This government became the de jure government of the Old Dominion and assumed temporary control of western Virginia. The Restored Government was expected to consent eventually to the division of the state.[21]

To lead the Restored Government, the Wheeling convention on June 20 selected as governor Francis Harrison Pierpont, an old Whig partisan and a successful Fairmont lawyer-businessman. He would serve until an election could be held. Pierpont, a powerful man in appearance with a large square face, ringed by a full head of curly brown hair and a thick set of chin whiskers, immediately reported to Lincoln on the convention's action. As "governor of this Commonwealth," he called on the president for aid in suppressing the rebellion and stopping the violence against Unionists.[22]

Lincoln was delighted with the action of the Wheeling convention. At a meeting of the Cabinet, the president secured its support for the Pierpont government as Virginia's legitimate government. Secretary of War Simon Cameron was instructed by Lincoln to honor Pierpont's request for a military force to assist in putting down the rebellion. The president expected Pierpont, like other loyal governors, to raise volunteers for the war effort, an expectation that Pierpont energetically fulfilled. The governor ultimately raised more than ten thousand troops for the defense of the Union in western Virginia. Cameron informed Pierpont that agents of the federal government in Virginia had been given instructions "to proceed hereafter under your direction." The secretary also indicated that Lincoln "never supposed that a brave and free people, though surprised and unarmed, could long be subjugated by a class of political adventurers always adverse to them; and the fact that they have already rallied, reorganized their Government and checked the march of these invaders, demonstrates how justly he appreciated them."[23]

With this ringing endorsement from the Lincoln administration, Pierpont called the "Virginia" legislature into special session. This assembly consisted of delegates to the Wheeling convention and members chosen in the regular General Assembly elections in May. Altogether, forty-nine members representing forty-eight counties assembled in Wheeling on July 1. Their main task was to select two United States senators to replace Robert M.T. Hunter and James M. Mason, who had vacated their seats to join the Confederacy. As the leading Unionist of western Virginia, Carlile was elected without opposition for the long term ending in 1865. Waitman T. Willey, a Union-Whig lawyer of Morgantown, was chosen for the short term, which would expire in 1863.[24]

When Congress met in special session on July 4, 1861, Lincoln told the lawmakers that the "loyal citizens" of Virginia "have, in due form," established a government. The president wanted Congress to admit immediately the Virginia representatives, who, in addition to the senators-elect, included three Unionists elected to the House of Representatives in May under the old state election laws. Lincoln, however, did not presume to instruct Congress in the matter except to insist that "this government is bound to recognize and protect" the Pierpont regime.[25]

The House of Representatives quickly moved to satisfy the president. With no significant opposition, it seated the three Virginia Unionists. In the Senate, however, a brief debate erupted when Senator Andrew Johnson of Tennessee presented the credentials of Carlile and Willey for admission. Border-state Democrats, reflecting an ultraconservative view that only a majority of a state's voters, whether rebel or Unionist, could legally act for the people, questioned the legitimacy of the Restored Government and the right of Carlile and Willey to Senate seats. Their objections were brushed aside by the Republican majority, including some senators who soon would be associated with the Radical wing of the party and opposed to Lincoln's reconstruction efforts.[26] John P. Hale of New Hampshire, in vigorously defending the Restored Government of Virginia, declared that it was the duty of federal authorities "to recognize the loyal and the true men that still cling to the Union and support the Constitution" in the state. The federal government, Hale insisted, should pour out men and money to sustain the Virginia Unionists who "are determined to stand by the cause of civil liberty in this hour of [the republic's] peril." Lyman Trumbull of Illinois echoed Hale's views. "If Virginia is in the Union," which he believed was the case, "her loyal men have a right to be represented here."[27]

On July 13 the Senate by a vote of thirty-five to five seated Carlile and Willey. In so doing, the Senate, along with the House, implicitly accepted not only the legitimacy of the Restored Government of Virginia, but also endorsed Lincoln's limited purposes in the war and his policy of encouraging Southern loyalists to establish nuclei governments looking toward a quick restoration of civil control. As time would prove, the Pierpont government's main action during the war was to arrange for the separation of western Virginia from Virginia. But in the summer of 1861 Lincoln and Republicans in Congress believed that Virginia's Restored Government would become a model for Unionists in other seceded states to adopt in their struggle, with the aid of Federal military forces, to overthrow rebel authority. As Senator Henry Lane of Indiana announced: "We expect soon to readmit Tennessee into the Union, as we have recently readmitted old Virginia; we expect soon to readmit North Carolina." Lane sanguinely predicted that within six months the rebellion would be crushed in every state.[28] Already, he knew, a movement was afoot in Tennessee to restore that state—or at least a part of it—to the Union.

Like Virginia, Tennessee left the Union only after Fort Sumter and Lincoln's call for troops to suppress the rebellion. As late as February 1861, Tennessee voters overwhelmingly had rejected a convention designed to take them out of the Union and into the newly formed Confederate States of America. Ten days after Lincoln's appeal for troops in April, the legislature met in special session and, at the urging of Governor Isham Harris, moved to sever the state's ties with the Union. Ignoring the state's constitutional procedure for such a fundamental change, the legislature framed "A Declaration of Independence" and a secession ordinance, both of which were submitted as a single proposition to a referendum on June 8. Governor Harris and the legislature, however, were impatient to align the state with the Confederacy. Before the election, they drew up a military agreement with the Confederate States, placing Tennessee troops under President Jefferson Davis's command.[29]

The actions of the state government stunned heavily Unionist East Tennessee. This section of the state had overwhelmingly voted for the Union in the February election. Unionist leaders now charged that Harris, who was from secessionist West Tennessee, and the legislature had defied the wishes of the people and had acted highhandedly to take the state out of the Union. Senator Andrew Johnson rushed home from Washington and joined his old Whig political foes Thomas A.R. Nelson and William G. "Parson" Brownlow to lead the fight against the secession ordinance. The fever for secession, however, was so high in Middle and West Tennessee that Unionists were intimidated, and Johnson and Nelson, who campaigned jointly, chose not to speak in those areas. In East Tennessee the vigorous canvass of these two party leaders succeeded in maintaining the Union cause there, despite the tug of loyalty that many Unionists felt toward "going with their state" and also their disquiet, at least at this time, about the antislavery Lincoln's determination to suppress the insurrection.[30] In the June 8 election, East Tennessee voted more than two to one against leaving the Union (32,923 to 14,780). The state, however, by a vote of 104,913 to 47,238 went for secession.

Such a dramatic reversal in state voter sentiment since February convinced East Tennessee Unionists that fraud and intimidation had been decisive in the election. They were only partly correct. Some incidents of intimidation and violence against Unionists did occur, even in East Tennessee. The election, however, fairly accurately reflected public sentiment, and secessionists did not owe their success to illegal or strong-arm methods. The secessionist triumph owed a great deal to the hysteria that gripped much of Tennessee after Fort Sumter and Lincoln's call for troops to suppress the rebellion in the lower South. Most white Tennesseans, already believing the worst about the "Black Republican" president, feared for their own safety and the institution of slavery, and this fear was expressed in the June 8 referendum.[31]

East Tennessee Unionists defiantly refused to abide by the election results. A hurriedly called convention of 292 Unionists met at Greeneville on June 17 to map out a strategy for resistance. The delegates arrived in Senator Johnson's home town with fire in their eyes. Bloodshed appeared imminent when squads of Confederate soldiers passing through Greeneville en route to Virginia harassed some of the "Tory" delegates and cut down the "enemy" flag. Their officers, however, intervened before violence occurred. Unintimidated by Confederate threats, Thomas A.R. Nelson, a former Whig congressman who assumed the mantel of leadership in the convention, proposed a stirring "declaration of grievances" against the secessionists and also put forth strong resolutions proclaiming that "the counties of East Tennessee and such of the adjacent counties as choose to act with them will still legally and constitutionally continue in the Union as the State of Tennessee." According to Oliver P. Temple, an active participant in the convention, Nelson's resolutions would have been adopted on the first day if they had not automatically been referred to a committee for study. By the time the committee completed its work three days later, the initial excitement and passion that had gripped the convention had subsided, and the committee's report reflected a more sobering mood among the delegates in view of the area's vulnerability to a Confederate occupation.

The Greeneville convention, instead of following the example of western Virginia in establishing a restored Union government for the state and asking Lincoln's approval, adopted a moderate statement petitioning the legislature in Nashville to consent to the separation of East Tennessee from the state. Like Kentucky Unionists in 1861, they expressed a strong desire to remain neutral in the war. After the convention had adjourned, the legislature dismissed East Tennessee's request for separation with the dubious explanation that the Greeneville meeting had not been authorized by the voters.[32]

The Greeneville convention also issued a declaration affirming East Tennessee's devotion to the Union. The statement carefully clarified the Unionist position in the South and was probably read by Lincoln and other Republican leaders. "We prefer to remain attached to the government of our fathers," the document declared.

> The Constitution of the United States has done us no wrong. The Congress of the United States has made no threat against the law-abiding people of Tennessee. Under the constitution of the United States, we have enjoyed as a nation more of civil and religious freedom than any other people under the whole

heaven. . . . The cause of secession has no charm for us, and its progress has been marked by the most alarming and dangerous attacks upon the public liberty. In other states, as well as our own, its whole course threatens to annihilate the last vestige of freedom.[33]

Although the Greeneville convention failed to establish a Union government for the state, East Tennessee Unionists in August 1861, participated in regular elections held under the authority of Confederate Tennessee. East Tennesseans voted in almost the same proportion (64 percent) for William H. Polk, the Conservative (formerly Union) candidate for governor, as they did against secession on June 8 (69 percent). They went to the polls believing that Polk, the brother of former President James K. Polk, would respect their neutrality in the war while remaining loyal to the Union. Some who had earlier supported the Union might even have acquiesced in the state majority's decision to secede provided a conservative like Polk led Tennessee and protected its rights in the Confederacy. Governor Harris, however, easily won re-election and soon moved to establish firm Confederate control over the disaffected region by dispatching a military force into the area under the command of Felix K. Zollicoffer.[34]

A greater anomaly in East Tennessee than the gubernatorial election was the August congressional contests. In the four districts of the region, which in the case of one district included counties in Middle Tennessee, Unionists ran against Confederates for seats in their respective congresses. Unionists Thomas A.R. Nelson and Horace Maynard easily defeated their "rebel" opponents, and both men secretly left for Washington to assume their seats in the federal Congress. Maynard, like Nelson a former Whig congressman and Knoxville lawyer, arrived without mishap and took his seat in the House of Representatives. Along with Senator Johnson, he quickly became an important confidant of President Lincoln regarding Tennessee affairs. Nelson, however, never arrived in Washington. He was arrested by Confederates while passing through Virginia; and though soon released, he returned home to Knoxville. In the other two East Tennessee congressional districts, both Unionists and Confederates claimed victory, and all four of the contestants left for their respective capitals to claim their seats. All were seated, though Unionist George W. Bridges, following numerous adventures, reached Washington a year later.[35]

Although Governor Harris was determined to suppress dissent in East Tennessee, General Zollicoffer adopted a conciliatory policy toward the Unionists. Zollicoffer, a former Whig congressman of Middle Tennessee and a native of East Tennessee, announced that Unionists would be protected in their rights, including freedom of speech and ballot, as long as they "pursue their respective avocations peacefully." Zollicoffer issued stern orders to his troops to leave Unionists alone and insisted that the military's purpose in East Tennessee was to insure peace and prevent "the horrors of civil war." His conciliatory policy had some effect in reducing opposition to Confederate control. Even the usually fierce Parson Brownlow, who was permitted to continue publishing his Unionist *Knoxville Whig,* for a time acquiesced in the new order of things.[36]

Events, however, were moving inexorably toward conflict in East Tennessee between Unionists and Confederate forces. In Washington, Senator Johnson, Congressman Maynard, and Republican friends of East Tennessee Unionists, notably Treasury Secretary Salmon P. Chase, rejected any accommodation with rebel authority. They pressed President Lincoln and the War Department for military aid for the Union cause. Lincoln complied insofar as his resources would permit. As early as June, he gave his approval to a plan to send arms to East Tennessee Unionists. Soon a military force was being raised in Kentucky to invade East Tennessee through Cumberland Gap.[37]

Reports of these preparations created alarm among Confederate officials in East Tennessee. They began to arrest Union leaders. Extreme Unionists, in anticipation of the Federal invasion in the fall and reportedly with Lincoln's approval, hatched a plan to burn nine important railroad bridges in East Tennessee. They succeeded in destroying five of the bridges, but no invasion occurred. Confederate authorities reacted vigorously to the bridge burnings by hanging some of the perpetrators, repudiating Zollicoffer's conciliatory policy, and clamping martial law on the area. More than fifty "Tory" ringleaders were apprehended and dispatched to the Confederate "Bastille" in Tuscaloosa. Brownlow was arrested and confined in Knoxville during the winter; in March he was released and sent through the lines to Federal-occupied Nashville.[38]

As a result of the Confederate repression, thousands of Tennessee Unionists fled to Kentucky, where they joined the Federal army. By the end of the war more than twenty thousand East Tennesseans had served in the army of liberation. Unionists who remained in East Tennessee in many cases sought sanctuary in the nearby mountain coves, where they organized guerrilla bands to prey upon Confederates.[39] Romanticized accounts of the East Tennessean struggle appeared in the North, exciting admiration for the "loyal mountaineers" and creating a demand for their early deliverance from Confederate oppression. Brownlow, even more than Andrew Johnson, became the leading propagandist for the East Tennessee cause in the

Northern states. Soon after his release from captivity, Brownlow went north, where at numerous public rallies he passionately recounted, frequently with exaggeration, the heroic struggle and sufferings of East Tennessee Unionists. Brownlow also rushed to print a narrative history of his adventures as well as those of other Tennessee loyalists. This book, published in Philadelphia in 1862 and entitled *Sketches of the Rise, Progress, and Decline of Secession,* immediately became what would have been called in the twentieth century a best-seller.[40]

East Tennessee Unionists had no greater champion in the North than Abraham Lincoln. The president was a native of nearby Kentucky and the product of a culture that was strikingly similar to East Tennessee. The Lincolns, Hanks, and their kin had come from the Valley of Virginia (or just east of the Blue Ridge, as in the case of Lincoln's mother), and had been neighbors of many subsequent settlers in East Tennessee. Before his marriage, Lincoln's father had lived briefly with an uncle in upper East Tennessee. Lincoln's ties to the area remained strong; even his speech reflected the region's vernacular.[41]

The vast majority of East Tennesseans, contrary to their reputation as poor mountaineers, lived on small farms and in towns in the Great Valley. By the time of the Civil War, small industries associated with mining and the production of grain had emerged in and around Knoxville, Chattanooga, and other towns. Like Lincoln and his circle of former Kentuckians in Springfield, Illinois, most East Tennesseans were old Whigs and held conservative social and political views. Their leaders in many cases were well-educated and well-read, although some of them, like Lincoln, were largely self-educated in the rural western tradition.

East Tennesseans were not as isolated from the main political and intellectual currents of America as historians have assumed. The routes up the valley and through Cumberland Gap, expanded by the completion during the 1850s of the railroad that went northward to Virginia, gave them relatively easy access to the border states and beyond. It also brought them economic contacts with the lower South through Chattanooga and Atlanta. Their contacts with the rest of Tennessee, however, were difficult, since the Cumberland Plateau hindered westward travel and communications.[42] By 1861, the history of East Tennesseans in the winning of American independence, especially their decisive role in the dramatic victory over the Tories at King's Mountain, had become a vivid part of their heritage and folklore. Their devotion to the Union was forged by this Revolutionary War tradition. Like Lincoln, they frequently recalled the greatness of the men who had led the fight for freedom and founded "the last best, hope of earth."[43]

East Tennesseans, including the Democratic followers of Andrew Johnson, differed with Lincoln on one important issue—slavery. With 27,539 slaves in their population of 297,596 in 1860, they opposed all antislavery agitation as destructive of the Union and the social fabric of the South. Many of the East Tennessee leaders, including Johnson, Horace Maynard, Oliver P. Temple, and Thomas A.R. Nelson, were slaveholders, and they frequently defended the institution on the stump and in the newspapers. Even William G. "Parson" Brownlow, though not a slave-holder himself, supported slavery and proclaimed that he "thoroughly identified with Southern institutions."[44] The proslavery sentiments of East Tennesseans, however, were not as strong as those of Southerners in heavy slaveholding areas. These Tennesseans were more willing than most South-erners to accept President Lincoln's early assurance that he was not an abolitionist and would respect Southern susceptibilities regarding slavery.

Early in the war Lincoln established a close bond with Senator John-son, Congressman Maynard, and other East Tennesseans in Washington. He frequently could be seen in their company. John Hay, Lincoln's secre-tary, noted in his diary a congenial meeting that the president had "with a couple of very intelligent East Tennesseans." "They talked in a very friendly way with the President," Hay wrote. "I never saw him more at ease than when he is with those first rate patriots of the border. He is of them really."[45]

Almost from the beginning of the war East Tennessee leaders urged Lincoln and the War Department to launch a campaign from Kentucky to liberate their homeland. Lincoln was sympathetic; furthermore, he quickly perceived the value of East Tennessee as a loyal nucleus around which a re-stored Union government could be formed. At first, however, he had more immediate military needs to meet, particularly preparations for the defense of Washington and the border states. But in September 1861, Lincoln directed the War Department to begin on about October 5 a military movement through Cumberland Gap and into East Tennessee in conjunc-tion with an operation against the South Carolina coast. Lincoln intended for the East Tennessee invasion to be the only major military operation in the West during the fall and winter of 1861-1862.[46] The campaign, how-ever, soon went awry. Logistical problems, including the difficulty of transporting an army over nearly impassable roads, and Commanding Gen-eral William Tecumseh Sherman's fear that his force was too small to defeat General Zollicoffer's troops, caused the invasion to be halted before it reached Cumberland Gap.[47]

The military setback bitterly disappointed East Tennessee Unionists. Charging mismanagement on the part of the Federal commanders in

Kentucky for the failure, they bombarded Johnson and Maynard in Washington with appeals for another, immediate operation to redeem East Tennessee. One Tennessee officer in camp in Kentucky assured Johnson that "there is nothing to hinder us from going to the relief of our people, but an order to march. . . . In God's name if it is in your power to do any thing to push us forward, do it at once, or our loyal & beloved E. Tennessee is forever ruined."[48]

Already Johnson was pressing Lincoln for a renewed military campaign through Cumberland Gap. Numerous accounts of Unionist suffering at the hands of Confederate authorities in East Tennessee reached the White House, increasing Lincoln's concern for the people of the area. On December 7, Johnson and Maynard, in company with General-in-Chief George B. McClellan, met with Lincoln and found him in firm support of a campaign to redeem East Tennessee. To facilitate the movement, Lincoln asked Congress to appropriate "as speedily as possible" the necessary funds for the construction of a railroad connecting East Tennessee with Kentucky. He insisted that "the work can be completed in a very short time; and when done, it will be not only of vast present usefulness, but also a valuable permanent improvement." Congress, however, with what appeared to be more practical financial needs to satisfy, refused the president's request.[49]

After their December 7 conference with Lincoln, Johnson and Maynard did not wait for the War Department to relay the president's directive to the military commanders in Kentucky. Immediately after the meeting, they telegraphed Gen. Don Carlos Buell, who had replaced Sherman in command, of the president's decision and admonished him to move quickly. Although Buell assured Johnson and Maynard that "I recognize no more imperative duty and crave no higher honor than that of rescuing our loyal friends in Tennessee," he found obstacles in the way of a successful East Tennessee campaign. When on January 4, 1862, no word of the movement had reached Washington, Lincoln impatiently telegraphed Buell inquiring about his plans. Buell replied that he was making preparations for the campaign; he also impertinently added: "I will confess . . . I have been bound to it more by . . . sympathy for the people of Eastern Tennessee, and the anxiety which yourself and the General in Chief have desired it than by my opinion of its wisdom." An attack on Nashville and Middle Tennessee, Buell informed the president, would be preferable to the proposed East Tennessee campaign.[50]

Lincoln was furious. The next day the president, after conferring with Johnson and Maynard, sent a dispatch to Buell declaring that his message "disappoints and distresses." He told the general that he "would rather have a point on the Railroad south of Cumberland Gap, than Nashville, first, because it cuts a great artery of the enemies' communication, which Nashville does not, and secondly because it is in the midst of loyal people, who would rally around it, while Nashville is not." Lincoln's reference to the need to cut the railroad was designed partly to appeal to the military instincts of Buell. His main reason for the operation was the redemption of a Unionist enclave in the Confederacy, an area like western Virginia that could serve as a nucleus for a loyal government and the restoration of the state to the Union. Lincoln, however, admitted to Buell that he was not competent to criticize military decisions and would not issue an order for the invasion of East Tennessee. The president conveniently forgot that he had earlier directed Buell to launch such a movement. Lincoln still declared: "My distress is that our friends in East Tennessee are being hanged and driven to despair, and even now I fear, are thinking of taking rebel arms for the sake of personal protection. In this we lose the most valuable stake we have in the South." Johnson and Maynard, Lincoln told the general, "will be upon me to know the answer, which I cannot safely show them. They would despair—possible resign" their seats in Congress "to go and save their families somehow, or die with them."[51]

General McClellan also told Buell that "the speedy occupation of East Tennessee [was] of absolute necessity." Buell still failed to move and was backed in his decision by Gen. Henry W. Halleck, commanding in Missouri. Halleck wrote Lincoln that military operations in remote areas like East Tennessee would certainly fail. When the president received Halleck's letter on January 10, he abandoned, at least temporarily, his insistence on the invasion. "It is exceedingly discouraging," he wrote, to be stymied in the East Tennessee movement. "As everything else, nothing can be done," he said.[52]

Within two months the capture of Nashville and much of Middle Tennessee by Federal forces under Buell and U.S. Grant provided a new opportunity for the restoration of Tennessee to the Union and, as Lincoln quickly perceived, a new base for the liberation of East Tennessee. Lincoln's confidence in Southern Unionism and his commitment to the conservative purposes of the war laid down in his inaugural address and his July 4, 1861, message to Congress had not been shaken by the early failure to redeem East Tennessee or by the prolongation of the rebellion. The success of his policy in western Virginia and reports of a returning loyalty on that state's Eastern Shore and along North Carolina's Outer Banks, where Federal military forces had seized control, convinced Lincoln that Southerners were coming to their senses and renewing their allegiance to the Union. As he told Congress in December 1861, "these things demonstrate that the cause of the Union is advancing steadily and certainly southward" with the progress of Federal arms.[53] However slowly the cause of the Union might advance in the South, Lincoln held firmly to the idea that the restoration of civil government in the hands of Southern Unionists should occur simultaneously with the armed suppression of the rebellion. Self-reconstruction, he believed, should be employed as an important weapon to end rebel resistance, provide for future loyal governments, and guarantee the permanency of "the noblest political system the world ever saw."[54]

2

A Presidential Initiative

Despite Lincoln's optimism as 1861 ended, Federal arms had not provided the president with the military successes necessary to encourage reconstruction efforts in the Southern heartland. Preoccupied with military preparations and realistic about immediate reconstruction prospects, Lincoln in 1861 gave no support to quixotic Unionist schemes on Virginia's Eastern Shore and North Carolina's Outer Banks. In the fall of 1861, Unionists in these areas, apparently without the president's knowledge, held elections in anticipation of obtaining recognition in Washington. In North Carolina, Charles Henry Foster, a native New Englander who had settled in the state in 1859, organized a "convention" of a half-dozen Unionists on the Outer Banks, and appointed a provisional governor for the state. Under the aegis of this pseudogovernment, a congressional election was held in November on Hatteras, and Foster, the only candidate, received the 268 votes that were cast. Lincoln, though heartened by the willingness of Outer Bankers to renew their allegiance to the Union, recognized the travesty of the Hatteras proceedings. He ignored the so-called provisional government of North Carolina, and Congress subsequently rejected Foster's claims for a seat in the House of Representatives.[1] On the Eastern Shore of Virginia, Joseph Segar, a conservative Union Whig, was "elected" to Congress in a sham contest in which only twenty-five votes were recorded. Congress initially refused to seat Segar. After Federal forces had secured firm control of the Eastern Shore, local elections were held in January 1862, and Union candidates won more than twelve hundred votes out of a voting population of two thousand. In May, Segar was seated in Congress after

Governor Pierpont, from the temporary Virginia state capital at Wheeling, certified his election.[2]

When Congress met in regular session in December 1861, members of Lincoln's own party seemed intent upon seizing the reconstruction initiative from the president. The war had raged for nine months, and during this period the revival of Southern Unionism had fallen far short of early congressional expectations. Some Republicans, who had cooperated with the president in his recognition of the Restored Government of Virginia and shared his belief that similar loyal governments could be organized in the South, now wanted Congress to lay down a thorough reconstruction policy for the insurrectionary states, one that would ignore Lincoln's self-reconstruction policy and include the abolition of slavery. Hardly had Congress met when bills were introduced with this purpose in mind. In early 1862 Senator Charles Sumner introduced a series of resolutions in the Senate designed to reduce the seceded states to territories and abolish slavery there. Another measure, introduced by James M. Ashley from the House Committee on Territories, also proposed emancipation, the confiscation of rebel property, and the proscription of the political rights of most Confederates. Although many Republicans favored the radical Ashley bill, a coalition of conservative Republicans, border-state Unionists, and Democrats, with Lincoln's support, defeated it in the House of Representatives.[3]

The Sumner-Ashley challenge to Lincoln in Congress caused the president a great deal of concern. He worried about the effect of any extreme federal measure upon Southern Unionists and also upon conservatives and Democrats in the loyal states. Bills and resolutions proposing the subjugation of the South and the forced emancipation of the slaves, Lincoln reasoned, could undermine the important support of non-Republicans and border-state men for his war policy. Already, by late 1861, he was in trouble with Democrats and many conservatives for his suspension of the writ of habeas corpus and other emergency actions that he had taken without congressional authorization. If he expected to maintain a united front behind the military effort to end the rebellion in 1862, he needed to avoid any appearance of radicalism on reconstruction or slavery. It was still not too late for the border states to reverse their decision to remain in the Union. Though unlikely, Lincoln could not be certain that these states or their citizens would remain loyal if confronted with a radical federal policy toward the South. The president believed that a policy of self-reconstruction directed by Southern Unionists was the only constitutional and politically sound approach to this important issue.

If Lincoln needed a reminder of the dire consequences of a radical policy, border state Unionists in Congress supplied it. Senator Garret Davis of Kentucky acted for almost all of his loyal border-state colleagues when he introduced a series of resolutions in the Senate declaring that the government's duty was to put down the rebellion, punish the guilty leaders, grant amnesty to the innocent masses, and give protection to the Unionists who would be charged with the immediate restoration of the legitimate state governments. Davis, an old Whig like Lincoln who had played a major role in saving Kentucky for the Union, maintained that the constitutional rights of Southerners were "fixed, permanent and immutable" and should be resumed immediately after the war with the same "force and effect as though they had not been suspended" by the rebellion. He warned against the confiscation of loyalist property or that of "any person whatever, unless for acts which the law has previously declared to be criminal."[4] Davis's resolutions, however, failed to pass, mainly because of a provision, which some conservatives could not agree to, threatening congressional action if the people of a state did not act. Nevertheless, the resolutions were designed to reaffirm the conservative position as the rebellion entered its second year and as pressure mounted for a federal reconstruction policy.

The conservative and moderate press expressed views similar to Davis's on the purpose of the war and reconstruction and warned against any territorial reorganization plan for the South. The *Washington National Intelligencer*, the bellwether of the old Whig party and an exponent of Lincoln's conservative war policy, claimed that the territorial proposals before Congress, in effect, recognized the "pestilent heresy of secession" because, like the Southern rebels, they adopted the theory that the states had left the Union. In an editorial entitled "The Work of Restoration," this newspaper maintained that "so soon as a State or portion of a State shall be reclaimed by the advance of our armies," the president should issue a general amnesty proclamation and, with congressional approval, establish provisional civil governments in the redeemed districts. These governments, in turn, would "summon the people to the work of restoration under the protection of Federal arms," paving the way for an early return of the states to their rightful place in the Union.[5]

In New York, William Cullen Bryant of the *Evening Post* reflected Northern moderate views when he declared that any movement toward extinguishing the rebel states or subjugating Southerners would excite sharp hostility in the North as well as in the South. Bryant contended that the Southern states governments "are held to be in suspense, but not annulled. As organizations, they have been perverted from their purposes, but not annihilated. They still exist *de jure*. As soon as enough people loyal to the Federal Constitution are gathered to put their machinery in operation, they will be revived." Nevertheless, Bryant, as well as other moderates and conservatives like Davis, demanded punishment for rebel leaders. These men, this New York editor explained, "have committed the most heinous offence against society which it is possible for a citizen to commit, and until they are in some way purged of the crime or punished for it, they are both incapable of civil rights and utterly unworthy of the enjoyment of them." Bryant's Republican neighbor, John B. Raymond of the *New York Times,* agreed that the Confederate "rulers" should be held responsible for the rebellion, but "the treason of the great mass [was] an act committed under duress." Raymond wrote that the "political leaders who have seduced the South into secession will either be hung by the National Government or driven into exile by the loyal citizens of their own States."[6] He would later, however, accept a less harsh fate for rebel leaders.

Aware of such sentiments, Lincoln and members of his party in Washington could ill afford in early 1862 to arouse suspicion among conservatives and others about their purposes in the war. These objectives were still limited to the suppression of the rebellion and the quick restoration of the states to the Union with all of their prewar rights. The successful prosecution of the war, especially in its early stages, depended upon placating conservative and ultraconservative elements in the North and border states. Furthermore, Lincoln's political and constitutional instincts were fundamentally conservative. He genuinely longed for the restoration of the old Union with the rights of the states and liberties of the people intact. Lincoln feared that the lessening of constitutional restraints, as secession had demonstrated in the rebel states, could lead to the destruction of popular government in the North and the impossibility of restoring true republican governments in the South. In his annual message to Congress on December 3, 1861, he pointedly told members of his party that "in considering the policy to be adopted for suppressing the insurrection, I have been anxious and careful that the inevitable conflict for this purpose shall not degenerate into a violent and remorseless revolutionary struggle."[7]

The federal government's position on slavery, of course, was a central issue in the debate over the war and reconstruction. Lincoln repeatedly had promised in 1861 that he would not interfere with the institution in the Southern states. In July, Congress had endorsed this position in the Crittenden-Johnson resolutions.[8] Although a number of Republicans already were concerned that the Southern states would return to the Union with slavery, until early 1862 no significant pressure for emancipation had developed in Congress. Senator Charles Sumner in his reconstruction resolutions, introduced on February 11, declared that Congress should insist on the abolition of slavery in the Southern "territory."[9] His resolutions failed to pass the Senate, but Lincoln, despite his promises on slavery and his fear that any action on his part against the institution might be misunderstood, no longer could ignore the growing demand among members of his party for federal action against the institution.

In March, Lincoln took two steps designed to satisfy Republicans on the slavery issue and to take control of reconstruction. His first step was to propose a plan for the gradual, compensated emancipation of slaves in the South. The president's proposal was designed not only to placate Republicans like Senator Sumner who opposed his reconstruction policy mainly because it contained no emancipation provision, but also to reassure conservatives that by making emancipation completely voluntary on the part of the states he had no intention of abandoning his nonintervention policy. On March 6 Lincoln submitted his compensation plan to Congress in the form of a resolution to be approved by the lawmakers. The scheme, directed at the border-slave states, offered financial aid to "any state which may adopt gradual abolishment of slavery." Such aid, Lincoln explained, would be used by the cooperating state "in it's [sic] discretion, to compensate for the inconveniences public and private, produced by such change of system."[10] If approved, the plan, which the president believed was practical and which reportedly had been endorsed by many influential border-state slaveholders, would not only fulfill the above objectives but, as Lincoln argued, would also shorten the conflict. He declared that if the Union slave states approved the plan, and thereby became free, the Confederacy could no longer be sustained by the hope of winning border-state allegiance. In an explanation that departed from his normally clear and logical thinking, the president insisted that to deprive the Confederacy of the hope that it could secure border-state support, "substantially ends the rebellion; and the initiation of emancipation completely deprives them of it, as to all the states initiating it. . . . I say 'initiation' because in my judgment gradual, and not sudden emancipation, is better for all."[11]

Lincoln insisted that his compensation plan "sets up no claim of a right, by federal authority, to interfere with slavery within state limits. . . . It is proposed as a matter of perfectly free choice" for the citizens of the states. At this point in the original draft of his March 6 proposal, Lincoln wrote this revealing sentence regarding reconstruction: "Should the people of the insurgent districts now reject the councils of treason, revive loyal state governments, and again send Senators and Representatives to Congress, they would, at once find themselves at peace with no institution changed, and with their just influence in the councils of the nation fully re-established."[12] Lincoln, in other words, promised the seceded states an immediate restoration to the Union with slavery preserved if they ceased their rebellion, a pledge that he had made earlier and now reaffirmed in the draft of his compensation proposal.

On the morning that he submitted the compensation message to Congress, Lincoln summoned Senator Charles Sumner to the Executive Mansion to review the draft. He correctly believed that Sumner, a leader of the emerging Radical faction in the Senate, would be pleased with the emancipation proposal, despite the fact that the Massachusetts senator desired direct federal action to end slavery. Sumner, however, was not so easily persuaded that slavery should be explicitly guaranteed by the federal government in any reconstruction plan, as Lincoln's draft provided. When Sumner read the sentence regarding reconstruction, he vehemently protested to the president. Rather than arguing with Sumner, Lincoln, who was in a hurry to send the message to Congress, bracketed the offending sentence for deletion from the proposal.[13]

Lincoln's border-state compensation scheme briefly gained broad support. One indication of this support was the fact that, probably for the only time during the war, all of the six major New York newspapers endorsed an initiative by the administration.[14] The *New York World,* an independent journal at this time, announced: "Here, then, is a hand stretched out to the border states to save them from the ruin, which they have half invited." The rebels "fail in their dearest hope" of gaining border-state support, and if they do not cease their rebellion, "their destruction must follow." This newspaper, which by late 1862 would be a leading Democratic critic of the Lincoln administration, informed its readers that the president in his message "takes it for granted that the abolishment of slavery, while it must be effected by the states, if done at all, must yet be done, and that, though the hand of the general government itself may never strike the blow at its deadly enemy, it may and must nerve the arm that strikes."[15] The Washington correspondent of the *World* reported that at the capital Lincoln's message was "generally regarded as a most ingenious and timely political movement." By striking the golden mean, this writer indicated that the president had undercut the opposition, especially the Radicals in Congress. "While conciliating the more moderate anti-slavery feeling of the country, [Lincoln] at the same time disabuses Southerners that he is bent on peremptorily destroying their domestic institutions."[16]

The *New York Times,* whose editor, Henry J. Raymond, soon would be closely allied with the Lincoln administration, published several articles and editorials in support of the president's emancipation scheme. The *Times* declared that Lincoln's plan "has hit the happy mean upon which all parties in the North and all loyalists in the South can unite." Privately, Raymond expressed a similar sentiment to the president. The message, he wrote, was "a master-piece of practical wisdom and sound policy" that should please all but the extremists. Lincoln thanked Raymond for his support but rebuked him for the comment that "the proposition . . . must fail on the score of expense."[17] Lincoln fully expected Congress for practical financial reasons, if for no other reason, to fund the compensation schemes of those states agreeing to participate. He indicated in his March 6 message that "in the mere financial, or pecuniary view, any member of Congress, with the census-tables and Treasury-reports before him, can readily see for himself how very soon the current expenditures of this war would purchase, at fair valuation, all the slaves in any named State." Nonetheless, the president provided no data to buttress his argument for the financial practicality of his plan, as he would do when, on December 1, 1862, he again appealed to Congress for support of a state-controlled compensation scheme.[18]

The conservative *Washington National Intelligencer*, though desirous of keeping the slavery issue out of national politics, also approved Lincoln's March 6 compensation proposal. "This proposition proceeds on the assumption that slavery is an institution not to be particularly conserved or perpetuated by the action or policy of the [federal] Government, which rather looks with favor on just and peaceful expedients that shall be directed toward its ultimate extinction—with the full consent and co-operation of the States."[19] On the Radical side, Horace Greeley's *New York Tribune* praised the plan and declared that it was the first step toward the eradication of slavery in the South. The *Tribune* sanguinely predicted that all sides, including the rebels, would accept the president's compensation offer. Even the fiery Radical Wendell Phillips, who rarely had a kind word to say about Lincoln's policies, announced his approval of the president's proposal as a move in the right direction toward emancipation.[20]

Lincoln's state-controlled emancipation scheme, however, soon foundered. Although a number of conservative newspapers like the *National Intelligencer*, with influence among Southern Unionists, called for the adoption of the president's proposal, the overwhelming majority of border-state representatives in Congress opposed it. They argued that its implementation would be an entering wedge for direct federal intervention against slavery in the South. The opposition of the influential John J. Crittenden of Kentucky, now in the House of Representatives, virtually insured that the border states would reject Lincoln's proposal. Although Congress approved it in principle on April 10, no border-state legislature accepted the plan.[21] A second rejection by the border representatives of the compensation scheme caused the president during the summer to adopt a direct approach to the eradication of slavery, not in the Union slave states but in the rebel states themselves.

Lincoln's second major step in March 1862 was the appointment of Senator Andrew Johnson as military governor of Tennessee, followed later in the year by similar appointments for North Carolina, Louisiana, Arkansas, and Texas. The president's purpose was to reestablish loyal civil governments in the seceded states as a start toward their full restoration to the Union. The stunning Federal capture of Nashville and occupation of much of Middle Tennessee in early 1862 provided Lincoln with a golden opportunity to seize the initiative in reconstruction. He expected the quick military liberation of Unionist East Tennessee, followed by the rebellion's collapse elsewhere in the state. Lincoln believed that success in restoring Tennessee to the Union would inspire the cause of loyalty throughout the South and, combined with the further penetration of Federal armies into the heartland of the Confederacy and the assistance of local Unionists, bring the insurrection to a rapid end.

With this plan in mind, on March 3 Lincoln appointed Andrew Johnson as military governor of Tennessee with the rank of brigadier general. Although Lincoln probably talked to Johnson about his responsibilities before he left Washington, the president's written instructions to him, through Secretary of War Edwin M. Stanton, were vague. The appointment letter consisted of one long sentence, which read:

> You are hereby appointed Military Governor of the State of Tennessee, with authority to exercise and perform, *within the limits of that state,* all and singular, the powers, duties and functions pertaining to the office of Military Governor (including the *power to establish all necessary offices and tribunals, and suspend the writ of Habeas Corpus*) during the pleasure of the President, or until the loyal inhabitants of that state shall organize a civil government in conformity with the Constitution of the United States.[22]

Although Lincoln had a general plan in mind, he was uncertain of the nature of military government and precisely how civil authority was to be restored. Never before in American history had military rule been imposed upon a state. Because it clashed with his basic conservative views on reconstruction, or what he insisted on calling restoration, and his theory that the Southern states had never left the Union, Lincoln was uneasy about the establishment of military control, even temporarily and in the hands of a prominent political leader like Johnson. Lincoln had not given Johnson detailed instructions because he did not know what the powers of a military governor should be. Nor did he have the time to study the matter. He was also unsure of how the transition should be made from a quasi-military government to civil authority. Of more immediate importance, the president did not indicate to Johnson what the lines of authority were between the military governor and the army commanders in Tennessee. Johnson's instructions from Lincoln to restore civil government as soon as possible could easily conflict with the army's efforts to defeat the Confederate army and suppress guerrillas. Despite his desire for an early restoration of civil government, Lincoln realized that the local political situation and military necessity would shape Johnson's authority and the pace of reconstruction in Tennessee. He seemed to understand that Washington was too remote to provide much practical guidance in the civil reorganization of Tennessee or of any Southern state. In essence, Lincoln gave Johnson a great deal of leeway in carrying out his reconstruction policy.

The Senate on March 4 overwhelmingly confirmed the popular Johnson's appointment as brigadier general without debating the role of the military governors in the reconstruction process. Support in Congress for Johnson's appointment was stronger than even the president could anticipate. When Johnson appeared in the Senate on the day of his selection, senators of all factions warmly congratulated him and wished him godspeed in Tennessee. Although many conservatives had vehemently opposed military interference in the border states, the Johnson appointment, according to a Democratic correspondent, was "an indication of what must be done at the start in every newly conquered Southern state. The state will be allowed to retain its name and status, but . . . the existing rebel authorities will be compelled to give way to the half civil, half military powers that will be placed over them until quiet is restored, and a sufficient body of loyalists are found to inaugurate a civil government." Lincoln's plan of reorganization, this observer confidently predicted, "will go forward through every Southern state, until all are returned to the Union."[23]

The Republican *New York Times* echoed the views of this correspondent. Johnson's appointment, the *Times* contended, was "the exercise of a right" by the president "incidental to the declaration of martial law" in insurrectionary areas. The imposition of martial law and the establishment of a "provisional military government" in Tennessee would be a preliminary step to the restoration of legitimate civil authority. The *Times* reported that Johnson had been instructed, evidently by Lincoln, to call a state convention of loyal men, which, "as was done by a similar body in Missouri, [would] organize a State Government and enforce its authority by all needful power." Once the convention's actions had been approved by the people, the provisional government would cease to exist, and "whatever remnants of rebellion might still exist in the State would be dealt with by

State authorities." The restored government, according to the *Times,* would conform to the state's constitution and existing laws, except as they may have been changed by the rebel government. The *Times* insisted that "the fewer violent changes that are made, and the less interference there is with local law, the sooner will the whole people adapt themselves to the altered order of things."[24] Lincoln's thinking when he appointed Johnson could not have been made clearer than that expressed by the *Times.*

On March 12 Johnson, accompanied by Congressman Horace Maynard and former Tennessee Congressman Emerson Etheridge, quietly slipped into Nashville, just two weeks after its fall to Federal forces. Postmaster General Montgomery Blair, a prominent advocate of a conservative Southern policy, wrote Johnson that "the eyes of the nation are upon you and its warmest feelings follow you" in the task of restoring Tennessee to the Union.[25] To many Northern and border-state supporters of the war, Johnson, who had stood tall for the Union in the Senate, was the ideal choice to launch reconstruction in the South. Even William G. "Parson" Brownlow, Johnson's old East Tennessee antagonist but now aligned with him in the movement to free the state from Confederate control, supported the appointment, believing that Johnson's courage and political prominence were essential characteristics for success against the fierce and determined rebels of Middle Tennessee.[26]

Union Whigs of Middle Tennessee, however, questioned the appointment of the Democrat who had long been their principal political rival in the state and who had supported John C. Breckinridge, the Southern Rights candidate for president in 1860.[27] They suspected that Johnson might use his power as military governor to attack his old political foes and revive party politics in the state. An East Tennessean, Johnson had demonstrated little interest in the affairs of Middle and West Tennessee, a sore point for Unionists of those areas. Gen. William Nelson of Kentucky, who entered Nashville with the vanguard of the Federal army, expressed the view of many Middle Tennessee Whigs when he wrote Salmon P. Chase warning against Johnson's appointment to a position of authority in the state. "Do not send Andy Johnson here in any official capacity. He represents a party. He is too much embittered to entrust with a mission as delicate as the direction of a people under the present circumstances."[28] The warning arrived in Washington after the appointment was made.

Johnson's main concern was the liberation of East Tennessee from Confederate control. In early 1862 he had opposed the diversion of Federal troops in eastern Kentucky for the invasion of Middle Tennessee, an opposition that created resentment among Middle Tennessee loyalists. The choice of these Unionists for military governor was former Whig governor and Mexican War hero William B. Campbell.[29] Because of the prominence of old Whigs in the Unionist coalition during the secession crisis of 1861 and the need to cultivate loyalty in Middle and West Tennessee, Lincoln might have been wise to have selected Campbell, a conservative of Lebanon, for the position. The president was probably unaware of Campbell's availability when he made his selection. Furthermore, Johnson, the only U.S. senator from a Confederate state to retain his seat, was the most prominent Tennessee Unionist and was personally known by the president. Lincoln evidently considered no other person for the state's military governor. At first, Middle Tennessee Whigs who had retained their loyalty to the old flag refrained from openly criticizing the appointment, hoping that Johnson, despite their concerns, would succeed in reestablishing a loyal civil government in the state, one that would reflect the conservative purposes of President Lincoln.

Johnson, like Lincoln and most Southern Unionists, believed that the majority of the Southern people had been misled into secession by designing politicians, editors, and "rebel priests." Although frequently associated by historians with yeoman hostility to the Southern planter aristocracy, Johnson, who owned eight slaves until Confederates seized them, in 1861-1862 found no slaveholders' conspiracy in the decision to destroy the Union. He repeatedly charged that the secession plot had originated among demagogues who had no respect for self-government or for the Constitution and laws of the United States. The conspirators, he asserted, had "simply selected" Lincoln's election "as an occasion that was favorable to excite the prejudices of the South, and thereby enable them to break up this Government and establish a southern confederacy." The Southern people, according to Johnson, never had a real opportunity to express themselves on the issue of secession, and rebel leaders after their brazen coup d'etat had quickly cut off debate and imposed a despotism in their states.[30] Not until 1863—after Lincoln's Emancipation Proclamation—did Johnson begin to hold slaveholding aristocrats responsible for the war and for Southern troubles.

Immediately upon arriving in Nashville, Johnson set out to reassure apprehensive Tennesseans that he came as their savior and friend, not their oppressor. On March 18 he issued a printed "Appeal to the People of Tennessee," indicating his conservative purposes as military governor. The Appeal, reportedly written before Johnson left Washington, reflected the conciliatory views of Lincoln rather than the fire and brimstone pronouncements against rebels that characterized Johnson's other public statements. Although no record exists of a meeting between the two men after Johnson's appointment and before his departure for Tennessee, the wording and tone of the Appeal strongly suggest that a conference occurred and that Lincoln broadly outlined to Johnson what he expected of him as military governor.[31] Citing the republican guarantee clause in the Constitution as the president's authority, Johnson told the people of Tennessee that he had been appointed "in the absence of the regular and established State authorities as Military Governor for the time being, to preserve the public property of the State, to give the protection of law actively enforced to her citizens, and, as speedily as may be, to restore her government to the same condition as before the existing rebellion." He "earnestly invite[d] all the people of Tennessee, desirous or willing to see a restoration of her ancient government" to unite with him "to accomplish this great end." Johnson announced that he would temporarily appoint Unionists to state and local offices. They will serve, he said, until Tennessee "shall be restored so far to its accustomed quiet, that the people can peaceably assemble at the ballot box and select agents of their own choice. Otherwise anarchy would prevail, and no man's life or property would be safe from the desperate and unprincipled."[32]

The Appeal also expressed Lincoln's position that all of the rights of the people "will be duly respected, and their wrongs redressed when made known." It promised that "the erring and misguided will be welcomed on their return." Johnson, however, admitted that "it may become necessary, in vindicating the violated majesty of the law, and in re-asserting its imperial sway, to punish intelligent and conscious treason in high places," but "no merely retaliatory or vindictive policy will be adopted." For those who only privately "have assumed an attitude of hostility to the Government," and were willing to become peaceful citizens, Johnson offered "a full and complete amnesty for all past acts and declarations."[33]

Johnson's first action as military governor was to appoint staunch Unionists to high state positions, including Congressman Horace Maynard, next to Johnson Tennessee's most prominent Unionist. Maynard became attorney general, but he soon returned to Washington and his congressional seat, where he lobbied vigorously for the early Federal redemption of East Tennessee.[34] Johnson's speedy appointment of state officers, though they possessed little authority at first, suggested that he sought to fulfill Lincoln's wishes for an early restoration of civil government in Tennessee.

On March 25 Johnson invoked Tennessee's constitutional requirement that all officeholders must take an oath to support the Constitution of the United States. When the city council demurred on the ground that municipal officers had not been required to do so before the war, the governor replaced its members and arrested Mayor Richard B. Cheatham for giving aid and comfort to the enemy. With Johnson's approval, the new council selected as mayor John Hugh Smith, a prominent Nashville Union Whig who had served in that office during the 1850s.[35] On May 22 an election was held in Davidson County (Nashville) for circuit judge. Although Johnson disapproved of the election, believing it premature, he did not take steps to prevent it. Turner S. Foster, the pro-Confederate candidate, defeated the Unionist candidate by a vote of 706 to 570. Many Unionists, however, declined to vote because they assumed that the election was unauthorized. Incensed by the election's outcome, Johnson arrested Foster for treason but only after giving him his commission as judge. Foster's incarceration was brief; he was released in the fall.[36]

When Johnson realized that he had made a mistake in permitting the Davidson County election, he sent messages to prominent local Unionists in the occupied area indicating that he would not recognize any election until "the Rebel Army [was] expelled and the jurisdiction of the State extended." The military governor acknowledged that he had been slow in appointing officials to vacant offices, but promised to act soon on requests for the reorganization of local government.[37] The fulfillment of his promise continued to be delayed because of the war as Tennessee became a major battlefield in the conflict. Johnson's view of the prospects for rebel redemption was not improved by the invective hurled at him and his "Tory" supporters by a large number of Confederates. Governor Isham Harris reportedly proclaimed: "When we catch Andy Johnson, we are going to flog him alive, & then tan his skin into leather," a threat that Johnson supporters took literally.[38]

True to his promise that disloyalty at the top would not be tolerated, Johnson took over the Bank of Tennessee and arrested officials who had continued to accept Confederate currency. The military governor also suppressed two pro-Confederate newspapers and arrested their editors.[39] He jailed several prominent citizens who, though holding no public office, had been instrumental in the secession movement and had played an active role in raising troops for the Confederacy. Three of these men, including two of the wealthiest persons in Middle Tennessee, were dispatched to Fort Mackinaw in Michigan, where they remained incarcerated until paroled in the fall of 1862.[40]

Ministers who had preached a secessionist gospel also experienced the wrath of Johnson. When he heard reports that six Nashville divines were using the pulpit to encourage defiance of Union authority, Johnson summoned them to his office in the state capitol and asked them to take the oath of allegiance to the United States. When they refused, Johnson sent two of them to a northern prison for a period of reflection, and the others were expelled to Confederate lines. He also arrested five Pulaski ministers and banished them to the Confederacy. Most clergyman, however, avoided Johnson's ire either by expressing their loyalty to the Union or by remaining silent on political issues. Nothing created more antagonism toward Johnson during his early tenure as military governor than his treatment of the Nashville and Pulaski ministers. Even staunch Unionists deplored his action toward the preachers. Johnson responded to the criticism in a blistering Fourth of July speech in which he announced that he had punished "these men, not because they are priests, but because they are traitors and enemies of society, law and order. They have pursued and corrupted boys and silly women, and inculcated rebellion, and now let them suffer the penalty." He made a similar explanation in a letter to a friend that he hoped Lincoln would see.[41] If the president read Johnson's letter, he probably feared that the arrest and imprisonment of the ministers would make martyrs out of them. Furthermore, the arrest of ministers was a bad constitutional precedent and could delay the return of loyalty among the citizenry. Later in the war Lincoln warned Federal commanders against the suppression of the Southern clergy.[42]

The question of loyalty in occupied Tennessee was foremost in the minds of Johnson and other Union officers. Although the state contained both diehard Confederates, at one extreme, and staunch Unionists, at the other, support for either cause ebbed and flowed, depending on the military situation in the area. When, for example, in mid-1862 Federal forces seemed in firm control of Middle Tennessee and able to protect citizens from Confederate retaliation, Unionism, or at least the outward expression of it, flourished. But when the Confederate army, as in late 1862, was successful or when rebel guerrillas and cavalry operated with virtual impunity in the area, the Union cause generally suffered. Loyalty to the Union also was influenced by the promise that the Federal occupation could bring the restoration of the local economy and its social institutions. Determining the extent of loyalty at any particular time or place often frustrated Federal officials. One Northerner reported soon after the occupation of Nashville: "I cannot tell whether there are twenty-five or twenty-five hundred loyal people in her population. There is a great deal of molasses and water loyalty here."[43]

During the early spring of 1862, open support for the Union grew as the Federal army penetrated deep into Middle and West Tennessee. The shocking battle of Shiloh, resulting in thousands of Southern casualties, including the death of Gen. Albert Sidney Johnston, severely damaged Confederate morale and led to the fall of Memphis on June 6. Governor

Johnson, though still intensely concerned about secessionists in positions of influence, exulted in military developments that he believed would soon complete the triumph of Unionism in Tennessee and the early restoration of civil government. "I am meeting with much greater success than I had expected," he happily wrote Secretary of State William H. Seward on April 19. "The Union sentiment is rapidly being developed." Since the Confederate defeat at Shiloh, Johnson reported, the people of the occupied areas no longer fear the consequences of a rebel return and "strong to union feeling . . . is daily being manifested. . . . I feel well assured that Tennessee, always against secession by the voice of her people, will, when the rebel soldiery shall be driven beyond her borders, wheel back into her old place in this glorious Union by a majority of tens of thousands."[44]

Johnson, seizing the moment to advance the Union cause, brought Samuel C. Mercer, a Kentucky editor, to Nashville and provided funding for his publication of a daily loyal newspaper in the city. The governor, through Secretary of State Seward, arranged for the newspaper, aptly called the *Daily Union,* to obtain the federal printing concession.[45] At the same time, Johnson and other Union leaders took to the stump to rally support for the Union and for reconstruction. On May 12 a large meeting of citizens "who [were] in favor of the restoration of the former relations of the State to the Federal Union" was held at the Tennessee capitol. The ex-governor and Whig patriarch William B. Campbell presided over the meeting. Upon taking the chair, Campbell reaffirmed Lincoln's conservative policy that "the Federal Government will pursue a kind, liberal, and benevolent policy toward the people of the South. . . . The Government intends no sweeping confiscation, nor wild turning loose of slaves, against the revolted States. It designs no infringement on the rights of property. [Unionists] bear no malice toward any one, but deep sympathy for the deluded."[46]

Following speeches by other Unionists, Johnson took the stand and spoke for three hours. He emphasized the bipartisan character of the Union rally and, turning to Campbell, his old political rival, exclaimed that it was the proudest moment of his life to stand by him in the Union cause. As he would do elsewhere in 1862, Johnson denied that slavery was an important issue in the war. The one great question that underlaid all others, he insisted, was free popular government; "all other issues were mere pretexts." Taking a more radical stance than Campbell, Johnson did not hold out the olive branch for all "deluded" rebels. He announced that his government would exempt from any penalties the Confederate masses who sincerely renewed their allegiance to the Union. But he would not compromise with the "leading traitors, who have drenched the land in blood." "Treason must be crushed out and traitors must be punished," he shouted to the throng at the state capitol.[47]

During the late spring Johnson made similar addresses, venturing to the periphery of Federal control in Middle Tennessee. He spoke at Murfreesboro, Shelbyville, and Columbia. At Murfreesboro, a Confederate cavalry force almost succeeded in cutting Johnson off from his escape route to Nashville and fulfilling Governor Harris's promise to "flog him alive" if captured. At Columbia he obtained an important convert to the Union cause when former Governor Neill S. Brown, whom Johnson had earlier arrested for treason but subsequently released, pronounced the rebellion "an utter failure" and announced his support for reconstruction. Declaring that the people had been deceived into a war that they did not have the resources to win, Brown asked Tennesseans, "Will you wait until an overwhelming force drives you into the ground" before ending the war?[48] Brown also spoke at a large Union rally at Pulaski, where people came from distant parts of the country, reportedly "eager to learn and anxious for the adoption of some plan by which the war may be ended and their sons and friends called home." The post commander extravagantly claimed that "were an election ordered here now, I don't believe ten votes would be cast in this County against reconstruction of the Union."[49]

Even in Memphis, an early hotbed of Confederate sentiment, Unionism seemed on the rise during the first few weeks of the occupation. Merchants pledged their loyalty mainly in order to resume business and revive the economic life of the town before it lost out to St. Louis and Cincinnati in the rivalry for the river trade.[50] The opportunity to make quick profits in Memphis and its heartland brought in Northern speculators who advertised their desire to buy cotton at its inflated war price. Many of them spread out into occupied West Tennessee seeking to purchase and ship northward the 1861 crop, which in most cases was still held by planters, farmers, and local merchants. Soon planters and farmers, with the connivance of Confederates who needed hard money, brought their cotton through the lines to Memphis. Many small town and rural residents took the oath of allegiance in order to do business.

Cotton was indeed king. One observer noted that "scarcely a day passes that hundreds of our 'country cousins' do not come with the article, which they are mighty willing to part with at prices ranging from thirty-five to sixty cents" a pound, more than triple the staple's prewar price.[51] The correspondent of the *St. Louis Missouri Republican* reported in July that the railroad cars near Memphis groaned with bales of cotton being transported to the North. According to official statistics, more than one hundred cars filled with the staple went north during the first few months of the Federal occupation. Some citizens who had fled the Memphis area when the Federal army approached returned to their homes, took a loyalty oath, and regained their property. Contributing to the desire of many rural inhabitants to take the oath was the local Confederate practice of indiscriminately burning property and sacking towns as they retreated. These depredations left a bitter taste in many mouths, causing them to abandon the rebellion. The Richmond government's institution of military conscription in early 1862 also contributed to a reaction against the Confederacy. After only three weeks of Federal military occupation, three thousand citizens of the Memphis area reportedly had taken the loyalty oath to the Union and others were reconsidering their commitment to the Confederacy.[52] Like in other Southern states, some Tennesseans who took the oath later violated it and again embraced the rebellion.

Federal commanders in the Memphis district, while threatening reprisals against those who aided Confederates, encouraged white support for the Union in a number of important ways. As elsewhere in the occupied South, they permitted the publication of competing loyal newspapers that frequently engaged in factional warfare and occasionally criticized federal policies and local military authorities.[53] The army commanders made it clear from the beginning that the military would return slaves to owners who demonstrated their loyalty. In addition, they put to work black refugees in closely supervised camps. These policies reassured many whites that the Northern purpose in the war was not to destroy slavery or incite black revolt.[54] Gen. Lew Wallace, the first Federal commander in Memphis, held back from imposing military rule in the belief that Governor Johnson or his surrogate would assume control of civil affairs in West Tennessee. Wallace and local Unionists pleaded with Johnson to come to Memphis and reorganize the local government, promising that "you will be more kindly welcomed here than you were at Nashville." Johnson, preoccupied with suppressing rebels in Middle Tennessee and gaining Federal support for the liberation of East Tennessee, never came. His lack of interest in West Tennessee affairs eventually became a sore point for Unionists of the area; they repeatedly asserted that the military governor's neglect impaired the work of reconstruction in the area.[55]

When Gen. William Tecumseh Sherman replaced Wallace on July 21, 1862, he established overall military control of Memphis and announced that he would not trifle with rebels. Despite his characteristic bluster, Sherman dealt gently with the town's citizens. Sherman continued to permit trade in noncontraband items with the surrounding countryside, and he allowed Mayor John Park, who had earlier supported the Confederacy, and other members of the city government to remain in office. In addition, the local police continued to function and the jurisdiction of the provost guards was restricted to military security. Sherman, who understood Lincoln's desire for an early restoration of civil government in the occupied areas, explained to Park that "I have the most unbounded respect for the civil law, courts, and authorities, and shall do all in my power to restore them to their proper use, viz, the protection of life, liberty, and property." He indicated, however, that because of the nearness of rebel forces, "the military, for the time being, must be superior to the civil authority, but it does not therefore destroy it."[56]

Army commanders elsewhere in West Tennessee, in keeping with Lincoln's desires and despite military emergencies and the hostility of many civilians, also went to considerable lengths in permitting civil governments to function. They even allowed elections to be scheduled to fill local offices, though the loyalty of some of the candidates was suspect. A raid by Confederate Gen. Nathan Bedford Forrest in December 1862 disrupted the first elections and only a few counties opened their polls. In an early 1863 congressional election authorized by Johnson, about one-tenth of the voters braved Confederate threats and went to the polls. Alvin Hawkins, a staunch Unionist of Carroll County, won the election with 1,900 votes cast in his favor. The House of Representatives, however, refused to seat him on the grounds that only a small portion of the district voted in the contest, and Governor Johnson did not certify Hawkins's election.[57] Except for Memphis, where a strong Federal base existed, local governments in West Tennessee continued to experience a precarious existence until the end of the war.[58]

Reports of the revival of Unionism in West and Middle Tennessee reached Lincoln in mid-1862, causing him to hope for an early restoration of the state. On July 3 he wrote Johnson encouraging him to hold elections as the first step toward civil reorganization. "If we could, somehow, get a vote of the people of Tennessee and have it result properly it would be worth more to us than a battle gained," he told his military governor. "How long before we can get such a vote?" he asked. Johnson bluntly informed him that the liberation of East Tennessee, with its large loyal population, must occur before a state election could be held.[59] Though disappointed, Lincoln apparently agreed with the governor that East Tennessee, or at least a part of it, should be redeemed before a reorganization election could be held that would "result properly" for the Union cause. Not until after the battle of Stones River (Murfreesboro) in January 1863 did Lincoln renew his appeal to Johnson for a state election.[60]

Efforts to restore civil government in the state ran into another obstacle: the Federal military command in Middle Tennessee balked at the full restoration of civil authority. The fact that the army commanders were charged by the War Department with conducting military operations created an ongoing tension between them and Johnson officials. When Lincoln received complaints from Johnson about military interference, he had to move with caution. The president could not undermine the operations of his commanders; at the same time he could ill afford to undercut his military governor, whom he had appointed to initiate the work of civil reorganization. In the case of the prickly Johnson, Lincoln also faced important political risks. The Tennessean was popular among Northern Democrats and among members of the powerful Senate Committee on the Conduct of the War, on which he had served before his appointment as military governor. Generally, the president hoped that the disputes between his military governor and his army commanders could be resolved without his involvement.

The first conflict occurred between Johnson and Gen. Don Carlos Buell, who commanded in Middle Tennessee in 1862. Though Buell sympathized with Lincoln's conciliatory policy toward the South and early promised Johnson that he would cooperate with him in the restoration of civil government, the general made it clear that he expected to exercise authority over all matters pertaining to the conduct of the war and the security of the occupied area.[61] Johnson insisted that he had authority from Lincoln to control Tennessee affairs, except as they pertained directly to the armies in the field. Because of the ambiguity of Johnson's instructions from Washington and the uniqueness of his position as military governor, a clash probably could not have been avoided. But the governor's sensitiveness and combative personality exacerbated the difficulties with military authorities. Furthermore, on several occasions Johnson went over the heads of Buell and other military officers and appealed directly to Lincoln and Secretary of War Stanton on purely military matters, a practice that greatly incensed Buell.

One week after the military governor's arrival in Nashville, Buell refused Johnson's request for a personal military force to assist in the work of reconstruction. The governor immediately appealed to Secretary of War Stanton, who ordered a reluctant Gen. Henry W. Halleck, the overall commander in the Mississippi Valley, to provide Johnson with an adequate force.[62] The need for troops for the Shiloh-Corinth campaign and elsewhere, however, gave Halleck and Buell good reason to ignore Stanton's order. They not only withheld men from the Tennessee governor but also stripped the Nashville area of its forces, including an Ohio regiment raised with Johnson's aid and bearing his name.[63]

A furious Johnson wired Horace Maynard, his agent in Washington, to see Stanton immediately and secure the return of the troops. "My understanding was that I was sent here to accomplish a certain purpose," he told Maynard. "If the means are withheld it is better to desist from any further efforts. . . . The effect of removing the troops is visible in the face of every secessionist." Johnson argued that until the redeployment order came, "secession was cooling down and [a] great reaction in favor of the Union was taking place." Stanton, after showing the telegram to Lincoln, asked Halleck and Buell for an explanation, whereupon Halleck informed the secretary that every available man was required on the front. "To send troops back to Nashville to accommodate Governor Johnson would be releasing our grasp on the enemy's throat in order to pare his toe-nails," Halleck declared. Buell in his reply simply dismissed Johnson's complaint as "absurd." Under the circumstances, Stanton decided not to interfere in the dispute.[64]

The military governor now appealed directly to Lincoln to keep the Ohio regiment in Nashville. He charged that "petty jealousies and contests between Generals wholly incompetent to discharge the duties assigned them have contributed more to the defeat and embarrassment of the Government than all other causes combined." "If I can be sustained in carrying out the object of the administration in restoring Tennessee to her former status in the Union," Johnson promised Lincoln, reconstruction "can be accomplished in less than three months." Lincoln, like Stanton, refused to override his commander in the field. He telegraphed Johnson that "Halleck understands better than we can here and he must be allowed to control in that quarter." The president, however, suggested that Johnson contact Halleck and express his concerns regarding the troops.[65]

Governor Johnson immediately sought Halleck's aid. He wired Halleck near Pittsburg Landing, Tennessee, and pressed upon him the importance of a force at Nashville, one "sufficient to exert not only a military but a moral power throughout Tennessee, which would be most salutary upon the public mind."[66] No record exists that Halleck replied to Johnson. This first crisis between the governor and the army, however, soon passed, though Johnson continued to blame the military commanders for the insecurity that plagued Middle Tennessee, contributing to his inability to restore local civil authority.[67] The fact that Lincoln and Stanton devoted so much attention to the dispute, including several conferences with Maynard and messages to the military commanders demanding that they justify their actions in withdrawing troops from Nashville, points to the influence that Johnson had in Washington and Lincoln's desire to accommodate him in hopes of securing the early restoration of civil government in Tennessee.

Lincoln's longing for the success of the state's reorganization soon worked in Johnson's favor in his relations with the military. When General

Buell in July 1862 backed the position of two subordinates in a dispute over authority in Nashville, the governor, to no one's surprise, appealed to Lincoln to sustain him. The president responded by ordering the removal of both officers and authorizing Johnson to appoint the provost marshal, or chief security officer, for the town. Lincoln also gave Johnson authority to raise military forces to protect Nashville. The governor, however, went too far when, in July 1862, he sought to move troops into Kentucky to protect the Louisville and Nashville Railroad, Middle Tennessee's lifeline to the North. The president gently rebuked Johnson for seeking to control military operations in the region. "Do you not, my good friend," Lincoln kindly wrote him, "perceive that what you ask is simply to put you in command in the West. You only wish to control in your own localities; but this, you must know, may derange all other parts." The president again recommended that he consult with General Halleck regarding military affairs in the area. Meanwhile, Lincoln sent a message to Halleck suggesting that he accommodate the governor's wishes as much as possible. "The Gov. is a true, and a valuable man—indispensable to us in Tennessee," the president reminded Halleck.[68]

Although Confederate cavalry continued to threaten Union security in Middle Tennessee during the summer and fall of 1862, Johnson maintained pressure on Washington for the liberation of East Tennessee.[69] Declaring repeatedly that East Tennessee was the key to the state's restoration to the Union, he criticized General Buell harshly for his delay in launching the planned summer invasion of the area. Lincoln also was anxious to get the campaign under way. On June 30, 1862, the president prodded General Halleck, Buell's superior, to begin the movement toward Chattanooga. He wrote Halleck that the occupation of East Tennessee was "fully as important as the taking and holding of Richmond." General Buell, however, had his hands full in checking Confederate forces in Middle and West Tennessee. Then, in September, Gen. Braxton Bragg's invasion of Kentucky made matters even worse for the Federal commander. Lincoln realized the military necessity for delaying the East Tennessee campaign, and, despite his prodding, he refused to interfere with Buell's plans.[70] But Johnson and his Unionist associates could not understand the reason for delay. The governor angrily wrote Lincoln that Buell "would never enter and redeem the Eastern portion of the State. I do not believe that he ever intended to, notwithstanding his fair promises." Unless Buell was removed from command, East Tennessee was doomed and the state's reconstruction delayed, Johnson told the president. This letter, written on September 1, may not have been seen by Lincoln until after his removal of Buell in

October, but he was well aware of Johnson's low opinion of the general. The governor's opposition to Buell weighed heavily in Lincoln's decision to find another commander for the army in Tennessee.[71]

Lincoln's preliminary Emancipation Proclamation, issued on September 22, gave many Tennessee Unionists (but not Johnson) additional cause to criticize the president. The story of Lincoln's decision during the summer of 1862 to abandon his early promise not to interfere with slavery in the South is a familiar one.[72] Pressed by antislavery elements in his party and frustrated by the border states' rejection of his voluntary compensation scheme and the failure of his armies to defeat the rebels, on September 22 the president announced that on January 1, 1863, slaves within any state or part of a state still in rebellion "shall be then, thence forward, and forever free." Anticipating criticism for this dramatic departure from his noninterference policy, Lincoln, in beginning the proclamation, reassured Southerners that, despite the change, "as heretofore, the war will be prossecuted [*sic*] for the object of practically restoring the constitutional relation between the United States and each of the [rebel] states." In a further effort to placate critics and perhaps satisfy his own constitutional concerns regarding the proclamation, Lincoln promised that when Congress met in December he would propose another compensated emancipation plan and seek the colonization of blacks outside of the country. The president also promised that the people in any state who held congressional elections and sent their representatives to Congress by January 1 would be exempted from the final emancipation proclamation.[73]

Tennessee Unionists, some of whom held slaves, were not placated by Lincoln's assurances. The more conservative Unionists even threatened to cast their lot with the rebellion because of the president's proclamation. Thomas A.R. Nelson, who had chaired the Greeneville convention of 1861 and subsequently was elected to the U.S. Congress, temporarily renounced his Unionism and issued a printed address to the people of East Tennessee attacking Lincoln's "infamous" proclamation. He charged that it violated the Constitution and opened the way for servile insurrection in the South. Nelson encouraged East Tennesseans to resist "the tyrants and usurpers of the Federal administration who have blasted our hopes and are cruelly seeking to destroy the last vestige of freedom among us." Many East Tennessee Unionists, however, refused to believe that Lincoln had changed his policy toward slavery; they rejected Nelson's address as a rebel forgery.[74]

Johnson, Maynard, and other East Tennessee leaders in late 1862 pleaded with Lincoln to abandon his emancipation policy, particularly as it pertained to Union men.[75] Writing from his native New England, Maynard criticized the president for his twin failures to stand by his conservative war policy and liberate East Tennessee. He harshly demanded that Lincoln,

> having provided for the freedom of the slaves, [should] in God's name, do something for the freedom of the white people of East Tennessee! Their tears and their blood will be a blot on your administration, that time can never efface, & no proclamation can cover up. We asked for a fish [liberation]; you gave us a serpent [emancipation]. For the moment you have satisfied the clamors of a seditious press & the partisans of a seditious leader [Charles Sumner?], at a terrible cost to us.
>
> For this, you, you Sir, are directly, individually responsible. There has been no time when an important word from you would have sent the people relief. But you have listened to the counsels of men . . . [who have] frightened you from your purpose.

In closing his bitter protest, Maynard told Lincoln that "for a long time I had confidence in you personally, & have labored hard to inspire it in the country. You can judge how cruelly I have been disappointed."[76]

Returning to Washington in December, Maynard immediately arranged for an interview with Lincoln. Based on a written statement he made to General Halleck a few days later, he evidently repeated to the president's face what he had said in his earlier letter. He also demanded that an invasion of East Tennessee be launched immediately from nearby Eastern Kentucky and not from relatively remote Middle Tennessee. As indicated in his statement to Halleck, Maynard, who ironically would support the Radical Republicans after the war, declared that the enforcement of emancipation "against the loyal men of East Tennessee would be such a cumulative outrage upon their rights that I think it derogatory to the President" for him even to attempt to defend it.[77]

Stunned by such criticism from his Tennessee friends, and fearful of losing their support, Lincoln exempted all of Tennessee from his final Emancipation Proclamation, despite the fact that no representative from the state would sit in Congress as the September 22 proclamation required.[78] This action produced a sigh of relief among Union leaders in the state. Johnson wrote the president on January 11 applauding his decision to exclude the state from the provisions of the proclamation and declaring that "the Exception in favor of Tennessee will be worth much to us."[79] In addition, as he had promised, Lincoln in his December 1, 1862, annual message to Congress proposed a scheme for the eventual federal compensation for Southern slaves, a gesture designed to reduce opposition to emancipation in Tennessee and elsewhere but soon rejected by Congress.[80]

Conservative Unionists were still unhappy with Lincoln's emancipation policy because of its implications for the future of slavery in Tennessee and the probability that it would cause the rebels to fight harder. These loyalists, perhaps with less intensity than the Confederates, feared the disintegration of the Southern social fabric if slavery ended suddenly. Most Tennessee Unionists, as well as those elsewhere in the South, however, accepted the president's position that military emancipation was designed only to secure the preservation of the Union and not to launch a social revolution. Before the end of 1863, they were providing positive support for emancipation, arguing that slavery was a blight upon the South that needed to be eradicated. Even Thomas A.R. Nelson, though still upset with Lincoln's proclamation, returned to the Union fold. In reality, Nelson, Maynard, and other Southern Unionists had no other choice but to accept emancipation, though not always with a strong commitment. Viewed as traitors by staunch Confederates, Unionists had tied their fortunes and perhaps their lives to the Washington government. Despite their own racial prejudices and their fear that returning Southern loyalty would be seriously retarded by emancipation, the majority of Union activists in the South realized that they could not oppose a major policy of an administration that controlled the government and served as their protector. Unionists also knew that their opposition to the president's emancipation policy would give encouragement to the rebels and contribute to division over the war in the loyal states.

Historians have long commented on Lincoln's need to move carefully on emancipation lest he lose support for the war in the border and Northern states. They have neglected to indicate the importance of Southern Unionists, particularly Tennesseans, in Lincoln's formulation of his emancipation policy. Lincoln understood that in order to prevent a large number of Southern Unionists from deserting the cause and undermining his hopes for the early restoration of the states to the Union he must not push too quickly or too hard on emancipation. It was a measure of Lincoln's political astuteness and skill that he succeeded in winning the active support of many Southern Unionists for emancipation. By the end of 1863, he was so secure in this support that he would make black freedom, but not black rights, an integral part of a new reconstruction plan.

Once he adopted emancipation as a means to win the war, Lincoln had departed from his original intention to preserve the Union and the Constitution as they were. This pragmatic president, however, apparently did not view his action on emancipation as a serious violation of the principle of local self-government or of Southern self-reconstruction. Lincoln left the process of emancipation and the status of blacks in freedom in the hands of local white Unionists, whom he expected to restore loyal, republican governments in their states and deal justly with blacks. Still, slavery was more than a local question for him. Since the 1850s Lincoln had insisted that slavery was a national issue and not merely a matter of state concern. According to Lincoln, the institution and the sectional division that it had spawned created compelling national issues that needed to be addressed in a constitutional and politically viable way. Before the war he had consistently expressed this position by vigorously opposing the expansion of slavery into the common territories of the United States while denying that federal authority could touch the institution in the Southern states.[81] However, when Southerners rebelled and used slavery to destroy the Union, Lincoln moved against the institution in the insurrectionary areas, but only after some hesitation while he weighed political and constitutional implications and sought alternatives (for example, his compensation scheme). In issuing his Emancipation Proclamation, he cited his war powers and the necessity for suppressing the rebellion. Lincoln "sincerely believed" his proclamation was "an act of justice, warranted by the Constitution, upon military necessity" for which he also was invoking "the considerate judgment of mankind and the gracious favor of Almighty God."[82] Though his approach was conservative, Lincoln viewed his action as serving a larger purpose—the ultimate destruction of the institution that violated the American creed set forth in the Declaration of Independence and had caused the terrible war.

3

North Carolina:
The Stanly Experiment

The positive reaction of the Northern and border states to Johnson's appointment in early 1862 encouraged Lincoln to dispatch military governors to other Southern states where Federal enclaves had been established. The first after Tennessee was North Carolina, where in February and March 1862 a Federal army under the command of Gen. Ambrose E. Burnside had seized the Albemarle and Pamlico Sounds region. On March 13 Burnside's forces took New Bern, the state's second largest town, strategically located at the confluence of the Neuse and Trent Rivers. In April, Fort Macon, guarding the Atlantic approach to Beaufort, fell to U.S. troops, and most of eastern North Carolina above Swansboro soon lay in Union hands. As in Tennessee, military raids and guerrilla activity continued to plague the occupied area, and repeated Federal attempts to extend the army's control west of New Bern failed. Likewise, Federal naval and military forces were prevented by the powerful guns of Fort Fisher from taking the important blockade-running port of Wilmington on the Cape Fear.

Like Tennessee, North Carolina had voted down secession in February 1861, and had left the Union only after Fort Sumter and Lincoln's call for troops to suppress the insurrection in the deep South. The state convention vote approving secession was unanimous. Lincoln did not realize the depth of North Carolinian outrage and fear toward his war policy and his antislavery sentiments. Without regard to party politics or class interests, the overwhelming majority of white North Carolinians, reflecting their intense colonial and revolutionary-era opposition to arbitrary power, sincerely believed that Lincoln's decision to preserve the Union by military force was the first step toward the establishment of an antislavery military despotism in the South. Despite Lincoln's promises in his inaugural address, they concluded that slavery and, paradoxically, liberty itself was at stake in the struggle.[1] Though not as radical in their defense of slavery as lower Southerners, North Carolinians like their white neighbors (and many Northerners also) considered liberty and slavery quite compatible, even claiming that the enslavement of blacks was essential to the liberty of whites.[2] Nevertheless, because of North Carolina's initial rejection of secession, the new president mistakenly believed that latent if not outright Unionism existed in the state. He concluded that North Carolinians, with proper encouragement from the federal government, would cooperate in the early reorganization of a loyal government in the occupied eastern part of the state. This government would serve as a nucleus for the extension of loyal control throughout the state until North Carolina had been restored to its proper place in the Union.

After consultation with Secretary of State William H. Seward, who, along with fellow Cabinet members Gideon Welles and Montgomery Blair, also favored a conservative reconstruction policy, Lincoln in April appointed Edward Stanly as military governor of North Carolina.[3] Stanly, the scion of a prominent eastern North Carolina family who had been living in California since 1853, had served several terms earlier as a Whig in the U.S. House of Representatives and in 1857 had run unsuccessfully as the Republican candidate for governor of California. He had affiliated with the Republican party mainly because of its opposition to the Democratic party, which he blamed for the sectional troubles. As a member of the House of Representatives, Stanly gained the reputation, according to former president and fellow congressman John Quincy Adams, for "quick perception, an irritable temper, and a sarcastic turn of mind, sparing neither friend nor foe. He [was] the terror of the Lucifer [Democratic] party." In 1851 Stanly had fought a bloodless duel with Representative Samuel W. Inge, an Alabama Democrat. This encounter was the last duel arising out of a congressional debate.[4] Stanly had mellowed by 1862, when he became military governor of North Carolina, but his partisan combativeness still existed, directed now at secessionists in the South and abolition "fanatics" in the North.

Stanly agreed with Lincoln in early 1862 that the only purpose of the war was to preserve the Union, not to disturb the institutions or laws of the Southern states. Like Lincoln, he believed that thousands of North Carolinians were ready to aid in the work of restoration provided radical or

Edward Stanly, Union military governor of North Carolina, 1862-1863
(courtesy of the North Carolina Division of Archives and History).

antislavery policies did not intrude. Although the president submitted the names of his other military gubernatorial appointees to the Senate for confirmation, he did not do so in Stanly's case. His omission resulted probably from Stanly's refusal of an army commission, and Lincoln did not see the need for asking senatorial approval of an appointment that was not covered by law. The president's failure to seek confirmation, however, later would be used by Stanly's opponents to discredit his efforts in North Carolina.[5]

When Stanly came east from California in mid-May, he first went to Washington, where he sought instructions from Secretary of War Stanton, who asked him to see Lincoln. But the president inexplicably referred him to Secretary of State Seward, who told the exasperated Stanly that he needed no instructions as military governor.[6] Finally, on May 20 Stanton sent him on his way with the same general charge that had been given Johnson in Tennessee, but with the additional comment that Lincoln would "confide in your sound discretion to adopt such measures as circumstances may demand." "Upon your wisdom and energetic action," Stanton informed him, "much will depend" in restoring North Carolina to the Union. Much to Stanly's relief, Stanton, evidently after conferring with Lincoln, directed General Burnside, commanding in North Carolina, to aid the governor in the task of reconstruction. "Between [Stanly] and yourself," Stanton informed the general, "the President expects cordial cooperation" in restoring Federal authority.[7]

General Burnside agreed with Lincoln and Stanly that the Old North State was ripe for reconstruction. While Stanly was in Washington, Burnside confidently reported to Lincoln that "there is much true loyalty here, and all the people are heartily sick of the war. . . . The arrival of Governor Stanley [sic] will, I hope, do a great deal of good."[8] Naval officers, who commanded gunboats that seized the small river towns in northeastern North Carolina, also reported a large measure of Union sentiment along the eastern waterways. One officer informed his superiors that at Plymouth, Elizabeth City, and Windsor "the loyal people are two to one against the disloyal." He maintained that "a little conciliation now may effect great things for the cause." In addition to a policy of conciliation, this officer recommended armed assistance for North Carolina Unionists. He predicted that if weapons were given to the Unionists "the State would soon return to her allegiance."[9] Such reports of Unionist strength in North Carolina were exaggerated, and Federal officers, who initially believed that they would be hailed as liberators, soon realized that they were unwelcome occupiers among a hostile white population.[10]

Immediately after the occupation of New Bern, Burnside, to further the cause of reunion, arranged for the publication of a Union newspaper in the town. Edited by George Mills Joy, a Massachusetts sergeant, this newspaper, the *New Bern Daily Progress,* expressed the conciliatory views of the commanding general and the administration in Washington. It repeatedly assured North Carolinians that the Lincoln government "shall not make war upon the peculiar institutions or reserved rights of a class, but shall adhere to all constitutional requirements under which our nation has thrived so long and happily." In an obvious appeal to Union Whigs, who in Confederate North Carolina had formed the Conservative party to resist secessionist transgressions on their rights, the *Daily Progress* declared that Lincoln was "an enthusiastic endorser of the progressive, gradual [emancipation] policy of the noble and lamented [Henry] Clay." This editor told North Carolinians that the president's rebuke of Gen. David Hunter in May for his proclamation freeing the slaves in his military department (South Carolina, Georgia, and Florida) was strong proof of Lincoln's hostility to the "radical abolitionist wing of the republican party." He urged "conservative men of the glorious old North State" to renew their allegiance and join with the president in the crusade to restore "the Union as it was."[11]

Unlike the cool reception that General Buell gave Andrew Johnson in Nashville, Burnside accorded Stanly a red-carpet treatment when the military governor arrived in New Bern on May 28. In a report to Washington after their first meeting, Burnside gushed with enthusiasm about the prospects for working with Stanly toward the reconstruction of the state. He wrote that his and the new governor's "views in reference to the course that should be adopted in this State by the General Government are remarkably coincident." Burnside promised to grant Stanly "every facility" in his power "to carry out these views."[12] He also invited the governor to make the *Daily Progress* his newspaper organ.

Even with Burnside's support, Stanly's task was formidable. Unlike Johnson in Tennessee, Stanly did not have a cadre of Unionists to assist in the work of reconstruction. Furthermore, though Federal forces had occupied much of the coastal area, their effective control extended little farther than the sounds and river banks where Federal gunboats patrolled. Virtual anarchy gripped the countryside. Federal forces sought unsuccessfully to seize the strategic Wilmington and Weldon Railroad, and Confederate forces, also without success, sought to expel the enemy from New Bern and other important positions. Federal raiders, seeking supplies and attempting to combat Confederate guerrillas, frequently preyed upon the people who had not yet fled to the relative security of the towns. Whites took refuge in Confederate-held interior towns, such as Raleigh and Hillsborough, and blacks flooded into New Bern and smaller eastern towns behind Federal lines. The army established camps for blacks and put able-bodied men to work on fortifications and other military facilities. With many rural communities almost depopulated, the production of agricultural products sharply declined, and foodstuffs were soon in short supply. Only New Bern and a few other eastern towns did not suffer, mainly because they were supplied by the navy and by army foraging raids.[13]

Stanly believed that salvation for North Carolina depended on the early restoration of civil government and the return of the state to the Union. He simultaneously moved, with little success, to protect citizens from plundering soldiers, restore the rule of law, and foster the growth of Unionism by satisfying whites that President Lincoln intended to reestablish the status quo antebellum. As he wrote Stanton soon after his arrival at New Bern, unless he could give North Carolinians "some assurance that this is a war of restoration and not of abolition and destruction, no peace can be restored here for many years to come. I am making efforts to induce Union men to come and talk with me. I feel confident I shall be successful in a few weeks."[14]

Three weeks after his arrival in North Carolina, Stanly took his message of conciliation and Union to the Pamlico River area north of New Bern. Speaking at Washington, North Carolina, to a large crowd, reportedly including representatives from seventeen eastern counties, he laid out an elaborate defense of Lincoln's policies toward the South and slavery and appealed to a returning sense of loyalty among the people of North Carolina. "Mr. Lincoln is no abolitionist," he assured his audience. "He is the best friend the South has got. . . . Has [Lincoln] not said over and over again, that he had no constitutional right to emancipate the slaves?" Stanly informed his listeners that he had been sent by Lincoln to "stand between you and all harm" and also to advise the president about "such terms as you could honorably accept." But he warned that, despite Lincoln's wishes, unless North Carolinians soon ceased their rebellion they would be "swept under" by Northern armies, and their institutions, including slavery, would be destroyed. If they agreed to reunion, not only would slavery be saved, Stanly told them, their republican liberties would be preserved, their seaports and rivers reopened, and their agricultural economy revived, ending the severe hardships caused by the war.[15]

After his tour of the Pamlico country and a stop along the coast, Stanly reported to Lincoln that he saw bright signs for reunion in North Carolina. Everywhere he went, Stanly informed the president, "I have been received with more than cordiality—with enthusiasm." Even many secessionists "are heartily sick of this war. A large majority of the people want the Union restored" and would be more open in their support if they did not fear withdrawal of Federal troops, leaving them at the mercy of "Secession ruffians." The anticipated success of Gen. George B. McClellan's Peninsula campaign against Richmond, he predicted, would provide North Carolinians with the kind of assurance that the state would not be abandoned by Union forces. Stanly also told Lincoln that most North Carolinians "would, if allowed to vote peacably [*sic*], express a preference for your plan of gradual [compensated] emancipation."[16]

Stanly, in his enthusiasm for an early reconstruction that would save the state from further ruin and also preserve slavery, had told Lincoln what the president had believed about Unionism in North Carolina since the beginning of the war. Both had been wrong. True Unionism was in short supply in the Old North State, including the occupied area, and McClellan's embarrassing failure to defeat Lee's army and take Richmond contributed mightily to the almost complete collapse of loyal sentiment in the state. Although most people wanted peace, they were unwilling to sacrifice Southern independence for it, particularly with the prospects high for an early Confederate victory in the war. The success of the Conservative party in the Confederate-held area of the state, which in August 1862 elected young Zebulon B. Vance as governor and won a majority in the legislature, did not portend the revival of Union strength in North Carolina. Secession Democrats, however, repeatedly charged during the campaign that the Conservative party, led by William Woods Holden, the powerful editor of the *Raleigh North Carolina Standard,* was lukewarm in its support of the Confederacy and, if Holden had his way, would reunite with the Union. Although Holden vehemently denied the charge, Stanly, the *New Bern Daily Progress,* and Northern journals wishfully concluded that the Conservative movement was "almost one of us."[17]

Based on Stanly's report and what he heard and read from other sources, Lincoln's hopes soared for an early end of the rebellion in North Carolina. After the Conservative victory in August, the president sent Stanly a "private" message, summoning him to Washington for consultation on the new political developments in the state. "I would very much like for you to see Col. Vance, the newly elected Governor of North Carolina, before you come, if such a thing is practicable," Lincoln told Stanly, perhaps not thinking that such a meeting with Vance could be construed as the recognition of a rebel-held election. The president also asked the military governor "to consider whether it would be advisable to order Congressional elections for accessible districts of North Carolina."[18] Not until after he had visited Washington and talked to Lincoln did Stanly attempt to arrange an interview with Governor Vance, only to be severely rebuffed. Stanly sent copies of his correspondence with Vance to the president, who must have been disappointed that the new administration in Raleigh, which Lincoln hoped had Unionist leanings, had rejected any movement toward peace or reunion.[19]

In fact, Stanly and Lincoln should have known that the Conservatives won in North Carolina because of popular discontent with the Davis administration in Richmond and its "destructive" allies at home, not opposition to the Confederate cause. Holden, Vance, and other Conservative leaders made it clear in 1862 and 1863 that North Carolinians never would accept peace terms short of Southern independence. In the *Standard,* Holden denounced Lincoln's appointment of Stanly as "a wicked attempt to subjugate our people," and he called on eastern North Carolinians to bear "their isolation from the rest of the State . . . with the courage and fortitude which becomes true men who are resisting the tyranny of their oppressors."[20]

Stanly also became embroiled in controversy in New Bern, which greatly weakened his position as military governor and undermined his policy to restore the status quo antebellum. The first trouble occurred when he reminded Vincent Colyer, the Burnside-appointed superintendent of the poor and the founder of two schools for blacks in New Bern, that the laws of North Carolina prohibited the education of blacks. Colyer, an idealistic New Yorker, immediately closed the schools, though Stanly advised him not to act hastily. Later, the military governor disingenuously claimed that he had no intention of ordering the closure of the schools but had only told Colyer that his approval of black education would place him in the difficult position of defying the state's laws, which he could not do without harming the Union cause in North Carolina.[21] Controversy also swirled when Governor Stanly, soon after his arrival in New Bern, returned the fugitive slave of a local citizen. The incident alarmed thousands of blacks in the New Bern area who had entered Federal lines with the approval of General Burnside and now feared that the military governor would assist slaveholders in the recapture of their slaves.[22]

Encouraged by antislavery friends in Burnside's army, Colyer rushed to Washington to complain about Stanly. Upon his arrival he met with Charles Sumner, leader of the emerging Radical Republican faction in the Senate. Sumner, a prewar political enemy of Stanly in Congress, was outraged by what he heard, and he immediately took Colyer to see Lincoln. They found him at the War Department. When Colyer began his report by condemning Stanly for closing the black schools, Lincoln irritably turned on Sumner and asked, "Do you take me for a School-Committeeman" who should deal with such matters? The president's tone, however, changed appreciably when Colyer informed him of Stanly's return of fugitive slaves to their masters. Lincoln at this point, according to Colyer's account of the interview, exclaimed that he had "always maintained, and shall insist on, that no slave who once comes within our lines a fugitive from a rebel, shall ever be returned to his master."[23] Evidently Colyer had concealed from the president the fact that Stanly had permitted the recapture of only one slave; and the slaveholder in that case was a professed Unionist, not a rebel.[24]

Lincoln, however, shrewdly refused to intervene in North Carolina without giving his military governor an opportunity to defend himself. Impatient for action, Republicans in Congress, led by Sumner and backed by a sympathetic Northern press, passed a resolution demanding to know if Stanly had prohibited the education of blacks and, if so, under what authority. An attack on Lincoln's military governments in the South accompanied the criticism of Stanly's regime. Sumner offered a resolution in the Senate, which passed, asking the administration to provide copies of the orders appointing military governors in North Carolina and Tennessee. In a second resolution, which was not approved, the Massachusetts senator insisted that Lincoln cancel Stanly's appointment. Sumner declared that the office of military governor "is without sanction in the Constitution and laws" and also "contrary to the spirit of our institutions, and in derogation of the powers of Congress." Republicans insisted that Stanly was not entitled to the office because Lincoln had never submitted his name to the Senate for confirmation.[25]

The president was shaken by this Republican criticism of his military governments. He knew that the real cause of conflict was not the issue of constitutional authority, as Sumner had said, but stemmed instead from a difference of policy between himself and members of Congress over slavery and reconstruction. Lincoln's confidence in Southern Unionists, many congressional Republicans now believed, was greatly misplaced. They concluded that his policy toward the rebel states and the slave institution, based on the delusion that loyalty could soon be restored and the war ended, had failed, and it should be replaced by an antislavery policy in the South. Middle-of-the-road Republicans, who held the balance of power in Congress, agreed with the Radicals that the federal government should not protect slave property belonging to the rebels. They also balked at the enforcement of antebellum slave codes by Federal officers. These Republicans declined, however, to join the Radicals in insisting that the Stanly regime be dissolved or that the abolition of slavery be made a condition for reconstruction.[26]

Emboldened by the failure of the Radical challenge, the president refused to repudiate his military governments in the South. If he upbraided

Stanly, Lincoln believed he would be committing himself to an antislavery policy that could squelch returning Southern loyalty and undermine support for the war among border-state and Northern conservatives. In the spring of 1862, Lincoln was not prepared to take such a step, although he continued to promote a voluntary state system of compensated emancipation, which, he reasoned, would not weaken support for the Union cause. Though irritated when Colyer complained to him that Stanly had closed black schools in North Carolina, the president agreed with members of his party that no barrier should be placed in the path of those persons seeking to educate African Americans in the occupied South. At the same time he publicly expressed confidence in Stanly and his policy regarding black education. Responding to the congressional resolutions opposing the North Carolina regime, Lincoln reported that "Governor Stanley [*sic*] has not been instructed by the Government to prevent the education of children, white or black, in the State of North Carolina," and, furthermore, he had "no official information that Governor Stanley [*sic*] has interfered to prevent the education of white or black children." The president, without comment, also sent Congress a copy of the letters appointing Stanly and Andrew Johnson to the office of military governor in their states.[27]

Still, Lincoln wanted private assurances that Stanly had not prevented the education of young blacks. He sought, through Stanton, an explanation from Stanly regarding his course toward the black schools in New Bern. The North Carolinian fired back a response that he had never acted to close the schools, despite Colyer's claims or reports in Northern newspapers, nor had he intimated that he would enforce North Carolina's slave code. He turned the issue around by blaming the administration for not providing him with the proper instructions to deal with the "great difficulties" that he faced in governing occupied North Carolina. Specifically, Stanly wanted to be told what action should be taken concerning the thousands of blacks flocking into Federal-held towns and the consequent collapse of the agricultural labor system in eastern North Carolina. He avowed that "if I am to act without instructions and not to be supported when I pursue the deliberate dictates of my judgment and conscience, then I ask . . . to be allowed to tender my immediate resignation."[28]

As one close to the scene, General Burnside came to Stanly's defense and called on the administration to sustain the governor. He wrote Stanton that Colyer had grievously misrepresented Stanly's policies toward blacks and insisted that the governor was "as sound on the Union question as you or I." Later Burnside met with Lincoln and Stanton and reassured them that Stanly was doing good work for the cause of Union in eastern North Carolina and that he was not the tool of rebel slaveholders as depicted in the North. Lincoln, fearful that his policy of appointing military governors and hastening the work of civil reorganization would be dealt a blow if Stanly resigned at this time, agreed and again expressed his confidence in the North Carolinian. The president's action deeply moved Stanly, inspiring him to write a letter of thanks to Lincoln.[29] Even Colyer agreed to write the Republican press indicating that he had misunderstood Stanly's intentions regarding blacks.[30] The Northern criticism of Stanly subsided, and congressional challenges to Lincoln's military governments faded.[31]

Neither Lincoln nor Stanton did anything to bolster Stanly's authority in eastern North Carolina after the Colyer incident. The military situation, however, probably had more to do with Stanly's lack of success than Radical criticism. Although Burnside and his successor John G. Foster were sympathetic to Stanly's efforts, the chaotic conditions existing in eastern North Carolina and the constant threat of Confederate excursions made unavoidable a continuation of the army's control of affairs in the occupied area. Even in relatively secure towns like New Bern and Beaufort, Stanly had little authority, and he made virtually no progress in restoring civil government or enforcing the antebellum laws of North Carolina. His pleas for instructions from Lincoln and Stanton regarding labor policy and the problem of black refugees in the towns went unanswered.[32] On an individual basis, he was successful in protecting the rights of citizens, including Confederate sympathizers, when complaints were made to him. Stanly repeatedly called to the attention of military authorities reports of depredations by Federal raiders in the area. He later claimed that he also protected blacks from soldiers who attempted to drive them from their homes or unjustly jailed them. Stanly declared that in numerous cases he granted permission to blacks to occupy and cultivate abandoned farms and plantations.[33]

Stanly's insistence on the protection of the rights and property of the people contributed to the issuance in January 1863 of strict regulations by General Foster's provost marshal for the conduct of troops in New Bern. These directives provided, for example, that troops on police duty in the town should insure that no private property was entered without proper authority and that no civilian was abused or insulted. Furthermore, any unauthorized soldier or sailor found in the streets after dark was to be arrested and jailed. The sale of liquor to troops or to blacks was strictly prohibited. The provost marshal's regulations went so far as to forbid fast driving in the streets and the hitching of horses to trees in town.[34] Although these regulations provided greater security for residents of New Bern, they did not improve conditions in the countryside. Nor did they convert many old citizens to the Union cause. Repeated Federal military defeats in Virginia continued to forestall cooperation with the Stanly government. At the same time Lincoln's decision to act against slavery increased Stanly's problems in creating a reliable nucleus of Unionism in eastern North Carolina.

Although Stanly appreciated Lincoln's conservative intentions toward the South and support of his own efforts in North Carolina, the governor, like Tennessee Unionists, was stunned by Lincoln's decision in September 1862 to make emancipation an objective of the war. In an interview with the president soon after the issuance of the preliminary Emancipation Proclamation, Stanly, who had privately endorsed Lincoln's gradual, state-controlled, and compensated plan to end slavery, expressed his disapproval of the action and indicated that he could not continue to serve as military governor if the proclamation was implemented. Lincoln assured Stanly that he had not abandoned his Southern Union policy and that he had not become an abolitionist. According to James C. Welling, editor of the *Washington National Intelligencer,* Lincoln informed Stanly that the proclamation had become "a civil necessity" to prevent congressional Radicals from openly embarrassing the government in the conduct of the war. The president reportedly—and disingenuously if true—told Stanly that the Radicals insisted if Lincoln did not come forth with the proclamation for which they had been clamoring, they would take the extreme step in Congress of withholding supplies for carrying on the war. At the same time, the president reaffirmed his support for the program of compensation to owners whose slaves were freed. He also indicated to Stanly that, as he had promised in his preliminary Emancipation Proclamation, the application of the final Emancipation Proclamation could be avoided in districts where congressional elections were held before January.[35]

Stanly, though still puzzled and uneasy about the proclamation, expressed satisfaction with the president's explanation. Two days after his interview with Lincoln, Stanly was further mollified when the president, in a note to him, praised his work in North Carolina. "Your conduct as Military Governor," Lincoln informed him, "has my entire approbation; and is with great satisfaction that I learn you are now to return in the same capacity, with the approbation of the War Department." Lincoln again urged him to hold congressional elections before January, but in the note he did not specifically indicate the relationship of these elections to emancipation.[36] He had already made this point clear to Stanly and also would do so in writing to other military governors in the South.

After his return to North Carolina, Stanly moved slowly toward holding a congressional election in the occupied area. One reason for the delay was the governor's desire that the initiative for the election come from local

Unionists.[37] But the main reason was the governor's wish to await the arrival in the state of Unionist Jennings Pigott, Stanly's candidate for Congress and a former Whig legislator who had been living in Washington. In advancing Pigott for the congressional seat, Stanly and other conservative Unionists sought to check the challenge of the radical and mercurial Charles Henry Foster who, since the summer of 1861, had intrigued to lead the reconstruction effort in eastern North Carolina. On December 10, 1862, the governor finally issued a proclamation scheduling the election for January 1. He did not require a test oath of loyalty for participation in the election, an omission that staunch Unionists and many military officers deplored. Instead, Stanly provided that all white men of at least twelve months' residence could vote and that the state's antebellum election laws would apply.[38] This meant that Federal occupation troops, including many ardent antislavery men in New England units who probably would vote for Foster, could not participate in the election, which, of course, was the conservative Stanly's purpose in setting forth voter requirements.

As expected, Pigott won the election. However, despite Stanly's efforts to get out the vote, only 864 ballots were cast, all in three counties. A "Free Labor" meeting at Beaufort on January 6 petitioned Congress to put aside the election and seek the removal of Stanly before proslavery rebels regained control of eastern North Carolina. After lengthy hearings that also considered congressional contests in other occupied districts of the South, the House of Representatives declined to seat Pigott.[39]

More importantly, the election occurred too late for Lincoln to exclude eastern North Carolina from the provisions of the Emancipation Proclamation. Dismayed by the president's decision to free the slaves, and sensitive to renewed Northern criticism of his policies as military governor, on January 15, 1863, Stanly submitted his resignation. He informed Lincoln that the Emancipation Proclamation had destroyed all hope for the success of his conciliatory policy in North Carolina, and he could no longer in good faith promise the people of the state that their rights and property would be protected by the federal government. Stanly predicted that the proclamation would prolong the war, spurring white Southerners to fight harder to prevent anarchy and ruin. Nevertheless, Stanly promised to continue to support Lincoln and his attempts to restore the Union and civil government in the South. He wrote the president: "Though I cannot approve of the measures you adopt, I know your motives are good and your purposes patriotic."[40]

Stanly's resignation left Lincoln perplexed and disappointed in North Carolina affairs. For three months, he considered appointing another military governor for North Carolina to continue the work of reconstruction.

On February 23, 1863, forty-four Republican members of the House of Representatives petitioned Lincoln to appoint Daniel R. Goodloe to replace Stanly. Goodloe, a former North Carolina editor who had fled the state before the war because of his antislavery views, was acceptable to both Radicals and conservatives in Washington. In April, in a final meeting with Stanly, the president indicated that Goodloe would be appointed if Stanton did not object.[41] There is no evidence that Stanton, who had approved of Stanly's efforts to restore civil rule, opposed the appointment, but Lincoln, with critical military campaigns pending, let the matter slide.

The president's unhappy experience with Stanly and the unwanted conflict with Radical Republicans over the quasi-civil regime in North Carolina contributed to his failure to send another military governor to the state. Lincoln preferred to wait for more substantial evidence of returning loyalty, coupled with emancipation sentiment, before encouraging a new reconstruction effort in North Carolina. Unlike the situation in East Tennessee and western Virginia, no enclave of staunch Unionism containing bold leaders existed in the Federal-controlled part of the Old North State. By 1863 Lincoln realized as a result of the Stanly experiment that ingredients for an early restoration were not available in eastern North Carolina. He hoped that the spring and summer military campaigns would extend the area of Federal control to include Raleigh, the political center of the state, where Holden's dissident *North Carolina Standard* held sway, and western counties, where opposition to the war was beginning to be heard. Not until military forces had penetrated the interior and Unionists asserted themselves would the state be ripe for a new reconstruction effort.

4

The Southwest:
An Uncertain Beginning

On May 1, 1862, New Orleans, the South's largest city and most important port, fell to Federal forces under the command of Flag Officer David G. Farragut and Gen. Benjamin F. Butler. Before the end of spring, Union troops controlled the region around New Orleans and as far upriver as Baton Rouge. General Butler occupied New Orleans with an especially heavy hand to restore order and to root out disloyalty. He appointed Col. George F. Shepley, a former U.S. district attorney for Maine, military mayor of New Orleans and gave him authority over all civil affairs in the city.

Soon after the expulsion of Confederate forces, Butler dispatched provost marshals into the occupied area to maintain order and to administer the oath of allegiance to individuals who wanted to affirm their loyalty. In most cases planters, with a great deal to lose in land and slaves if they did not cooperate with Federal authorities, swore fealty to the Union. Many claimed that they had never actively supported the rebellion—a claim that probably was true in numerous cases. The occupied parishes had voted overwhelmingly for John Bell and Stephen A. Douglas, the Unionist candidates, in the presidential election of 1860, and a relatively large number of the residents, though dismayed by the triumph of the sectional Republican party, had not supported secession. As New Orleans fell, many stalwart Confederates fled the area, carrying their slaves with them and leaving behind Unionist neighbors who expected Federal forces to protect them and respect their rights. By August 1862 eleven thousand citizens had taken the loyalty oath in the Federal-held area. By early 1863 sixty thousand had reportedly sworn allegiance to the Union. Many of them, like residents of Memphis and other occupied towns, did so to resume commercial activities and secure the protection of their property.[1]

Occupied Louisiana, with its strong Union base and cosmopolitan population, offered Lincoln a promising site for an important test of his reconstruction policy. On June 10 Lincoln appointed Shepley military governor of Louisiana. Although "other persons were strongly urged" for the position, Lincoln, with Stanton's concurrence, selected Shepley because Butler had already appointed him mayor of New Orleans. The president probably did not want to risk offending the sensitive and politically influential commanding general by rejecting Shepley, a close associate. Like Johnson in Tennessee and Stanly in North Carolina, Shepley received vague instructions from Washington, and these were sent through Butler. Secretary of War Stanton simply told Shepley that he was "to re-establish the authority of the Federal Government over the State of Louisiana and to secure to the people protection until they can establish a civil government consistent with the Constitution of the United States." Stanton informed him that "it is not deemed necessary to give any specific instructions, but rather to confide in your sound discretion to adopt such measures as circumstances may demand."[2]

Time would prove that Lincoln's appointment of Shepley was a mistake. The colonel (later general) viewed the duties of military governor primarily as that of administrator under the authority of the commanding general. Unlike Johnson in Tennessee and Stanly in North Carolina, Shepley neither understood that he had a role in initiating reconstruction nor comprehended that he should encourage local political action. His close ties with Butler, who soon became a focus of controversy, and the fact that, unlike other military governors, he was not a Southern Unionist also made it difficult for him to lead in the work of reconstruction.

Military authorities soon found themselves overwhelmed by black refugees fleeing the grip of slavery. This situation left Butler in a quandary. President Lincoln had not yet embarked on a policy of freeing the slaves and, when he did in the Emancipation Proclamation, he specifically exempted occupied Louisiana. To make matters more complex, many slaveholders claimed to be Unionists; they therefore expected military authorities to protect their property and return runaway slaves to them. Congress, however, on March 13, 1862, had prohibited the army from "returning fugitives from service or labor, who may have escaped" their masters. This prohibition implicitly extended authority to Federal commanders to provide sanctuary for blacks entering their camps. Earlier, in Virginia, Butler had adopted a policy of retaining as "contraband" of war

Andrew Jackson Hamilton, Union military governor of Texas, 1862-1865; provisional governor of Texas, 1865-1866 (courtesy of Archives Division, Texas State Library).

the few hundred slaves who had been deserted by their Confederate masters or who had labored on rebel fortifications then escaped to Union lines.
In Louisiana, however, the large number of black and white refugees and
indigent persons, especially in New Orleans, caused Butler serious problems. Butler, though privately sympathizing with the fugitive slaves, attempted to stop the flow of blacks into the army camps and the city. Gen.
John W. Phelps, an abolitionist who commanded at one of these camps,
however, insisted on giving refuge to blacks within his lines.[3]

When the president received complaints that Phelps's policy damaged
the Union cause in Louisiana, Lincoln, four days after he had announced
to his Cabinet his intention to free slaves in the rebel states, indignantly
reacted. In a letter marked private to Reverdy Johnson, a prominent Maryland Unionist whom he had sent to New Orleans to investigate charges
against Butler by foreign consuls, Lincoln declared that "the people of
Louisiana—all intelligent people every where—know full well, that I never
had a wish to touch the foundation of their society, or any right of theirs."
Yet "they forced a necessity upon me to send armies among them, and it is
their own fault, not mine, that they are annoyed by the presence of General Phelps." The president told Johnson that they could "remove the
necessity of his presence" by "simply [taking] their place in the Union upon
the old terms. If they will not do this, should they not receive harder blows
rather than lighter ones?"[4]

Still agitated by Unionist complaints against Phelps and other excuses
for the lack of progress toward reconstruction, on July 28 Lincoln wrote a
sharply worded letter to New Orleans Unionist Cuthbert Bullitt, the scion
of a prominent Kentucky family and an old acquaintance of the president.
Lincoln asked Bullitt that if the majority of the people of the occupied district were loyal, which he believed was "probably true," why did not they
form a government and manage their own affairs rather than complain
about the mistakes of federal authorities? "The paralysis—the dead palsy—
of the government in this whole struggle," Lincoln told Bullitt, was due to
the fact that the loyal people of Louisiana "will do nothing for the government, nothing for themselves, except demanding that the government shall
not strike its open enemies, lest they be struck by accident. . . . Of course
the rebellion will never be suppressed in Louisiana, if the professed Union
men there will neither help to do it, nor permit the government to do it
without their help." The solution, the president insisted,

> does not lie in rounding the rough angles of the war, but in re-
> moving the necessity for the war. The people of Louisiana who
> wish protection to person and property, have but to reach forth

their hands and take it. Let them, in good faith, reinaugurate the national authority, and set up a State Government conforming thereto under the constitution. They know how to do it, and can have the protection of the Army while doing it.

As he had written Reverdy Johnson, Lincoln promised Bullitt that the army would be withdrawn as soon as a loyal state government "can dispense with its presence; and the people of the State can then upon the old Constitutional terms, govern themselves to their own liking. This is very simple and easy." On the other hand, if Louisianans "decline what I suggest, you scarcely need to ask what I will do. What would you do in my position? . . . Would you deal lighter blows rather than heavier ones?" he asked. "Would you give up the contest, leaving any available means unapplied"?[5]

Despite his almost simultaneous decision (though at that time unannounced) to eradicate slavery in the Confederate states, Lincoln's threat in the Johnson and Bullitt letters was not serious. When no civil reorganization occurred, the president did not deal heavier blows against Louisiana. His fulminations reflected more frustration over the failure of Louisiana Unionists to take hold of reconstruction and reorganize the state government than an intent to act harshly, thereby undermining white loyalty in the state and elsewhere in the occupied South. No doubt some of Lincoln's frustration could be attributed to the border-states' failure to accept his compensation plan for ending slavery and thereby, as he believed, undermining the rebellion itself. Furthermore, the Federal military situation, which seemed bright in the spring, had deteriorated, creating a greater demand by Northern Republicans for action against slavery and its rebel retainers. Everything seemed to conspire against Lincoln's conservative purposes in the war. The heavier blows for Louisiana that Lincoln had threatened in his letter to Bullitt referred not to what he thought was right but what he feared would be forced upon him by events and Northern Republican pressure. Except to suppress the armed rebellion and politically proscribe its leaders, Lincoln did not believe that he—or, for that matter, the federal government—had the constitutional authority to strike heavier blows against the South. As explained earlier, his emancipation decision, which would be limited in its application, was justified on the grounds of "military necessity" for the purpose of suppressing the rebellion. Lincoln promised Louisiana Unionists that whatever action he took, "I shall do nothing in malice. What I deal with is too vast for malicious dealing."[6]

A few days later, in response to still another Unionist criticism of his failure to indicate what he expected of Louisiana, Lincoln angrily declared that if the complainant wanted to know his policy he should read his inaugural address, his messages to Congress, and "minor documents" that he had issued. These materials, Lincoln inferred, plainly demonstrated his conservative purposes in reconstruction. The president went on to repeat the substance of what he had written Bullitt. "Broken eggs cannot be mended," he declared; "but Louisiana has nothing to do now but to take her place in the Union as it was, barring the already broken eggs. The sooner she does so, the smaller will be the amount of that which will be past mending. This government cannot much longer play a game in which it stakes all, and its enemies stake nothing."[7]

Despite Lincoln's admonition for them to act, Louisiana Unionists, lacking specific instructions from the president or encouragement from Military Governor Shepley, made no move to organize a government. For more than two months during the late summer of 1862, Lincoln focused his attention on the critical military engagements in Virginia and Maryland and also on his new emancipation policy. During this period he ignored affairs in Louisiana. When Lincoln did become involved again, he had changed his emphasis from insisting on the immediate formation of loyal governments in the South to the holding of elections for seats in Congress. The president had been disappointed in the slow pace of state reorganizations. He concluded that the only attainable step toward reconstruction at this time was the election of loyal congressmen in the occupied districts. If Congress accepted these representatives, Lincoln believed that the process of state reorganization would be significantly advanced. As he had promised in his preliminary Emancipation Proclamation of September 22 and had told Military Governor Stanly of North Carolina and others, congressional districts that held elections and sent their representatives to Washington would be exempted from emancipation. Lincoln now used the threat of emancipation to persuade Southerners to abandon the rebellion, send loyal representatives to Congress, and restore Union governments in their states. For Lincoln, bringing the Emancipation Proclamation to bear upon the reconstruction process would be an immediate and practical demonstration of his constitutional justification that he acted out of "military necessity" for the purpose of restoring the Southern states to the Union. Though the secretive Lincoln did not always reveal his purposes, particularly those of a political nature, he might have believed that his promise to exempt loyal districts from the provisions of his proclamation would reduce conservative opposition to his emancipation decision in the North and the border states, as well as among Southern Unionists. With state and local elections scheduled in the fall, Lincoln must have been concerned about the fate of his party and also support for the war in the

Union states. For political reasons, he probably believed that he needed to show progress, especially in Louisiana, in his efforts to restore the wayward South to the Union.[8]

On October 14 Lincoln sent John E. Bouligny, the only Louisianan to remain in Congress when the state seceded, to New Orleans with instructions to Butler and Shepley to organize congressional elections as soon as possible. They were specifically directed to aid Bouligny in arranging the contests. The people, Lincoln wrote, by holding elections would "avoid the unsatisfactory prospect before them," namely emancipation, and will "have peace again upon the old terms under the constitution of the United States." The president also thought that the time might be ripe for elections for state officers and United States senators, but he did not insist on this point. "In all available ways," he declared, "give the people a chance to express their wishes at these elections. Follow forms of law as far as convenient, but at all events get the expression of the largest number of the people possible. All see how such action will connect with, and affect the proclamation of September 22nd."[9]

When no steps had been taken by early November to schedule elections, Lincoln wrote Shepley that he was "annoyed" by the delay. "I wish elections for Congressmen to take place in Louisiana," he pointedly told Shepley; "but I wish it to be a movement of the people of the Districts, and not a movement of our military and quasi-military, authorities there. I merely wish our authorities to give the people a chance—to protect them against secession interference." The president preferred that local Unionists "fix a day and a way" for the elections, but if they did not act, he instructed Shepley to "fix these things for them by proclamation. And do not waste a day about it; but, fix the election early enough that we can hear the result here by the first of January." In another letter to the military governor, Lincoln warned against the election of outsiders to represent Louisiana in Congress. "To send a parcel of Northern men here, as representatives, elected as would be understood, (and perhaps really so), at the point of the bayonet, would be disgusting and outrageous." Under the circumstances, Congress would probably refuse to seat them. "What we want is the conclusive evidence that respectable citizens of Louisiana, are willing to be members of congress & to swear support to the constitution; and that other respectable citizens there are willing to vote for them" and send them to Washington.[10]

Actually, a few days earlier Shepley had ordered an election for December 3 in the two congressional districts under Federal control. The Union Association of New Orleans, organized during the summer, seized the initiative in the brief campaign and nominated candidates for the seats.

Clear political lines over emancipation and other issues that would be raised later were not drawn in the contest. The only significant issue in the campaign was the candidates' loyalty to the Union in 1861 and early 1862 when the secessionists controlled the area. As Lincoln had directed, the military did not interfere with the election, though General Butler "persuaded" Dr. Thomas Cottman, a conservative sugar planter, to withdraw from the race because he had signed the state's ordinance of secession. Butler admitted that the doctor was "a good Union man now," but he thought that it was wise that Cottman withdraw, since "the Government should not be put to the scandal of having a person so situated elected" to Congress.[11]

In the election Benjamin F. Flanders, a New England native who had settled in New Orleans in 1842, and Michael Hahn, a native of Germany, easily defeated their opponents. Flanders, who would soon become a leading radical in Louisiana, had the support of General Butler's friends, while Hahn, who would later lead a more moderate or conservative faction, lacked their endorsement. Hahn's successful candidacy was clear evidence that Butler and the military did not control the election. The turnout at the polls was impressive, especially in view of the fact that many of the two districts' 1860 electorate were in the Confederate army. Seven thousand, seven hundred, and sixty citizens cast ballots in the two congressional districts—60 percent of the number that had voted in the last prewar election for the seats.[12]

When Flanders and Hahn arrived in Washington to take their places in Congress, they found themselves at the center of controversy. Although they were greeted warmly by Republicans, a debate raged in Congress over the whole issue of seating representatives from the Confederate states before loyal civil governments had been established. Many Republicans, including almost all of the Radical faction, now had second thoughts about their earlier support for or acquiescence in Lincoln's military governments in the South and the seating of members from Tennessee and Virginia in 1861 and early 1862. They were particularly distraught over the president's frantic efforts in late 1862 to hold congressional elections in occupied areas for the purpose of encouraging reconstruction without emancipation. Furthermore, Radicals believed that Lincoln in his preliminary Emancipation Proclamation had opened the floodgates to unreliable white voters by exempting from freedom those states or parts of states where "a majority of the qualified voters" had participated in congressional elections. This provision suggested a departure from his policy of recognizing only the loyal element as the body politic in the rebel states. Actually, the president probably inadvertently omitted an important word in this provision. He probably intended to say a majority of the *loyal* voters of a district must go

to the polls for the election to count. At any rate, Lincoln now was willing
to approve elections, and thus the exemption from emancipation, of districts where only a minority who were presumably loyal cast ballots,
specifically in Virginia, North Carolina, and Arkansas.[13]

In Congress, Democrats, for different reasons, joined dissident Republicans in arguing that Lincoln lacked constitutional authority to create
military governments in the South. His policy of military rule in the
South, though designed to be temporary, and his Emancipation Proclamation (which became final on January 1, 1863) caused Democrats and
many anti-Republican conservatives (mostly ex-Whigs) to charge that the
president had adopted the Radical policy of Southern subjugation as the
purpose of the war. Daniel Voorhees, Democratic leader in the House
of Representatives, declared that the seating of members from military
enclaves in the South would be "a total subversion of the principles of representative government." Democrats also charged that in securing the
election of friendly representatives from rotten Southern boroughs, the
president sought to strengthen the Republican party in Congress.[14]

Without noting Democratic criticism, Lincoln denied any such partisan intention. "We do not particularly need members of congress" from
the South "to get along with legislation here," he informed George F. Shepley in Louisiana.[15] Lincoln's purpose was to jump-start efforts toward
self-reconstruction in the Federal-occupied areas. Employing the threat of
emancipation, he believed that congressional elections in these districts
would motivate local Unionists, with the backing of the military, to go a
step further and hold elections for reorganized governments in their states.

On February 9, 1863, the Committee on Elections, chaired by Republican Henry L. Dawes of Massachusetts, recommended that Flanders
and Hahn be seated. The decision of the committee hinged on the members' belief that all of the requirements of Louisiana law except one had
been met in the elections and also the fact that a large number of antebellum voters—in this case a majority—had voted. The only exception to
the state's election law was that Lincoln's military governor, not a civil authority, had issued the call for the elections. This action, however,
constituted no serious violation of a free ballot. Nevertheless, the committee admitted that it was uneasy about clothing the position of military
governor in the South with legitimacy, and it mildly rebuked Lincoln for
failing to enlighten Congress on this officer's role in Louisiana. "The committee sought, as the House well knows, to obtain from the President what
sort of commission be [he] clothed this military governor with—without
success however," Dawes informed his colleagues. "The office of military
governor is not very clearly defined," though "I suppose it has its origin in

necessity," specifically the need to prevent chaos after the military occupation of an area and also to assist in the restoration of self-government. Regardless, Dawes argued, the only practical way for reconstruction to be launched in the Southern states was for Lincoln's military governors to issue writs of election, which Shepley had done in Louisiana.[16]

After several days of debate, the House approved—by a wide margin of 92 to 44—the committee's recommendation to seat Flanders and Hahn. Lincoln and members of Congress were surprised by the overwhelming vote in favor of the Louisianans. The key to the committee's easy victory was the House's decision to permit Hahn, on the day of the vote, to speak on the floor in his and Flanders' behalf.[17]

The decision to allow a claimant for a seat in Congress to state his case before the chamber was unprecedented. In this case, it probably was influenced by the Republican need to reverse the growing disillusionment with the war in the North during the winter of 1862-63 and to demonstrate to Northerners that loyalty existed in the South, a loyalty that Republicans of Lincoln's persuasion believed must be sustained and encouraged. Leaders of the war party insisted that Southern Unionists, who had shown their mettle in defense of the nation, had a claim on Northerners to fulfill their commitment to the reestablishment of a republican form of government in the South, as guaranteed by the Constitution for every state.

Republicans already had solid evidence of the powerful emotional effect of Southern Union orators on Northern audiences. Speaking extensively in the North in 1862 and 1863, Andrew Johnson and Parson Brownlow of Tennessee, Andrew Jackson Hamilton of Texas, Flanders of Louisiana, and other prominent Southern loyalists had graphically—and frequently with a cavalier disregard for the facts—described the Unionist struggle to overcome rebel oppression and restore loyal governments in the South. In every speech, they confidently predicted the eventual triumph of the cause, which, they proclaimed, would redound to the glory of the nation for generations to come. All that was required to achieve this noble goal was a united North and the suppression of Northern "croakers" and copperheads, or peace Democrats. Most speakers even expressed their approval of Lincoln's emancipation policy provided the destruction of slavery was necessary to save the Union. Nevertheless, because of the opposition of their constituents to emancipation and the need for the support of most Northern Democrats and conservatives who insisted on the restoration of "the Union as it was," Southern speakers played down Lincoln's antislavery policy. When they mentioned emancipation, they argued that the secessionists, in continuing their rebellion, had forced Lincoln to take action

against the institution. A major exception to the Unionists who soft-
pedaled the slavery issue was Hamilton of Texas, who, beginning with
Lincoln's preliminary Emancipation Proclamation, persistently and vigorously argued that the end of slavery would be a positive good for the
South.[18]

In his important address to the House in early 1863, Hahn ignored
the slavery issue in a stirring appeal for members to demonstrate support
for Louisiana Unionists by admitting their representatives to Congress. He
claimed that the majority of the old citizens of New Orleans and Southern
Louisiana "have never voluntarily done anything that could in the least
taint them with disloyalty." Hahn informed members of the House that
the people of the area had historically produced sugar and vegetables and
had never been a part of the cotton culture of Northern Louisiana that had
caused secession. Not only had Southern Louisiana voted for Union candidates in the 1860 presidential election, it was "a notorious fact," Hahn
argued, that under Confederate control "the jails of New Orleans were
crowded with the loyal citizens of Louisiana who refused to approve the
treasonable doings and submit to the authority of the rebel government."
Other Unionists, he declared, were "ruthlessly driven from their homes and
families" and into exile in the North. Hahn told House members that, although Lincoln had ordered Shepley to call for elections, the citizens of the
two congressional districts had long pressed for such action. In response to
those who argued that Lincoln's military governors had no authority under
law, Hahn maintained that the Unionists of Southern Louisiana recognized
Shepley as their governor and approved of his administration. The Louisianan insisted that his primary interest in a House seat was not personal
ambition but his conviction that the reconstruction of the Bayou State
and other Southern states would be dramatically advanced by his admission to Congress.[19]

Lincoln must have been elated with Hahn's speech, followed by the
action of the House in seating the Louisianans. Despite opposition from
both ends of the political spectrum, the large House majority in favor of
Flanders and Hahn suggested to the president that his reconstruction
policy and his conservative approach to emancipation had been accepted
by Congress.[20] Though increasingly preoccupied with the war as the spring
campaigns began, after this victory Lincoln expected the process of reconstruction to accelerate in the occupied areas of the South. He hoped that
his military governors and local Unionists would assume more initiative
than they had earlier. Lincoln particularly expected Louisiana to move
toward the restoration of civil government and the extension of Federal
control throughout the state. The president, however, soon was disap-

pointed, both by his friends in the South who, for a variety of reasons, failed to act, and also by Congress, which, despite the seating of the Louisiana representatives and its recognition of the Restored Government of Virginia, had never really given Lincoln carte blanche for his evolving reconstruction policies. Congress in fact became increasingly reluctant to cooperate with him. Flanders and Hahn would be the last representatives from the South to be seated during the war. The absence of Southern representatives in Congress left Lincoln's reconstruction program incomplete.

Although Lincoln focused most of his attention in 1862 on the reorganization of Tennessee, North Carolina, and Louisiana, during this period he also made tentative efforts at reconstruction in two other states, Arkansas and Texas. The situation in Arkansas appeared especially promising as the military campaigns of 1862 unfolded. After defeating Confederate forces at Pea Ridge in March 1862, a Federal army under the command of Gen. Samuel Curtis swept into northern Arkansas. Batesville fell on May 4, and Confederate Governor Henry M. Rector, believing that the capture of Little Rock was imminent, fled the state capital. Confederate reinforcements, however, saved Little Rock but not before Southern morale in Arkansas had been seriously weakened. The high tide of the 1862 Union campaign in the state was reached on July 12 when General Curtis's forces captured Helena on the Mississippi River.[21]

Like Southern Louisiana, Arkansas had given a majority of its votes in the 1860 presidential election to Union candidates Bell and Douglas. Southern Rights nominee John C. Breckinridge, however, carried the state by winning a plurality of the votes. Arkansas resisted secession until Fort Sumter and Lincoln's call for troops to suppress the Southern insurrection. Even after the state joined the Confederacy, hundreds of Arkansans, especially in the northwestern hill country, remained loyal to the Union. An even larger number began to have second thoughts about secession when the terrible consequences of war were brought home to them in 1862. The "arbitrary and tyrannical acts" of rebel officers in enforcing the Confederate conscription law and destroying cotton and other property as they retreated caused bitter resentment throughout northern Arkansas.[22]

Like East Tennesseans, many Arkansas Unionists joined the Federal army while their families either remained at home to face a life of hardships, including the threat of guerrilla reprisals, or fled to Missouri or the Midwest, where they became impoverished and unwanted refugees. By the end of the war, approximately ten thousand Arkansans had served in the Union army. Most Arkansas Unionists, like their compatriots in East Tennessee, were nonslaveholders (as, for that matter, were most

Confederate soldiers), but they hardly fitted the stereotype of the oppressed poor-white hill dwellers who saw the war as an opportunity to avenge past wrongs suffered at the hands of the lowland slaveholding aristocracy. "In reality, with scarcely an exception," according to the Union editor of an Arkansas newspaper, the state's Federal troops "were owners of farms, of cattle and [were] well to do in the world." They were also educated and patronized newspapers more than did residents of the slaveholding counties.[23]

Sufficiently impressed by reports of resurging loyalty in Arkansas, on July 19, 1862, Lincoln appointed John S. Phelps, a longtime Democratic congressman from Missouri, military governor of Arkansas with the rank of brigadier general. Phelps's instructions from Secretary of War Stanton were identical to those given Lincoln's other military governors.[24] Phelps, a slaveholder who one week prior to his appointment had joined nineteen other border-state members of Congress in rejecting Lincoln's compensated emancipation proposal, made his way slowly to Helena, where he established his "government," consisting of himself and a secretary.[25]

By the time of Phelps's arrival, the Federal offensive in Arkansas had ground to a halt in the face of a relentless counterattack by Confederate Gen. Thomas C. Hindman using guerrilla tactics. Instead of presiding over a reorganized state administration in Little Rock, which he expected to do by the end of the year, Phelps found himself, along with ten thousand Federal troops, hemmed in and harassed at Helena by Hindman's forces. When General Curtis refused, for sound logistical reasons, to complete the conquest of Arkansas, Phelps bitterly complained to Stanton. He charged that military operations in the state had been delayed in order to aid "officers and cotton traders in making fortunes with the blood of our brave men." By Christmas, the governor, sick and disillusioned with the situation in Arkansas, had returned to St. Louis to await the redemption of the state. Before Phelps had an opportunity to assume control of reconstruction in Arkansas, Lincoln, dismayed by setbacks in the state, revoked his appointment as military governor.[26]

Despite the unsettled military situation in Arkansas in late 1862, Lincoln, as he had done elsewhere, urged the state's Unionists to hold congressional elections before January 1. The president sent the same message regarding elections to Gen. Frederick Steele, commanding Federal forces in Arkansas, and Military Governor Phelps that he had earlier sent to authorities in Tennessee and Louisiana, including the comment that "all see how such action will connect with and affect the [emancipation] proclamation of September 22d."[27] Lincoln also dispatched William M. McPherson to Arkansas with instructions to encourage and aid Unionists in organizing and holding elections. McPherson, a politically obscure individual who apparently was a prewar resident of the state, first went to St. Louis where, after conferring with Arkansas Unionists, reported to Lincoln that he was "greatly encouraged at the prospect of getting an election" in northern Arkansas, provided "the people can be sufficiently protected by the movements of the army." He told Lincoln that "a majority of the people north of the Arkansas River are truly loyal and would prove it by their votes if allowed without fear to go to the polls." McPherson indicated that General Curtis, the department commander, believed that a new military operation into northern Arkansas, which would take several weeks, was needed before the area could be cleared of Confederate guerrillas and Unionist fears relieved. Recalling the deadline for the issuance of the Emancipation Proclamation and confronted by Unionists who wanted an exemption from its provisions, McPherson urgently asked Lincoln for a postponement of the election. "Can I give the people assurance that if they act in good faith and elect a member within the month of January that it will save them?" he inquired. Before he could receive a response from the president, McPherson, after a two-week visit to the Federal enclave at Helena, changed his mind about the practicality of immediately holding a congressional election. He reported to the president that Union forces did not occupy any county in the eastern part of the state and that guerrillas continued to harass loyal people elsewhere.[28] With this bleak report in hand, Lincoln dropped his insistence on an election, or elections, in Arkansas.

After his proclamation of January 1, Lincoln's interest in Southern reconstruction temporarily declined. Along with his attention to military affairs, his relative inactivity on reconstruction matters, continuing until the late summer of 1863, partly was influenced by the fact that the threat of emancipation—a weapon he had used largely unsuccessfully to secure congressional elections—was no longer available. The Emancipation Proclamation had been issued freeing slaves, if only on paper, in those districts of the Confederate South that had not held elections to send representatives to the U.S. Congress.

In Arkansas, however, an unusual opportunity seemed to open for Lincoln to combine emancipation with the readmission to Congress of one of the state's antebellum senators. In late July 1863, William K. Sebastian, who had resigned from the U.S. Senate when Arkansas left the Union, indicated his intention to go to Washington and claim his seat. Based on this information and the further report that Sebastian had the support of Arkansas Unionists, Lincoln immediately wrote Gen. Stephen A. Hurlbut, commanding in Memphis, where Sebastian lived: "I understand that Senator Sebastian of Arkansas thinks of offering to resume his place in the Senate. Of course the Senate, and not I, would decide whether to admit or reject him. Still I should feel great interest in the question. It may be so presented as to be one of the very greatest national importance," particularly, Lincoln suggested, if admission were tied to both reconstruction and emancipation. Although he reaffirmed that "the emancipation proclamation applies to Arkansas [and] I think I shall not retract or repudiate it," Lincoln indicated that he would accept any plan from Arkansas—and, by implication, any Confederate state—that provided for the gradual emancipation of slaves who had not yet been freed. Still, Lincoln insisted, emancipation "should begin at once, giving at least the new-born, a vested interest in freedom, which could not be taken away. If Senator Sebastian could come with something of this sort from Arkansas, I at least should take great interest in his case; and I believe a single individual will have scarcely done the world so great a service." General Hurlbut, an old friend of Lincoln's, conveyed the message to Sebastian, but the former Arkansas senator refused to cooperate.[29] Disappointed by this failure, Lincoln never again proposed such a scheme. But the president did not abandon completely the notion of gradual emancipation.

Texas was the last state to receive a Lincoln-appointed military governor. The situation in the Lone Star State, however, was even less promising for success than in Arkansas, though Texas Unionists and influential northeasterners with economic interests to serve argued otherwise. In the beginning of the war, a relatively large number of Texans, particularly in the Austin area, remained loyal to the Union and for almost a year were usually successful in resisting Confederate encroachments upon their liberties. By the spring of 1862, however, Confederate authorities and local vigilante committees had gained the upper hand and had launched a vigorous campaign to suppress Unionist dissent. Lacking arms and unable to organize for defense because of the vast distances separating settlements, Unionists had no choice but to flee persecution and, in many cases, death. Hundreds of them, frequently leaving their families to the tender mercies of their Confederate neighbors, hid out in the hills or desperately sought sanctuary across the Rio Grande. Some refugees were pursued by Confederate cavalry into Mexico. In August 1862 more than twenty German-Americans were killed in a pitched battle with Confederate troops on the banks of the Nueces as they sought unsuccessfully to escape to Mexico. Crowds of Union refugees huddled in Matamoros, Mexico, near the mouth of the Rio Grande, waiting, usually in vain, for rescue by United States vessels off the coast. In northwestern Texas, a more bloody Confederate campaign against Unionists occurred. Almost one hundred Unionists or suspected "traitors" were lynched in the area when Confederates discovered a Unionist plot to raise a military force, seize arms and supplies, and march to join the Federal army in Kansas.[30]

Escaping Unionists rushed to Federal-occupied New Orleans and then to the North to give grim accounts of loyalist suffering in Texas and urge the liberation of their state. They found thousands of Northern listeners eager to hear about the latest exploits of Southern Unionists in their heroic struggle to resist rebel tyranny. No man was more powerful in his appeal than Andrew Jackson Hamilton, a former Democratic congressman and the leader of the loyalists in the Austin area. Born and raised in Alabama, "Colossus Jack" Hamilton moved with two slaves to Texas in 1846 and became one of the most prominent lawyers in the Southwest. Though he supported the institution of slavery, by 1860 he possessed no slaves. When the war came, Hamilton abandoned his support of slavery. As he declared in 1862, "the very moment [slavery] sought to tear away from me the only protection I have ever had, or hope to leave my posterity—the flag of my fathers—for the purpose of building another government upon slavery, as its cornerstone—that moment I changed my relationship [to it]." He then became an abolitionist.[31]

Driven from his home by Confederates in 1862, Hamilton and a few friends crossed the Rio Grande in mid-summer, escaping several Confederate ambushes in northern Mexico before reaching safety. By late September he was in New York, where romantic accounts of his adventures preceded him and where he received a warm welcome from the National War Committee of the Citizens of New York.[32] This committee, consisting of prominent Republican merchants and other leading advocates of the war in the city, was organized to foster support for the Union cause and, though not one of its stated objectives, to advise the administration in Washington on ways to win the war. In addition to its patriotic purposes, the war committee also represented the economic interests of New York, which had suffered because of secession and the city's loss of the cotton trade. Reports that thousands of cotton bales were stored in Texas awaiting shipment by Confederates across the Rio Grande and on to Europe in exchange for war goods excited both the patriotism and the material instincts of members of the war committee. Before Hamilton's arrival, committee members had been approached by "some Texas gentlemen" in New York about cotton prospects in their state and the need for "aid in bringing the subject to the attention of the Government."[33] After Hamilton's arrival, the New York war committee held a large rally on October 3 at Cooper Institute to obtain support for the early redemption of Texas. Hamilton was the only speaker at the meeting. With such prominent New Yorkers as Mayor George Opdyke,

David Dudley Field, and Francis Lieber on the platform, Hamilton passionately appealed for aid for Southern Unionists in general and Texas Unionists in particular. He also called for the vigorous prosecution of the war, contending that unless the rebellion was thoroughly suppressed in the South, it someday would directly afflict New York and other Northern centers. Hamilton was more forthright than other Southern Unionists in declaring that slavery was the cause of the war and that it should be eradicated as a prerequisite for reconstruction.[34]

Inspired by the Texan's speech and his private solicitation for arms and money, the New York war committee dispatched a delegation to Washington, along with Hamilton, to obtain the Lincoln administration's approval of a Texas campaign. The delegation, headed by John Austin Stevens, Jr., met first with Secretary of Treasury Salmon P. Chase because Stevens was a friend of Chase and Hamilton had a letter of introduction to him from a Texas kinsman. Chase was greatly impressed with the tall and rugged Texan who professed strong antislavery views and also the need for a true political reconstruction of the South. Except to advocate the political proscription of rebel leaders and officials at all levels, Hamilton was vague as to what he meant by a true political reconstruction.[35]

On October 9 the New York delegation, Hamilton, and other Texans met with Lincoln. They urged the president to issue "a proclamation announcing the policy of the Government to be simply the restoration of the national constitutional Government where it has been subverted." Reflecting the conservative purposes of the New York committee, the proposed proclamation would make no mention of emancipation. The delegation claimed that large numbers of Southerners—and Texans specifically—would flock to the old flag and take up arms against the rebels if they could be assured of Federal assistance.[36] Hamilton told Lincoln that a Federal army of five thousand men, combined with armed Texas Unionists, some of whom, he reported, had already been organized in New Orleans, could defeat the Confederates and restore constitutional authority. He proposed that the force land at the mouth of the Rio Grande and march to the Rio Nueces, where it would be joined by a state Unionist force for the final offensive against the rebels. Hamilton and his associates informed the president that not only would Texas be redeemed from "anarchy and barbarism" by a successful military campaign, the large Confederate exchange of cotton for contraband along the Rio Grande would be disrupted. The stoppage of this trade, they insisted, would contribute significantly to the suppression of the rebellion. Furthermore, the delegation reminded Lincoln of the growing French threat in Mexico. A United States army in Texas, they contended, would cause the French to abandon any territorial designs that they might have in the area and would strengthen Benito Juarez's position in the Mexican war of liberation.[37]

Lincoln expressed a strong desire to aid the Texas Unionists but declared that he would have to study the delegation's proposal before acting. In an effort to put additional pressure upon the president, the delegation talked to Cabinet members about the enterprise and gained the unequivocal support of Postmaster General Montgomery Blair, whose strong faith in Southern Unionism even exceeded that of Lincoln. Secretary of State William H. Seward, with an eye on the French in Mexico and in the Gulf, also favored the scheme.[38] In early November Lincoln again conferred with Hamilton, and a few days later the Texan was appointed military governor of his state with the rank of brigadier general. Lincoln, however, with other military priorities to meet, was still unprepared to approve the proposed Texas expedition. Hamilton's written instructions were identical to the vague directives that Stanton had given other military governors. Stanton shed a little more light on Hamilton's responsibilities when he wrote Gen. Nathaniel P. Banks, the new military commander of the Department of the Gulf, that the governor's duty was "to re-establish and maintain, under military form, the functions of civil government, until the loyal inhabitants of Texas shall be able to assert their constitutional rights and privileges." The secretary of war directed Banks to provide Hamilton with a sufficient military force "to maintain peace and enforce respect" for the law. Hamilton also received permission to organize and command two cavalry regiments that would be raised upon his arrival in Texas.[39]

Meanwhile, support for the Texas expedition had grown. New England merchants and manufacturers had felt the pinch of the cotton shortage even more than New York businessmen. By late 1862 only about 25 percent of the spindles in New England textile mills were operating, and manufacturers were desperately looking for a steady, reliable supply of cotton. Since the beginning of the war, area merchants had recognized Texas's potential for meeting their need for cotton, and a few of them had early urged an expedition to restore the state to the Union. They were joined in this interest in Texas by northeastern antislavery elements who viewed the vast, sparsely populated territory of the state as ideal for the use of both black and white free labor in the cultivation of cotton and other crops. After Lincoln's preliminary Emancipation Proclamation, the antislavery dream for Texas became a realistic objective. Both New England businessmen and antislavery stalwarts who were usually one and the same believed that the conquest of Texas and the creation of a free state should be accompanied by the infusion of a large number of northeastern and European settlers. These immigrants, along with the relatively large German

population already in the state, would bring white enterprise to the production of cotton and insure the future success of freedom and Union.[40]
As the *New York Times* expressed it, "New-England had the capital, the
enterprise and the labor to push this fact [plan] to the full extent of development, and emancipate the world from the delusion that slave labor is
necessary to the production of the world's staples. . . . Texas needs to be col-
onized."[41]

Lincoln could not have been oblivious to the commercial motives
behind the proposed Texas campaign, or unaware of the importance of a
steady cotton supply for the Northern war effort. The Stevens delegation
had called the president's attention to the economic distress in the Northeast caused by the cotton shortage and the need to fulfill military contracts
with its products. Furthermore, ambitious cotton dealers and their associates in Washington, such as Senator Orville H. Browning of Illinois,
arguably Lincoln's closest friend in the capital, impressed upon the president the financial value of cotton to the Union cause.[42] In addition,
Southerners like Hamilton and Michael Hahn told the president that the
reestablishment of the cotton trade would influence misguided rebels to
renew their allegiance to the Union in order to exchange their valuable crop
for goods and specie. Hahn, who would soon become governor of Louisiana, wrote the president summarizing the benefits from the trade. If the
traffic were fostered, Hahn declared, "the Federal treasury will reap an im-
mense benefit, the markets of the North and the world will receive a large
supply of cotton, and the people here will become satisfied that the rebellion is at an end."[43]

The president took the advice of Hahn and others and encouraged a
regulated trade in the staple, despite the fact that an increasing amount of
the traffic illegally went through the lines and to the aid of the Confederacy. General Grant and other military commanders attempted unsuccessfully to put a halt to the illicit trade. When Gen. Edward R.S.
Canby, commanding in the lower Mississippi Valley, protested against the
abuse, Lincoln informed him that the cotton trade had become "im-
mensely important to us" and noted: "if pecuniary greed can be made to
aid us" in the war, "Let us be thankful that so much good can be got out
of pecuniary greed." Though the president supported the trade and authorized Hamilton and his friends to bring out Texas cotton, he did not accept
the argument that the traffic could be used directly to advance the cause of
reconstruction.[44]

Historian Gabor Boritt suggests a contrary thesis, arguing that
Lincoln had great faith in the cotton trade as an important instrument
of reconstruction. He contends that Lincoln, a good Whig who "saw

commerce as a glue that bound the Union together," believed that "the South could be seduced into peace via the economic charms" of the nation. In Lincoln's thinking, federal agents and Northerners with trade permits would purchase the valuable cotton of those planters who had taken the oath of allegiance and had indicated a willingness to support reconstruction. Hard-pressed to market their crops, planters would agree to Lincoln's terms. In the end, according to Boritt, "the grand policy of making peace via economic incentives failed" to turn many planters into Unionists. Boritt, admits, however that the president never publicly revealed the true intent of his trade policy, for to do so "would have undercut its effectiveness with Southerners." Instead, to Secretary of Treasury Chase and other skeptics in the administration, Lincoln defended the cotton trade "for its bearing on our finances." The president, Boritt writes, argued the good effect that the acquisition of cotton would have on the country's gold reserve, the control of inflation, and the reduction of the war debt.[45]

Boritt exaggerates the importance of economic assumptions in Lincoln's reconstruction policy. Though aware that "pecuniary greed" played an important role in human affairs, Lincoln overwhelmingly perceived of loyalty to the Union in political terms. Concurrently with the suppression of rebel arms, Lincoln believed that returning loyalty and a desire for reunion rested on a Southern reverence for the American past (or mystic chords of memory, as he eloquently expressed it), a commitment to the nation's constitutional heritage, and a longing for the restoration of a civil government that would protect traditional rights and prevent social disorders. Had Lincoln placed much faith in material self-interest to gain support for reconstruction, he would not have adopted an antislavery policy which, despite his willingness to compensate slave owners for their financial loss, was sure to threaten that interest and reinforce Southern resistance to reunion.

During late 1862, when prominent New Englanders with cotton on their minds learned of the efforts of Hamilton and the New York war committee to secure the Lincoln administration's approval for a Texas expedition, they threw their support behind the movement. Governor John A. Andrew of Massachusetts promised to raise eight regiments for the invasion of Texas and suggested to Lincoln and the War Department that John C. Frémont, an antislavery hero, be given command of the expedition. The administration agreed to accept the troops, and implicitly promised that they would be used to redeem Texas. But instead of Frémont, Gen. Nathaniel P. Banks, who more nearly reflected Lincoln's conservative political views, was placed in command of the expedition. The troops were hastily raised as nine-month volunteers with the promise by Governor

Andrew that they would be granted land in Texas after the conquest and the expiration of their enlistments.[46] The prospect of land and cotton clearly motivated Massachusetts men to volunteer for the army, men who had earlier resisted the blandishments of recruiting rallies and campaigns. By joining the Texas campaign, these Massachusetts volunteers, as well as troops from other New England states and New York, expected not only to improve their economic prospects but also to avoid the horrors of battle then occurring in Virginia and in the Mississippi Valley.

When the expedition sailed from New York on December 3, 1862, with Banks, Hamilton, and John Austin Stevens, Jr., of the New York war committee on board, the New England troops believed that their destination was the Texas coast. Much to their chagrin, however, they discovered while at sea that the War Department, with Lincoln's approval, had ordered the expedition to go directly to New Orleans. The lower Mississippi River had not yet been cleared of Confederate forces, and Midwesterners were clamoring for the opening of this important commercial artery. Banks, instead of commanding an amphibious assault on Texas, was ordered (probably as a political necessity) to give top priority to a campaign up the Mississippi. Not only were the New Englanders angry with the change in plans, Hamilton and his friends, including Stevens and other New York cotton speculators who accompanied the army, were furious. After landing in New Orleans they badgered Banks until he agreed to send a small expedition to take Galveston Island, a strategic position on the Gulf coast where a regiment of Texas troops (U.S.) had recently established a beachhead.[47]

Ill-equipped and poorly trained, the Galveston expedition in late December, 1862, was a disaster for the Union cause. General Banks blamed the defeat upon Hamilton and his associates for their insistence upon a premature campaign to liberate Texas. He complained to his superiors in Washington that Hamilton, though not a bad man himself, "does not manifest great force of character, and is surrounded by men who came here on the Government transports, unbeknown to me, for base, speculative purposes and nothing else. . . . He explains their presence by saying that in the North he became indebted to them for pecuniary assistance."[48]

The failure of the Galveston assault did not deter Hamilton and friends from their efforts to launch a Gulf coast invasion, though the enthusiasm of the New England troops for a Texas campaign noticeably cooled after this setback. Hamilton now urged Banks to implement the original plan of dispatching a force of five thousand men to the mouth of the Rio Grande, where they would be joined by Unionists encamped across the border. When Banks refused, Hamilton hurried north for another round of speaking and lobbying in behalf of his plan for Texas's redemption from rebel control. He again spoke at Cooper Institute and then traveled on to New England, where he ended his tour with a rousing anti-slavery and Union speech in Boston's Faneuil Hall. The Texas military governor-in-exile, with the praises of Republican editors and politicians vibrating in his ears and demanding action by the Lincoln administration to liberate the Lone Star State, went to Washington to make what he claimed would be his final appeal before returning home to share the bitter fate of his Union comrades.[49]

At the capital Hamilton had little success until the fall of Vicksburg and Port Hudson during the summer of 1863, securing Federal control of the Mississippi and releasing troops for operations elsewhere. By this time French imperial designs in Mexico had become open and aggressive. In June 1863 a French army had marched into Mexico City, causing Benito Juarez to flee northward. At the suggestion of the Confederate commander in Texas, the French agreed to move on Matamoros along the Rio Grande. Rumors were afloat that the French intended to continue their campaign into Texas and also occupy the United States territories taken from Mexico during the 1840s.[50]

These reports created dismay in Washington, renewing demands for a campaign to restore Texas to the Union and to quash French designs. Hamilton and other members of the "Texas lobby" saw their opportunity. From New York, "Colossus Jack" wrote a long letter to Lincoln in which he sought to curry favor with the president and thereby secure his approval for a Texas expedition. Hamilton devoted most of the letter to a vigorous defense of Lincoln's emancipation policy and an opposition to any compromise with the rebels. The letter, which was printed by the Loyal Publication Society of New York, an adjunct of the New York war committee, contained a pointed warning of the French danger in the Southwest. The French "usurper is already triumphing over the ruins of republican government" in Mexico, Hamilton told Lincoln, and was in league with the antidemocratic rebels north of the border. Hamilton claimed that "at the moment, negotiations are pending, if not consummated, between the leading rebels in Texas who despair of success by the so-called Confederacy, and parties in northern Mexico, for a union of Texas with the States of Tamaulipas and Nuevo Leon and Coahuila for the formation of a new government under the imperial sanction and favor of Louis Napoleon."[51]

Lincoln needed no prompting from Hamilton to act against the French threat. Before he could have received Hamilton's letter, on July 29 the president directed Secretary of War Stanton to organize an expedition to sail for coastal West Texas.[52] Although Generals Grant and Banks, commanding in the lower Mississippi Valley, wanted top priority given to an attack on Mobile, the president told Stanton: "I believe no local object is now more desirable" than the immediate occupation of some portion of Texas. A few days later Lincoln wrote General Banks that "recent events in Mexico, I think, render early action in Texas more important than ever." However, he left the planning for the operation in the hands of Banks and the War Department.[53]

Spurred to action by the president, Banks prepared an amphibious expedition to take Houston through Sabine Pass and use it as a staging base for the liberation of the Lone Star State. On September 5, the day after his forces sailed from New Orleans, Banks informed Lincoln that the Sabine was the key to success in Texas. Once the Sabine had been taken, the general confidently told the president, "we can secure every position to the Rio Grande." Banks promised that Texas would be reorganized and restored to the Union within a year. Buoyed by Banks' confidence, Lincoln on September 19 sent this message to the general:

> In strong hope that you have the old flag flying in Texas by this time, we are about sending Gen Hamilton to act as Military Governor there. . . . I really believe him to be a man of worth and ability; and one who, by his acquaintance there, can scarcely fail to be efficient in re-inaugurating the National authority. He has suffered so long and painful an exile from his home and family that I feel a deep sympathy for him; and I scarcely need say I am sure he has received, and will receive the same from you.[54]

The Sabine Pass attack failed due to the poor performance of the naval units, shattering the hopes of Lincoln and the Texas Unionists that the state would soon be restored to the old government. Undeterred by this setback, Banks in November dispatched an expedition to seize the mouth of the Rio Grande and nearby points along the coast. This time Banks's forces succeeded. On December 1 a jubilant Hamilton, whose support by the president the politically astute Banks could not ignore, arrived in Brownsville to inaugurate his government. He sanguinely reported to Secretary of Treasury Salmon P. Chase, his benefactor in Washington, that the rebellion had been broken in Texas. In many areas, Hamilton declared, Texans were successfully resisting conscription officers and refusing to permit the impressment of grain for the rebel army. "Nothing but the most rigorous military despotism keeps [rebel] soldiers in arms," he told Chase. Hamilton claimed that a force of twenty-thousand Union troops could march from the coast to anywhere in the interior without serious opposition and speedily end the rebellion.[55]

Despite such optimism, Gen. N.J.T. Dana, who commanded Federal troops along the Rio Grande, knew that Hamilton's roseate view of the military situation was wrong. Dana, who was busy contending with rebels and brigands in the area, soon clashed with Hamilton over authority. He heatedly complained to his superiors that the governor was interfering with military matters. Hamilton also raised the ire of Secretary of State Seward when, in a toast at a reception in Matamoros, he promised American aid to the Juaristas. Despite apprehension regarding the French threat, the Lincoln administration was scrupulously trying to avoid offending France. Seward, after consulting with Lincoln, wrote General Banks that the governor should not be permitted to deal with Mexican authorities. Banks was "authorized to suspend the Military Governor from his command if the public interest should at any time seem to require it." Although Stanton endorsed this directive to Banks, Seward had overstepped Lincoln's position in giving the general carte blanche authority to remove Hamilton. Banks sensed that this was the case, and he ended the matter by writing the Texan a friendly note, reminding him of the delicacy of relations with Mexico while assuring Hamilton of his continued support for him as military governor.[56]

By early 1864 the Union redemption of Texas had foundered, primarily due to the Federal army's failure to penetrate the interior. Hamilton, however, continued to issue ineffective proclamations and appoint a few civil officers in the Brownsville area. He also made speeches in support of emancipation and the Union. In late 1864 the governor again visited the North to canvass for Lincoln and the Republican party. The Red River campaign of 1864, which Lincoln vigorously supported, was partly designed to put Hamilton in control of Texas and to restore the state to the Union. Commanded by Banks, the Federal assault up the Red River in the spring was checked forty miles South of Shreveport by Confederate forces under Gen. Richard Taylor. The humiliating retreat of Banks's army damaged the Union cause in Texas as well as in Louisiana and Arkansas and stymied for the remainder of the war Hamilton's efforts to establish a loyal government in the Lone Star State. After the war Hamilton served as provisional governor of the state under President Andrew Johnson's program of reconstruction. He later affiliated with the conservative wing of the Republican party.

In 1862-1863 Hamilton's advocacy of emancipation had won the praises of Northern Radicals like Salmon P. Chase. The support for emancipation by this popular Southern Unionist also contributed during the mid-period of the war to Republican acceptance of Lincoln's conservative reconstruction policy that included dependence upon temporary quasi-military governments, the initiative of Southern Unionists, the early revival of self-government, and a cautious approach to ending slavery. Despite their often shrill rhetoric and desire to cleanse their states of rebel influence, Hamilton and other Southern Unionists did not seek a political revolution in the South. On the contrary, following Lincoln's lead, they favored the quick restoration of the Union as it existed in 1860, but with loyal men in control and, in the case of some like Hamilton, without slavery.

5

Stalemate

By 1863 President Lincoln had become frustrated by the lack of progress in the organization of loyal governments in occupied areas. The main problem was the failure of the army to expand Federal control and provide security for Unionists. Military setbacks in late 1862 and early 1863, particularly in Virginia, where Gen. Ambrose E. Burnside had suffered a disastrous defeat at Fredericksburg in December 1862, cut deeply into northern morale, alarming Lincoln and requiring him to devote almost all of his attention to the war and the critical political situation at home. Conversely, in the South, Confederate military successes raised morale, inspired greater sacrifices for independence, and silenced many Unionists. Lincoln continued to have an interest in reconstruction, but military success in the spring and summer campaigns of 1863 was necessary before he could press ahead on Southern reorganization.

The president's Emancipation Proclamation, issued on January 1, 1863, gave the war a new purpose, inevitably causing Lincoln to reassess his position regarding the relationship of black freedom to reconstruction. The recruitment of black troops, which he provided for in the proclamation, weighed heavily in the president's reassessment, increasing his commitment to emancipation. Though desiring to link emancipation with reunion, Lincoln was uneasy about his constitutional authority to interfere with slavery, especially in the Federal-occupied areas that he had exempted from the Emancipation Proclamation. When Salmon P. Chase asked him to extend freedom to these areas, the president in a September 2, 1863, letter reminded his treasury secretary that the "original proclamation has no constitutional or legal justification, except as a military measure. The

Michael Hahn, Union congressman of Louisiana, 1863; Union governor of Lousiana, 1864-1865 (courtesy of the Louisiana Collection, State Library of Louisiana, Baton Rouge).

exemptions were made because the military necessity did not apply to the exempted localities. Nor does that necessity apply to them now any more than it did then." Lincoln posed a series of rhetorical questions to Chase that revealed his constitutional conservatism and the serious consequences he feared if he acted against slavery in the exempted areas. "If I take the step" that you want, "must I not do so, without the argument of military necessity, and so, without any argument, except the one that I think the measure politically expedient, and morally right?" Lincoln asked. "Would I not thus give up all footing upon constitution or law? Would I not thus be in the boundless field of absolutism? Could this pass unnoticed, or unrestricted? Could it fail to be perceived that without any further stretch, I might . . . change any law in any state? Would not many of our own friends shrink away appalled? Would it not lose us the elections, and with them, the very cause we seek to advance?"[1]

Even while denying that he could proclaim emancipation in the exempted districts, Lincoln was moving quietly to secure local action on freedom in those areas. However, not until late 1863 did he insist that reconstruction should include emancipation. By then Federal armies had ceased to flounder in the South, creating hope for an early end of the war. Lincoln probably now realized that unless he acted soon to make emancipation a requirement of reconstruction, reunion could occur with slavery still in existence in the South, despite the Emancipation Proclamation. This realization ultimately impelled the president to overcome his commitment to a nonintervention policy and require emancipation as a condition of reconstruction.

Making the decision easier for Lincoln were indications from the South that Unionists who had earlier opposed Republican antislavery policies were moving closer to his position on the issue. In 1863 a number of Union leaders in the occupied areas, including Governors Andrew Johnson and Francis H. Pierpont, shocked by the terrible toll that the war was taking and fearful that the rebels might prevail, yielded to the president's cautious antislavery proddings. Even before Lincoln had made black freedom a requirement for reconstruction in December 1863, they announced their support for emancipation as a war measure.[2] Unlike Lincoln, Southern Unionists used racist language to explain their antislavery conversion. Beginning in August 1863, Johnson repeatedly said that he favored emancipation because it freed white men, not blacks, from rebel oppression. He declared that if in order to end the rebellion "slavery must go, I say, let it go," as Lincoln had proclaimed. "If either the government or slavery must go, I say give me the Government. Rather than have [the Union] destroyed I would send every Negro back to Africa." John R. Hood of Chattanooga announced that he favored "blotting the institution" of slavery "from the face of the earth . . . not because we love the negro, but because we love the Government and hate the domineering fiendish spirit that slavery breeds." Writing in 1863, Virginian James W. Hunnicut indicated that he had been a proslavery man, but circumstances "have made me a thorough anti-slavery man. When traitors to God and their country threw African slavery into one end of the scales and their country to the other end, and ask me which I would choose, slavery without my country, or my country without slavery, my answer was, is, and always will be, my country."[3] Although official emancipation did not occur in any of the Southern states until 1864 (except in newly created West Virginia), Lincoln was encouraged by the early support for freedom that he received from prominent Southern Unionists.[4]

During 1863 Virginia, Tennessee, and Louisiana held promise for progress in the reorganization of loyal governments. Virginia was unique because it already had a loyal civil government recognized by both Lincoln and Congress. Until 1863 Pierpont maintained the Restored Government of Virginia in Wheeling, across the mountains and remote from the eastern part of the state. While orchestrating statehood for West Virginia, Pierpont continued to claim authority over eastern Virginia and visited the occupied area on several occasions. During these visits, he usually conferred with Lincoln, who insisted that the governor keep him informed of his actions.[5] Over the course of the war, Lincoln spent more time conferring with Pierpont than with any of his Southern governors, partly because Pierpont had a prickly personality that he frequently had to stroke. The governor was particularly sensitive regarding his authority, expecting to receive the respect due to past governors of the Old Dominion. Lincoln made a special effort to promote Pierpont's status in the North. He secured an invitation for the Virginia governor to attend the Altoona, Pennsylvania, conference of Union governors on September 24, 1862, called for the purpose of developing support for the war in the wake of the Army of the Potomac's repeated failures. When the conference convened, the recently issued preliminary Emancipation Proclamation became a focus of debate. Despite conservative opposition to emancipation, an address signed by a majority of the governors, including Pierpont, endorsed the proclamation and Lincoln's war policies. A committee of three governors, again including Pierpont, presented a copy of the address to the delighted president.[6]

The Lincoln-Pierpont relationship was made easier by the fact that both were natives of border states and former Whigs who favored a conservative approach to the rebellious South. Although the proximity of Virginia to Washington made possible their frequent meetings, the conferences between the two men reflected the importance of Virginia to the president and conversely Pierpont's dependence upon Lincoln for support.

After the admission of West Virginia to the Union in 1863, Pierpont, moved the temporary capital of the Restored Government to Alexandria, across the Potomac from Washington. He issued a proclamation outlining the parameters of military and civil authority as the process of redemption occurred. "In those portions of the State occupied by the military, and in which civil government has not been established under the authority of the organized government of Virginia," the governor announced, "the people will have to endure military rule and submit to the orders of the Generals commanding the military departments." But in areas where "the restored Government has been organized by the election of the various civil officers required by the laws of the State . . . the officers will discharge their duties in conformity with the laws." Pierpont told Virginians that President Lincoln "manifests the most lively desire for the restoration of order in this State and a disposition to assist, by every means at his command, to restore the civil government and produce harmony."[7]

In 1863 Pierpont's domain included only the Eastern Shore, the Norfolk area, and the counties across the Potomac from Washington. Until Lee's army surrendered in 1865, the governor's authority would not extend much beyond this small area. Because of its Lilliputian size and its pretensions of authority, from the beginning the Restored Government was subjected to severe ridicule. A border-state editor referred to it as the "Alexandria usurpation," while Senator Charles Sumner characterized it as "little more than the common council of Alexandria," an epithet that was repeated by its opponents.[8] Nevertheless, the Pierpont government provided Lincoln with the kind of nucleus of loyal authority that he believed, in combination with the military's advance, could rapidly restore the state to the Union and spark civil reorganization efforts elsewhere.

Pierpont's determination to follow the forms of Virginia's prewar election laws, despite the small size of the occupied area and the disruptions caused by the war, contributed to the derision hurled at his government. His own election and reelection as governor proved to be an easy target for critics. In May 1862, Pierpont without opposition was elected by 14,824 votes to fill the unexpired term of Governor John Letcher, though he had already been appointed to that office by the Wheeling convention. Only four of the thirty-two counties voting in the election would remain in Virginia after statehood was granted to the western part of the state. The following May, Pierpont, again without opposition, stood for election to a regular four-year term as governor; this time he only received 3,755 votes, all in occupied eastern Virginia. His new term began on January 1, 1864.[9]

The Restored Government also held elections in 1862 and 1863 for local offices, the state legislature, and Congress. Lincoln approved of the Virginia elections, insisting that the loyal voters of the state, no matter the number, constituted the electorate. Still, in March 1862 he cautioned Pierpont to "make haste slowly" in the work of reorganizing local governments, at least until the Federal army had firm control.[10] In May 1862, Pierpont, even before he had moved his headquarters to Alexandria, issued a proclamation calling for local elections in several eastern counties, including a few that Federal arms had not secured. Voters had to take a simple loyalty oath pledging future allegiance to the Union; it closely resembled the one that Lincoln later required in his Proclamation of Amnesty and Reconstruction.[11]

The voter turnout in these and subsequent wartime elections in Federal-occupied Virginia was light. Though martial law still existed in their domain, members of the Restored Government insisted that the citizens were loyal and civil authority should take precedent over the military.[12] Lincoln seemed to agree; he avoided, however, any policy statement on who had ultimate authority in Virginia. In November 1862, he told U.S. Commissioner of Internal Revenue George S. Boutwell that the Eastern Shore counties were loyal and should be treated like any other loyal district.[13]

However much he might tilt toward civil authority, the president permitted army commanders in Virginia, as well as in other occupied areas of the South, to arrest and try civilians charged with attacks on military personnel. The most celebrated case involved Dr. David M. Wright, who, enraged by the presence of black troops on the streets of Norfolk in July 1862, shot and killed the army officer marching at the head of his unit's column in a downtown parade. Convicted of murder and sentenced to be executed, prominent Virginia Unionists, including Senator Lemuel Bowden and Congressman Joseph Segar, appealed to Lincoln to set aside the conviction on the ground that Wright was insane at the time of the murder. No issue was made on the jurisdiction of the military in the case. Lincoln dispatched a physician who was an authority on insanity to Norfolk to investigate carefully the question of Wright's mental state, "both at the time of the homicide, and the time of your examination." Based on the physician's report, statements from Wright's counsel, and a recommendation from the judge advocate general, Lincoln ruled that Wright at no time suffered from insanity. He approved the conviction and sentence, and on October 23 Wright was hanged.[14]

Despite the close proximity of major military operations and the presence of a large number of Federal forces, only one important civil-military conflict occurred in occupied Virginia before late 1863 and the irascible Benjamin F. Butler's resumption of command in the Norfolk area.[15] In August 1863, Governor Pierpont, who jealously protected the authority of the Restored Government, appealed to Lincoln to prevent Gen. Henry M. Naglee, the local commander, from countermanding a special rental fee that Portsmouth officials had placed on the property of Confederate sympathizers. The purpose of the fee or tax was to support the town's destitute. Although Lincoln recognized the civil authority of the Restored Government over all of occupied Virginia, he refused to intervene. However, he wrote Gen. John G. Foster, Naglee's superior, that the two generals should meet with Pierpont and try to reach an understanding on this and other issues. "Governor Pierpont is a good man," he told Foster, "and if you will place him in conference [confidence?] and amicable relations with the military authority in the vicinity, I do not doubt that much good will come of it." Prompted by Lincoln, Naglee met with the governor. Pierpont admitted to Naglee that Portsmouth officials had no authority to condemn property and collect rents, a concession that resolved the main issue between them. However, Naglee, according to his account of the meeting, refused Pierpont's demand that the military confiscate the property of all citizens who did not take an oath of allegiance to the Union and the Restored Government of Virginia.[16] After this incident Naglee and his subordinates took care not to interfere in local civil affairs.

Meanwhile, Governor Pierpont's antislavery stand endeared him to Lincoln. In addition to his role in the Altoona conference, Pierpont in December 1862 devoted his annual message to the General Assembly to a defense of Lincoln's preliminary Emancipation Proclamation. Like the president, he focused on its utility as a war measure for the purpose of suppressing the rebellion. The governor, however, declined to recommend that the General Assembly, a "rump" body of twenty-four members, act to end slavery in Virginia. A later legislative session, prodded by Pierpont, issued a call for a state constitutional convention, which in early 1864 abolished slavery in Virginia.[17]

Despite his antislavery stand, Lincoln reaffirmed to Virginians his promise that districts holding congressional elections before January 1, 1863, when the Emancipation Proclamation would go into effect, would be exempted from its provisions. With northern morale plummeting and opposition to emancipation growing, Lincoln clearly placed a greater premium on Union-held elections in Virginia and elsewhere in the South than on black freedom. The Virginia Eastern Shore easily reelected Congressman Joseph Segar, and the district that included Alexandria held an election that was subsequently contested by the loser. When, on the day before he was to issue his proclamation, Lincoln had not received a report of an election in the Norfolk district, he hurriedly wired Gen. John A. Dix, the area commander. "I hear not a word about the Congressional election of which you and I corresponded," the president declared. "Time nearly up." Dix then telegraphed Lincoln that he had just received the returns from the election, and John B. McCloud, the victor, would leave immediately for Washington to take his seat. Dix reported that the Union men of the district hoped to secure "their exemption from the penalties of disloyalty, by electing a member of Congress so as to be represented by the 1st Jany. 1863."[18] The next day Lincoln, as he had promised, included the counties of occupied Virginia in his list of areas exempted from the provisions of the Emancipation Proclamation.

Though he had arranged for the elections, Lincoln carefully maintained a hands-off policy when the House of Representatives in early 1863 considered the credentials of the newly elected congressmen. He repeatedly declared that Congress was the sole judge of its membership. The House Committee on Elections, chaired by Henry L. Dawes, who during the same session supported the seating of Louisianans Hahn and Flanders, recommended that the House reject the Virginia claimants on the ground that the war had prevented a majority of the loyal voters from going to the polls. Dawes denied that the principle of free elections had been violated in the seating of Hahn and Flanders or even that of Segar, who had been admitted to his seat in 1862 after having been elected in 1861. The Dawes committee disallowed Segar's reelection on the ground that sixteen of the twenty counties in his district were under rebel control, which, the committee asserted, prevented the majority of the Union men from casting ballots.[19]

After a vigorous debate, the House of Representatives accepted the Dawes committee report and refused to seat the Virginians. Lincoln, however, continued to exempt the occupied area from the provisions of the Emancipation Proclamation. The rejection by the House of the Virginia aspirants, along with one from Tennessee, did not reflect an important division between Lincoln and congressional Republicans over reconstruction. Certainly, many Republicans, particularly Radicals like Sumner, Benjamin Wade, and Henry Winter Davis were concerned about a presidential policy that permitted "bogus" elections and exacted few guarantees of loyalty. But they were not in a position in 1862 and 1863 to challenge Lincoln and his approach to reconstruction. Most Republicans generally acknowledged the legitimacy of the Restored Government of Virginia, and at this time, except for questions about Stanly's administration in eastern North Carolina, offered no serious criticism of Lincoln's Southern regimes. Furthermore, the Dawes rule on who constituted the electorate of an area did not conflict with Lincoln's view that Unionists, even though a minority of the total number of antebellum Southern voters, were the body politic and capable of electing representatives to Congress and to state and local offices. The war had reached a critical stage by 1863, and the majority in Congress awaited the outcome of military campaigns in Virginia, Tennessee, and elsewhere before turning their attention to reconstruction matters. Whether Republicans of the president's party in Congress challenged Lincoln on his reconstruction policy would be determined by military events and northern political developments. Congressional action would also be affected by the course of reconstruction in the South under Lincoln's guidance and the perception that Republicans and others had of Southern affairs.

In 1863 Lincoln, after setbacks in Louisiana and elsewhere, expected Tennessee to become the first Southern state to be completely restored to the Union. As 1862 ended, Gen. William S. Rosecrans, who had replaced Gen. Don Carlos Buell in October, after considerable prodding from Lincoln left Nashville with forty-two thousand men to attack Gen. Braxton Bragg's army at Murfreesboro. The military movement's ultimate objective was to liberate Unionist East Tennessee and thereby complete Federal control of the state.[20] In a bloody three-day battle near Murfreesboro, Rosecrans drove Bragg from his position, forcing him to retreat toward Chattanooga. In this winter of northern discontent, Rosecrans's victory gave Lincoln something to cheer about. In addition to its military significance and the boost it gave to Union morale, the battle of Stones River, as it was known, renewed the president's hopes, which had been dashed by General Buell's earlier failures, that the rebel armies would soon be expelled from Tennessee, elections held, and the state regain its proper place in the Union.

With this in mind, Lincoln, on January 8 and again on January 10, telegraphed Military Governor Andrew Johnson inquiring "as to the effect the late operations about Murfreesboro, will have upon the prospects of Tennessee."[21] Johnson happily informed Lincoln that Rosecrans's success "has inspired much confidence with Union men of the ultimate success of the Government, and has greatly discouraged rebels." He indicated that "if the rebel army could be expelled from the State, and Union sentiment developed without fear or restraint, I still think Tennessee will be brought back into the Union by [a] decided majority of popular vote." But Johnson reminded Lincoln that East Tennessee must be redeemed from rebel control "before confidence can be inspired with the mass of the people that the Government has the power to assert and maintain its authority in

Tennessee." As he had done before, Johnson made it clear to the president that he would not attempt statewide elections and the restoration of popular government until Confederates had been driven from the eastern counties and the large Union population there could vote to elect a loyal state government. The governor also informed Lincoln that, despite the exemption granted Tennessee in the Emancipation Proclamation, his policy regarding black freedom had damaged the Union cause in the state. Nevertheless, Johnson said that he did not think that Lincoln's antislavery action would seriously retard the work of restoration.[22] Indeed, by the late summer Johnson himself and his political supporters were promoting the cause of emancipation in the state.[23]

While preparing for his advance on Bragg at Chattanooga, Rosecrans became embroiled with Governor Johnson in a conflict over authority in Nashville. By early 1863 Johnson, primarily through appointments to office, had restored civil government in Nashville and in several Middle Tennessee counties. He and other Tennessee Unionists also had persuaded President Lincoln to reestablish the federal court system for the state's middle district. However, Rosecrans, as part of his effort to secure his rear lines before launching the East Tennessee campaign, had created a military police force and a provost court in Nashville for the purpose of rooting out "traitors," spies, and "rascals" who, he believed, had infiltrated his central army depot and communications center. Similar to his conflict with Buell, Johnson soon clashed with Rosecrans's provost marshal in Nashville over the military's highhanded seizure of property and the arbitrary arrest of individuals. The governor complained to Rosecrans that the actions of his officers "have not only excited [incited] a feeling of indignation among the more conservative portion of the community, but have greatly impaired the confidence of the loyal men . . . in the correct intentions of the Government."[24]

When Rosecrans refused to jettison his police system, Johnson appealed to Washington. General-in-Chief Henry W. Halleck, probably after consulting with Lincoln, wrote a long letter to Rosecrans reminding him that the president had sent Johnson to Tennessee "to mitigate as much as possible the evils resulting from a government purely military, and to restore to the loyal people, and to those who are willing to return to their allegiance, the benefits of a civil government." Johnson had largely succeeded in this purpose, Halleck told Rosecrans, "and the civil authorities so organized or restored are as much to be respected as those of Kentucky, Missouri, or any other State in which war is waged and military operations carried on." The military authorities in Tennessee, Halleck directed, "will not interfere with the authority and jurisdiction of the loyal officers of the State government, except in cases of urgent and pressing necessity."[25]

Rosecrans bristled at Halleck's admonition and order. In a telegram to the general-in-chief, he vehemently denied that a conflict existed and impertinently declared that "if the Governor would report at Gallatin," a small town near Nashville, "I should be pleased to put him in command. Nashville is too important a post for me to intrust to his command at this time." Upon receiving this message, the usually mild-mannered Halleck exploded in anger. He wired Rosecrans that "your telegram in regard to General Johnson indicates very plainly that you have not considered my letter of the 20th. General Johnson was not appointed a brigadier-general to command a brigade in the field, but . . . to organize and administer the civil government of the State until a constitutional government could be organized." Shaken by the strong rebuke from Washington, Rosecrans told Halleck that he would do all in his power to assist Johnson in his civil capacity. He immediately sought a conference with the governor to resolve their differences.[26] The conflict between the general and the military governor soon eased, a reconciliation that was advanced by Rosecrans's concern for Johnson's alcoholic son serving in his army and also the general's renewed efforts to drive rebel forces from Tennessee.[27]

By the early summer of 1863, Rosecrans had cleared Middle Tennessee of Confederate forces, and West Tennessee momentarily was free of rebel raiders. Unionists in the occupied area, along with East Tennessee exiles, launched a movement for a convention that would lead immediately to the state's restoration to the Union and the election of a civil government. Memphis Unionists, including a number of Northerners who had followed the army into town, were especially active in the convention movement. They bombarded a reluctant Johnson with appeals for him to issue a call for a convention. These Unionists forthrightly impressed upon the military governor that Memphis's economy could not fully recover until the state shed its secessionist image, returned to the Union, and secured the removal of trade restrictions. As Benjamin W. Sharp, a federal official in West Tennessee, wrote in urging Johnson to call a convention: "Our State is regarded and treated as disloyal, while it is known to the World to be as truly Loyal to the Constitution and Laws of the United States, and to the Administration as the states of Indiana and Illinois. Our City is made to suffer much in Commercial relations in consequence to the status that is imputed to the State, by denouncing it 'Insurrectionary.'"[28]

Without Lincoln's urging or Johnson's encouragement, fourteen Tennessee Unionists issued a call for a state convention of "fellow citizens who desire to maintain the State Government in connection with the Federal

Union as it stood prior to the rebellion." More than "two hundred duly accredited delegates," chosen in most cases by local Union meetings and representing forty-three counties, responded to the call and met in the state capitol on July 1.[29] Sharp division, largely along old regional lines, immediately occurred in the state Union convention. Conservative Unionists, mainly from West and Middle Tennessee, demanded that the convention bypass Johnson, whose emancipation and proscriptive tendencies they opposed. They wanted the convention to authorize an August election of a loyal state government and members of Congress as provided by the antebellum constitution. East Tennessee delegates and friends of Johnson in the convention vigorously opposed the conservative scheme. These Unionists, who had long chafed at the western domination of the state, argued that to hold an election for governor before the eastern counties were liberated and free to vote inevitably would mean that a minority of Unionists, or pretended Unionists, from the western part of the state would select the next governor. After an extended debate, the convention agreed to a compromise of sorts. It requested that Johnson arrange for an election in August for members of a state legislature that would convene in Nashville on the first Monday in October. No mention was made either of a gubernatorial or congressional election or of emancipation. Finally, the convention pledged to Military Governor Johnson its "hearty co-operation and support, in whatever measures may be requisite for the restoration of Tennessee and her people to their Civil and Federal relations."[30]

Many of the conservatives refused to accept what they considered to be a one-sided compromise in favor of the Johnson forces. They particularly resented the defeat of their scheme to hold a gubernatorial election in August. Anxious to thwart what they perceived to be a Johnson conspiracy to retain power and end slavery despite Lincoln's exemption of the state from the provisions of his Emancipation Proclamation, conservative Unionists intrigued to run a candidate for governor simultaneous with the October legislative election. Emerson Etheridge, a former congressman from West Tennessee, and a handful of conservatives, most of whom were old Whigs and bitter antebellum opponents of Johnson, met and nominated William B. Campbell for governor. They planned after the election to ask Lincoln to recognize Campbell as governor and pronounce the state restored to the Union with its old constitution intact. Etheridge and his faction secured the support of the *Nashville Press* and founded the *Memphis Journal* as their newspaper organ in the West. Both papers were edited by former Whigs.[31] Clearly, old political and regional divisions, as well as conflict over reconstruction and emancipation, were deeply involved in the strife among Tennessee Unionists that occurred in 1863. Such fissures would complicate Lincoln's efforts to restore the state to the Union.

Johnson, warned of the conservative scheme to elect a governor, refused to issue writs of election for the legislative seats. Goaded by the challenge of his old enemies while ignoring them publicly, in an August 22 speech at Franklin, Johnson announced that he supported emancipation as a military necessity to suppress the rebellion. In an effort to deflect rising criticism of his actions, the military governor assured loyal Tennesseans that he would call an election "as speedily as it is practicable to hold one." He also promised that "one by one all the agencies of your State government will be set in motion."[32]

Despite Johnson's refusal to authorize the election, the Etheridge forces managed to organize one in a few counties anyway. In this farcical contest, a total of about twenty-five hundred ballots were cast for Campbell, a former Whig governor who was declared the winner over Edmund Cooper. Etheridge, who once had Lincoln's ear, on September 28 wrote the president asking him to recognize Campbell's election. He explained that all of West Tennessee and much of Middle Tennessee were within Federal lines, and despite the fact that Johnson "strenuously opposed the election of a governor," thousands of votes had been cast for Campbell in these counties. Local judges and justices of the peace had been elected in several counties, Etheridge told Lincoln, but they could not take office under Tennessee law until commissioned by a civil governor. Claiming to represent "the best and truest Union men," Etheridge declared that without a legitimate government anarchy would soon engulf the state.[33]

Lincoln, realizing that his endorsement of Campbell would mean repudiating Johnson and his East Tennessee friends, refused to approve Campbell's election. Etheridge, alienated by what he perceived to be the president's conversion to radicalism, in December plotted in the U.S. House of Representatives, where he was the acting clerk, to omit fourteen Republican members from the roll call and replace them with ultraconservatives and Democrats.[34] This scheme also failed, ending Etheridge's influence in Tennessee reconstruction and damaging the conservative Unionist effort to discredit Johnson. It also ended Etheridge's relationship with Lincoln. In 1864, when Republican newspaperman Whitelaw Reid suggested to the president that he should publish something that would further damage Etheridge's reputation, Lincoln advised him not to do so. "Emerson ain't worth more than a squirrel load of powder anyway," he explained in his characteristically folksy way.[35]

While Etheridge intrigued to put Campbell in the governor's mansion, dramatic events were occurring in East Tennessee. On September 3

Gen. Ambrose E. Burnside, operating out of Kentucky with an army of twenty-four thousand men, marched into Knoxville. A few days later General Rosecrans entered Chattanooga as Bragg's army retreated to the hills of North Georgia. East Tennessee at last appeared on the verge of liberation. Lincoln could hardly suppress his delight. He jubilantly wrote Johnson: "All Tennessee is now clear of armed insurrectionists. You need not to be reminded that it is the nick of time for re-inaugerating [*sic*] a loyal State government. Not a moment should be lost." At the same time Lincoln indicated that he would not dictate the method that Tennessee should follow in the reorganization of its government. "You and the co-operating friends there," he informed Johnson, "can better judge of the ways and means, than can be judged by any here. I only offer a few suggestions. The reinauguration [*sic*] must not be such as to give control of the State, and it's [*sic*] representation in Congress, to the enemies of the Union. . . . The whole struggle for Tennessee will have been profitless to both State and Nation, if it so ends that Gov. Johnson is put down, and Gov. [Isham] Harris is put up." In the same letter, Lincoln praised Johnson for his recent public statement in favor of emancipation, and advised: "Get emancipation into your new State government—Constitution—and there will be no such word as failure for your case."[36]

Cheered by military successes in East Tennessee and urged to act by the president, Johnson contemplated the issuance of writs for a general election in October. But he abandoned the plan when Rosecrans was defeated at Chickamauga on September 19-20 and driven in hasty retreat into Chattanooga. Soon Confederate forces under Gen. James Longstreet were threatening the gains that Burnside had made in upper East Tennessee. Confederate morale revived throughout the state and elsewhere, spawning rebel raids and guerrilla attacks in many areas of Tennessee. Under the circumstances, Johnson again postponed plans for an election. In defending the governor's decision, the *Nashville Union,* Johnson's newspaper organ at the state capital, declared that the rebels "are foes not to be voted down, but fought down by the armies of the United States."[37]

Lincoln, who was almost obsessed with a desire to liberate East Tennessee, was undaunted by Federal setbacks and the precarious position of Rosecrans at Chattanooga. In August he had written East Tennesseans who sought his assistance that "I have all the while done, and shall continue to do the best for you I could, and can. I do as much for East Tennessee as I would, or could, if my own home, and family were in Knoxville."[38] Although dismayed by the Union defeat at Chickamauga, Lincoln impressed upon Rosecrans the importance of East Tennessee to the suppression of the rebellion. "If we can hold Chattanooga and East Tennessee," he wrote the general, "I think the rebellion must dwindle and die. I think you and Burnside can do this."[39]

The president also telegraphed Johnson to come to Washington "and have a personal consultation with me." The governor, however, found it impossible to leave Tennessee at that time, though he understood that the president was formulating a new reconstruction plan and wanted his advice. Johnson did write Postmaster General Montgomery Blair, an old political friend who had been an important influence in the development of the president's conservative policies, warning the administration against any proposition to convert the Southern states into territories, a view that Radical Republicans like Charles Sumner and Thaddeus Stevens were advocating. "The institution of slavery is gone," Johnson told Blair, "& there is no good reason now for destroying the states to bring about the destruction of slavery." As a pointed aside, the Tennessee governor informed Blair that "if [Lincoln] steers Clear of th[e] extreme, his election to the next Presidency is without a reasonable doubt."[40] Not until after Lincoln had issued his Proclamation of Amnesty and Reconstruction in December and after a second invitation—almost a summons—did Johnson visit Washington.[41]

If Johnson had met with Lincoln prior to the formulation of his reconstruction proclamation, he might have influenced the plan's provisions. The president had a high regard for the governor's views and his courageous stand in Tennessee. Furthermore, Lincoln knew that Johnson's popularity was high in the North, particularly among War Democrats of his old party and Republicans who applauded his conversion to emancipation. Lincoln must have realized that it would be politically wise to listen to the governor's opinions. At the same time Johnson, while strongly supporting Lincoln's self-reconstruction policy, reflected the kind of hard-nosed policy toward rebels that many Republicans desired and found wanting in the president's efforts. Lincoln knew that Johnson's high-handed actions in Tennessee had upset conservatives in the North and in the border states. The *Louisville Journal*, which usually expressed conservative border-state opinion, aimed its editorial guns at Johnson during the fall of 1863. The *Journal*, in a long editorial on October 20, charged that because of the course of "the so-called Military Governor" the work of restoring Tennessee

to her constitutional relations to the Union appears to be at a stand-still or to be going backward rather than forward. . . . His simple task was to protect and second the people in reorganizing their local government as it was under the local constitution. . . . But unhappily he has not confined himself to this task. He has departed from it. . . . He has called upon the people . . . not merely to resume their constitutional relations in the Union but forthwith to abolish slavery. . . . Without formally asserting the [territorial] theory of Sumner and [William] Whiting and Butler, he is vigorously carrying it out in practice.

The *Journal* also lambasted Johnson for his opposition to Campbell's election. It asserted that the motive behind Johnson's actions was clear: he had struck a bargain with antislavery leaders in the North to make Tennessee a free state in exchange for the presidential nomination in 1864.[42]

Meanwhile, during the late fall Federal forces had regained the initiative in East Tennessee. In November, Grant, who had replaced Rosecrans, drove Bragg's army from the heights around Chattanooga and into North Georgia. Federal forces also repulsed Longstreet at Knoxville and consolidated their position in the area. Lincoln believed that this time East Tennessee would be completely liberated. On December 7, one day before he revealed his new reconstruction plan, Lincoln announced the success of Union arms in East Tennessee, proclaiming it "of high national consequence."[43] The issuance of the two documents at the same time probably was coincidental, since Lincoln had timed his reconstruction proclamation to coincide with his annual message to Congress on December 8, not military events in Tennessee. Nevertheless, the president's expectation that East Tennessee would soon be liberated was important in his decision to take a major step in the restoration of the Southern states to the Union.

As before, the loyal reorganization of Tennessee proved more difficult than Lincoln anticipated. Though Bragg's army was permanently expelled from East Tennessee, Longstreet's forces continued in the upper counties until May 1864, living off the land and wreaking havoc on Unionists. Poverty and insecurity became the lot of East Tennesseans. Thousands of them fled the area to escape the war's heavy hand, delaying further the reconstruction of the state.[44]

Lincoln in 1863 also expected Louisiana to move rapidly toward the restoration of civil government. With reconstruction objectives partly in mind, the president in December 1862 appointed Gen. Nathaniel P. Banks to command the Department of the Gulf, which included occupied Louisiana. When Banks arrived in New Orleans on December 14, he was appalled by what he found. Gen. Benjamin F. Butler, his controversial predecessor, and Gen. George F. Shepley, military governor, had restored order and induced thousands of citizens to swear allegiance to the Union. But Banks found corruption rampant and the citizens mistreated. After one month's experience in New Orleans, he despondently wrote his wife: "I never despaired of our country until I came here," he told her. "Our affairs have been terribly managed. . . . Every body connected with the government has been employed in stealing other people's property." Banks wrote that trade with the enemy had been extensive and had been tolerated by officials. Though the people of Louisiana were sympathetic to the Confederacy, "a firm & just government would have their acquiescence & support." He feared, however, that it might be too late to gain their loyalty in view of the harshness and corruption of Butler's regime.[45]

Influenced by his antipathy to Butler, Banks exaggerated the condition of affairs in New Orleans. A truer history of Butler's administration would credit the general with some success in providing occupied Louisiana, particularly New Orleans, with a reasonably fair and efficient government. Citizens who did not resist military authority were not mistreated, and only a few army officers and government officials made personal fortunes in trading with the enemy.[46] Nevertheless, the looseness with which Butler permitted trade, especially in valuable cotton, opened a Pandora's box to rampant violations of commercial regulations and the virtual impossibility of stopping the flow of goods across the lines. New Orleans, which had long been known as a city of shady opportunities, rapidly became the center of illicit trade in the lower Mississippi Valley, and many supposedly honest citizens blamed the sordid state of affairs on Butler.[47]

Little progress, however, had been made toward reconstruction in Louisiana, despite the holding of congressional elections in the fall of 1862 and the subsequent seating of Michael Hahn and Benjamin F. Flanders by the House of Representatives. Lincoln clearly expected Banks to employ the carrot rather than the stick to restore the state to the Union. As George H. Hepworth, a subordinate of Banks, wrote, employing a different metaphor: "Our overcareful President was desirous to conciliate. There had been harsh measures enough in the department; and since Butler had stroked the cat from tail to head, and found her full of yawl and scratch, it was determined to stroke her from head to tail, and see if she would not hide her claws and commence to purr."[48] Banks seemed almost perfect for the task. Like Lincoln, he was moderate in his temperament and whiggish or conservative in his view of military authority. His military record was less than perfect, given his embarrassment by Stonewall Jackson in the Shenandoah Valley and at Cedar Mountain. But Banks, a political general who had served as Speaker of the U.S. House of Representatives, had the confidence of the War Department, and Lincoln hoped that in the Louisiana cauldron his political skill would rise to the occasion and compensate for his mediocrity as a military commander.

Banks, however, made an early blunder that cost him dearly and contributed to a sharp division among Unionists in occupied Louisiana. On January 30, 1863, he issued a military order establishing a so-called free labor system for blacks in the state. Banks's order created a halfway station between slavery and freedom. Contracts were to be drawn up in which planters were required to pay wages to their laborers and provide housing, food, and clothing for them and their families. Planters were also to permit black children to attend schools organized by army personnel in the area. Blacks, however, could not leave the plantation or farm without the approval of the military and could have their wages withheld as a penalty for not working.[49]

Since Lincoln's Emancipation Proclamation excluded occupied Louisiana from its provisions, Banks's free-labor order was an important step toward the destruction of slavery in the state. It also provided some protection for blacks while the war raged and rural society tottered on the brink of anarchy and racial conflict. But staunch antislavery men did not see it in that light. Ignoring the area's exemption from Lincoln's emancipation policy and Banks's own antislavery sentiments, the general's opponents in New Orleans bombarded their abolition friends in the North with charges that Banks had sold out to the "slavocrats." Horace Greeley's *New York Tribune*, as well as other Radical newspapers, gave prominence to these charges. The *Tribune* declared that "Gen. Banks appears to have yielded without hesitation or reluctance to every demand which the grasping avarice, the hostility to freedom, the hatred to the policy of the Government, the cunning selfishness and the inhumanity of the Louisiana slavemasters can have induced them to make."[50]

Banks, however, had his defenders in the North, mainly among conservative Republicans and friends of Lincoln. The *New York Times* observed that Banks's labor system "holds out the hope that Slavery may be thus quietly put aside without a severe shock to society and industry." The general himself later wrote a long letter to William Lloyd Garrison's *Liberator* responding to the criticism directed at his labor system. Contrary to what Greeley, Wendell Phillips, and other northeastern Radicals had charged, Banks informed readers of the *Liberator* that Louisiana planters, then meeting in New Orleans, "had nothing to do with perfecting or devising the system." It was presented to them as a fait accompli, which if they rejected it, "other persons" would be found to cultivate their lands, Banks said. He revealed that the only group he had consulted prior to issuing his order were black leaders whose suggestions he "implicitly followed." Banks declared that his purpose in the labor policy was three-fold: "to quiet the public mind," both white and black, regarding relations between the races;

"to restrain owners in assertion of their claims" to black labor; and to "secure the negroes in the undisturbed possession of their liberty." He also was concerned about the dissolution of family unity and the problem of public health among black refugees fleeing plantation slavery.[51]

Although in general agreement with Banks's labor system, Lincoln wisely stayed out of the controversy. He had not yet given emancipation the importance in his Southern policy that he would later. The president's main interest lay with the reorganization of Louisiana's government and the acceptance of the state's representatives in Congress. The seating of Hahn and Flanders in the House of Representatives, he believed, was a major breakthrough toward the success of his policy. Already, in late 1862, Lincoln had moved to reestablish a court system in Louisiana. By executive order on October 20 he created a "provisional court" for the state, which would have "all such powers and jurisdiction as belong to the district and circuit courts of the United States." He also suggested that the court, unique in American history, would have authority over purely state matters, following the "customary" procedures of the state courts. Lincoln, despite his aversion to "strangers" holding civil office in the South, selected Charles A. Peabody, a former New York state supreme court justice and a conservative, as provisional judge.[52] Peabody arrived with Banks in December and early in the new year organized the court. The provisional court was designed to replace the military's provost court, but in fact the two courts existed side-by-side, creating confusion in the enforcement of the laws.[53] A few months later, on May 20, 1863, the president, upon Hahn and Flanders' recommendation, appointed Edward H. Durell U.S. district judge of the eastern district of Louisiana, terminating most of the functions of the provisional court system.[54]

Despite the appointment of the politic Banks, Lincoln in 1863 had little success in his effort to nudge military authorities and Louisiana Unionists toward a reorganization of the state government. Rapidly developing divisions among loyal men and officials were a major reason for the delay. General Banks's policies particularly spawned contention and factionalism. The commanding general's conciliatory gestures to Confederate sympathizers and to some Louisianans who reputedly only took the oath of allegiance to avoid the confiscation of their property and to be able to engage in business, created concern among staunch Unionists. Furthermore, Banks' attempt to stop the illicit commerce through the lines brought down the wrath of numerous speculators, bankers, merchants, and officials who were engaged in the trade. Some of these opportunists also professed antislavery sentiments, having been appointed by Secretary of Treasury Salmon P. Chase to U.S. Customs and Treasury offices in

Louisiana. Banks tended to associate his antislavery opponents with the rampant speculation in cotton and goods. One month after issuing his labor order, he reported to his wife that "all the abolitionists here assist me, except those engaged in speculation."[55] Actually, all elements in wartime Louisiana engaged in the lucrative and illegal traffic with Confederate-held areas. Banks, however, preferred to believe that the opposition to his labor policy was mainly motivated by the pecuniary interests of antislavery Chase appointees who sought to discredit him in the eyes of Northern Republicans. Though Chase would maintain a low profile in the Louisiana conflict, his radical supporters seized the gauntlet thrown down by the general and early but unsuccessfully clamored for Banks's removal from command.[56]

Conservative Unionists, representing the interests of sugar planters, also opposed Banks's free-labor policy. They feared with good reason that it was the first step toward emancipation. Determined to hold onto southeastern Louisiana's exemption in Lincoln's proclamation, these conservatives failed to control the "various Union associations" of the New Orleans area that met in May 1863 to initiate the work of reorganization. The General Committee of the associations asked Military Governor Shepley to approve and assist in the call for a state convention to frame a new constitution that would reflect "the change of circumstances and conditions produced by the rebellion."[57] Proslavery conservatives interpreted this to mean emancipation, as did the committee's leader, Thomas J. Durant, an antislavery lawyer of New Orleans, who urged the Union associations to adopt a free state or emancipation platform. Durant also riled the conservatives of the plantation counties by proposing that representation in the convention be based on the white population in each parish. If adopted, this plan would give New Orleans a majority of the delegates in the convention. The power of the interior would be broken in a constitutional convention dominated by the city. Furthermore, many of the New Orleans delegates would probably be antislavery newcomers from the North and unacceptable to the old citizens. Although within a year Durant and several other antislavery members of his committee would support qualified black suffrage, their 1863 proposal recommended that only "loyal free white male citizens" be allowed to vote for delegates to the state convention.[58]

Except to order a voter registration under Durant's supervision, Military Governor Shepley refused to act until he had received explicit instructions from Lincoln or the War Department. When Secretary Stanton failed to answer Shepley's request for instructions, the governor went to Washington to confer with his superiors. Meanwhile, two delegations of conservative Unionists sought Lincoln's support for the reorganization of a state government based on the old Louisiana constitution. Arriving in the capital in mid-June, both groups—one representing Louisiana planters and the other conservative Unionists of New Orleans—presented plans for the "full recognition of all the rights of the State, as they existed previous to the passage of an act of secession."[59]

Warned by Michael Hahn and others that Louisiana Unionists were divided over reconstruction, the president did not give the conservative delegations the answer that they wanted. When pressed for a response, Lincoln wrote Thomas Cottman, the leader of the planter delegation, that "reliable information has reached me that a respectable portion of the Louisiana people, desire to amend their State constitution, and contemplate holding a convention for that object. This fact alone, as it seems to me, is a sufficient reason why the general government should not give the committal you seek, to the existing State constitution." As for an election in the fall, the president told Cottman that "there is abundant time, without any order, or proclamation from me just now" to hold one.[60]

Lincoln saw Shepley in early August. The president learned from the military governor that Durant, who had been appointed provisional attorney general for the state, was preparing a voter registration preparatory to the election of delegates to a constitutional convention. On August 5 he wrote Banks that this action "appears proper." He told Banks that he "would be glad for [Louisiana] to make a new Constitution recognizing the emancipation proclamation, and adopting emancipation in those parts of the state to which the proclamation does not apply. And while she is at it, I think it would not be objectionable for her to adopt some practical system by which the two races could gradually live themselves out of their old relation to each other, and both come out better for the new. Education for young blacks should be included in the plan." The president also affirmed his support for Banks's free-labor contract arrangement "for this probationary period" between slavery and freedom, though he made it clear to the general that "I shall not, in any event, retract the emancipation proclamation" or return anyone to slavery "who is free by the terms of that proclamation" or acts of Congress. Lincoln, however, carefully explained to Banks that his views constituted advice, not an order, regarding reconstruction. "While I very well know what I would be glad for Louisiana to do," he wrote, "it is quite a different thing for me to assume direction of the matter." Still, "I think the thing should be pushed forward, so that if possible, it's [*sic*] mature work may reach here by the meeting of Congress" in December when, Lincoln implied, Louisiana's representatives would be seated and the state government's reorganization completed.[61]

On August 24 Secretary of War Stanton sent instructions to Shepley, who had returned to New Orleans, regarding the work to be done. Stanton informed the general that the instructions came from the president, but in their transmittal he ignored Lincoln's repeated promise not to dictate regarding Louisiana reconstruction. The war secretary directed—not advised—Shepley to hold an election for delegates to a constitutional convention. Although Stanton declared that the convention could pass "all needful ordinances and laws" to restore a loyal civil government in the state, he stopped short of recommending that it abolish slavery. He ordered the election to be held after the completion of the voter registration and not less than thirty days after Shepley had issued an election proclamation.[62]

What followed was a comedy of errors. Banks wrote Lincoln on September 5 that "there will be no serious difficulty in the restoration of this State to the Union" by the end of the year. This prediction fell far short of fulfillment. Preoccupied with a Federal invasion of Texas, Banks left the preparations for the fall elections to Shepley, who in turn awaited the completion of the voter registration begun by Durant during the summer. Durant encountered numerous problems in the registration of a loyal electorate in the occupied rural parishes. His registrars, who represented the free-state Union Association, applied a rigid test of past loyalty, which many conservatives could not or would not take. In a letter to Lincoln on October 1, Durant also blamed the local U.S. provost marshals for the failure to register a loyal electorate, though he did not indicate why they refused to cooperate in the registration. Durant recommended that the provost marshals in each occupied parish be directed to aid "the formation of a free state government." Yet, like Johnson in Tennessee, he complained that not enough territory had come under Federal control to warrant the holding of elections.[63]

Almost simultaneous with his receipt of Durant's letter, Lincoln received other reports that the work of reconstruction in Louisiana was at a standstill. Both Flanders and Hahn went to Washington in October to describe the situation to Lincoln. Flanders, representing Durant and the Union Association, blamed Banks and the military for the delay.[64] Hahn, on the other had, defended Banks and blamed Durant and radicals in the Union Association for the failure. However, like Durant, he favored an end of slavery by a state constitutional convention but criticized a recent meeting of blacks in New Orleans that petitioned General Shepley for the right of their race to vote in the next election. Supported by a handful of antislavery radicals, the demand for black suffrage, Hahn told Lincoln, could defeat "all our efforts."[65] Shepley, who finally had begun a registration of voters on his own, apparently agreed; he refused to permit blacks to register.[66]

To complicate matters even more, on November 2 a faction of Louisiana conservatives held an election of sorts in the rural parishes and, without Shepley's approval, "elected" Thomas Cottman and A.P. Field to Congress. The scheme to admit these two men to the House was a part of the Emerson Etheridge conspiracy to seat conservatives and exclude radical members. Although historians have concluded otherwise, no clear evidence exists that Lincoln, who helped to foil the plot, directly associated Cottman and Field with Etheridge's intrigues. Indeed, both men, who were admitted provisionally to seats in the House, supported Lincoln and the Republicans in the affair.[67] Neither, however, was subsequently seated by the House.

After several months of waiting for Louisiana Unionists to organize a loyal state government, by October 1863 Lincoln finally had become exasperated. When Flanders in an October conference with the president argued that not enough of the state and its population had been redeemed by Federal arms to justify an election, Lincoln shot back that so great was his anxiety to restore civil government and Louisiana to the Union that he would recognize and sustain a loyal government organized by any significant part of the state that Federal forces controlled. He asked that Flanders report this view to Louisianans upon his return to the state.[68] On November 5 Lincoln angrily wrote General Banks that the failure of Louisianans to act "disappoints me bitterly." He pointedly told Banks that he and the Unionist leadership should "go to work [immediately] and give me a tangible nucleus which the remainder of the State may rally around as fast as it can, and which I can at once recognize and sustain as the true State government." The president worried that if delay occurred "professedly loyal men shall draw the disloyal about them" and set up a government that would preserve slavery, a concern that was becoming increasingly important to him. Lincoln declared that he could not recognize a state government that fell short of emancipation, though he would accept "a reasonable temporary arrangement, in relation to the landless and homeless freed people." Ignoring occupied Louisiana's exemption from the Emancipation Proclamation, Lincoln in his November 5 letter made his strongest statement yet on freedom as a requirement for reconstruction. Nevertheless, he still did not insist on the election of a state convention, which the radicals desired, as the mechanism for effecting emancipation.[69]

When Banks returned in early December from an unsuccessful military campaign on the Texas coast, he received Lincoln's letter and was stunned by its contents. He immediately wrote the president, denying that he had been given the responsibility for holding elections and blaming Shepley, Durant, and others for the failure. "Had the organization of a *free* state in Louisiana been committed to me under general instructions," he told Lincoln, "it would have been complete before this day. It can be effected now in sixty days—let me say, even in thirty days, if necessary." Banks made it clear to the president that he must be given the authority to act if he expected favorable results.[70]

On December 24 Lincoln gave Banks the power that the general wanted. In granting this authority and responding to the general's lament, Lincoln did not mention his proclamation of December 8 initiating a new reconstruction plan, though he believed it would spur a greater effort toward reorganization in the state. In his message to the general, he referred to the peculiar and tangled situation in Louisiana. "I deeply regret to have said or done anything which could give you pain, or uneasiness," he wrote the overly sensitive Banks. "I have all the while intended you to be *master*" in the reorganization of the Louisiana government. "My error has been that it did not occur to me that Gov. Shepley or any one else would set up a claim to act independently of you." Lincoln explained that instructions had been given directly to Shepley "merely to spare you detail labor, and not to supersede your authority. . . . I now distinctly tell you that you are master of all, and that I wish you to take the case as you find it, and give us a free-state re-organization of Louisiana, in the shortest possible time."[71]

With this ringing affirmation of authority from the president, Banks began his own preparations for the restoration of Louisiana to the Union. Lincoln, confident that the task in the Bayou State would be accomplished soon and efficiently by Banks, turned his attention to other occupied areas of the South where he expected his December Proclamation of Amnesty and Reconstruction to create a strong movement toward reunion and civil reorganization.[72] Little did he know in December 1863 that the political imbroglio in Louisiana was just beginning. The president's desire to restore Louisiana quickly and completely to the Union soon would go awry.

Part 2

Second Phase

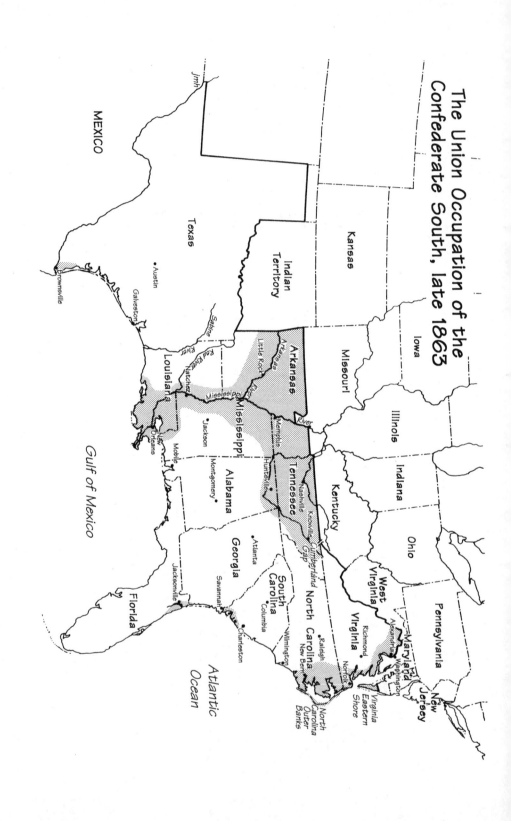

The Union Occupation of the Confederate South, late 1863

MEXICO

Texas

• Austin

Galveston •

Brownsville •

Rio Grande

Sabine River

Red River

Natchez

Louisiana

New Orleans •

Mobile •

Gulf of Mexico

Indian Territory

Little Rock •

Arkansas

Arkansas River

Mississippi River

Memphis •

Jackson •

• Montgomery

Alabama

Mississippi

Huntsville •

Nashville •

Tennessee

Knoxville •

Cumberland Gap

Atlanta •

Georgia

Jacksonville •

Florida

Savannah •

South Carolina

Columbia •

North Carolina

Wilmington •

Raleigh •

New Bern •

Charleston •

Atlantic Ocean

North Carolina Outer Banks

Norfolk •

Virginia Eastern Shore

West Virginia

Richmond •

Virginia

Alexandria

Washington

Maryland

Pennsylvania

New Jersey

Ohio

Indiana

Illinois

Kentucky

Missouri

Iowa

Kansas

6

A New Presidential Initiative

By the fall of 1863, the Confederacy appeared to be on its last legs. Vicksburg and Port Hudson had fallen to Union arms, clearing the Mississippi of rebel strongholds. Little Rock and Fort Smith had been occupied by Federal armies in September, and by the late fall the collapse of Confederate authority in Arkansas seemed imminent. Despite fears of French intervention, General Banks's forces were poised to take the Texas coast. Andrew Jackson Hamilton and other Texas Unionists predicted that Banks's campaign would strike the death blow to the Confederacy in the Southwest. Farther east, Federal forces, though they had experienced a temporary setback at Chickamauga in September, occupied the heart of East Tennessee and, by late November, had driven the main rebel army into North Georgia. They now prepared to march on Atlanta. In the Eastern theater, Lee's army had suffered a devastating blow at Gettysburg in July, followed by a series of smaller defeats after its return to Virginia. Demoralized and short of provisions, Confederate forces now numbered fewer than one-half those of the Union.

The time thus appeared ripe for a new presidential initiative on reconstruction, one that would provide a plan of action for Unionists and foster the loyal sentiment that Lincoln believed existed just below the surface of Southern society. Though the president would develop a general plan for the South, reorganization would still be in the hands of a loyal nucleus of Southerners. These Unionists would be recognized by Lincoln as

General Nathaniel P. Banks, commander, Department of the Gulf, 1862-1865 (courtesy of the United States Army Military History Institute, Carlisle Barracks, Penn.).

the body politic of their states and serve as the instrument for the self-reconstruction of the South.

Lincoln's hopes for the rapid collapse of the rebellion soared during late 1863. The president's address at Gettysburg on November 19 reflected his upbeat mood when he proclaimed in closing that because of the sacrifices made on that battlefield four months earlier "this nation, under God, shall have a new birth of freedom—and that government of the people, by the people, for the people, shall not perish from the earth." Whether Lincoln's vision for America included biracial democracy and equality is a question that historians have long debated. Clearly, the essence of republicanism for Lincoln was loyalty to the Union, respect for the Constitution, self-government, and freedom. In late 1863, his attention focused on winning the war, restoring loyal white governments in the South, and taking steps toward ending slavery in the rebel states. The president also expected loyal governments in the border states, inspired by the army's success and his administration's commitment to freedom in the South, to move rapidly toward emancipation. These steps had to take place before the greater vision for America outlined in his Gettysburg Address could be fulfilled.

Lincoln's optimism was fueled by news of widespread disaffection in the South and resurgent Unionism. Even in the heartland of the Confederacy, the president received reports of increasing war-weariness and a desire for reunion. From Alabama, reports reached Lincoln that August state elections indicated the people were ready for the restoration of the old government. Edmund Fowler, a Montgomery physician in exile in New York, told the president that a majority of loyal men had been elected to the Alabama legislature, insuring the approval of a resolution calling for the immediate return of the state to the Union.[1] Armistead Burwell, a prominent Vicksburg Unionist, wrote the president that along the lower Mississippi River "there are many bold and talented men, once men of wealth and influence, who at all hazards are willing to raise the old standard, and follow it to the death." Burwell, a substantial property holder before the war, told Lincoln that "it is a great error into which ignorant and prejudiced men [of the North] fall that those who do not come out boldly for the Union are its enemies, or in the modern phrase, disloyal. There are thousands in Miss: who desire most ardently the restoration of the United States Government, who yet see no way, in which their sentiments can be safely or beneficially expressed." Burwell pleaded with Lincoln to take immediate steps to restore Mississippi to the Union. He informed Lincoln that the institution of slavery provided no real barrier to reunion, since its demise was being accomplished by "the practical operation of war."[2] Lincoln received a similar report from Adj. Gen. Lorenzo Thomas, who visited the Natchez area in October 1863. Thomas found "a growing Union feeling" in the riparian counties of Mississippi, and the prominent citizens, who in most cases had been Whig opponents of secession, "are extremely desirous of bringing the State back into the Union." Like Burwell, Thomas indicated that planters recognized the inevitability of emancipation and were prepared to compensate the freed blacks for their labor.[3]

According to information reaching Washington, many Southerners favored reunion in order to avoid the calamity of race war and the complete collapse of their labor system. After traveling through several Confederate states in August and talking to "former prominent politicians" in those states, a Lincoln supporter reported that the "danger of the annihilation" of slavery and the Federal employment of black troops "bear more heavily upon [Southerners] than anything else connected with the war." In order "to escape this now apparent inevitable fate," Southerners whom the traveler talked to "expressed a willingness to any terms which shall not humiliate and degrade them." They repeatedly declared that "if the President were to issue a proclamation holding their leaders to a strict accountability for the rebellion, and offer the people protection in person and property, leaving the institution of slavery to the constitutional immunity of State laws, they will not only accept it, but will hail the act as magnanimous, noble, and great."[4]

Political events in Arkansas and North Carolina during the summer and fall of 1863 gave Lincoln considerable hope that these states were moving toward reunion. Developments in Arkansas looking toward reconstruction occurred quickly after the Federal occupation of Little Rock and Fort Smith in September. Arkansas Unionists held a series of meetings designed to encourage a returning loyalty among the people and to seek the quick restoration of civil authority. Letters and newspaper clippings reporting these meetings flooded Washington asking for support for the restoration of civil government in the hands of Arkansas's "unconditional Unionists."[5] An Arkansas correspondent of the *Cincinnati Gazette* wrote: "When the war broke out there was a strong Union party in favor of staying in the Union, but they were out of sight in the vortex of secession. When the war began to be oppressive many men fled to the mountains for security from conscription, or came to our lines and joined our service." Other Arkansans, he declared, remained at home, hoping to be left alone. Now they desire to return to the Union and hold elections "as soon as it is safe to do so without fear of interruption by guerrillas or overawing of any kind."[6] The *Memphis Bulletin* confirmed these reports: "We have conversed with persons of that State from various conditions of life, from the woodchopper to the planter, the soldier and the civilian, Unionists and

Secessionists, natives of the State and visitors to it from North and South, and we find all agree that the people of Arkansas are for the Union."[7]

The most dramatic case of returning loyalty among Arkansans occurred a few months before the fall of Little Rock, when Brig. Gen. Edward W. Gantt, who had commanded Confederate forces at New Madrid, announced his abandonment of the rebellion. Gantt had been elected to the U.S. Congress in 1860 but did not take his seat. After becoming a prisoner of war in June 1863, Gantt proclaimed his support for the Union. He visited Lincoln in mid-July and told the president that the Southern masses, particularly Arkansans, were sick of the war and the reign of terror by Davis and his "minions." Gantt impressed upon the president the growing desire for peace and reconstruction in Arkansas and insisted that "it is the first State among those which clearly seceded that can be induced to return to its allegiance." Hoping to encourage such sentiment, Lincoln assured Gantt that he would deal gently with former Confederates and would support any effort to restore a loyal government in Arkansas once Federal arms had taken Little Rock and provided security for Union men. The president evidently also reminded Gantt of his determination to enforce the Emancipation Proclamation in Arkansas. After Little Rock fell to Gen. Frederick Steele's forces, Gantt returned to the state and issued a printed address to the people urging them to throw off the yoke of the Davis "despotism" and rejoin the Union. Although a slaveholder himself, Gantt called on Arkansans to recognize that the war had "well nigh accomplished" the end of slavery, and he concluded that the state would be better off without it.[8] After having his address printed and circulated, Gantt returned to Washington, where he was pardoned by Lincoln. Using the national capital as his base, Gantt, who, according to one source, "stands high with the President," continued to lobby in behalf of Southern Unionism and spoke at several war rallies in the North before returning to Arkansas.[9]

Arkansas Unionists, acting on the momentum created by loyal meetings in the state and encouraged by Lincoln, met at Fort Smith on October 30 and laid plans for the restoration of civil government in the state. Representing twenty counties, the delegates passed resolutions expressing their desire to return to the Union and form a government that would recognize freedom for blacks. With these purposes in mind, they called for a state constitutional convention composed of loyal men to meet in Little Rock on January 4. Local Union meetings chose delegates to the constitutional convention, though at least in one county an election was held and 814 votes were cast. The selection of delegates was under way in late 1863 as Lincoln contemplated a new reconstruction initiative. Encouraging reports of reconstruction activities in Arkansas, even without his or General Steele's direct involvement, contributed to Lincoln's decision in December to take another important step in Southern reconstruction.[10]

Events in North Carolina during the summer and fall of 1863 further reinforced Lincoln's view that the tide of Southern Unionism was surging. A peace movement, organized after Gettysburg by William Woods Holden of the *Raleigh North Carolina Standard,* caused the president as well as other Northerners to believe that Unionism was rapidly gaining strength in that state. Though Edward Stanly, who resigned as military governor in early 1863, had failed to make progress toward restoration, later reports of discontent in North Carolina filled the columns of the *Washington Chronicle,* the president's newspaper organ, and revived interest within the Lincoln administration for a new reconstruction effort in the Old North State.[11] Even the usually skeptical Salmon P. Chase agreed with Attorney General Edward Bates during the summer that "North Carolinians are just now beginning to discuss the subject of disconnecting their State from the Confederacy."[12] Lincoln's hopes regarding North Carolina rose, prompting him to give his "entire approval" of a letter to Governor Zebulon B. Vance proposing peace based on reunion, emancipation, and "the full reinstatement of every Confederate citizen in all the rights of citizenship in our common country."[13]

Elsewhere in the South, the success of old Union Whigs, or conservatives, in fall elections lent additional support to Lincoln's belief that the Confederacy was coming unglued.[14] Moreover, Copperheads or peace Democrats in the North and the border states, whom Lincoln thought had shamefully helped to keep the rebellion alive in the South, suffered heavy losses in the fall elections. John Hay, the president's secretary, quoted Lincoln as saying that Jefferson Davis's only hope now for maintaining the rebellion was his army, "not only against us, but against his own people. If that were crushed out, they would be ready to swing back to their old bearings."[15]

Lincoln, however, in his anxiousness for an end to the war and the quick restoration of the Union, had missed an important point regarding most Southern disaffection. The success of conservative ex-Whigs in the 1863 elections did not represent a broad Southern desire to return to the Union. Governor Vance of North Carolina ignored Lincoln's overture of peace. Even Holden's militant peace movement, which did not significantly spread beyond North Carolina's borders, was designed to preserve Confederate independence through a negotiated peace before slavery and Southern society were destroyed.[16] Southern political disaffection in 1863 mainly reflected a bitter dissatisfaction with secessionist leaders for their failures to defeat the Northern armies, respect individual and state rights, and prevent social disorder.[17] Though some Confederate dissidents may have concluded that reunion was preferable to subjugation and ruin, they still hoped that independence could be achieved. Lincoln, however, preferred to believe the roseate and misleading reports of Southern Unionists like Fowler and Burwell. He rejected the contention of many members of his own party, particularly the Radicals, that only a small minority of Southerners actually sought the restoration of the old government.

The president, by the late fall, with his political flank in the North secure, began to formulate a new reconstruction plan, one that would require emancipation while preserving the essence of self-reconstruction. He was more convinced than ever that he could find a large nucleus of Southerners in almost every state to rally behind a conservative plan that would also gain the support of Congress and the border-state and Northern people. Timing was crucial for Lincoln in the announcement of a new Southern policy. He admitted as much in an October 4 reply to a suggestion by Gen. William S. Rosecrans that he should soon offer a general amnesty to rebels. Lincoln agreed with Rosecrans, declaring "I intend doing something like what you suggest, whenever the case shall appear ripe enough to have it accepted in the true understanding, rather than a confession of weakness and fear."[18]

Members of Lincoln's party were aware that the president was preparing a new policy for the South. All political persuasions in the Republican party—from Radicals like Chase, who wanted full freedom for blacks included in the state constitutions as a reconstruction requirement, to conservatives like Senator James Dixon of Connecticut, who wanted the restoration of the status quo antebellum—bombarded Lincoln with their views.[19] Chase and other Radicals were aware of Lincoln's support for an apprenticeship system for emancipated blacks, which would leave them at the tender mercies of their former owners and fall short of actual freedom. A few days after issuing the Emancipation Proclamation, Lincoln had indicated to General John A. McClernand that, though he would not retract the proclamation, he would accept the Southern adoption of "systems of apprenticeship for the colored people, conforming substantially to the most approved plans of gradual emancipation." Then, in his angry November 5 message to General Banks chastising Louisianans for their failure to reorganize their government, the president made it clear that he now expected the Southern states to adopt emancipation as a part of any reconstruction settlement. Nevertheless, as the Radicals feared, Lincoln told Banks that he would accept "a reasonable temporary arrangement" for the freed people in the South. In a November 25 letter to Lincoln, Chase warned the president not to make such a concession in his reconstruction policy lest it be perverted into a new form of slavery.[20]

Postmaster General Montgomery Blair, the leading conservative in the Cabinet and a Lincoln confidant, attempted to relieve some of the Radical pressure on the president with a shrill and ill-advised speech at Rockville, Maryland. Entitled a "Speech on The Revolutionary Schemes of the Ultra Abolitionists, and in Defense of the Policy of the President," Blair, though supporting emancipation, charged that the Radicals "would make the manumission of the slaves the means of infusing their blood into our whole system by blending with it 'amalgamation, equality, and fraternity.'"[21]

Issued as a pamphlet, Blair's Rockville speech created a sensation in the North, leading to an angry Radical counterattack on the postmaster general and the threat to undercut Lincoln's control of reconstruction. Blair had clearly overshot his mark in his biting criticism of the Radicals. Actually, by late 1863 Lincoln, with the war decidedly in his favor, had the upper hand in his party, and no united front existed in Congress to challenge his authority over reconstruction. The issue of civil and political equality for blacks, which Blair claimed was the objective of the Radicals, had hardly been broached in Congress.[22] Though they wanted clear guarantees for black freedom and white loyalty in the insurgent states, Radicals in late 1863 looked to the president for leadership on reconstruction. Charles Sumner, the most vocal Radical in the Senate, indicated to Blair, an old friend despite their political differences, that his main desire was "to get the rebel region back under the national govt" and in the hands of loyal men. Since both supported emancipation, Sumner told Blair that "I have not yet been able to comprehend the difference between us" on the question of reconstruction.[23] Sumner overstated his agreement with Blair on reconstruction policy. The Massachusetts senator had no faith in Southern Unionism, though he was unclear how reconstruction should proceed in the South without Unionists in control. He had sweepingly called for an end to the "perverse pretension of State Rights," the political oblivion of rebels, and guarantees for black freedom before the insurgent states could be restored to the Union. Unlike most Republicans in 1863, he insisted that Congress, not the president, should formulate a reconstruction policy.[24]

A few weeks after Blair's Rockville address, Henry J. Raymond, editor of the *New York Times* and a leading middle-of-the-road Republican, sought to soften the blow of the postmaster general's remarks and deflect both Radical and ultraconservative criticism of the president's approach to reconstruction. In a speech at Wilmington, Delaware, Raymond indicated that "the question of reconstruction cannot become a practical question until the rebellion is conquered. Until then we have nothing to reconstruct." He believed, however, that the day was rapidly approaching when the rebellion would be quelled. Like Lincoln, Raymond insisted that individuals, not the states as Radicals asserted, had rebelled against the Union. Once the insurrection was suppressed, he declared that the rights of the Southern states would be protected by the national government.

Raymond also maintained that, contrary to what many critics charged, Lincoln had been consistent in his objective to restore the Union and not to end slavery by federal decree. Citing the president's August 22, 1862, letter to Horace Greeley, in which he declared that his paramount object was to save the Union and neither to save nor destroy slavery, Raymond insisted that Lincoln had been true to this purpose in his emancipation policy. The sole reason for the Emancipation Proclamation was "the salvation of the Union, and not the abolition of slavery." Lincoln, according to Raymond, by late 1862 realized he could not preserve the Union, and, by implication win the war, without some action against slavery that would weaken the military forces of the rebellion. This prominent Lincoln ally explained that "if the rebels persist in their rebellion, and compel the National Government to send its armies into all the Slave States, . . . the whole territorial area of the rebellion" will be brought "under the practical workings of the Emancipation Proclamation." Again, in keeping with Lincoln's position, he assured the Union slave states that the federal government had no right to interfere with "the peculiar institution" in their states. Raymond, however, expected these states to enact "the law of freedom" and eventually provide equal rights for all of their citizens, black and white.[25]

Reinforced in his thinking on reconstruction by Raymond and other prominent Republicans,[26] on December 8 Lincoln issued a proclamation outlining the method by which Southerners heretofore engaged in the rebellion could "resume their allegiance to the United States" and "reinaugurate loyal State governments." Known as the Proclamation of Amnesty and Reconstruction, the presidential edict granted "a full pardon" and the restoration of all rights, except the ownership of slave property, to former rebels who would take an oath of allegiance to the Union and agree to abide by all congressional and presidential proclamations regarding slavery.[27] In his annual message to Congress, which Lincoln completed on the same day that he issued his proclamation, the president carefully explained why he required the test on slavery. The Civil War laws and proclamations on slavery, he declared,

> were enacted and put forth for the purpose of aiding in the suppression of the rebellion. To give them their fullest effect, there had to be a pledge for their maintenance. In my

judgement they have aided and will further aid, the cause for which they were intended. To now abandon them would be not only to relinquish a lever of power, but would also be a cruel and an astounding breach of faith. . . . While I remain in my present position I shall not attempt to retract or modify the emancipation proclamation; nor shall I return to slavery any person who is free by the terms of that proclamation, or by any of the acts of Congress. For these and other reasons it is thought best that support of these measures shall be included in the oath.

Though Lincoln indicated that as president he had the "clear constitutional power" to require oaths in return for pardons, he admitted that the part of the pledge regarding slavery could be modified or abrogated by Congress or the Supreme Court.[28]

After writing the draft of his Proclamation of Amnesty and Reconstruction, the president inserted in the document a list of categories of high-ranking rebel military and civil officials who were excluded from amnesty. He also denied clemency to Confederates who had not lawfully treated black soldiers or their officers as prisoners of war.[29] The proclamation offered no process by which the banned classes could be pardoned, though the assumption existed that individuals seeking amnesty must apply directly to the president. A few days after the issuance of the proclamation, Edward W. Gantt, former Confederate general of Arkansas and prisoner of war who had announced his support for reunion, became the first officer to seek and received a pardon from the president. Lincoln displayed no reluctance in granting clemency to the few rebels like Gantt who sought pardons. A year later the president informed Congress that all voluntary applications of persons in the excepted class had been approved. Near the end of the war, he was even disposed to turn the matter over to Federal commanders in the field, evidently without requiring final presidential approval.[30]

Finally, in his December 8 proclamation, Lincoln outlined a method to reconstruct the state governments. The method was simple, taking up only a paragraph in his proclamation. Lincoln indicated that whenever one-tenth of the number of voters in any rebel state in the 1860 presidential election had taken the oath of allegiance and had not subsequently violated it, they could "re-establish a State government which shall be republican" in character. He did not explain why the Ten Percent formula was chosen, but, eager to get the process under way, he probably believed that while the war raged this percentage of 1860 voters would constitute a reasonable nucleus to launch loyal state governments. Nor did the president explain what he meant by "republican," though he cited the republican guaranty clause in the Constitution, which provided that "The United States shall guaranty to every State in this Union a republican form of government, and shall protect each of them against invasion." Because the Restored Government of Virginia had been recognized by both the president and the Congress, Lincoln excluded that state from the provisions of his proclamation. The president, however, expected his new initiative to inspire a greater reconstruction effort in the Old Dominion, particularly as the army penetrated the state's interior during the spring campaign.

The only other reconstruction requirement in Lincoln's proclamation was that each restored state government should "in no wise contraven[e]" the loyalty oath taken by the voters. Because the oath contained a promise to abide by all federal laws and presidential proclamations regarding slavery, this requirement in effect directed members of the new government to seek the abolition of slavery in their states. In a separate paragraph, however, Lincoln indicated that he would not object to "any provision which may be adopted by such State government in relation to the freed people of such State, which shall recognize and declare their permanent freedom, provide for their education, and which may yet be consistent, as a temporary arrangement, with their present condition as a laboring, landless, and homeless class." This meant that the states could adopt an apprenticeship system for blacks that would serve as a transition from slavery to freedom. Such a system, though peculiar to each state, perhaps could be patterned after General Banks's labor order in Louisiana in which blacks were nominally free but required to make labor contracts and remain on the land. Indeed, Lincoln probably had Banks's policy in mind when he wrote this provision in his proclamation.

The president made it clear that each state's prewar boundaries, constitution, and laws would be retained, "subject only to the modifications made necessary by the [above] conditions" and provisions "which may be deemed expedient by those framing the new state government." Lincoln also reaffirmed that Congress was the sole judge for the admission of Southern members to seats in that body. He further declared that his plan of reconstruction was the best that he could suggest, but "it must not be understood that no other possible mode would be acceptable."[31] This qualification did not necessarily mean, as historians have suggested, that the president would accept a more rigid plan emanating from Congress. Lincoln understood that some Unionists might reorganize their states at variance from his Ten Percent Plan. He would accept any scheme that did not violate the spirit of his proclamation, particularly regarding emancipation, and that conformed to the principle of self-government controlled by a loyal minority.

Lincoln clearly did not intend to undercut the progress toward reconstruction that had been made in Tennessee and Louisiana, where military governors still held forth, or in Arkansas, where Unionists at the time of his proclamation were poised to hold a constitutional convention. His proclamation was designed to accelerate the work in these states and spur reconstruction efforts elsewhere. As he explained in his annual message to Congress: "In some States the elements for resumption seem ready for action, but remain inactive, apparently for want of a rallying point—a plan of action." The proclamation "may bring them to act sooner than they otherwise would." His plan, he said, "will save labor and avoid great confusion."[32]

Notably missing in the proclamation was any mention of a future role for military governors. Earlier, when he did not reappoint governors for North Carolina and Arkansas, Lincoln implicitly acknowledged that this hybrid civil-military arrangement was not the best mechanism to launch the self-reconstruction of the Southern states. Although he was generally satisfied with Andrew Johnson's efforts in Tennessee, his recent frustrating experience with Louisiana, where Military Governor George F. Shepley and army commander Nathaniel P. Banks were at cross-purposes, caused Lincoln to question the wisdom of using military governors. To a delegation of Arkansas Unionists who visited him in January 1864, the president explained that he had chosen not to appoint any more military governors because of the constant misunderstandings and conflicts between the governors and the district commanders. Lincoln indicated that in the future he would entrust the task of temporary civil administration to the army commander in each state. The president expected, however, that "a formal organization of the State Government[s] under the terms of the Amnesty Proclamation would speedily be made by the people" and the necessity for military rule soon ended.[33]

Lincoln must have been pleased by the reaction in the North and in the border states to his proclamation. Republicans representing all factions praised the document and predicted that it would produce an early end to the rebellion and to slavery. Declaring that Lincoln's reconstruction edict "gives, probably, more general satisfaction than any message since the days of Washington," newspaperman Noah Brooks reported that it "has pleased the radicals and satisfied the conservatives by plainly projecting a plan of reconstruction which is just to popular rights, to the cause of liberty, and to the loyal people of all sections of the Union."[34] George Templeton

Strong, an antislavery New Yorker, on December 11 observed with some exaggeration that "Uncle Abe is the most popular man in America today. The firmness, honesty, and sagacity of the 'gorilla despot' may be recognized by the rebels themselves sooner than we expect, and the weight of his personal character may do a great deal toward restoration of our national unity."[35]

Radicals, or those leaning toward a radical position, emphasized Lincoln's reliance on military power rather than conciliation or latent Southern Unionism to bring the South back into the Union. The *Chicago Tribune* declared that "the President holds out the olive branch to the main body of the rebels," but "he wisely places our main present reliance on the sword. . . . The tender shoots of loyalty cannot put forth where the rigors of rebel rule are as yet unbroken. We must occupy, overshadow, and protect all."[36] Most Radicals stressed the part of Lincoln's reconstruction plan requiring Southerners to renounce "that monstrous idol of slavery" in order to have their rights restored.[37] Even though he had doubted the power of the president over reconstruction and had earlier advanced the state-suicide concept of reconstruction, Senator Charles Sumner hailed the president's proclamation because it "fastens emancipation beyond recall." At the same time Thaddeus Stevens, also in support of Lincoln's plan, asserted that it endorsed what he had been proposing in the House of Representatives since 1861. "In details we may not quite agree," Stevens told his colleagues, but Lincoln "proposes to treat the rebel territory as a conqueror alone would treat it." The Pennsylvania Radical's claim that Lincoln's plan called for the subjugation of the South must have fallen on skeptical ears in the House. Stevens, however, admitted that "the President may not strike as direct a blow with a battering-ram against this Babel as some impetuous gentlemen would desire; but with his usual shrewdness and caution he is picking out the mortar from the joints until eventually the whole tower will fall."[38] The editor of the *National Anti-Slavery Standard* predicted that Lincoln "will receive high honor from the lovers of freedom and the haters of slavery everywhere" for his commitment to emancipation in the December proclamation.[39]

Conservative and middle-of-the-road Republicans, as expected because of their close ties to Lincoln, expressed strong support for the Proclamation of Amnesty and Reconstruction. Unlike the Radicals, they emphasized its conciliatory tone. Henry J. Raymond's *New York Times* profusely praised the plan "as another signal illustration of the practical wisdom of the President."[40] The *Washington Chronicle*, which rarely differed with the administration on any issue, noted that Lincoln in his proclamation had again demonstrated "his kindness to and sympathy with the people of the South" and offered pardons to all except those "who have been flagrant in rebellion." "The President sees beneath the absolute and unyielding tyranny" of the Confederate regime and knows that "the true element of Southern society [has] no heart in the war. . . . When the yoke is lifted," the Southern people "will arise. Our armies are lifting the yoke— and the President offers his hand to assist them." In a similar vein, the *Boston Advertiser* predicted that the proclamation will "divide the enemy" by separating "the misled from the treacherous leaders, and make the interest of the many our powerful ally in defeating the purposes and punishing the crime of the selfish few" in the South. The taking of Lincoln's oath of allegiance, the *Washington Chronicle* approvingly told its readers, would restore all of the rights of Southerners and would exempt them from the penalties of the Confiscation law except for slave property. "We wish to preserve the Constitution as it is, and the Union as it was, with slavery left out by the State action of the loyal people of the slave States," this editor declared.[41]

The *St. Louis Missouri Republican,* the organ of many border-state conservatives, praised the president's proclamation for "stopping a long ways short of the Chase, Sumner, and [William] Whiting radical dogmas." The plan "recognizes fully the sovereignty of the States subordinately to the Union; intimates nothing in regard to reducing the rebellious country to a territorial condition; and it proposes terms upon which certain classes in the South may save themselves from penalties named in the Confiscation and other laws of Congress." Furthermore, Lincoln did not require the immediate emancipation of the slaves, since his proclamation provided that they could be temporarily held "in a serving condition." The *Missouri Republican* editor agreed with Lincoln that an apprenticeship arrangement for blacks was wise because it would avoid "throwing the slaves landless and homeless upon the world." He doubted, however, that "the reconstruction programme thrown out by President Lincoln [was] practical within the time that seems to have been contemplated" by him. "We must break the military power of the Southern Confederacy" before the plan can be carried out in most of the South, this editor wrote.[42]

Not all Northern political elements, however, were happy with Lincoln's reconstruction edict. Although most Radicals expressed their pleasure with the president's commitment to emancipation, many were uneasy about how the reconstruction plan would be implemented.[43] They feared that the president, in permitting an apprenticeship transition to freedom, had left the door open for broad state action delaying true liberty for blacks. Furthermore, these Radicals believed that his amnesty policy was too lenient and would unfortunately lead to a premature restoration of rebel political rights and property. Radicals, the *Washington Chronicle* reported, "complained that the proclamation unwisely gives back to the great mass of the rebels their forfeited property, which," they proposed, "should be confiscated and devoted to the redemption of the public debt."[44] The *Boston Commonwealth* reflected Radical concerns when it protested that the proclamation endowed former rebels "with the right of suffrage, which carries the right to organize another rebellion with all the forms of law in [their] favor. It can never be safe to enfranchise these rebels until they have been governed by a power outside of themselves long enough to make the rehabilitation of slavery impossible."[45]

Some Radicals contended that freedom for the slaves could not be secured until blacks had obtained the ballot, their own land, and education. Wendell Phillips, Lincoln's most vociferous critic, went up and down the East Coast during the winter denouncing the president's reconstruction plan and declaring that before Northerners left the black man to shift for himself "we ought to leave him on his own soil, in his own house, with the right to the ballot and the school-house within reach."[46] Few white Northerners, however, agreed with such a radical position in 1863 and 1864.

Frederick Douglass and other black spokesmen, though more circumspect in expressing their position, agreed with Phillips that Lincoln's reconstruction policy was a grievous mistake, since it did not provide for black rights and suffrage. Douglass, who had two private conversations with Lincoln during the war, unsuccessfully sought the president's support for the enfranchisement of black males. The president seemed indifferent to Douglass's appeal. Indeed, Lincoln at no time solicited black opinion regarding reconstruction policy or the rights of the race in freedom. Douglass was so disappointed with the president that he joined in the dissident Republican call to meet at Cleveland on May 31, 1864, to find a Radical candidate to oppose Lincoln in the fall election.[47]

In March a free-black delegation from Louisiana visited Lincoln and presented a petition asking for the right to vote for their race. Two months later five North Carolina blacks talked to the president and appealed to him to require black suffrage in their state as a part of his reconstruction settlement. These men reminded Lincoln that they had voted in North Carolina prior to the state constitutional changes of 1835. Though the interviews with both delegations were "pleasant," with Lincoln expressing his "assurances of sympathy," he was noncommittal and made no changes in his reconstruction policy.[48]

The Democrats, as Lincoln must have expected, provided the harshest criticism of the reconstruction proclamation. Referring to the proclamation as a "despot's edict," the *New York News* pronounced it "a wild, unjust, and impracticable plan for the consummation of Abolition" that would destroy self-government and the Union rather than preserve the Constitution and the republic. Governor Horatio Seymour in his annual message to the New York legislature claimed that Lincoln's policy would fasten a military despotism upon the South, which would eventually be extended to the whole country.[49] The *New York World* and the *New York Journal of Commerce* provided a similar indictment of the proclamation, with the *World* concluding that "Mr. Lincoln's scheme is not only preposterous in itself, but it is the very height of absurdity to pretend to find authority for it in that part of the Constitution which guarantees to the States a republican form of Government."[50] The *Washington Constitutional Union* contended that the president's plan for establishing minority governments in the South would violate a cardinal principle of republicanism—majority rule. Lincoln's real purpose in issuing the proclamation, Democrats charged, was to win Southern electoral votes in 1864.[51]

Although maintaining a discreet public silence, military leaders privately expressed their uneasiness with the proclamation. Gen. William Tecumseh Sherman wrote his brother, Senator John Sherman, that Lincoln's plan was senseless, since it would prolong the war "by seeming to court peace."[52] Gen. James H. Wilson, who had been sent on a mission to Washington by Grant, in a report to his commander deplored "the feverish anxiety on the part of the Government to bring back or reorganize the state governments in the conquered territory with as little delay as possible." Wilson suggested that reconstruction objectives would dictate military decisions. "We must destroy his armies before we begin to reerect the broken machinery of the states."[53] As usual in political matters, Grant, who would soon assume command of all Federal troops, kept his views on reconstruction to himself.[54]

Staunch Confederates wasted no time or effort in attacking Lincoln's Proclamation of Amnesty and Reconstruction. Catherine Ann Edmondston of North Carolina feigned incredulity at the notion that Lincoln would "offer us pardon. Pardon for what? Forgiveness for what? Forgive us for having himself invaded our land, ravaged & desolated our homes? Forgive us for his own sin!" The South, Edmondston defiantly proclaimed, would never return to the Union.[55] In a similar vein, the *Richmond Sentinel* declared that Lincoln's "miserable attempt to divide and conquer us will be contemptuously resented as the insult which it is. . . . This infamous proclamation will arouse us to new zeal and new efforts."[56] Citing Northern newspapers like the *New York Herald,* the Confederate press reported that the proclamation is "universally laughed at, and will prove revolting even to reconstructionists" in the North. Confederates contended that Lincoln's real aim in issuing the proclamation was to gain European support for his aggression rather than provide a liberal plan for Southerners to return to the Union.[57]

William Woods Holden, who had led the peace movement in North Carolina and who many Northerners believed favored reconstruction, denounced the proclamation as an effort to ferment civil war within his state. Like Democrats in the North, this long-time Southern Democratic editor charged that the Ten Percent requirement for selecting a new government was "opposed to the fundamental principle of the right of a majority to govern." "Whatever may happen," Holden defiantly promised, "North Carolina will act as a *State,* by a majority of her people," and not in conformity with Lincoln's proclamation.[58]

In the Confederate Congress, Representative Henry S. Foote of Tennessee offered a resolution declaring that the proclamation was "truly characteristic . . . of the imbecile and unprincipled usurper who now sits enthroned upon the ruins of constitutional liberty in Washington City." Foote, who ironically before the end of another year would seek asylum and clemency within Union lines, exclaimed that "there has never been a day or a hour when the people of the Confederate States were more inflexibly resolved than they are at the present time never to relinquish the struggle of arms in which they are engaged until the liberty and independence for which they have been so earnestly contending shall have been at last achieved." Inexplicably, Foote's resolution, as well as a similar but less defiant one by a colleague, was laid on the table and not acted upon by the Confederate House of Representatives.[59] The thunderous criticism that Confederates hurled at Lincoln's proclamation revealed their fear that it might have a damaging effect on the Southern war effort. Events would demonstrate that their fear was not entirely unfounded.

Southern Unionists, of course, expressed a decidedly different view of the proclamation. They hailed Lincoln's plan and predicted that it would lead to an early restoration of the Southern states to the Union.[60] Even conservative Unionists—despite the proclamation's emancipation provision, which they opposed—indicated their satisfaction with the plan. J.L. Riddell, a Louisiana conservative, wrote Lincoln, predicting that his plan "will be endorsed and accepted throughout the length and breadth of [his] state." Thomas Cottman, another Louisiana conservative, who was in Washington at the time Lincoln issued his proclamation, visited the White House on December 15 and informed the president that he would be guided by his "wishes" on reconstruction when he returned home. After the interview Lincoln outlined in a letter to Cottman just what his wishes were. The president wrote: "I deem the sustaining of the emancipation proclamation, where it applies, as indispensable." Lincoln informed Cottman that in areas exempted from the Emancipation Proclamation he "would esteem it fortunate" if the people would free the slaves there "and then, if in their discretion, it should appear best, make some temporary provision for the whole of the freed people, substantially as suggested in the [reconstruction] proclamation."[61]

Lincoln explained to Cottman that "I have not put forth the plan in th[e] proclamation, as a Procrustean bed, to which exact conformity is to be indispensable." He declared that he wished "labor already done, which varies from [his] plan in no important particular, may not be thrown away." The president told Cottman that "I have publicly stated certain points, which I have thought indispensable to the reestablishment and maintenance of the national authority; and I go no further than this because I wish to avoid both the substance and the appearance of dictation." He suggested that, though "the particulars of what I may think best to be done in any state" might be at variance with the actions of the loyal people, he would not interfere. The message seemed clear to Cottman and other Unionists: Lincoln would permit the loyal white element in the South to control affairs in their states and make their own provisions for the freed black population. In effect, the president's only significant reconstruction requirement was an emancipation that did not threaten white political supremacy or Southern white society.

Though Southern Unionists generally accepted emancipation as a reconstruction requirement, they raised objections to the amnesty oath required by Lincoln's proclamation. Many of them complained that the president's oath was too lenient, since rebels by taking it could have their property (except for slaves) and political rights restored. Some Unionists, including Military Governor Andrew Johnson of Tennessee, like stalwart Republicans in the North wanted the door left open for the confiscation of rebel land and its distribution among Southern white loyalists. These Unionists mainly feared that rebels would take advantage of Lincoln's liberal amnesty policy and overwhelm the loyal element at the polls.[62] Tennessee Unionists explained to Lincoln the political implications of his oath and demanded that a stringent test for voting required by Johnson be retained. Johnson's oath required voters to swear that they "ardently desire the suppression of the insurrection" and would actively support the Union against its enemies. Commenting that "of course Gov. Johnson will proceed with re-organization as the exigencies of the case appear to him to require," Lincoln permitted the Tennesseans to apply their own oath for election purposes. "I do not apprehend [Johnson] will think it necessary to deviate from my views to any ruinous extent."[63]

The contrast between the president and the governor's oaths, however, continued to create confusion, prompting Johnson to complain to Lincoln that his "Amnesty will be seriously detrimental in reorganizing the state government, and that Tennessee should be made an exception. . . . As it now operates, its main tendency is to keep alive the rebel spirit in fact reconciling none. This is the opinion of every real union man here." Lincoln telegraphed Johnson that he would respond to his complaint in a day or two. But no subsequent message has been found, and the president's liberal amnesty policy, with the concession to Johnson's voting requirement, remained in force.[64]

Staunch Southern Unionists also objected to the proclamation's requirement, as they interpreted it, that they, like the rebels, must take Lincoln's oath before their rights could be restored. Others, mainly in Louisiana who had taken earlier oaths, complained that their citizenship already had been restored, and they resented having to reaffirm their loyalty. The president informed Secretary of War Edwin M. Stanton that, as a matter of principle, he disliked "an oath which requires a man to swear he has not done wrong" as a matter of principle. "It rejects the Christian principle of forgiveness on terms of repentance," Lincoln added. "I think it is enough if the man does no wrong *hereafter.*"[65] In practice, Lincoln directed that the "loyal as well as disloyal should take the oath, because it does not hurt them, clears all question as to their right to vote, and swells the aggregate number who take it, which is an important object." Nevertheless, when Unionist opposition to the loyalty test mounted, Lincoln retreated from this position and left the matter to local civil and military authorities.[66] It is reasonable to assume that most Unionists who objected to reaffirming their loyalty were never required to take the oath.

The Republican Congress, impressed by the initial support in the nation for Lincoln's Proclamation of Amnesty and Reconstruction, adopted a wait-and-see attitude toward the new policy. In the Senate the president's proclamation was simply referred to the Judiciary Committee, where no action was forthcoming.[67] In the House of Representatives a committee—called the Select Committee on the Rebellious States—was appointed on December 16 to monitor reconstruction developments under Lincoln's plan and if necessary recommend changes for consideration by the full body. It was chaired by Henry Winter Davis, who bristled at Lincoln's tilt toward his rival in Maryland politics, Postmaster General Montgomery Blair.[68] Davis, however, did not openly oppose Lincoln until the summer of 1864, when the political current turned against the president; then he became the most vehement opponent of the administration's reconstruction policy.

Five days after the appointment of the select committee, two measures challenging the president's plan were introduced into the House. A set of resolutions offered by Representative George H. Yeaman of Kentucky advanced the ultraconservative alternative to Lincoln's proclamation. These resolutions declared that the Southern states had never left the Union and no formal restoration procedure or requirements should be imposed on the South by either the president or Congress. All questions regarding property—presumably Yeaman meant slavery—should be settled by the courts after Southerners reestablished their allegiance. Since the Yeaman resolutions represented the ultraconservative or Democratic minority position, the Davis committee to which they were referred quietly ignored them.[69]

A more important challenge to the president was a bill introduced by James M. Ashley, an Ohio Radical. The measure, which in most particulars followed the broad outline in Lincoln's proclamation, departed drastically from the president's plan in a provision opening the door to black suffrage. This provision ordered the enrollment as voters of "all loyal male citizens of the age of 21 years." Although the bill abandoned the early Radical insistence that the Southern states had reverted to territories by virtue of rebellion, Ashley called for the appointment of provisional military governors to rule over the South until state constitutional conventions could meet and guarantee a republican form of government, including bona fide black freedom. In addition to the suffrage provision, these requirements exceeded those of President Lincoln, who by this time had abandoned the policy of appointing military governors for the South and, moreover, had indicated that the question of calling constitutional conventions was a matter for state Unionists to decide, not federal authorities.[70] Referred at first to the Davis committee, an attempt in January to put the Ashley bill on the House agenda for consideration failed to pass, ending for a time the Radical threat to Lincoln's policy.[71]

The future of Lincoln's reconstruction plan, as outlined in his December 8 proclamation, would be determined by the course of the war, national political developments during the 1864 presidential campaign, and the skill in which the president's policy would be implemented in the occupied South. Lincoln had laid down the challenge to the South, a challenge he expected many war-weary Southerners to accept: to take action to lay the foundation for the reestablishment of loyal republican governments in their states.

7

A Flurry of Activity

After his proclamation of December 8, 1863, Lincoln moved quickly to set his new reconstruction plan in motion. By not imposing more than the minimum guarantees of loyalty and emancipation upon the South, he hoped to secure an early restoration of the southern states to the Union. As usual for Lincoln, timing was of essence in the implementation of his reconstruction proclamation. The winter of 1863-64 had brought even greater demoralization and war-weariness to the embattled Confederacy than had the military setbacks of the preceding summer and fall.[1] Lincoln expected the military power of the Confederacy to be crushed during the spring and summer campaigns of 1864. In view of weakening southern morale, he reasoned that his clemency and reconstruction policy would contribute to the early capitulation of Davis's armies. Lincoln's reconstruction policy then would go hand-in-hand with the military effort to destroy the rebellion.

According to Lincoln's scenario, as Federal armies accelerated their penetration of the South in 1864, Unionists would organize and form a "tangible nucleus" around which the masses who were willing to reaffirm their loyalty could rally. Although still a minority, southerners who took the oath would vote to reorganize civil governments in their counties and states. Lincoln assumed that, though Union control might not yet extend to all areas of a southern state, the rapid progress toward reconstruction, combined with his emancipation requirement, would insure the seating of the state's representatives in Congress. The president believed that his "tangible nucleus" approach, which he had adopted at the outset of the war when he recognized the Restored Government of Virginia and had expanded upon in 1862 with his appointment of military governors for the

Francis H. Pierpont, governor of the Restored Government of Virginia,
1861-1868 (courtesy of the West Virginia and Regional History Collection,
West Virginia University Libraries).

occupied areas, would be invigorated by his Proclamation of Amnesty and Reconstruction. Despite his disappointment with the slow progress in the states where he had appointed military governors, Lincoln now expected these states, with the stimulus provided by his proclamation, to act immediately on reconstruction. States where reorganization efforts had been launched, specifically Louisiana, Tennessee, and Arkansas, could serve as models for the restoration of loyal governments in areas that would soon be occupied by Federal forces.

Although Lincoln could not control the pace of reconstruction in the states themselves, he acted quickly to implement the amnesty provisions of his December 8 proclamation and thereby provide the necessary loyal nucleus for the success of the policy. On Christmas Day, 1863, as John Hay recorded, Lincoln "got up a plan for extending to the people of the rebellious districts the practical benefits of his proclamation." He had "record books" prepared "to receive subscriptions to the oath," the form for which Lincoln evidently drafted. Certificates of loyalty would be given to each person taking the oath. Lincoln also prepared a "placard," or poster, giving public notice of the amnesty procedure and the wording of the oath. He sent the record books first to Governor Pierpont in nearby Alexandria for distribution.[2] The president then dispatched agents with clemency forms and instructions to Union officials in other occupied areas.[3] The Union press in Nashville, Little Rock, New Bern, Memphis, New Orleans, and other Federal-held towns repeatedly printed the December proclamation and optimistically predicted that large numbers of war-weary southerners would soon take Lincoln's oath.[4]

Lincoln also instructed the War Department to have commanders in the field circulate his amnesty proclamation and have the books available for persons willing to subscribe to the oath. The War Department's special commissioner appointed for this purpose directed that each commanding officer "shall see that on all occasions of expeditions, raids, or reconnaissances into the enemy's lines, a sufficient number of men are detailed for the purpose of distributing the proclamation broadcast among rebel soldiers and people."[5]

Some commanders were more zealous than others in carrying out the War Department's directive. In a raid through nine Virginia counties in March 1864, an officer on Gen. Judson Kilpatrick's staff left copies of the proclamation in temporarily abandoned houses, shops, and churches and "in every conceivable nook and corner" where people could find them.[6] Several commanders sent printed handbills of the proclamation through the lines and to Confederate soldiers. When Gen. John G. Foster, commanding Federal forces at Knoxville, had his troops distribute copies to rebel pickets, Gen. James Longstreet, the Confederate commander, indignantly wrote Foster, complaining that he had acted in an improper way. "The few men who may desert under the promise held out in the Proclamation can not be men of character or standing," Longstreet told Foster. "If they desert their cause they degrade themselves in the eyes of God and of man. They can do your cause no good, nor can they injure ours." Longstreet asked Foster in the future to communicate "any views that your Government may have upon this subject through me, rather than by handbills circulated among our soldiers." Surprisingly, Foster agreed "that it would have been more courteous to have sent these documents to you for circulation"; and he promptly provided Longstreet with twenty copies for distribution. The Longstreet-Foster exchange was so bizarre that even Lincoln doubted the genuineness of newspaper reports of it. Nevertheless, when he learned the truth, he did not upbraid Foster.[7]

Lincoln demonstrated his eagerness for the early success of his amnesty program when he offered release from prison camps of rebels who would take his oath. Having received reports that many Confederate prisoners of war were anxious to abandon the rebellion, the president on December 27 visited Point Lookout, a large camp for prisoners in coastal Maryland. Gen. Gilman Marston, the camp's commandant, told Lincoln that from one-third to one-half of the prisoners would subscribe to the president's oath of allegiance if given the opportunity. On January 2 the president dispatched John Hay to Point Lookout with the oath forms and record books. He instructed Hay, along with Gen. Benjamin F. Butler, commanding Federal troops along the Mid-Atlantic coast, to grant amnesty to all Confederate prisoners who took the oath and either lived within Union-occupied areas or were willing to "enlist in our service."[8]

No record has been found of precisely how many prisoners at Point Lookout or elsewhere in Butler's military department actually obtained amnesty and were released from captivity. Federal officers, however, were soon flooded with requests for clemency, and they administered Lincoln's oath to hundreds of prisoners. A Tennessean incarcerated at Rock Island, Illinois, prison camp probably typified the thinking of many Confederate prisoners who applied to take the oath when he wrote: "Having seen the President's Proclamation, and thinking for myself that the best interests of society, humanity and civilization demand that this wicked, unnatural war *close*," he desired to renew his American citizenship and go home. By remaining in prison, death was certain, "reducing my wife to widowhood, my children to orphanage and want."[9] Complaints soon reached Lincoln that many prisoners who sought amnesty did so only to be able to rejoin the rebel army. Lincoln at first defended his clemency policy for prisoners, informing Secretary of War Stanton that more good than harm would come from it. Nevertheless, when reports of amnesty violations continued and criticism of his policy mounted, Lincoln reversed himself. On March 26, 1864, before the amnesty policy had become general, he issued a proclamation withdrawing the privilege for prisoners of war or Confederates under parole in the South.[10]

Confusion over the question of property confiscation also created complications for the president's amnesty policy. Lincoln never really approved of the laws of 1861 and 1862 confiscating rebel property, though he went along with the 1862 act after Congress agreed in an explanatory resolution that judicial proceedings under it would not "work a forfeiture of the real estate of the offender beyond his natural life." Such a forfeiture, Lincoln believed, would violate the provision in the Constitution prohibiting the confiscation of a "traitor's" property except during the life of the attainted person. The president, however, failed to obtain a congressional amendment to the bill authorizing him to restore the condemned property of rebels who were granted presidential clemency.[11] Lincoln was concerned not only about the constitutional implications of confiscation but also about the unsettling effect that it might have on his conservative reconstruction efforts in the South.

Lincoln left the enforcement of the confiscation laws to his conservative attorney general, Edward Bates, and the federal court system.[12] United States courts, of course, did not exist in the Confederate South, and not until 1863 were they reestablished in the Union-occupied areas. United States marshals and judges in occupied Louisiana and Tennessee followed Lincoln and Bates's wishes and ignored the confiscation laws, to the chagrin of many Northern Republicans and Southern loyalists who wanted confiscation enforced as a punishment for the crime of rebellion. Except for a few Radicals, Republicans shied away from advocating confiscation as an instrument of revolutionary change in the South, though many of them desired the seizure and emancipation of rebel slaves. Even some conservative Unionists, while warning against a general emancipation policy, urged the government to confiscate the slave property of rebels.[13] Nevertheless, as the historian of wartime confiscation concludes, the primary intent of Congress in passing the Confiscation Act of 1862 was to expropriate rebel lands, not free slaves.[14] Confiscated property, except for slaves who would be freed or put to work by the military, would be distributed among Unionists and Northern soldiers in the South or sold by the government to pay the war debt.[15]

One federal judge in the occupied South took the confiscation laws seriously. Appointed by Lincoln upon the insistence of Secretary of Treasury Salmon P. Chase, John C. Underwood, judge of the Eastern District of Virginia, ignored the administration's policy on nonenforcement and pressed suits against rebel property in his district. Although his wife was a cousin of Stonewall Jackson, Underwood, a native of New York who had lived in Virginia for more than thirty years, announced that "retributive justice" should be meted out to rebels, including the loss of their slaves. "With the extinction of slavery," he predicted in a Fourth of July 1863 address, "will come the confiscation, sale, and subdivision of the old rebel plantations into farms, owned and cultivated by soldiers and other loyal men."[16]

Even before his judicial appointment, Underwood as an official in the Treasury Department had seized rebel property, including that of General Lee, for nonpayment of federal taxes. As a federal judge, he improved on his record.[17] His court at Alexandria soon groaned under the weight of confiscation cases. Contrary to Lincoln and Bates's view of the Confiscation Act, Underwood held that the law permitted forfeiture of rebel property in fee simple, that is, forever. He insisted that neither the Constitution nor the explanatory resolution in the 1862 congressional act prohibited the permanent forfeiture of property, provided the court issued the confiscation order during the lifetime of the offender.[18] Following this dubious reasoning, Judge Underwood during the 1863-64 winter term ordered the confiscation of more than two hundred Virginia estates. In the spring of 1864, he took his court to Norfolk, where in three days he issued decrees against the property of fifteen prominent rebels. Altogether, before the war ended, Underwood arranged the forfeiture of several million dollars of property, the proceeds of which went into the federal treasury. After the war, in a murky 1870 decision, the United States Supreme Court rejected Underwood's position that the property of rebels could be permanently alienated.[19] Little property, however, was returned to the heirs of rebel offenders because of this ruling.

Neither Lincoln nor Governor Pierpont acted to halt the confiscation proceedings in Underwood's court. Pierpont ignored the issue, probably because he was in sympathy with the judge's efforts but did not want to alienate Attorney General Bates, an important friend of the Restored Government, by supporting confiscation. For his part, Lincoln, after the issuance of his Proclamation of Amnesty and Reconstruction, saw no compelling reason to protect the property of leading rebels who refused to take his loyalty oath. He hoped that the mere threat of confiscation would cause rebels to renew their allegiance to the Union and prevent the loss of their real property. A presidential conflict with Underwood might have occurred had the judge rejected Lincoln's position that once a person had subscribed to the oath of allegiance no forfeiture decree could be issued against his property.[20]

Still, many federal authorities, including powerful Republican congressmen, insisted that taking Lincoln's oath did not automatically exempt a person from confiscation proceedings, either by the courts or the military. Fears abounded among Republicans and Southern loyalists that rebels would perjure themselves in order to save their lands while continuing their opposition to the Union. William H. Sorrells of Tennessee reflected these fears when he wrote: "If rebels are suffered for nearly three years to do all they can to break down the Government, and then when they are conquered, come forward and take a hypocritical oath to save property, an awful doom awaits the loyal portion of the American people."[21] No doubt some Southerners, including women, took the oath primarily to avoid confiscation, though they were usually circumspect about expressing this reason. William E. Woodruff of Little Rock was not so careful. Woodruff wrote a friend that he would take "the oath of allegiance to Old Abe's Government" in order to retain his boarding house and collect the rents, his only source of income. "I shall take it tomorrow [as] a matter of necessity—not of choice," Woodruff candidly told his friend, "and I shall be quite as strong a Rebel after taking it as I ever have been." When this letter fell into the hands of Gen. Frederick Steele, he ordered Woodruff expelled from Union lines and his property seized and held for military uses.[22]

Despite such abuses of the oath, Lincoln stood firm on the position that a Southerner regained all of his or her rights, including property rights, upon swearing future loyalty to the Union. On February 21, 1864, he directed acting Attorney General Titian J. Coffey to issue a circular letter to U.S. district attorneys explicitly exempting from the Confiscation laws any Southerner who took the oath, as long as there was no clear evidence that he had perjured himself.[23] Coffey's letter, widely circulated in the press, settled the issue for the moment, but many Republicans continued to question the policy out of concern that Lincoln was too soft on Southern rebels and was inadequate for the task of reconstruction as the war entered its final stages.

Meanwhile, by early 1864, reports had reached Washington that Floridians were ready to take advantage of Lincoln's Proclamation of Amnesty and Reconstruction.[24] The state, with a white population of only 77,747 in 1860, most of whom lived in the Northern panhandle, suffered greatly during the war from military raids, guerrilla attacks, and the general social disruption caused by the war. Unionists, residing mainly in the Atlantic coast towns where many Northerners had settled before the war, consisted of between 5 and 10 percent of the white population.[25] In the interior, a relatively large number of Floridians, living a hardscrabble existence in rural isolation, sought to avoid the war, desiring only security and a return of peace. When conditions became deplorable under Confederate rule, they were eager to renew their allegiance to the old government, escape the ex-actions of the "rebel despots," and restore their livelihoods. Along with the Unionists, they wanted assurances that they would be protected from the wrath of Confederates if they cooperated in the state's reconstruction.

The first attempt at the restoration of Florida occurred in March 1862, when Federal troops occupied Jacksonville. Encouraged by the commander of the force, local Unionists, reportedly consisting of most of the town's residents, met and issued a call for "a convention of all loyal cit-izens . . . for the purpose of organizing a State government of the State of Florida."[26] The convention was never held. Three weeks after the meeting, Federal forces abandoned Jacksonville, leaving the Unionists of the town, including some who had returned with the army, at the tender mercy of the Confederates. The evacuation of Jacksonville, the most important Florida town, ended for almost two years any serious effort to restore the state to the Union, though Federal forces seized and continued to hold St. Augustine, Fernandina, Pensacola, and other coastal communities. The lesson from the Jacksonville debacle was clear, the *Washington National In-telligencer* declared: "There must be no promises of protection on the part of the Government, followed by speedy desertion, as in the case of Jack-sonville. We lose by one such example more than we can regain by the redemption of many engagements."[27]

News of Lincoln's Proclamation of Amnesty and Reconstruction in December 1863, however, spurred St. Augustine Unionists to meet and call for a state convention to assemble on March 1 for the purpose of comply-ing with the president's requirements for restoration. They also petitioned Lincoln to send a military force sufficiently strong to liberate the state.[28] Al-though these Unionists probably did not know it, a Federal expedition was already being outfitted at Hilton Head, South Carolina, to retake Jack-sonville and march into the interior of Florida.

When Lincoln received reports of Unionist stirrings in Florida and the military's preparations to retake Jacksonville, he immediately saw an opportunity to gain an early success for his new reconstruction plan.[29] He again turned to John Hay for help. This time he dispatched his young sec-retary, whom he commissioned a major in the army, to Florida with amnesty oath forms and record books for the purpose of aiding local Unionists in initiating reconstruction. Lincoln's parting words, according to Hay, were: "Great good luck and God's blessing go with you."[30] The president also sent along instructions to Gen. Quincy A. Gillmore, the de-partment commander, describing Hay's mission and indicating that all

should cooperate in the effort "made by some worthy gentlemen to reconstruct a loyal state government in Florida. . . . I wish the thing done in the
most speedy way possible, so that, when done, it [will] lie within the range
of the late proclamation on the subject." As he had told General Banks a
few weeks earlier, Lincoln informed Gillmore that "if irreconcilable differences of opinion shall arise, you are master."[31] General Gillmore assured
Lincoln of his wholehearted support for Hay's mission and indicated that
a major purpose of his Florida campaign would be to restore the state to
the Union. "The plan now being pursued by General Banks in Louisiana
impresses me very favorably, and can doubtless in its principal features be
both easily and speedily applied in Florida."[32]

At first the military operation went well. Gillmore's forces under the
command of Gen. Truman Seymour entered Jacksonville on February 7
and occupied the adjacent west bank of the St. Johns River.[33] Two days
later John Hay arrived in Jacksonville and immediately posted Lincoln's
Proclamation of Amnesty and Reconstruction on buildings throughout the
town. Both in Fernandina, where he had first landed, and in Jacksonville,
Hay found "a most gratifying unanimity of sentiment" for the Union
"among the few leading men I have met." Even old secessionists, he informed Lincoln, "are heartily in favor of your plan." As for the masses,
"they are ignorant and apathetic. They seem to know nothing and care
nothing about the matter. They have vague objections to being shot and
have their houses burned, but don't know why it is done. They will be very
glad to see a government strong enough to protect them against these every
day incidents of the last two years." Although Hay reported that "the state
is well-nigh depopulated," he gave Lincoln "the best assurance that we will
get the tenth required" to inaugurate reconstruction.[34]

Hay's effort to restore Florida to the Union soon ran aground. Although several hundred Floridians, including many Confederate prisoners
of war, took Lincoln's oath, the defeat of Federal forces under General Seymour at Olustee on February 20 dealt a blow to the young secretary's hopes
that he would be able to enroll the 10 percent of voters required by the
president's proclamation. In the aftermath of Olustee, few Floridians dared
risk the wrath of resurgent Confederates by taking the oath and participating in the state's restoration to the Union. Complicating Hay's work was
the presence of Lyman D. Stickney, who came to Florida as a direct tax
commissioner but was more interested in promoting the political fortunes
of his boss, Secretary of Treasury Salmon P. Chase, than in cooperating
with Lincoln's representative. In supporting Chase, who Stickney believed
would be the Republican candidate for president in 1864, he expected
his own political and material fortunes to be advanced. Stickney, however,

concealed his purposes from Hay and ingratiated himself with the president's secretary while working behind the scenes against him and other Lincoln supporters in the state. After the Olustee disaster to Union arms, Stickney cleverly persuaded Hay that his mission had failed and his continued presence in Florida was unnecessary.[35]

Northern criticism of his purposes also contributed to Hay's disillusionment with Florida affairs and his desire to leave the state. Even before the Olustee defeat, Democratic newspapers charged that Hay had been sent to Florida to win support for Lincoln in the forthcoming presidential contest. The *New York World,* the bellwether of the eastern Democratic press, repeatedly claimed that Hay's mission and Gillmore's military operation in Florida were part of a grand Republican strategy to carry the 1864 election, a rather far-fetched charge in view of the fact that the state only had three electoral votes. "Florida has been marked out as one of the rotten borough states which is to help make Mr. Lincoln President," the *World* declared. "The war for the Union is first perverted into a war for abolition, and now it is a war for the Republican succession." Sharp criticism of his mission by the *New York Herald,* a newspaper that claimed to be politically independent, especially stung the sensitive Hay.[36] The *Herald* stridently charged that "brigades of our brave armies are being sent into rebellious states to water with their precious blood the soil that may produce Presidential votes."[37]

After the failure of Union arms at Olustee, the *Herald* and the Democratic press increased their attacks on Lincoln and his purposes in Florida. The army's defeat, they charged, occurred because the administration rashly pushed Seymour into the Florida interior in time to organize a Lincoln party in the state and send delegates to the national Republican convention in June. Friends of the administration indignantly replied that the sole aim of the Hay mission was to restore Florida to the Union and provide for civil government in the state. The military expedition, they argued, could not have been inspired by partisan concerns, since General Gillmore had made preparations for the campaign before he received Lincoln's instructions regarding Hay's mission.[38]

Lincoln had more important things to attend to in 1864 with the approach of an all-out military campaign to bring the Confederate government to its knees. The military effort would be followed by critical fall elections in the North. On his return to Washington, Hay found that the president "thoroughly understood the state of affairs in Florida and did not seem in the least annoyed by the newspaper falsehoods about the matter."[39] Lincoln must have been concerned, however, about the failure of this early attempt to implement his reconstruction proclamation. If repeated elsewhere, such a defeat could cause serious doubts regarding the practicality of his restoration policy. Criticism of Lincoln's reconstruction effort could create political problems in the North for his war policy and his reelection bid. Lincoln accepted the fact that Florida could not be restored to the Union until Federal military forces had occupied the interior of the panhandle and provided security for the organization of the loyal citizens. Although a "convention of Loyal citizens" meeting in Jacksonville in May urged Lincoln to authorize elections for a restored Union government in Florida, he evidently gave little or no thought to the matter.[40]

North Carolina seemed a more likely state for an early implementation of Lincoln's reconstruction plan than Florida. Federal forces had occupied the northern and central coast and sounds since early 1862, and the mountains of the western part of the state were rapidly becoming a haven for Unionists and others attempting to escape the war. Although William Woods Holden's well-publicized peace movement had failed in the late summer of 1863, North Carolina dissidents during the winter organized a campaign to call a state convention for the purpose of negotiating a separate peace with the Washington administration if the Confederate government did not act. This movement, however, was behind Confederate lines, and its leaders, including Holden, who soon became a candidate for governor against Zebulon B. Vance, denied that they sought reunion with the Lincolnites.[41]

Unionists in Federal-occupied North Carolina and many Northerners hailed the state convention movement as a major "stepping-stone back into the Union" for the Old North State. They claimed that such a convention, when it met, would withdraw the state from the Confederacy, leaving North Carolina no choice but to return to the Union. Unionists in the occupied area credited Lincoln's liberal Proclamation of Amnesty and Reconstruction and the contrasting tyranny of the Davis administration with "the decided revolution now going on in public sentiment" in North Carolina.[42] Unionists also claimed that slavery, at least in Eastern North Carolina, was no longer a significant deterrent to the state's reconstruction. The *New Bern North Carolina Times* reported that "wherever the Federal Flag floats in the Eastern part of the State, Slavery has been utterly demolished." Slaveholders who had lost their slaves "seem to be entirely reconciled by the change," this newspaper indicated.[43] Indeed, many eastern North Carolina slaveholders, stunned by the course of events, acknowledged the reality of the new situation. But they were hardly reconciled to the change in the status of blacks. Some probably concluded, like many Southern Unionists, that Lincoln's apprenticeship provision in his reconstruction proclamation would permit them to continue a master-slave relationship after the war.

Lincoln, however, did nothing to advance his reconstruction plan in North Carolina. When former Military Governor Stanly in California, having received a report from New Bern of "important movements on foot in the interior," telegraphed the president that he was ready to return to North Carolina to aid the work of reorganization, Lincoln quickly replied that he had no plans at the moment for the state.[44]

Lincoln's reluctance to foster a reorganization effort in Federal-occupied North Carolina was probably influenced by the embarrassment that he had received in his earlier attempt to establish a loyal nucleus under Stanly's leadership and the failure of Federal forces to advance beyond the virtually depopulated coastal counties. Possibly the president also wanted to await the results of the state convention movement before seeking the implementation of his proclamation in North Carolina. As it stood, Union leadership in the occupied area was weak and unreliable on emancipation. The state convention movement, which sought the continuation of slavery, not its demise, collapsed during the summer, when Holden lost the gubernatorial election to Vance. The election occurred at an unpropitious time for the convention cause. Northern morale was faltering as victory appeared remote, filling North Carolinians with renewed hope for the political defeat of Lincoln and his war party in the fall election and causing them to reject overwhelmingly the defeatist convention party. After Lincoln's election, a peace proposal, which implied reunion, was introduced in the state legislature. This failed, leaving North Carolina in the Confederacy until the end of the war.[45]

Alabama Unionists, also without direct encouragement from Lincoln, sought to take advantage of the reconstruction proclamation and act quickly to restore their state to the Union. In the secession crisis of 1860-1861, Alabama had been divided essentially along north-south lines. South Alabama, though dotted with small farms, was dominated by the plantation-slave society of the Black Belt. Similar to East Tennessee, North Alabama was primarily a land of yeoman farmers living in the hills and valleys of the area.[46]

Inspired by the fiery rhetoric of William Lowndes Yancey, South Alabamians were united for separation after Lincoln's election. On the other hand most north Alabamians, despite the presence of prominent local secessionists like Senator Clement C. Clay, Jr., and Leroy Pope Walker, supported a policy of cooperation with other Southern states before rushing madly into secession. In addition, some residents of this region wanted to see what policy Lincoln would pursue toward the South: if he made no threats against slavery or the South, they were prepared to remain in the Union.

After the adoption of the secession ordinance, followed by Lincoln's decision to use force to preserve the Union, most North Alabamians joined in the fight for Confederate independence, though not as enthusiastically as their compatriots in the southern part of the state. Traveling through the area during the summer of 1861, George S. Houston, a Union Whig congressman for two decades who retired from public life during the war, probably exaggerated when he wrote Governor Andrew B. Moore that he "found no organization or the trace of one indicating a purpose of hostility to the Confederate Government," and he was "very confident" that North Alabamians "entertain no such purpose." Houston was more accurate in reporting that most North Alabamians "were reluctant to give up the old Union, and while some of them express regrets upon that subject now, they at the same time avow a determination to stand by the South."[47] Unlike East Tennessee, where several influential politicians persisted in their support for the Union, only one prominent North Alabama leader, Judge George W. Lane of Huntsville, continued to heap scorn on the secessionists and the Confederacy until he was driven into exile.[48] Indeed, in 1861 Lane accepted an appointment by Lincoln as U.S. district judge for North Alabama. Lane, however, never held court.

Loyalty to the old republic began to reassert itself when Federal forces penetrated the area in early 1862. In February, an officer on the first Federal gunboat that moved up the Tennessee River as far as Florence reported that his crew "have met with the most gratifying proofs of loyalty every where" on their frequent stops. "Men, women, and children several times gathered in crowds of hundreds, shouted their welcome, and hailed their national flag with an enthusiasm there was no mistaking; it was genuine and heartfelt."[49] To become a political force, this Unionism needed security from Confederate retaliation and the support of local leaders, many of whom had been Unionists or cooperationists in 1860-1861 but after secession "fell into the current, and sided with the Rebellion," as one of them later expressed it.[50] The two requisites for local Union success began to appear in April 1862, when a Federal force under Gen. Ormsby M. Mitchel occupied much of the Tennessee Valley of North Alabama, including Huntsville. At the same time Confederate efforts to enforce conscription also contributed to the revival of Union sentiment in North Alabama as it did in Arkansas and East Tennessee. General Mitchel, hopeful that a Union nucleus could be found to restore civil government in the area, recommended to the War Department the appointment of Judge Lane as military governor of Alabama, "when the time comes."[51] Lincoln either did not know of Mitchel's suggestion or ignored it. Probably because of the precariousness of Federal military control in North Alabama, no military governor was appointed for the state. Lane died in Louisville in 1863 and was succeeded as federal judge by Richard Busteed of New York, who evidently, except for Judge Charles A. Peabody of the "provisional court" of Louisiana, was the only "carpetbagger" that Lincoln appointed to federal office in the South.[52]

The war soon began to take a dreadful toll upon north Alabamians. Repeated cavalry raids by both sides spawned social disarray and political instability throughout the area. The hill country became infested with deserters, conscript evaders, and Unionists, all of whom were trying to escape the war. Many of these disaffected Southerners formed bands that preyed upon their enemies and upon their helpless neighbors. Families, with able-bodied men away in the Confederate army or in the hills, suffered deprivations and insecurity. Many of them, including blacks, fled to Huntsville or other towns in the Tennessee Valley where they could find a modicum of sustenance and security. It became increasingly clear to a large number of north Alabamians that secession had failed and their only hope for the future lay with the Union.[53]

Prominent cooperationists of 1860-1861 stepped forward to lead the Union movement. Jeremiah Clemens, a former Whig senator who in 1861 had been placed in charge of organizing troops to defend Alabama against the Lincolnites, was the most important addition to the cause. In 1862 Clemens, a cousin of Samuel Langhorne Clemens (Mark Twain), quickly shifted from raising state forces to recruiting Federal troops. Largely due to his efforts and those of William H. Smith, who also had briefly served the Confederacy, hundreds of north Alabamians, both from the hills and the Tennessee Valley, enlisted in Federal units from other states or joined the First Alabama Cavalry (USA). Altogether, approximately three thousand white Alabamians, most of them from North Alabama, served in the Federal army during the war.[54]

Huntsville became the center for Union activity in North Alabama. After the Confederates had temporarily reoccupied the town in late 1862, Alabama Senator Clement C. Clay, Jr., reported from his Huntsville home that "this city is the place where Union feeling most prevailed and where it now most exists. It has given tone to the political sentiment of North Alabama."[55]

Following the battle of Gettysburg and the fall of Vicksburg in 1863, a network of secret peace societies, apparently with Huntsville as its center, sprang up in North Alabama. These societies sought an early end to the war and Alabama's restoration to the Union. The August election of former Union Whig Thomas Hill Watts as governor encouraged North Alabama reconstructionists who, along with many Unionists outside of the state, mistakenly believed that Watts would be receptive to peace overtures from the Lincoln administration.[56]

The Federal reoccupation of Huntsville and other Tennessee Valley towns in 1863, followed by Lincoln's Proclamation of Amnesty and Reconstruction, brought the reconstructionists into the open. Clemens, David C. Humphreys, and other cooperationists of 1860-1861 flooded North Alabama in early 1864 with letters and printed addresses calling for the reorganization of the state under the president's plan. The *Louisville Journal* reported that north Alabamians "are becoming outspoken, and that among them are many men of influence, who once were trusted with high office." This editor was confident that the 10 percent of the state's 1860 electorate required by Lincoln's proclamation could be obtained by the summer in the northern counties alone, provided "the rebel cavalry and guerrillas [were] driven from the State." Meanwhile, hundreds of area residents were taking Lincoln's amnesty oath in preparation for reorganization and the restoration of their rights.[57]

As a preliminary step toward reconstruction, Huntsville Unionists met on March 5 and called for a convention of North Alabama loyalists to meet one week later at the Madison County Courthouse. Jeremiah Clemens presided over both meetings, which, according to an observer, were well attended by "men of wealth and respectability." General John A. Logan, commanding Federal forces in the area, ordered his troops to provide security but not to participate in the meetings. Humphreys, a Douglas elector in 1860 who subsequently served as an officer in the Confederate army, provided the main leadership for the movement. In an early February address to North Alabamians, which was widely circulated, Humphreys declared that his motive in seeking reconstruction under Lincoln's plan was to avoid further bloodshed and ruin. He reminded the people that the only terms that Lincoln demanded was the end of slavery. If the war continued, he declared, the whole Southern labor system would be destroyed. With the president's apprenticeship provision in the proclamation in mind, Humphreys announced that immediate reunion "will secure to the State the right to dispose of its labor system in the way and manner that shall accord with the circumstances surrounding us."[58] In other words, as he declared in a later and more elaborate printed address, "the restoration of the Government will give to the State the power to regulate its social relations and domestic affairs."[59]

The Union meetings passed resolutions calling for Governor Watts to order an election for the selection of delegates to a state convention to end Alabama's participation in the rebellion and restore the state to the Union. Though Watts had been elected on an anti-Davis platform, North Alabama Unionists had little hope that he would agree to such a convention.[60] As expected, the governor ignored the resolutions, whereupon the Clemens-Humphreys party asked Lincoln what action North Alabama Unionists should take to restore the state under the old flag. Clemens wrote Secretary of State William H. Seward, whom he had served with in the Senate during the early 1850s: "We have taken steps in Alabama to organize a civil government, but before proceeding further, we thought it best to ascertain the views of the President." Confederate cavalry, Clemens informed Seward in May, had overrun much of North Alabama south of the Tennessee River, and the people in those counties dared not act until General Sherman's army cleared the area of rebel troops. Meanwhile, the counties north of the river "are in a condition to act" and to form a nucleus "around which others may rally." Clemens wanted Lincoln's support for such action and also asked for the appointment of federal officials for the area. After showing the letter to the president, Seward informed Clemens that "military events [were] occurring in Georgia, which may very essentially modify the situation in Alabama, and enable the government to profit by your advice."[61]

Sherman's campaign in northwest Georgia, however, did not modify the situation in Alabama. The clash of the major armies above and around Atlanta during the spring and summer spawned raids and military operations in North Alabama, prolonging the social breakdown and political uncertainty in the area. Then in the fall, General John B. Hood's army, defeated in Georgia, moved into North Alabama, living off the land and preparing for a desperate assault upon Federal forces at Nashville. Although the time was hardly propitious for the reconstruction of the state, Lewis E. Parsons, leader of the peace faction in the legislature, introduced a resolution in October demanding that the state open negotiations with the federal government based on the peace platform drawn up by the Democrats at Chicago. Parsons, along with many proslavery or conservative Unionists, wishfully believed that, despite Lincoln's improving political prospects after the fall of Atlanta, the Northern Democrats with General McClellan as their standard-bearer would win the election. The Democratic success, they predicted, would be followed by an armistice and a convention of the states that would restore the South to the Union with slavery intact. The legislature, vigorously supported by Governor Watts, by a vote of 45 to 32 rejected the Parsons resolution.[62]

The 1864 election determined that Lincoln, not McClellan, would control reconstruction when rebel authority collapsed. Several north Alabama Unionists, who had supported Lincoln and had warned that the Chicago platform was a chimera, went north to seek the president's approval for their reorganization schemes. The most aggressive of these loyalists was Clemens. This former U.S. senator outlined a plan of reconstruction for Alabama similar to that of Lincoln. He proposed the appointment of a military governor, with himself obviously in mind, who would select officials and "set the machinery of law in motion" in the upper one-third of Alabama. This reorganization would become the nucleus for the restoration of loyal government throughout the state. The only significant difference between the president's plan and Clemens's proposal was that the Alabamian would have a state convention rescind Alabama's secession ordinance. The president objected to such an action because it suggested that the state had been out of the Union, an admission that he could never make. As to slavery, Clemens thought that it should be "cut up root and branch," despite the fact that he was a large slaveholder, whose blacks were still "at home & at work." He told Andrew Johnson that "the Secessionists deserve" the abolition of slavery "as a punishment for their guilt, & the Union men would rather part with it (slavery) now & forever, than run the risk of its bringing on their children the evils with which it has cursed us."[63]

When Clemens went to Washington to see the president in early February, Lincoln was in Virginia with the troops. Sick and discouraged, the Alabamian left Washington and died in Philadelphia soon after the war.[64] The task of initiating Alabama's return to the Union would await the end of the conflict and the leadership of another president, Andrew Johnson.

Reconstruction rumblings after Lincoln issued his December 8, 1863, proclamation could also be heard in Georgia and Mississippi. Efforts to restore these two states to the Union, however, were weaker and more scattered than in North Alabama. Still, in Georgia discontent had become widespread as the war took a dreadful toll on families and communities. Like North Alabama, the hills of northern Georgia became infested with bands of deserters, conscript dodgers, and others trying to escape the war. Virtual anarchy gripped some areas of Georgia, and criticism of Confederate and state authorities became rampant. Dissatisfaction and a desire for reunion, however, were not synonymous in the minds of Georgians, though these two sentiments tended to blend when the state became the scene of major fighting in 1864.[65]

The first movement toward reconstruction in Georgia occurred after Sherman occupied Atlanta in September. With the general's encouragement,

Augustus R. Wright, a former United States and Confederate congressman of Northwest Georgia, and another prominent Georgian met with Sherman in Atlanta. Wright, who was anxious to recover two hundred bales of cotton confiscated by the Federal army, agreed to work for the state's restoration under Lincoln's plan. Sherman sent him to Washington, where, according to Wright's account, he had several interviews with the president. In each interview Lincoln expressed his sympathy for the people of the South in their calamities and reaffirmed that his main objective was the quick restoration of the Union. Lincoln wanted blacks freed and protected in their freedom, Wright recalled, but "he did not talk as if he thought the negro was capable of self-government." Wright received no specific instructions from the president on how reconstruction should proceed in the state. The Georgian later claimed that had Lincoln lived he would have been appointed provisional governor.[66]

When Savannah fell to Sherman in December, a Unionist meeting in the town adopted resolutions demanding that Governor Joseph E. Brown call a convention to end Georgia's participation in the rebellion. Inspired by the Savannah resolutions, Union organizations, some of which were secret, sprang up throughout the state and were soon augmented by dispirited "deserters" from Lee and Hood's armies. Brown and other state Confederate leaders, however, refused to act under Lincoln's plan, and when the war ended, they were forced from office and, in some cases, briefly imprisoned.[67]

In Mississippi, the Federal occupation of the river counties in 1863 set the stage for a reconstruction boomlet on the Natchez-Vicksburg axis. Many planters of this area had opposed secession, and when Federal gunboats appeared on the river, they raised the old flag and gave material assistance to their liberators. In addition, by late 1863 the normally sparsely populated piney woods of southeastern Mississippi were teeming with deserters, refugees, and poverty-stricken local inhabitants who wanted an end to the war, even if it meant reunion and emancipation. A correspondent to the *Washington Chronicle* reported that "the people of Mississippi are getting tired of the war, and, if they had their own way, would probably come back very soon to the Union. . . . They would emulate the example now being set by Arkansas, and endeavor to return a free State."[68] Adjutant General Lorenzo Thomas, who was on an inspection tour of the lower Mississippi Valley, also found that Natchez area inhabitants were "extremely desirous of bringing this State back into the Union, and they are doing all in their power to accomplish this very desirable object. The strong undercurrent of Union feeling is daily growing, and the time is not far distant when it will rise to the surface and assert its proper sway."[69]

Before Lincoln issued his reconstruction proclamation, Natchez Unionists attempted to persuade William L. Sharkey, former chief justice of the state's high court, to lead a movement for Mississippi's restoration to the Union. Though Sharkey met with General Sherman, who commanded in the state, to discuss the prospects for reunion, he declined to participate at this time, indicating that such a movement would be premature. Even after the president's proclamation, Confederate military control of most of the interior and the collapse of communications between the river counties and the disaffected backcountry made it impossible for Mississippi Unionists to coordinate their efforts to establish a loyal government in the state.[70] Though a few hundred Mississippians would take Lincoln's oath and serve in the Federal army, the Union reorganization of the state would await the end of the war.

Closer to home, in Virginia, Lincoln hoped that his Proclamation of Amnesty and Reconstruction would immediately boost the efforts of Governor Pierpont to extend his authority and advance the Union cause in the state. The Restored Government's Lilliputian size had been somewhat of an embarrassment to Lincoln and its friends in Washington.[71] Since 1861, however, both the president and Congress had recognized the Restored Government, and it continued to be represented in the U.S. Senate. One of its senators, Lemuel J. Bowden of Williamsburg was popular in Washington, though not influential. When he died in early 1864 of smallpox, Lincoln attended the funeral.[72] Bowden would not be replaced until after the war. John S. Carlile, Virginia's other senator, became a thorn in Lincoln's side when he joined the ultraconservative opposition to emancipation. In the House of Representatives, the Restored Government's claimants for seats in 1863 and again in 1864 were rejected on the ground that their elections were not representative of the loyal voters of the districts, since either rebel occupation or the general disruptions of war prevented the opening of most of the polls.[73] Both Lincoln and Governor Pierpont believed that this setback was only temporary. They expected that as Grant's offensive toward Richmond progressed in the spring of 1864 thousands of Virginians would take the loyalty oath and participate in the elections to restore civil authority and elect members to Congress.

Lincoln's renewed interest in Virginia was further bolstered by the likelihood that the Old Dominion probably would become the first Confederate state to abolish slavery. The key to emancipation was Pierpont. The governor, who had earlier secured Lincoln's exemption of the occupied counties from the provisions of the Emancipation Proclamation, converted to the antislavery cause in 1863, partly due to the influence of his antislavery wife. He explained to Lincoln in September 1863 that the exemption had not induced loyalty, as he had earlier thought, and the president should revoke it on grounds of military necessity.[74] Though unsaid, the governor's conversion to emancipation was probably also caused by his realization that Lincoln and other powerful backers of the Restored Government, including Salmon P. Chase, now expected the Union regimes in the South to abolish slavery in their states. A commitment to emancipation on his part, Pierpont hoped, would check the decline in support for the Restored Government in Washington.

Encouraged by Pierpont's conversion, Lincoln, instead of revoking his exemption for the occupied counties as the governor recommended, foresaw an even greater opportunity for emancipation in Virginia, one in which Virginians, not he, would bring about the end of the institution in the state. State action in the liberated areas of the South would be in keeping with Lincoln's commitment to self-government as exercised by the loyal population. In conferences with Pierpont he secured the governor's approval of a plan by which the Restored Government would abolish slavery in the state's constitution. Following this plan, Pierpont called the General Assembly into session on December 7—one day before Lincoln issued his reconstruction proclamation. At the governor's urging, the General Assembly, consisting of only seventeen members representing thirteen counties, called for elections for a constitutional convention to meet in Alexandria on February 13. The main purpose of the convention would be to abolish slavery in Virginia.[75] Irregular elections for delegates were held on January 21, and seventeen men, some of whom were chosen by fewer than one hundred votes, were sent to represent their districts in the convention. Most of the delegates were educated, middle-class Unionists who were moderate former Whigs; a few were natives of the North who had settled in Virginia before the war.[76]

The state convention proceeded with alacrity to adopt a new constitution for Virginia. On March 10 the convention approved a provision abolishing slavery, making Virginia the first Confederate state to provide for emancipation in its fundamental law. Freed blacks, however, received no rights in the new constitution. The delegates even rejected a proposed section that provided for black testimony in court. They created, at least on paper, Virginia's first system of public schools and directed that it enroll white children only. In addition to denying blacks the right to vote—a concept that was far too radical for Southern Unionists in 1864—the constitution disfranchised Virginians who gave voluntary aid to the rebellion after January 1, 1864. This provision went beyond Lincoln's Reconstruction and Amnesty Proclamation requiring a simple loyalty oath for the restoration of all rights. The legislature, however, received the authority to restore voting rights to those who were disfranchised. A more rigid disqualification was the constitution's requirement that no person who had held office under the Confederacy or "any rebellious State government," except in a local position, could serve in a public post. No provision was made for the removal of this disability.[77]

A vigorous convention debate occurred over a measure reducing to one year the residency requirements for voting and officeholding.[78] The provision, which ultimately passed, enabled northern settlers and returning Unionists to take part in the Restored Government. The constitution also directed that all property should be taxable in proportion to its value, a measure designed to end the privileged tax status of landowners.[79] Except for this provision, the section abolishing slavery, which Lincoln clearly favored, and the paper establishment of the public school system, the Constitution of 1864 hardly could be classified as a progressive document. The disfranchisement of large numbers of whites (though this disability was removed soon after the war), the failure to provide blacks with any rights other than freedom, and a provision granting the governor the power to appoint judges did not provide a sound foundation for postwar Virginia.[80] Furthermore, the new constitution, at the insistence of Governor Pierpont, who feared that perjured rebels and proslavery Unionists would vote it down, was not submitted to the people for ratification.

The Pierpont constitution, as it was sometimes called, went into immediate effect. The governor issued a proclamation declaring all county offices vacant and calling for elections in May. Despite the disruptions created by the war, regular elections were held in the occupied counties and in at least one southwestern county where the shadowy Heroes of America, a militant Unionist society, contested Confederate authority.[81] On the Eastern Shore, Unionists complained that former secessionists took advantage of the confusion over the loyalty oath requirement for voting—some thought Lincoln's oath was adequate—and won control of Accomac County.[82] Though the vote totals were low, the elections in the occupied area provided the Restored Government and, by implication, the new constitution with a vote of confidence. The constitution adopted in 1864 survived the war and continued as the fundamental law of Virginia until it was replaced in 1870 by a document promulgated under congressional or military reconstruction.

Despite the Virginia constitution's shortcomings, Lincoln was delighted with the convention's work, particularly the provision abolishing slavery. His delight, however, soon was tempered by a growing conflict over authority between the Restored Government and the military. At the center of the conflict was Gen. Benjamin F. Butler, who attracted controversy in the South like a magnet. Given Butler's highhanded approach to problems wherever he was assigned, a clash with a strong-willed civil official like Governor Pierpont was virtually inevitable; and it began soon after he assumed command of the Department of Virginia and North Carolina in November 1863. Butler's command included the lower James Peninsula and the Eastern Shore, but not the occupied area along the Potomac. His headquarters was at Fort Monroe near the important military and naval staging base at Norfolk. Although Alexandria on the Potomac, like Norfolk, was an important center for the Federal army, President Lincoln informed Gen. John P. Slough, the local commander, that he should not interfere in civil affairs unless imperatively demanded by military necessity, a directive that the general largely obeyed. Even before the adoption of the new constitution, elections had been held in Alexandria and the regular functions of local government had been restored.[83]

Governor Pierpont and other members of Virginia's Union government expected a similar policy in the Norfolk area and on the Eastern Shore. Lincoln, however, did not clarify with either Butler or Pierpont the proper relationship of the military to the Restored Government. When a crisis of authority arose between the general and the governor, Lincoln found himself in a difficult political situation, particularly in view of the approach of a presidential campaign. He could not risk antagonizing Butler, who was popular with the Radicals and with many War Democrats whose support Lincoln needed in the election. At the same time the president could not afford to undercut the Restored Government, which represented his handiwork and also had important supporters in Congress and in the Cabinet.

Hardly had Butler assumed command when he began to interfere with the civil administration in Norfolk and nearby Portsmouth. Butler restored the authority of the provost or military courts in the two towns and levied a tax to support "a provost marshal's fund." Governor Pierpont, after returning to Alexandria from the Tidewater, where he had investigated complaints against Butler, angrily wrote the general charging that his provost courts "were intermeddling with the civil authorities of the cities in a most licentious manner." Pierpont told Butler that the reestablishment of military authority over purely civil matters in the Norfolk area had nothing to do with suppressing the rebellion or rendering the army more efficient, "but, upon the contrary, its very tendency is to keep up the rebellion, to exasperate Union men as well as rebels, and mix everything in inextricable confusion." The governor demanded that Butler dissolve the military courts and cease intervention in civil affairs.[84]

In response, Butler ignored Pierpont's main contention that he had superseded civil authority in the Norfolk area and declared that the governor had been "misinformed" regarding the facts. Furious at the general's reply as well as reports of additional military interference, Pierpont immediately saw Lincoln and insisted that the president put a halt to Butler's "subversion of good government." In his conference with Lincoln, Pierpont focused his criticism on two recent orders of the general interfering with the collection of revenue by civil officials and threatening to assume control of local banks. Lincoln, agreeing with the governor that Butler's actions exceeded military necessity, directed the general "to suspend these measures, until you can state, . . . in writing or otherwise, your views of the necessity or propriety of them."[85] The president made no mention of the provost courts, an omission, inadvertent or not, which suggested to Butler that he could still exercise military authority in the Norfolk area. Instead of explaining his actions to Pierpont, whom he referred to as "the supposed governor of Virginia," Butler wrote a long letter to the president defending in detail his course. Again, the general ignored the question of military necessity in the controversy or the larger issue of the effect of his interference on Lincoln's reconstruction policy. The thrust of Butler's explanation was that he had restored efficiency, good order, and prevented rebel sympathizers from attacking Federal officers and suppressing true Union men.[86]

Butler's explanation did not sit well with the president. It was at this time that Lincoln reportedly told a visitor that "I think you agree with me that General Butler is not fit to have a command." When the general learned of the comment, Lincoln, recognizing the political gravity of the situation whether he actually made the comment or not, dispatched a memorandum to Butler expressing "confidence in [the general's] ability and fidelity to the country *and to me* and I wish him sustained in all his efforts in our great common cause subject only to the same supervisions which the Government must take with all Department Commanders." Lincoln, however, would not write, as Butler wanted him to do, that he never made the derogatory comment about the general's competence.[87]

The president later admitted that he should have acted more forcibly to forestall Butler's transgressions on civil authority. But for most of 1864, as military campaigns and the national election occupied much of his time, he remained silent while the general became bolder in his interference with the Pierpont government. In March Butler placed the issuance of commercial licenses under military control and granted a whiskey monopoly in Norfolk to northeastern friends, much to the chagrin not only of Pierpont but also local liquor dealers who had previously controlled the lucrative traffic. He also seized a local press and converted it into his own newspaper organ in Norfolk, assigning a member of his staff and several enlisted men to publish it.[88]

Governor Pierpont struck back with a fifty-five page printed letter to the president and Congress detailing Butler's "abuse of military power." The governor contrasted his relationship with Butler with the friendly and cooperative association he had had with several military commanders in both western and eastern Virginia, all of whom, he claimed, had respected civil authority. Pierpont told the president and Congress that, from the beginning, based on Butler's record in New Orleans, "I was satisfied he was going to abrogate civil government if he could; that Unionism availed nothing if it lay between him and his object." Butler, the governor declared, "was the seventh vial poured out to try the faith of the saints." In addition to the whiskey monopoly, Pierpont described other instances in which the general at the expense of native Unionists had granted his friends exclusive rights to do business. The governor declared that Butler's oppressions, which, he charged, also prevailed in eastern North Carolina, "have done more to unite the rebels in the south and retard Union sentiment there, though confined to a narrow compass, than any thing that has occurred since the rebellion has commenced." He called on the president and Congress to relieve the people of Butler's arrogance and restore civil government. Each member of Congress received a copy of the governor's letter on the day it was printed. Pierpont also directed state officers to ignore military orders that interfered with their functions.[89]

The governor had overshot his mark with his lengthy and strident indictment of the general. The *Washington Chronicle* criticized Pierpont for "his elaborate attack upon General Butler," charging that it had been done "in the worst and narrowest spirit." The editor lamented that "it is a melancholy prospect to see a soldier of the Republic, now in the midst of battle and contending with the enemies of this country, thus assailed and denounced." When the war was over would be time enough for criticism of the republic's military commanders, this editor declared.[90]

Reinforced by apparent Republican support and aware of Lincoln's reluctance to become involved, General Butler during the summer moved to end the authority of the Restored Government in the Norfolk area. His action was triggered by a grand jury indictment of thirty liquor dealers who had failed to obtain Virginia licenses and had refused to pay the required state taxes. All of the offenders had received permits from the military to do business in the area. Pressed by the indicted whiskey dealers, Gen. George F. Shepley, who at Butler's request had left Louisiana to assume direct command in Norfolk, issued an order for a late July election to determine whether the people wanted to discontinue the local civil government, including the state court. The election would be conducted by the provost marshal and would clearly be stacked against the friends of the Restored Government.[91] Butler followed with an order abolishing civil government in Norfolk until the election could be held.

Pierpont, angered by what he referred to as a violation of the federal constitutional guarantee of a republican form of government for the state, warned loyal citizens not to participate in the election.[92] In addition, on several occasions the governor and other officials of the Restored Government unsuccessfully sought a meeting with the president to protest Shepley's order and have the "election" canceled. Attorney General Bates, who was similarly outraged by the election order, also attempted in vain to obtain the ear of the president on the issue.[93] Lincoln had just returned from visiting the armies in Virginia, where he found prospects poor for the success of the summer campaign.[94] Dismayed by the military situation and under a great deal of political pressure as his support in the North eroded, the president had no desire at the moment to tangle with Butler over affairs in Norfolk. Already a movement was afoot to replace Lincoln with Butler as the National Union or Republican candidate for president, a fact that the politically astute president could not ignore.[95]

Finally, on July 20 the president discussed the Norfolk imbroglio with his Cabinet. According to Bates, Lincoln made a long statement on the history of the conflict between Pierpont and Butler, but said little about Shepley's election order or Butler's directive abolishing civil government in the port town. When Lincoln had finished, Cabinet members leaped to the support of the Restored Government, including Secretary of War Edwin Stanton, who, despite his hard-nosed reputation, favored the president's policy of restoring civil government in the South as soon as possible. Stanton told Lincoln that Butler's assumption of authority was "a high-handed measure" and ought to be overruled by the administration. The president, however, refused to act, explaining only that if he revoked the general's orders, Butler will "raise a hubbub about it."[96]

Attorney General Bates, Pierpont, and friends of the Restored Government were mortified by Lincoln's failure to countermand the election order. "The President knows as well as I do," Bates complained, "that General Butler's proceedings to overthrow the Civil Law at Norfolk, and establish his own despotism in its stead, is unlawful and wrong, and without even a pretence of military necessity, and yet he will not revoke the usurping orders, for fear General Butler will 'raise a hubbub *about it.*' . . . My heart is sick, when I see the President shrink from the correction of [this] gross and heinous wrong."[97] When Bates again brought the issue to

the attention of Lincoln, the president, Bates sorrowfully noted, "was im-
passive as water."[98]

As expected, the military-held election in Norfolk approved
Butler's revocation of civil authority. Pierpont immediately complained
to Lincoln that of the 303 votes cast for ending civil government, 139
were secessionists, 111 nonresidents, mainly liquor dealers, and 33 were
government employees who were threatened with the loss of their jobs if
they did not support Butler's position.[99] Judge Edward R. Snead and
state attorney Charles H. Porter, however, refused to accept the results of
the military election. They proceeded to try in Snead's court the indicted whiskey dealers, whereupon Butler ordered their arrest on the
grounds, as he wrote Lincoln, that they sought to embarrass the military
government and inaugurate a conflict between the civil and military
authorities of the United States. Snead immediately resigned his judge-
ship.[100] Despite an elaborate—and typically evasive—explanation by
Butler of his actions, Lincoln could not continue to ignore the general's
highhandedness. He quickly responded to an appeal from Pierpont by
ordering the release of Snead "to go to his family on [the] Eastern
Shore."[101] Lincoln, however, did not order the reinstatement of Snead to
his judicial post.

The president on August 9 also drafted a letter to Butler chastising
him for his institution of military rule for reasons other than military necessity. "Nothing justifies the suspending of the civil by the military
authority, but military necessity," Lincoln wrote, "and of the existence of
that necessity the military commander, and not a popular vote, is to decide.
And whatever is not within such necessity should be left undisturbed." The
president confessed that he should have given explicit instructions on this
matter earlier, when Butler's conflict with the Virginia government erupted.
He mildly chided the general for his war on Pierpont and also his attack on
Bates, whom Butler had criticized for his meddling in the controversy. Lincoln reminded the general that Pierpont was "the loyal governor of all
Virginia" and "was as earnest, honest, and efficient to the extent of his
means, as any other loyal governor." He admitted, however, that the extent
of the governor's current control "gives a somewhat farcical air to his dominion; and I suppose he, as well as I, has considered that it could be
useful for little else than a nucleous [sic] to add to." Finally, in a pointed
reference to charges of corruption brought by Pierpont and others against
the Butler regime, Lincoln told the general that "you should so keep accounts as to show every item of money received and how expended."[102] A
later investigation would reveal that the charges of corruption had some
foundation in fact.[103]

With the political situation worsening for the administration during the late summer, Lincoln withheld the letter to Butler. After the release of Snead, no new incidents occurred that demanded presidential action, though Governor Pierpont talked to Lincoln on August 20 and pressed him to "set things right at Norfolk." The president, as usual, was sympathetic but refrained from action.[104] Pierpont went north to campaign for Lincoln, and Butler devoted himself to military operations in his department. After his victory in the election, Lincoln no longer had a political reason to tolerate Butler's suppression of civil authority in the Virginia Tidewater or his military incompetence. He could now, if given renewed cause, remove Butler from command.

In December, Butler gave the president cause to act. On November 15 Col. Frank J. White, provost marshal on the Eastern Shore, reported to Butler that "a number of the most influential citizens" of the area "wish to repudiate any connection with the so-called Restored Government of Virginia," claiming that Pierpont "has done all in his power to excite dissension between the military and civil authorities." Later, in a meeting with White, Butler gave him permission to hold an election similar to the July one in Norfolk, asking the loyal citizens if they desired to replace the Restored Government with military authority.[105] White immediately issued an order for such an election. When shown a copy of it, Lincoln on December 21 wrote Butler directing him to suspend White's order, "at least until conferrence [sic] with me, and obtaining my approval." He also enclosed the August letter with the comment that "it embraces the views I then entertained, and still entertain. A little relaxation of complaints made to me on the subject, occurring about that time, the letter was not finished and sent."[106] Left unsaid was Lincoln's political reason for not sending the letter when it was written.

Butler denied that either he or any officer in his command had ordered an election for the Eastern Shore.[107] An exasperated Lincoln shot back that he had seen a copy of the order. A few days later Provost Marshal White reminded Butler that he had issued the order "in obedience to what I supposed to be your instructions."[108] On January 7 the president removed Butler from command. Though the main reason for his removal was his disastrous failure to take Fort Fisher in North Carolina, Butler's subversion of civil authority and Virginia's Restored Government contributed to his undoing. He was replaced by Gen. Edward O.C. Ord, a native of Maryland, who permitted civil officials to resume their functions. On February 16, 1865, Governor Pierpont had his moment of triumph when he appeared at a large rally of supporters in Norfolk, congratulating them on the restoration of civil government in the area.[109]

Despite Pierpont's ultimate success in establishing civil authority over the Federal military, the area controlled by the Restored Government had not appreciably expanded since Lincoln's issuance of the proclamation of Amnesty and Reconstruction in December 1863. The governor would have to await the final collapse of Lee's army before he could enter Richmond, establish a truly restored government for the state, and put into effect the 1864 constitution abolishing slavery. Like reconstruction movements in Florida, Alabama, Georgia, and Mississippi following the announcement of the president's new policy, the ambitious efforts of Virginia Unionists to achieve Lincoln's objectives faltered because, to a great extent, they could not control the state's political center. This was not the case in Louisiana, Tennessee, and Arkansas, where a more active body of Unionists, occupying the main political centers and aided by the military, assumed the initiative in the reorganization of civil government and the emancipation of blacks. Nevertheless, difficulties, including military setbacks, factionalism among Unionists, and opposition in Congress, confounded the efforts at self-reconstruction and prevented the complete restoration of these three states to the Union before the end of the war. Louisiana, since the beginning of the occupation of New Orleans in 1862, had created more problems for Lincoln than any Federal-controlled area, and it would continue to do so even as local Unionists, encouraged by Gen. Nathaniel P. Banks, moved rapidly in early 1864 to provide the president with a loyal free-state government.

8

Louisiana: A Tangled Skein of Reconstruction

Beginning in the 1960s, historians devoted a great deal of attention to wartime reconstruction in Louisiana, usually to the neglect of restoration efforts elsewhere. Their interest in the state is understandable in view of the relevance of black freedom and equality in Civil War Louisiana to the twentieth-century civil rights movement. Occupied Louisiana, with its educated free black leadership and its polyglot, urban white population, including recently arrived antislavery Northerners, offered a promising setting for the early success of a reconstruction program based on black equality. Though intensely committed to the struggle for black rights, historians have sharply differed on the reasons for the failure of Louisiana to establish a biracial democracy. Except for Joseph G. Tregle Jr., they are in agreement only on one point: Lincoln had radical objectives in mind for Louisiana, but he failed to achieve them because of the division and mismanagement of federal officials and Union men in the state. Herman Belz, whose fine book on reconstruction theory and policy during the war appeared in 1969, wrote that Lincoln, faced with a choice between Unionist factions in Louisiana, aligned with the radical group led by Thomas J. Durant. Belz, however, does not explain why, in view of the president's presumed support, the radicals lost out in the struggle to control Louisiana reconstruction.[1]

Almost a decade after Belz's book appeared, Peyton McCrary wrote an account of wartime Louisiana reconstruction in which he blamed the derailment of Lincoln's radical plan for the state on Gen. Nathaniel P.

Banks. McCrary argued that Banks, who was committed to a moderate re-construction program, misled Lincoln on the political situation in Louisiana, and for a time the president acquiesced in the general's policy. According to McCrary, a radical approach would have been more in tune with political realities in the state and in the nation. He indicates that Lincoln, after attempting for more than a year to obtain congressional acceptance of the Banks-controlled regime, finally came out in the last public address of his life for the radical position in Louisiana.[2]

Joseph G. Tregle Jr. goes even further in making the radicals—and specifically Durant—the heroes of the reconstruction melodrama in Louisiana. In company with Banks, Louisiana moderates, and conservative planters, Tregle adds an unlikely person to his list of villains—Abraham Lincoln. He asserts that the president in late 1864 betrayed Durant, whom he had earlier supported, by making General Banks "master of all" in the implementation of the state's reconstruction. Tregle suggests that if Lincoln had not abandoned Durant and the radicals the "sequence of disasters" in postwar reconstruction would have been avoided.[3]

LaWanda Cox presents an entirely different view of Lincoln, Banks, and Durant. In her study of *Lincoln and Black Freedom,* which focuses on Louisiana, Cox writes that the president employed both the carrot and the stick to move the state's Unionists from support of emancipation to black suffrage. According to Cox, Lincoln had the cooperation of General Banks but not the Durant faction whose suspicions of the president's intentions and Banks's military methods caused radicals to oppose the president's plan. Durant and the radicals, though a minority among Louisiana Unionists, ultimately forestalled the readmission of the state to the Union by convincing enough Republicans in Congress of the unworthiness of the Lincoln-Banks government.[4]

These interpretations overlook an important political reality in occupied Louisiana. Although most Louisiana Unionists followed Lincoln's lead in supporting emancipation, black equality was not the central issue in wartime reconstruction in the state, despite the fact that it generated considerable debate in the 1864 constitutional convention. Only the politically impotent free-black leadership in New Orleans and a handful of white radicals sought political rights for African Americans prior to the struggle for control of Louisiana's reconstruction in 1864.[5] Other considerations were more important in white Unionist alignments on reconstruction. Perceptions regarding the war's progress, past and future loyalties, republican constitutionalism, commercial interests, personal rivalries and ambitions, local political alliances, and presidential politics bore heavily on the complex history of Louisiana reconstruction.

In early 1864 Lincoln discovered how tangled the political skein was in Louisiana, even with a sympathetic political general like Nathaniel P. Banks in charge. Having made Banks "master of all" and directed him to "give us a free-state reorganization of Louisiana, in the shortest possible time," Lincoln expected quick results.[6] Rebuked earlier for not taking charge, when the new year began Banks sprang into action to give Lincoln what he wanted. He even delayed assuming command of a military campaign on the Texas coast in order to put Louisiana's reconstruction wheels in motion.[7] On December 30, 1863, he optimistically wrote the president that he could establish within thirty to sixty days a state government under a plan that followed the outlines of Lincoln's December 8 proclamation. Banks proposed a two-step procedure: an election for a state government, followed by a second election for delegates to a state constitutional convention that would provide for "the absolute extinction of slavery." Thus slavery would be ended "with the general consent of the people." Nevertheless, Banks would not submit the question of emancipation "to the chances of an election," particularly the first election. His procedure, he declared, would be practical and more readily accepted by all classes of Southerners than holding a state convention before a civil government was in place, as Durant and other members of the Free State Committee or radical faction insisted. The general even held out the greater prospect: "If this plan be accepted in Louisiana, . . . it will be adopted by general concurrence, in Texas, Arkansas, and Mississippi, and in every other southern state."[8] These were words Lincoln wanted to hear. On January 13 he wrote Banks that the general's "confidence in the practicability of constructing a free state-government, speedily, for Louisiana, and your zeal to accomplish it, are very gratifying. . . . I am much in hope that . . . you have already begun the work, [and] proceed with all possible despatch" to carry out your plan.[9]

Even before Lincoln indicated his approval, Banks launched his two-step election procedure for Louisiana's reconstruction. On January 11 he set February 22 for the election of a governor and six other state officers, and a second election on the first Monday in April for delegates to a state convention whose purpose would be to "harmonize" Louisiana's organic law "with the spirit of the age." Qualified voters under the state's antebellum election laws who had taken Lincoln's loyalty oath could vote in the elections, as well as Union soldiers who were citizens of the state, though a provision of the Constitution of 1852 prohibited men in uniform from casting ballots in state elections. Banks estimated that almost ten thousand Louisiana whites had joined the Federal army or navy, most of whom were stationed in the state and were eligible to vote under his ruling.[10] Since

African Americans were not viewed as "citizens," black soldiers could not participate in the 1864 elections.

Though Banks recognized the antebellum election laws, he foolishly announced in his proclamation that "the fundamental law of the State is martial law." Such a pronouncement was unnecessary in view of both his and Lincoln's commitment to the rapid phasing out of military power except where army operations were affected. He also unwisely declared, in a remark that could have been taken as a warning to radical opponents, that "when the national existence is at stake and the liberties of the people in peril, faction is treason." Both remarks were seized upon by radicals and other opponents of his plan to demonstrate to Northern friends that Banks had established a military despotism in Louisiana and unless checked would impose a puppet government upon the state.[11]

Louisiana radicals, who mainly lived in New Orleans, had other reasons to be concerned about Banks's plan. Though they differed in their motivations, radicals generally agreed that the old state constitution should be replaced as soon as possible with a new document that would abolish slavery, provide protection for black freedom, and insure that rebels would pay a price in their political and property rights for their crime against the Union. New Orleans radicals desired a reapportionment of congressional and legislative seats to reduce the power of the rural or plantation districts. These actions, they insisted, should be taken before the restoration of the state government. Through Gen. George F. Shepley, who technically was still the military governor of the state, radicals had attempted to gain Lincoln's support for a convention election. The president, however, having made Banks "master of all," refused to intervene.[12]

The day after Banks issued his election proclamation, the Free State Committee, representing the various Union clubs in occupied Louisiana, met in New Orleans and called a nominating convention for February 1 to select candidates for the state election. Although unhappy with Banks's plan, radicals participated in local meetings to nominate delegates to the Free State convention, mistakenly assuming that their strong base in the New Orleans Union clubs would permit them to control it. When the delegates assembled in the city's Lyceum Hall, a majority supported Banks's plan and his candidate for governor, former congressman Michael Hahn. After a rancorous exchange between the radicals and the Banks or Hahn faction, the radicals bolted the convention and, meeting nearby, nominated Benjamin F. Flanders for governor.[13] Conservative Unionists, many of whom still harbored hopes that slavery or the substance of slavery could be retained and wanted no federal intervention in their affairs, chose J.Q.A. Fellows as their candidate.

The campaign was brief but lively, characterized by large torchlight rallies with transparencies, musical bands, and long-winded orators. Flanders and other radical speakers declared that they represented the true free-state movement in Louisiana while playing down their support for black rights. They wrote their friends in the North that a victory for the Banks-Hahn forces would threaten the liberty of blacks and loyal whites. They charged that Hahn's success in the election would restore rebel sympathizers to power and undercut the work of radical change, though they were vague as to what changes they sought. Radicals also repeatedly charged that Hahn had acquiesced in the rebellion before the Federal occupation of New Orleans. The former congressman, they claimed, was simply the stalking horse of a Federal military commander who was determined to maintain his power.[14]

Although they exaggerated Banks's purposes and the military's influence in the election, the radicals were correct in claiming that the general aided the Hahn campaign. Banks promised not to interfere in the contest, but he had told Lincoln even before the February 1 nominating convention that he was certain that Hahn would win the gubernatorial election. His troops, scattered in garrisons throughout the occupied area extending above Baton Rouge and westward to Bayou Teche, understood their commander's preference in the election. Hundreds of troops appeared at Hahn rallies, permitting the moderate candidate to campaign in areas that Flanders and Fellows did not dare or care to visit. A Hahn rally in Baton Rouge on February 15 reportedly was the largest political gathering in the history of the town. This gathering was augmented by people from the countryside, who, either out of loyalty to the Union or out of curiosity, flocked to the main square to hear the speakers and to be entertained.[15] The outpouring of white citizens at these rallies confirmed the Banks-Hahn contention—and Lincoln's also—that Southerners were war-weary, impoverished, and willing to accept the security that Federal forces could provide. Fear of Confederate reprisals no longer caused overriding concern. Many whites had close family members still fighting in the rebel army who were now more anxious about the social disorder at home than about winning the war. As Banks repeatedly claimed, by 1864 many interior inhabitants were prepared to accept the restoration of a Union government, even if it meant emancipation, in order to avoid greater evils.[16]

Hahn also had the major New Orleans newspapers on his side. Of New Orleans's six newspapers, only the *Tribune,* the journal of the black community, supported Flanders. Suspected of disloyalty, the *Picayune* largely ignored the political contest. Hahn himself owned the *True Delta,* which he had purchased in early January 1864 in anticipation of his candidacy for governor and probably with the encouragement of General Banks. The *True Delta* was the only New Orleans newspaper that circulated throughout occupied Louisiana, providing loyal voters with the Hahn-Banks version of issues and candidates.[17]

Hahn and his supporters focused on the moderate objectives of their faction. They made clear their support for immediate emancipation while reassuring white Louisianans that "instantaneous and universal emancipation" in the hands of the Free State party would not mean black equality. They declared that General Banks's labor policy, requiring freed slaves to work, would be enforced by the new government. Some moderates, sounding a great deal like the conservative Unionists who supported Fellows, used the race issue against Flanders, claiming that he stood for black equality. (Actually, Flanders supported black suffrage with a property and education qualification.) On the day after the election, Hahn's newspaper, the *True Delta,* which had been relatively restrained in its appeal to white racial fears, perhaps revealed its true sentiments when it referred to the radical slate of candidates as "the Negrohead ticket." The *New Orleans Bee* proclaimed Hahn "the true conservative candidate for Governor," since he did not believe in black equality. The German-born Hahn and his associates also repeatedly claimed that only their party had the support of President Lincoln, and its defeat would postpone the restoration of civil government and the state's representation in Congress.[18]

Presidential politics played an important part in the February election. Supporters of Secretary of Treasury Salmon P. Chase, who was expected to challenge Lincoln for the Republican nomination in 1864, held most of the positions in the New Orleans Custom House and served as special treasury agents (tax collectors) in the occupied area. They intrigued to send a Chase delegation from Louisiana to the national Republican convention in June. Chase men naturally opposed the Banks-Hahn party, since it favored Lincoln's reelection. Outside of the Treasury officialdom in Louisiana, radicals like Thomas J. Durant supported Chase because he served as a counterweight to Lincoln and Banks's conservative reconstruction policy. Their staunch antislavery stand, which fell short of advocating black political equality during the campaign, owed a great deal to Chase's concern for African-American rights and the need to harmonize their position in Louisiana with that of the treasury secretary. Durant, for example, was a recent convert to the cause of black rights. He had been a slaveholder and a Confederate sympathizer before the Federal occupation. When Lincoln repudiated his reconstruction efforts in late 1863 and turned to Banks, Durant raised the standard of opposition to the president in Louisiana and attached himself to the Chase faction, claiming that the Lincoln-Banks party would sell out the antislavery objectives of the war.[19] Banks characterized Durant as "an honest man, and able in his profession, but he is without knowledge of the world, is without power to originate, blindly following precedents, and in spirit wholly impracticable."[20] The general might have been partly correct in his characterization of Durant. But the Louisianan's main failing, as soon would be clear, was his decision to join the Chase faction and become a vociferous critic of the dominant Lincoln-Banks party in the state.

It is difficult to determine who threw down the presidential gauntlet first in Louisiana, and how much encouragement the aspirants themselves gave to their partisans. Chase, whose ambition for the presidency was obvious, had used his control of Treasury offices to build up a loyal political faction in a number of states, including Louisiana and Florida. Such political conduct was neither out of line with accepted nineteenth-century practices nor was it always viewed as an act of disloyalty to the incumbent president.[21] Chase, however, realized the political risk of openly promoting his candidacy through his Treasury appointees. The secretary, though no match for Lincoln, was more politically astute than most historians have judged. In early 1864, and until after the February election, Chase wisely warned his zealous Louisiana supporters not to challenge General Banks or the president's reconstruction policy in Louisiana because such action would be premature and could backfire. At the same time, Chase discreetly indicated to them that he was deeply troubled by Banks's failure immediately to call a state convention to abolish slavery. The treasury secretary also expressed dismay at the division among Unionists that Banks's policies had caused. Yet he professed friendship for the general and expressed the hope that differences among Louisiana Unionists could be resolved. At least two Treasury officials in New Orleans, George S. Denison, a kinsman, and B. Rush Plumly, a Philadelphia abolitionist, advised Chase to establish close ties with Banks, explaining that both stood for the same antislavery principles. They wishfully told Chase that the general, if properly cultivated, would arrange for the delivery of Louisiana's national convention delegation to him.[22]

Lincoln men, however, had the edge over Chase partisans. The prospect of office and influence undoubtedly played a part in their support of Lincoln. To them, the president was firmly in control of reconstruction and the government in Washington. Furthermore, with the prospect that Federal forces would soon rout the rebel armies, they reasoned that Lincoln was virtually assured of the Republican nomination and victory at the polls. Hahn and members of his Free State party had tied their political fortunes to Abraham Lincoln and his largely hands-off reconstruction plan. They also believed that the president's racial views and support for local self-government reflected those of most Southern white Unionists. In his first issue as proprietor and editor of the *True Delta,* Hahn announced that he would "use his whole influence to maintain power in the hands of the patriot who stands immovably at the head of the national administration."[23] Hahn, Cuthbert Bullitt, and other Lincoln activists repeatedly contrasted the president's "conservative principles" on race and reconstruction with those of the Radicals in the North and in Louisiana "who would pull down the whole government" in an attempt to place blacks "on a perfect equality with the white race." Radicals, they charged, "[were] not willing, like the president, to wait and try the effect of education and freedom on the negro race, but they must rush headlong into a vortex of anarchy and confusion."[24]

Friends of the president formed "Pioneer Lincoln Clubs" to promote not only their champion's candidacy but also the Free State ticket in Louisiana. In their public expressions of support for the president, they profusely claimed that Lincoln, who "has thus far carried the country safely through the greatest perils that have ever surrounded it, [was] worthy to be ranked side by side in our affections with the immortal Father of his Country." Few Americans, including Republicans, in 1864 accorded the Illinois rail splitter this high distinction.[25]

Hahn and his friends let Lincoln know that their cause was his cause in Louisiana.[26] They asked the president to signal his support for their party by granting patronage to them. Specifically, they asked the president to appoint Edward H. Durell, an antislavery moderate, as U.S. district judge and replace the radicals in the Treasury offices with Lincoln-Hahn supporters. At first Lincoln did not respond, but when Hahn wrote him that Durell's appointment prior to the election was crucial to his party's success, the president sent his name to the Senate for confirmation. Lincoln, however, fearing the repercussions within the Republican party if he conducted a presidential purge of Chase's Treasury officials in Louisiana, refused to act further. Disturbed by Lincoln's indifference to their situation, Cuthbert Bullitt, a conservative, informed him that Flanders as the chief Treasury official in the state was "decapitating every subordinate believed or suspected of being in the least tainted with Lincolnism." Bullitt told Lincoln that "the failure of Washington to stand by the true friends of the President is producing great discouragement here, and unless a change takes place, and that at a very early day, in the distribution of patronage . . . the Lincoln party will be seriously damaged."[27] Despite this plea, Lincoln remained unmoved, through he subsequently appointed Bullitt U.S. marshal for Louisiana.

Still, the appointment of the influential Durell with his well-known ties with Banks, Hahn, and Bullitt signaled to Louisiana voters that Lincoln favored the Free State party in the February election. Even some radicals now swung to the support of the Hahn party. A few Chase-appointed officials, having received no clear instructions from their chief, informed their friends that they had made a mistake in bolting the Free State party and supporting Flanders. An important radical addition to the Hahn faction was Anthony P. Dostie, who would die in the bloody New Orleans riot of 1866. He joined with moderates and conservatives in attacking the Flanders-Durant faction and claiming that support for Lincoln's plan, though it did not go far enough, would insure freedom and the Union cause in Louisiana.[28]

The election returns provided the reconstruction mandate in Louisiana that Lincoln and Banks wanted. Voter turnout was impressive, with a total of 11,411 ballots cast. Hahn won by a wide margin, receiving 6,183 votes to 2,996 for the conservative Fellows and 2,944 for the radical Flanders.[29] Though Fellows was the conservative candidate, he ran as well in New Orleans as he did in the rural or plantation parishes.[30] Despite the disruptions created by the war, including the absence of men in the Confederate armies, the vote, augmented by the participation of refugees from rebel-held parts of the state and by Louisiana soldiers, approximated the normal turnout for antebellum elections in the occupied parishes. It constituted about one-fourth of the prewar electorate of the whole state, which easily exceeded the one-tenth required by Lincoln's reconstruction proclamation.[31]

The large turnout reflected not only the intensity of Union divisions in the occupied area but also Banks's efforts to motivate potential voters to take Lincoln's oath and participate in the election. Indeed, the general virtually ordered—or so a February 3 directive signed by his adjutant could be interpreted—that Union men must vote or be penalized. "Men who refused to defend their country with the ballot-box or cartridge box," this officer declared, "have no just claims to the benefits of liberty regulated by law." Though insisting that "opinion is free," the adjutant warned that "indifference will be treated as crime, and faction as treason."[32] Banks's involvement in drafting this part of the order remains problematical. The harsh language used was uncharacteristic of Banks, who sought to conciliate Louisianans of all persuasions and former loyalties. Furthermore, the order mainly dealt with labor regulations and was lengthy; the part about the election appeared at the end of the document and probably signified nothing more than the rhetorical excess of a young staff officer. However, many Louisianans viewed the order as directing them to vote or face punishment. After analyzing the returns, Banks boasted that between two-thirds and three-fourths of the voting population in the occupied area participated in the election.[33]

The general immediately informed Lincoln of the contest's outcome. He told the president that the election had been waged fairly and free of military interference. Banks declared that every voter had taken Lincoln's oath. "There is no sounder basis for a State government in the country than is presented by this population," Banks asserted. "I need not say, what you know, that Mr. Hahn and the gentlemen *elected* with him are earnest, faithful and efficient friends of your administration who wait [the] opportunity to serve your interests, and that of the whole country." The general confidently predicted "the absolute extinction of slavery upon which the election has proceeded, and to which every voter has assented, and provide for such extension of suffrage, as will meet the demands of the age." He closed by calling for the immediate recognition of the Louisiana government.[34]

Hahn's *True Delta* crowed that the vote "was a full and emphatic response to and endorsement of the president's plan of reinstituting civil governments in the seceded States, as it has been faithfully followed by Gen. Banks." Louisiana, according to a New Orleans correspondent of the *New York Times,* had set an example for "the remainder of the States now held by a [rebel] military despotism." The Louisiana voters carefully steered "between the two extremes, accepting a Free State Constitution as a basis of action, untainted by ultra Abolitionism or incipient sympathy with the spirit of the rebellion."[35] Unionists elsewhere predicted that the election in Louisiana of a civil government on an antislavery platform would serve as an example for other Southern states to follow immediately.[36]

Not all Louisiana Unionists rejoiced over the February election results. Durant wrote Lincoln that he was "deeply mortified that you should treat us in this way," permitting Banks to assume military control of the state's reorganization. Durant asked the president to correct his error by refusing to recognize the gubernatorial election and by immediately ordering an election of delegates to a constitutional convention. Lincoln never replied.[37] Durant and Flanders also protested to friends in Washington that Banks and the military had carried the election for the Hahn ticket. Durant wrote Salmon P. Chase that the election, if it stood, "will inaugurate a system favorable to nothing but military despotism and corruption." He confided that Banks's real aim was to win the state for Lincoln in the presidential contest. Having failed to obtain Lincoln's intervention, the Durant radicals asked Congress to invalidate the election and take control of reconstruction. They even intrigued with Fellows and the conservative Unionists to have the election set aside. But this strange collaboration between radicals and proslavery "Copperheads," as their opponents labeled them, never materialized.[38]

In Washington, Chase sympathized with the radicals, but he had been placed on the defensive in the Republican party by the recent publication of the Pomeroy circular touting him for president. As a member of the Cabinet, he now could ill afford to criticize Lincoln or his party in Louisiana. The treasury secretary cautioned his Louisiana allies to wait and see what action the Hahn government would take before attacking it. Chase informed them: "If Mr. Hahn redeems his pledges, and goes in earnest for a prompt establishment of a Free State, unsullied by compromises in the form of negro apprenticeships or like devices for the continuance of servitude, there can be no ground for permanent division" among Louisiana Unionists.[39] In early 1864 neither Chase nor the Radicals in Congress had sufficient strength to challenge the president and his reconstruction program. The majority in Congress was content to wait and see if the Hahn government and the promised state convention would unequivocally abolish slavery and take other action to insure the fruits of Union success.

On March 2 the new government, with a great deal of pomp and ceremony, punctuated by a one-hundred-gun salute, took office in New Orleans. In his inaugural address Hahn, who came from Germany to Louisiana as a boy, hailed the restoration of the state government, but with General Banks sitting on the platform, declared that "for the moment civil government must necessarily harmonize with military administration." Hahn, however, promised that the military "will interfere but little with individual action," and the process of restoring civil functions and economic prosperity will be rapid. Like Union leaders in other Southern states by 1864, he condemned slavery as the cause of the present troubles. Slavery, Hahn told a largely sympathetic inaugural crowd, "founded on a great moral, social and political evil, and inconsistent with the principles of free government, . . . is opposed alike to the rights of one race and the interests of the other; it is the cause of the present unholy attempt to break up our government; and, unpleasant as the declaration may sound to many of you, I tell you that I regard its universal and immediate extinction as a public and private blessing." Hahn indicated that the constitutional convention scheduled to meet in April would abolish slavery, establish a system of public education for both races, and provide for the meeting of a state legislature whose main business would be to deal with "the absorbing labor question" created by emancipation. The new governor ignored the issues of black rights in freedom and the political status of former rebels in postwar Louisiana.[40]

Attention in Louisiana now turned to the convention election to be held not in April as Banks had originally announced but a few days earlier, beginning on March 28. Governor Hahn and the moderates clearly had the upper hand. Most radicals, who were challenging the legitimacy of the Lincoln-Banks-Hahn government and seeking congressional intervention, boycotted the election of delegates. The "Conservative" or "Copperhead" party dissolved after the February election, and many of its followers temporarily cast their lots with Hahn's Free State party.[41] Although the turnout was light, the moderate victory in the convention contest was even more impressive than in the February election: supporters of Hahn won all but four seats in the convention.[42] The governor jubilantly reported to Lincoln that the election "virtually ends the contest here, and makes Louisiana a Free State."[43]

Banks proclaimed the dawn of a new era for Louisiana. Writing on the day of the convention election, the general told John Hay, Lincoln's secretary, that in Louisiana "we have changed all of the elements of society—in labor, trade, social organization, in the church, and in the army." He declared that "those of our friends in the North who think the experiment in Louisiana is premature, or might be postponed, are utterly mistaken."[44] The only specific change that he noted was the "utter extinction" of slavery. Banks, who had a penchant for unsubstantiated claims, exaggerated the effects of developments in the Bayou State. Some change had occurred because of the disruptions created by the war, the willingness of many Louisianans to accept Union authority, and the general's rather benign labor policy, but these had hardly been as far-reaching or as deep as Banks claimed. Only the issue of slavery had been settled.

When the state constitutional convention met in April, the question of what rights blacks should have in freedom had emerged as an important issue. Lincoln himself had a major hand in raising the question by making a startling recommendation to Governor Hahn. On March 13, in a letter marked *Private,* the president, after congratulating Hahn "on having fixed your name in history as the first-free-state Governor of Louisiana," suggested that the state grant suffrage to blacks. "You are about to have a Convention which, among other things," Lincoln said, "will probably define the elective franchise. I barely suggest for your private consideration, whether some of the colored people may not be let in—as, for instance, the very intelligent, and especially those who have fought gallantly in our ranks. They would help, in some trying time to come, to keep the jewel of liberty within the family of freedom. But this is only a suggestion, not to the public, but to you alone."[45]

Lincoln, who was so intent on achieving emancipation, restoring loyal governments in the Southern states, and winning the war, had not given much thought earlier to the matter of black political rights. He was prompted to make his March 13 suggestion by an interview ten days earlier with a free-black delegation from New Orleans, who presented him with a petition asking for the right to vote for members of their race. The delegates, Arnold Bertonneau and Jean Baptiste Roudanez, were cordially received by the president. The two men made a favorable impression upon Lincoln, and perhaps for the first time the president considered the desirability of suffrage as an element of black freedom and an instrument of loyal control. Louisiana with its able and educated black leadership seemed to Lincoln an ideal Southern state for a modest experiment in black political participation under the tutelage of moderate white Unionists like Governor Hahn. At any rate Lincoln told Bertonneau and Roudanez that he had no personal objection to the enfranchisement of intelligent black men, but as president he had a paramount responsibility for suppressing the rebellion. Lincoln informed the delegation that if he imposed a suffrage requirement upon Louisiana, he would jeopardize the Union purpose in the war. He said that he could not act solely on moral grounds, as the petition emphasized; he must be guided by military necessity alone. However, he did promise Bertonneau and Roudanez that he would refer the question of black suffrage to the Louisiana convention.[46]

Notwithstanding his support for emancipation and the preeminent sovereignty of the nation, Lincoln, along with the great majority of Northerners, believed that the granting of political rights rested with the people acting in their states. The president's commitment to republican self-government would be violated if federal authorities dictated a suffrage requirement for a state, in this case Louisiana, where a loyal state government was being restored. The tentative and private nature of his suggestion to Governor Hahn reflected his "wish to avoid both the substance and the appearance of dictation" in the reconstruction process, as he had expressed to Thomas Cottman on December 15. The only exception that Lincoln would make, as he had done with emancipation, was if federal intervention became a necessity for suppressing the rebellion. The formation of Union governments in Louisiana and elsewhere, however conservative they might be, meant that justification for such action by Lincoln on grounds of military necessity would be remote.

When the Louisiana convention met on April 6, Governor Hahn showed Lincoln's suffrage letter to leading delegates and evidently appealed to them to grant the president's wishes.[47] Banks, though with the army along the Red River, also conveyed his view that the convention should approve some form of black suffrage as well as other rights for the freedmen. On the day the convention opened, Banks wrote federal judge Edward H. Durell, who would be chosen president of the convention, recommending the enfranchisement of intelligent and property-holding blacks. The general told Durell that much interest existed in Washington regarding black suffrage, and he advised the judge to "give the subject your best consideration." He made a similar suggestion to another delegate.[48] However, in the draft of a long letter to James M. McKaye, a staunch antislavery member of the American Freedman's Inquiry Commission who had visited Louisiana, Banks seemed more interested in schools and a free and stable labor system for blacks than political rights.[49]

The constitutional convention, dominated by middle-class New Orleans Unionists, stopped short of enfranchising blacks. By a 70 to 16 vote, the delegates adopted a clear-cut emancipation ordinance; most of the sixteen dissenting delegates favored holding out for federal compensation for slave property. After a heated debate, characterized by vigorous opposition to black political rights, the convention adopted a provision authorizing the legislature to enfranchise blacks on the basis of military service, payment of taxes, or intellectual fitness. Even so, only the lobbying efforts of Governor Hahn, supported by General Banks from his headquarters on the Red River, saved the authorization provision.[50]

Although the delegates did not enact black suffrage, as Lincoln had suggested, the president's March 13 letter, according to Hahn, "had great effect on the action of the Louisiana Convention in all matters appertaining to the colored man."[51] The convention directed the legislature to "provide for the education of all children of the State," including blacks, made all men equal before the law, required the enrollment of both blacks and whites in the militia, recognized the interest of labor in the state, and ruled that seats in the legislature must be apportioned according to the number of eligible voters, not the white population as had been the case before the war. The latter provision was designed to reduce the power of rural parishes and increase that of New Orleans.[52] The new framework of government also prescribed that "all property shall be taxed in proportion to its value" and directed the legislature to impose an income tax on businessmen and artisans. A provision placing a special tax on blacks to support their schools was deleted from the final draft. Though the changes were significant, the convention largely retained the antebellum constitution. Unlike Virginia's 1864 constitution, in Louisiana former Confederates faced no voting or officeholding restrictions, provided they had taken Lincoln's loyalty oath. One change, however, moved away from the democratic features of the old constitution. The convention increased the governor's appointive power. Like Unionists throughout the South, framers of Louisiana's constitution feared the voting strength of returning rebels, but were unwilling to disfranchise them or adopt black suffrage as a counterweight. Instead, in order to prevent a disloyal electorate from winning control of local governments, the Louisiana convention gave the governor extensive authority to fill offices.[53] After the war this provision proved to be a broken reed with an ultraconservative in the governor's mansion.

Before adjourning on July 22, the Louisiana state convention directed the governor to call an election for September 5 to vote on the constitution and, assuming that it would be ratified, for congressional and legislative representatives under it. Leaving the management of the election to Lieutenant Governor J. Madison Wells, Governor Hahn left immediately for Washington to give Lincoln a copy of the document and lobby for its acceptance.[54] In a letter to Lincoln, Banks, with typical overstatement, praised the new Louisiana constitution as "one of the best" ever framed and informed the president that "the work of reconstruction in this state is all that you could desire." The general triumphantly declared: "The emancipation is instantaneous and absolute without a condition or compensation and nearly unanimous." Furthermore, Banks told Lincoln that blacks had been placed "upon an equal footing with the whites before the law," and he predicted that the legislature would soon enfranchise them. The general reported that only Treasury officials and a few U.S. district officers opposed the constitution; he requested that Lincoln remove these men from office. Finally, Banks praised Hahn and asked the president to give the governor's suggestions, which he would soon make in person, "your most favorable consideration."[55]

When Hahn arrived in Washington, the political situation in the national capital was not as propitious for the president and his reconstruction policy in the South as it had been in the spring. The Federal military offensive had faltered, with Sherman mired above Atlanta; Grant, after a series of bloody engagements, stymied in Virginia; Banks defeated along the Red River; and Washington itself the scene of an audacious raid by Confederates under General Jubal Early. Although Lincoln had been renominated for president by the Republican party, now styled the National Union party to broaden its appeal, he was blamed for the Federal failure to achieve the knockout blow that Northern and border-state people had anticipated when the 1864 offensive began.[56] Lincoln's political prospects and those of his party declined as the summer progressed and military casualties mounted. Northern Copperheads, who opposed the war and emancipation, stood poised to capture the Democratic party and win the fall election.

Republicans were deeply troubled and feared that their cause—and that of the Union—was lost if Lincoln remained the party's candidate. Some Radicals had already deserted to the camp of John C. Frémont, while many conservative war-supporters, mainly of Whig antecedents, threatened to bolt to the Democrats or stay at home on election day. Talk of replacing Lincoln with Gen. Benjamin F. Butler or Salmon P. Chase could be frequently heard when Radicals, as well as many Republicans who had never associated with the Charles Sumner-Benjamin Wade faction, conferred in congressional corridors or hotel rooms. About the only bright spot for Lincoln was the fact that dissident Republicans could agree neither on how nor with whom to replace him as their candidate.[57]

Radicals in Congress, whose opposition to presidential reconstruction had grown with the decline of Lincoln's political fortunes, sought to take advantage of the president's vulnerability and enact a stringent plan for the restoration of the rebellious states. Their motives and purposes regarding reconstruction, however, were mixed; also alignments on the issue frequently shifted with some Radicals supporting moderate positions. Most Radicals were genuinely concerned about the direction, or misdirection as they charged, that reconstruction had taken under Lincoln and his surrogates in the South. They had little confidence in Southern Unionism, except perhaps in Tennessee, where Andrew Johnson was pursuing a deliberate policy designed to insure Unionist control after restoration. Henry Winter Davis charged in the House of Representatives that no reliable evidence existed of "any respectable portion of the people of the southern states" who were willing to accept even such terms as Northern Democrats might offer them.[58] Radicals wanted a more thorough and less hurried political settlement for the rebel states, one in which former rebels, especially their leaders, could not take part. They sought certain guarantees for black rights in freedom, rights that Lincoln did not require. Only a few Radicals such as Sumner publicly insisted on black political equality as part of a reconstruction settlement. The recent failure of Congress to initiate a constitutional amendment freeing all slaves made Radicals more determined to oppose the president's lenient reconstruction policy despite Lincoln's commitment to such an amendment.

After early failures to obtain a majority for a congressional plan of reconstruction, the Radicals, joined by a few other Republicans, secured the passage on July 2 of a reconstruction bill introduced by Henry Winter Davis in the House and Benjamin Wade in the Senate. It passed easily in the House, but only by an 18-to-14 vote in the Senate.[59]

The Wade-Davis bill provided for the appointment by the president of a provisional governor when each rebellious state came under Federal control. The provisional governor, unlike Lincoln's earlier military governors, would have to be approved by the Senate and would serve until Congress had recognized the new state government. "So soon as the military resistance to the United States shall have been suppressed" in the state, the provisional governor was directed by the bill "to enroll all white male citizens of the United States resident in the State [and] request each one to take the oath to support the Constitution." If the persons prescribing to the oath were a majority of the persons enrolled, the provisional governor was required to issue a proclamation inviting the "loyal people" to elect delegates to a state constitutional convention. No person who had held office "under the rebel usurpation" could vote. To serve in the convention, delegates would have to swear that they had never given aid or comfort to the rebels. Furthermore, the convention must disfranchise and disqualify from serving as governor or legislator all persons who had held high civil or military positions in the Confederacy. It must also abolish slavery and repudiate the Confederate debt. Other provisions, not inconsistent with the United States Constitution, could be included in the new state document. A ratification election then would be held, along with officers for a state government under it if the constitution were approved by the loyal voters and Congress.[60]

The president pocket-vetoed the Wade-Davis bill. Some contemporaries expressed surprise that Lincoln, four months from the critical presidential election of 1864, would risk the wrath of powerful members of his party by disapproving the bill.[61] Realists in Congress knew, however, that had the president signed the bill it would have meant abandoning the work of reorganization that had occurred in Louisiana and elsewhere, and probably postponing reconstruction until after the war, when 50 percent of the voters required by the bill would be willing to take the loyalty oath. Lincoln's commitment to civil reorganization as the Federal armies liberated areas of the South thus would have been rendered useless had the bill become law. Approval of the Wade-Davis bill would also have cost Lincoln important conservative support in the North and the border states, because it would have put the party at odds with growing sentiment during the summer that peace and reunion could only be achieved if Southerners were assured that they would not be subjugated by a victorious Union. Conservatives believed that the enactment of the Wade-Davis bill, setting forth a rigid formula for reunion, would unfortunately send a message to Southerners that the North was now determined to impose a harsh settlement upon them. Though the bill provided for black freedom, its approval might actually have delayed emancipation in Louisiana, Arkansas, and perhaps Virginia, where constitutional provisions already had been made for the immediate end of the institution and where Lincoln had a strong commitment to antislavery Unionists. Conceivably, adoption of the Wade-Davis bill would have invalidated the new constitutions, thus requiring the process of state emancipation to begin anew.

Whereas his action toward the Wade-Davis bill perhaps was predictable, Lincoln's proclamation of July 8, explaining the pocket veto, was unusual. Presidents do not normally issue proclamations indicating why they have pocket-vetoed a congressional measure. In this case, Lincoln acted in an attempt to diffuse opposition in Congress and restore party unity. With the approach of the presidential election, Lincoln saw the need to placate Republicans who were dissatisfied with the veto. However, he did not believe that the Radical leadership could be appeased by any concession that he was willing to make. The president confided to John Hay that if the Radicals in Congress "choose to make a point upon [the veto] I do not doubt that they can do harm. They have never been friendly to me and I don't know that this will make any special difference as to that. At all events, I must keep some consciousness of being somewhere near right; I must keep some standard of principle fixed within myself."[62]

Lincoln's July 8 proclamation maintained that principle while offering a concession to disaffected members of his party. The president declared that the Wade-Davis bill not only would set aside the established free-state governments but also conflicted with his purpose in the Amnesty and Reconstruction Proclamation not "to be inflexibly committed to any single plan of restoration." He could not agree to "a constitutional competency in Congress to abolish slavery in [the] States," as provided for by the bill. Lincoln hoped, however, "that a constitutional amendment, abolishing slavery throughout the nation, [would] be adopted." Still, he was "fully satisfied with the system for restoration contained in the Bill, as one very proper plan for the loyal people of any State choosing to adopt it." He promised to assist people in those states desiring to be reconstructed under the congressional plan.[63] Lincoln must have known that Southern Union leaders who had attached themselves to him and his reconstruction policy would not want to switch to the more complicated and stringent Radical plan. It would have been strange indeed if Southern states had pursued reconstruction under a plan that had no legal basis, since the Wade-Davis bill did not carry the force of law.

Radical leaders, as Lincoln expected, refused to be placated by his offer to cooperate if Southern Unionists chose to adopt the Wade-Davis plan. They denounced his "usurpation" of congressional powers and predicted that the veto would damage the party in the election. Radicals assumed that Lincoln's veto of the Wade-Davis bill and his explanatory proclamation had more to do with presidential politics than with recon-struction. Thaddeus Stevens expressed this view when he wrote that the only purpose of the president's "infamous proclamation [was] to have the electoral votes of the seceded States," specifically Tennessee, Arkansas, Louisiana, Florida, and perhaps North Carolina. Nonetheless, Stevens warned Radicals to avoid public criticism of Lincoln in view of the forth-coming election and the critical need to maintain party harmony in order to defeat the Copperheads. He suggested that Radicals "condemn privately" and await their opportunity to strike back at Lincoln.[64]

Wade and Davis, however, were not prepared to wait before striking a blow at Lincoln's presidential candidacy. Indeed, they sought just such an opportunity as the president's proclamation to put another nail in Lincoln's political coffin, making inevitable his replacement as the Republican stan-dard bearer in the fall election. On August 5 Wade and Davis, who had long disliked Lincoln, issued through the columns of the *New York Tribune* a statement charging that Lincoln's July 8 proclamation was "a political manifesto against the friends of the Government," and "so far as it pro-poses to execute the bill which is not a law, it is a grave Executive usurpation." The Wade-Davis Manifesto, as it is known, criticized the presi-dent's recognition of "shadow governments" in Arkansas and Louisiana. "They are mere creatures of his will, . . . imposed on the people by military orders under the form of election, at which generals, provost marshals, sol-diers and camp-followers were the chief actors, assisted by a handful of resident citizens, and urged on to premature action by private letters from the President." Employing statistics that were probably supplied by Thomas J. Durant, then lobbying in Washington for the defeat of the Louisiana constitution, Wade and Davis denounced "the farce called an election" in the Bayou State and acidly declared that "nothing but the fail-ure of a military expedition deprived us of a like one in the swamps of Florida." They scornfully predicted that before the fall presidential election governments similar to the one in Louisiana would be "organized in every rebel State where the United States has a camp." The president's veto, they indignantly charged, was "a blow at the friends of the Administration, at the rights of humanity, and at the principles of Republican Government." Lincoln was advised to "confine himself to his Executive duties . . . and leave political organization to Congress."[65]

Although a few dissident Republicans privately applauded the man-ifesto, Wade and Davis had overshot their mark.[66] The shrillness and obvious political purpose of their protest caused most Republicans either to ignore or repudiate it and criticize its authors.[67] Lincoln privately ex-pressed outrage, and, according to a report, wondered aloud if Wade and

Davis "intend openly to oppose my election—the document looks that way."[68] Lincoln's political prospects, however, did not appreciably benefit from the Republican reaction to the manifesto. On the day after its publication, the astute Thurlow Weed, a conservative backer of the president, ruefully admitted to a Radical: "Lincoln is gone, I suppose you know as well as I."[69]

Ironically, the Banks-Hahn reorganization effort, which the Radicals in Congress were determined to defeat, benefited from the reaction to the Wade-Davis Manifesto. B. Rush Plumly reported to Banks after seeing Lincoln that the "president's blood is up on the Wade-Davis protest," insisting to all that he "stands by you firmly."[70] The day after the appearance of the manifesto, Governor Hahn arrived in Washington and delivered a copy of the new state constitution to the president. Lincoln expressed his hearty approval of the document. On August 9, Lincoln, almost in defiance of his critics, wrote General Banks: "I am anxious that it shall be ratified by the people." He made it clear that federal officials, including Treasury agents in the Durant faction, should support the ratification of the constitution upon penalty of losing their positions. "I will thank you to let the civil officers in Louisiana, holding [office] under me, know that this, is my wish," Lincoln pointedly told Banks, "and let me know at once who of them openly declare for the constitution, and who of them, if any, decline to so declare."[71] The president also asked Cuthbert Bullitt, whom he had appointed U.S. marshal for the eastern district of Louisiana and who in June had headed the state's Lincoln delegation to the Republican national convention, to inform him of the Treasury officials who did not support the constitution.[72] The implication was clear: He would remove these obstructionists.

Despite the fact that success in putting down the rebellion seemed remote and his political troubles were multiplying, in the summer of 1864 Lincoln seemed determined, as in the case of emancipation, to achieve an early and complete reconstruction success in Louisiana. The dark days of August 1864 had not caused him to back down on his reconstruction plan or desert his Union supporters in Louisiana and elsewhere who were in the process of reorganizing their state governments.

Buoyed by the president's support, Louisiana Unionists ratified the new constitution on September 5. The vote was 6,836 in favor of the constitution to 1,566 opposed, which was comparable to the turnout in the April election for convention delegates but three thousand fewer than the more heated gubernatorial contest in February.[73] Though 1,178 of the votes were cast by Louisiana troops, Banks, in response to Durant and other critics, vigorously denied that the military had influenced the election's outcome.

He immediately informed Lincoln of the election results and declared that it had been "conducted with perfect freedom." Army officers, he claimed, were either indifferent or divided over the ratification question. The moderate Free State party, or as Bullitt called it, the Lincoln party, also won control of the new legislature and captured the four congressional seats that were decided by the election.[74] Ever the optimist, Banks jubilantly told Lincoln that "history will record the fact that all the problems involved in the restoration of States and the reconstruction of government have been already solved in Louisiana with a due regard to the elevation of the black and the security of the white race. Your policy here will be adopted in other states and work out in the end the re-establishment of the Union."[75]

Hahn supporters in their moment of success, which they believed would be sustained in Washington if Lincoln won the presidential election, were determined to be rid of their political enemies in the U.S. Treasury offices. Lincoln had already done their bidding by replacing radicals in federal judicial and law-enforcement positions with moderates and at least one conservative, Bullitt. Though Chase was no longer their superior, local Treasury officials, encouraged by Durant and his Radical friends in Congress, held deep-seated resentments against the Banks-Hahn regime. A few had supported the new constitution because it abolished slavery and contained other progressive features, but most Treasury officials had remained silent during the brief campaign, hoping to avoid removal by Lincoln. Still others defied the president and worked to defeat the constitution. Banks claimed that the Durant-Flanders party used tricks "to make the vote small." He told his wife that "but for the opposition of the men in service of the [federal] government, we should have had 15,000 votes," instead of the eight thousand that were cast.[76]

Whatever the case, Governor Hahn and his supporters demanded that Lincoln fulfill his promise to remove obstructionist officials. Soon after the election, Hahn reported to the president that federal appointees in Louisiana, with few exceptions, "gave us no aid whatsoever and acted just as if it was the object of the government not to restore Louisiana to the Union, or to seek the triumph of the principles embodied in our new Constitution." He reminded Lincoln of "our understanding before I left Washington" that these officials would be replaced, "and I now earnestly appeal to you to make [the] changes. We must have true Union, free State men in office in this quarter if we desire to maintain our principles along the Mississippi River and the Gulf."[77] Lincoln, however, having restored intraparty harmony in the North by removing Montgomery Blair, the bête noire of congressional Radicals, delayed any purge of the U.S. Treasury in the state, at least until after the presidential election.[78]

Meanwhile, General Banks and U.S. District Judge Edward H. Durell, with Hahn's blessings, left for Washington to plead for the immediate recognition of the Louisiana government.[79] Though Banks and Durell had Lincoln's support, Congress, which would not be in session until after the fall election, still had to apply the final touch to Louisiana's reconstruction—the admission of its representatives. This step proved far more difficult than anticipated by the Hahn forces or by Lincoln. At the president's insistence, Banks remained in Washington for four months, lobbying for congressional approval.[80]

In Louisiana, the Hahn government expected to carry on its functions as if reconstruction had been completed. On October 3 the newly elected legislature met in New Orleans with 25 senators and 104 representatives present. One week later the legislature elected R. King Cutler to the U.S. Senate for a full term and Charles Smith for the short term to expire on March 3, 1865. Hahn dutifully sent their election credentials to the Senate, and the two men went to Washington to take their seats when Congress convened in December. At Governor Hahn's suggestion, the legislature, in a highly irregular action without benefit of a general election, selected "seven good Lincoln men" as presidential electors. Congress, however, refused to count the Louisiana electoral vote on the ground that no real election for president had been held in the state.[81]

The governor called on the legislature to implement those provisions in the new constitution freeing blacks and "eliminating from the old system every vestige of human inequality." As Lincoln had wanted and the state constitution provided, Hahn asked the legislature to provide equal education for both races. However, he did not raise the explosive issue of racially mixed schools with the legislature. Like many nineteenth-century Americans, including Lincoln and Southern Union leaders, Hahn believed that "without general education, liberty had no guarantee, society is always menaced, and virtue itself is without a safeguard." According to this view, the preservation of republican institutions, based on freedom and virtue, depended upon an enlightened system of education for blacks and whites alike.[82]

Following the governor's recommendation, the Louisiana legislature, meeting in late 1864 and early 1865, considered giving "certain rights to some of our colored population," as Hahn explained to Lincoln on November 11. He did not specify what rights were under consideration, but he clearly had in mind suffrage. Hahn asked for permission to publish Lincoln's private letter of March 13 suggesting that the constitutional convention enfranchise "the very intelligent" blacks and black army veterans. The letter if published, Hahn explained to the president, might "prove of some service to the colored race and do you no harm." Lincoln, however, did not respond to Hahn's request.[83]

At this time it is problematical whether Lincoln's influence in behalf of African-American political rights would have persuaded the Louisiana legislature to adopt qualified black suffrage. The threat by former rebel voters to Union control in postwar Louisiana was not yet clear. With the return of Confederates after the war, Lincoln might well have provided the support for black rights as a guarantee for freedom and loyalty that staunch Unionists like Hahn wanted.

In the end, the legislature, consisting of moderate and conservative Unionists, failed to act on the question of black rights. A bill known as the "Quadroon Bill," because it only would enfranchise mulattoes, failed in the state Senate by a vote of 20 to 4. Even the African-American editor of the *New Orleans Tribune* opposed the measure, arguing that the bill if enacted would increase class divisions among blacks. This editor, as well as other blacks, mainly objected to the bill on the ground that it did not extend the right to vote to all black male adults. Only unqualified black suffrage, they believed, would fulfill the need for an adequate safeguard for African-American freedom and rights. A convention of "Colored Men" of Louisiana, meeting in January 1865, indignantly attacked the legislature for its failure to enfranchise their race and petitioned Congress to grant universal black suffrage. The *New Orleans True Delta*, the newspaper organ of the moderate Hahn faction, warned that, though the Congress might initiate the pending Thirteenth Amendment abolishing slavery, "the right of suffrage will probably always be determined by individual states."[84] Louisiana blacks, however, did not abandon the effort to secure political rights, seeking both state and federal action in their behalf. Not until 1867, when Congress enacted the Military Reconstruction bill, did they realize success.

The Louisiana legislature, despite Hahn's appeal, also postponed the establishment of a public school system on the ground that adequate financing could not be obtained until after the war, when the full taxing authority of the state would be restored. Neither Governor Hahn nor President Lincoln insisted that the Louisiana lawmakers honor this and other promises to blacks made or implied in the 1864 state constitution. The legislature, however, in February 1865 ratified by an almost unanimous vote the Thirteenth Amendment to the U.S. Constitution, an action that had the highest priority for Lincoln. Louisiana thus became one of the first states to approve the amendment.[85]

With the sympathetic Banks away in Washington, the Hahn government soon ran into trouble with the military in Louisiana, further complicating the complete restoration of civil authority. Even before the Massachusetts general's departure, Gen. Edward R.S. Canby, who had replaced Banks in overall command of the Trans-Mississippi West, had clashed with civil authorities when he ordered the release from jail of editor Thomas P. May. This editor had been arrested by order of the constitutional convention for referring to certain delegates as drunkards. Banks, in command of the Gulf Department, had endorsed the action of the convention, but did not protest when Canby released May.[86] In October, Gen. Stephen A. Hurlbut, Banks's temporary replacement and an Illinois political friend of the president, began to interfere in the municipal administration of New Orleans. When civil officials reminded him that the military no longer had control over such matters, Hurlbut denied that civil authority prevailed and wrote General Canby, seeking support for his position. Hurlbut, an erratic former Whig who inclined toward conservatism in his political views, told Canby that the civil officials were engaged in "scandalous abuse under cover of legislation upon an impoverished and exhausted people. My own view of the matter is simply this: that the present civil government of Louisiana is an experiment liable to be cut short at any time by military orders, and that until approved and received by Congress they are wholly within the scope of martial law. . . . It would be far better for all concerned that military government prevail."[87]

Canby agreed with Hurlbut's assessment of the Louisiana situation. Without consulting his superiors in Washington, he informed Hurlbut that "all attempts at civil government, within the territory declared to be in insurrection, are the creation of military power, and, of course, subject to military revision and control." Canby even told Hurlbut that if he deemed it necessary he could suspend any action of the legislature, then in session, until the disputed matter could be submitted to the president.[88]

Governor Hahn, outraged by what he perceived as military arrogance, appealed to Lincoln, demanding that he order the army to cease its interference in civil affairs. "The military officers now in power in this Department," Hahn wrote, "seem not only to ignore all civil authority, but their acts look as if they are determined to prevent the organization of a loyal State government, and to extinguish as much of it as has been established." The governor insisted that he was not complaining of the military responsibilities of army officers in crushing the rebellion, but he could not "remain silent when I see the most barefaced and *unnecessary* attempts made to crush out a State government which was formed to aid the country and the administration." He also asked Lincoln to return Banks immediately to command in Louisiana.[89]

Lincoln was furious. Having seen copies of the Hurlbut-Canby exchange (probably from the hands of Banks), he dispatched a sharply worded letter to Hurlbut. "Few things, since I have been here," he angrily informed his old friend,

> have impressed me more painfully than what, for four or five months past, has appeared as bitter military opposition to the new State Government of Louisiana. . . . A very fair proportion of the people of Louisiana have inaugurated [*sic*] a new State Government, making an excellent new constitution—better for the poor black man than we have in Illinois. This was done under military protection, directed by me, in the belief, still sincerely entertained, that with such a nucleous [*sic*] around which to build, we could get the State into position again sooner than otherwise. In this belief a general promise of protection and support, applicable alike to Louisiana and other states, was given in the last annual message. During the formation of the new government and constitution, they were supported by nearly every loyal person and opposed by every secessionist.

Lincoln told Hurlbut that "every Unionist ought to wish the new government to succeed, and every disunionist must desire it to fail. It's [*sic*] failure would gladden the heart of [John] Slidell in Europe, and of every enemy of the old flag in the world. Every advocate of slavery naturally desires to see blasted, and crushed, the liberty promised the black man by the new constitution. But why Gen. Canby and Gen. Hurlbut should join on the same side is to me incomprehensible," Lincoln wrote.[90]

Lincoln reaffirmed in his letter to Hurlbut that "the military must not be thwarted by the civil authority" in its efforts to defeat rebel forces. At the same time, he maintained that it should not interfere in civil affairs. He cited several instances of military intervention that should not have occurred, including the release from confinement of editor May. "The military necessity for insulting the [state] Convention, and forcibly discharging the editor," Lincoln said, "is difficult to perceive." He warned that any effort "to crush out the civil government will not be overlooked."[91]

Stunned by Lincoln's disapproval, Hurlbut showed the letter to General Canby, whose headquarters was also in New Orleans. Canby wrote the president, defending his action in the May case and complaining of the "bitter animosity" toward his military administration expressed in Lincoln's letter. "It is proper that your Excellency should be advised," Canby declared, that in matters "that will ultimately, come under the control of the State Government, are now so complicated with questions of military administration, that, in the changes to be made, differences of opinion may arise, which should not subject officers of the army to the imputation of opposition or animosity."[92]

Lincoln, though in a more conciliatory tone than before, had the last word. "I think it is probable that you are laboring under some misapprehension as to the purpose, or rather the motive of the government" in Louisiana, he wrote Canby. It was not, as Hurlbut and Canby seemed to believe, to create "a piece of machinery merely to pay salaries, and give political consideration to certain men. But it is a worthy object to again get Louisiana into proper practical relations with the nation; and we can never finish this, if we never begin it. Much good work is already done, and surely nothing can be gained by throwing it away."[93]

In this exchange with Hurlbut and Canby, Lincoln was more emphatic than ever in demanding that his military commanders cooperate with local authorities in their reorganization efforts and avoid putting obstacles in the way of civil restoration when no clear military necessity existed. With military victory in sight and his re-election behind him, the president expected an early completion of reconstruction in Louisiana as well as in other states where reorganization was occurring. Success in Louisiana could spur peace and reconstruction efforts elsewhere in the South, advance emancipation, and influence Congress to act quickly in seating representatives from the former Confederate states. Though minor clashes over authority in Louisiana continued to occur (for example, a dispute regarding Hurlbut's appointment of a drainage officer), military officers curbed their interference and hostility toward the Hahn government.[94] Like General Rosecrans in Tennessee in 1863, Hurlbut and Canby understood after their exchange with Lincoln that he fully intended for them to cease interfering with Union civil officials who were trying, as the president said, to restore Louisiana to its "proper practical relations with the nation." By December 1864 the focus of attention for Lincoln's Louisiana government had shifted to Washington. The state's senators and representatives, along with those from Arkansas, stood ready to take their seats in Congress. The president's reelection in November seemed to have made their seating inevitable, thereby gaining congressional acceptance of the work of reorganization in Louisiana and promising further successes for Lincoln's plan of amnesty and reconstruction.

9

Arkansas:
An Unfulfilled Promise

Arkansas also provided Lincoln with an important early test for his new re-construction initiative. Though not as significant in the eyes of the nation as Louisiana, success in this large, sparsely populated state could inspire Unionists and disaffected rebels elsewhere to move boldly, with Federal military assistance, toward the civil reorganization of their states. Arkansas Unionists acted quickly to meet the president's requirements for restora-tion. William D. Snow of Pine Bluff, who would be elected to the U.S. Senate in early 1865, wrote Lincoln on December 25, 1863, that his proclamation "opened a practical and easy door to rapid reconstruction." He sanguinely told the president that "the crisis in Arkansas is past. All are alike anxious for the early inauguration of a state government."[1] A large Union rally in Little Rock resolved that Arkansas's reorganization, set to begin with the meeting of the recently elected state constitutional conven-tion on January 4, would conform "to the demands of loyalty and the proclaimed policy of the Government," including emancipation. The Little Rock gathering dispatched a delegation to Washington, including Snow's brother and former Confederate Gen. Edward W. Gantt, to confer with Lincoln and gain his support for their actions.[2]

Gen. Frederick Steele, the Federal commander in Arkansas, at first believed that it was premature to hold a state convention so soon after the occupation of Little Rock and before the countryside had been pacified. But he soon warmed to the idea of an early Unionist reorganization of the state government. He even placed most of his troops in town garrisons,

Isaac Murphy, Union governor of Arkansas, 1864-1868 (courtesy of the Arkansas History Commision).

where they would be available to protect loyal men, rather than using them to expel the remaining Confederate forces in Arkansas.[3] Steele also adopted a conciliatory though firm policy toward Confederate sympathizers. Some Unionists believed that the general went too far in befriending rebel women and giving "superb parties," attended by "beautiful ladies and gallant gentlemen." Most Unionists, however, supported Steele's conciliatory policy, secure in the belief that he would aid in the quick restoration of civil government under their control.[4]

On January 4, 1864, the Arkansas state convention, with General Steele's encouragement but without any official recognition from Washington, assembled at the state capitol in Little Rock. In a message to the delegates, Steele confidently predicted that Lincoln would approve the convention's work. Only twenty-six delegates answered the roll call on the first day; the number ultimately reached forty-five. They represented twenty-three of the state's fifty-seven counties, some of which were still being contested by Confederate guerrillas. Unsettled conditions within Federal lines prevented a number of counties from sending delegations. The convention required that the delegates take Lincoln's oath of allegiance, which included the pledge that they would honor the Emancipation Proclamation.[5] Evidently all of the delegates, including thirteen who were former slaveholders, took the oath.

The convention proceeded rapidly to draft a new constitution. On January 19, by a unanimous vote, the delegates adopted a document that, as they informed the people, "is simply your old Constitution, with some few amendments, according to the most approved free State constitutions." Slavery was abolished "because of the now almost universal belief that a peace, made on any other plan, would be of short duration." The convention also directed that the legislature should pass no law "prohibiting the education of any class of the inhabitants" of the state, which seemed to meet Lincoln's requirement in his reconstruction proclamation that the reorganized states should provide for the education of the freedmen. Again consistent with the president's plan, the Arkansas convention implicitly authorized the legislature to establish an apprenticeship system for young blacks. Finally, it reserved the right of suffrage for "white male citizens of the United States."[6]

The convention set March 14 for a ratification vote on the new constitution. At the same time elections were to be held for state officers and for members of the U.S. House of Representatives in case the constitution was approved. Meanwhile, Isaac Murphy, a sixty-one-year-old lawyer and teacher from northwest Arkansas, was chosen to serve as provisional governor until the March election.[7] In 1861 Murphy, a small slaveholder before the war, had cast the only vote against secession in the Arkansas state convention, rebuking friends who pressed him to vote for separation and warning them: "No, I am a slaveholder, like most of you; and I tell you that Secession will be the death of slavery."[8] Soon after the adjournment of the 1864 convention, Provisional Governor Murphy was nominated for governor by a state Union committee.[9]

On the day that the convention adopted the free-state constitution, the Arkansas delegation to Washington, chosen at Little Rock in December and headed by Gantt, met with Lincoln to discuss the state's reorganization. They continued their discussion the next day and again two days later. Lincoln developed a fondness for Gantt, partly because the former rebel brigadier assured the president that he would work for the abolition of slavery in the state. Pleased with the delegation's report on political conditions in Arkansas, Lincoln wrote General Steele, informing him that once emancipation had been accomplished, "the constitution and laws of the State, as before the rebellion, . . . [will be] in full force." The president also expressed pleasure with what he had heard regarding the progress toward civil reorganization in the state, though news of the convention's actions had not yet reached Washington. In addition, he indicated his strong support for Steele's conciliatory approach. At the urging of both the delegation and Congressman John B. Steele, a New York Democrat and the general's brother, Lincoln in order to facilitate matters placed Arkansas in a separate military district with General Steele in command.[10]

Unaware that the state convention had scheduled elections for March 14, Lincoln in consultation with the Arkansas delegation instructed General Steele to call an election for governor on March 28 to be held under the state's prewar constitution and laws.[11] A few days later the delegation informed the president that the convention's work might conflict in a few details with his plan. He immediately wrote Steele that the convention, "having the same general object, has taken some action, which I am afraid may clash somewhat with my programme. I therefore can do no better than to ask you to see Mr. Gantt immediately on his return, and with him, do what you and he may deem necessary to harmonize the two plans into one, and then put it through with all possible vigor."[12]

On January 30, Lincoln learned that the convention had fulfilled his only requirement for approval by adopting a free-state constitution. He again wrote the general: Arkansas Unionists "seem to be doing so well, that possibly the best that you can do would be to help them on their own plan—but of this, you must confer with them, and be the judge." He gave Steele some political advice: "Of all things, avoid if possible, a dividing into cliques among the friends of the common object."[13] To the Gantt delegation, the president expressed his warm support of the convention's actions and predicted that Arkansas would be the first wayward state to return to the Union.[14]

Still, Lincoln's instructions to Steele regarding a gubernatorial election on March 28 conflicted with the convention's plan for a March 14 election to ratify the new constitution and select civil officials under it. On February 2 General Steele asked the president to "harmonize matters" by ordering the election for March 14, since "the convention has dispersed and cannot change the day" that it had set for it. On February 8, Provisional Governor Murphy reminded Lincoln that the call for the March 14 election had already gone to the counties, and the ensuing confusion might insure the failure of both plans. The president agreed. On the same day, Lincoln wired Murphy that he would withdraw his order to Steele and defer to the convention's election plan.[15]

When he continued to receive telegrams from Arkansas asking him "to postpone the election to a later day than either fixed by the convention or me," Lincoln became irritated. He wrote William M. Fishback, an Arkansas Unionist and a former acquaintance in Illinois, that he had "been constantly trying to yield [his] plan" to the convention's arrangement, and he had sent two letters to General Steele informing him that he "must be master, but that it will probably be best for him to merely help the convention on it's [sic] own plan." "Some single mind," he told Fishback, "must be master, else there will be no agreement in anything, and General Steele, commanding the Military, and being on the ground is the best man to be that master. . . . This discord must be silenced." Lincoln in a letter to Gen. John M. Thayer, a subordinate of Steele, indicated that the commanding general should assist, not dictate to, Provisional Governor Murphy and the convention in the preparations for the March election and the restoration of civil government. "I yield to the convention," the president wrote Thayer, "and have so notified General Steele, who is master, and is to cut any knots which cannot be untied."[16] Lincoln's intent in making Steele "master," as in the case of Banks in Louisiana, was to use the military to jump-start civil reorganization in Arkansas, not control the elections or the state government that would be formed.

Meanwhile, Lincoln had taken the initiative, as he had done elsewhere, to give Arkansans the opportunity to take his oath of allegiance preparatory to voting. In early January he sent Gen. Nathan Kimball to Arkansas with blank amnesty books and forms for distribution. The president, in informing General Steele of Kimball's mission, directed him to issue the forms "immediately at such points as you may think likely to give success." He also asked Steele to report the results to him.[17] When Kimball arrived with the forms, Steele ordered the provost marshals at nine posts to administer the oath to willing citizens and appointed Kimball to supervise the work. Hundreds of Arkansans immediately descended upon the Federal posts to take the oath, including a few who had held offices in the Confederate and rebel state governments.[18] No record has been found indicating that Steele reported to Lincoln precisely how many Arkansans took the oath, though the March election returns gave evidence that more than ten thousand had sworn allegiance.

Despite this enthusiasm, the election campaign hardly could have been characterized as normal. In some counties Union rallies nominated candidates for office; in others, individuals simply announced their candidacy. The Union state ticket headed by Murphy had no challengers in the election. Only in the second congressional district, whose main centers were Pine Bluff and Little Rock, did the campaign resemble an old-styled political canvass. In this district, Unionists held separate meetings and nominated their favorites for Congress. These candidates launched a vigorous campaign in which they endorsed the new constitution, including emancipation, but spent most of their time questioning their opponent's loyalty. The issue of past loyalty seemed to have been the only issue raised in the campaign by any candidate for office.[19] The Arkansans ignored Lincoln's warning against disputes among those supporting reconstruction, and the factionalism that erupted on this issue continued after the election, creating a severe division in the Arkansas leadership, a schism that would be detrimental to the restoration of the state to the Union.

As the date for the election neared, Lincoln became anxious. He probably knew that Confederate guerrillas, with orders from Gen. Edmund Kirby Smith, were doing all in their power to disrupt the election. Smith wrote Gen. T.H. Holmes, commanding the Confederate enclave of southwestern Arkansas, that "great good may be accomplished" if the Union election could be disrupted.[20] General Steele fully understood the importance of protecting the polls and also Lincoln's desire that there should be a large turnout of voters. To satisfy the president, Steele even delayed plans for his army to rendezvous with Gen. Nathaniel P. Banks's forces for the important Red River campaign. He explained to Banks on February 28: "An election for State officers is ordered for the 14th proximo, and the President is very anxious that it should be a success. Without the assistance of the troops to distribute the poll books with the oath of allegiance and to protect the voters at the polls, it cannot succeed." Steele told Banks that "the rebels contemplate making a dash for the purpose of breaking up the election. They have a large mounted force, and their horses are represented to be in fine condition." To counter this Confederate effort, Steele dispatched a cavalry detachment with orders also to distribute three thousand copies

of Lincoln's amnesty proclamation among the people in the threatened areas. When informed of the reason for Steele's delay to join Banks,
Gen. William Tecumseh Sherman, who was also responsible for providing
troops for the Red River campaign, disgustedly wrote Steele: "If we have to
modify military plans for civil elections, we had better go home."[21]

On February 29 General Steele urged the people of Arkansas to go to
the polls on the fourteenth. He declared that it gave him "the highest grat-
ification to be able to say that . . . peace has, so far been restored in your
midst as to enable you to institute proceedings for the restoration of the
civil government, by which order may be firmly established and the rights
of persons and property secured against violence and the dangers of anarchy." The general reminded Arkansans that "to render the election valid"
under the president's Ten Percent requirement, 5,406 votes must be cast.
Steele sent a copy of his address to Lincoln, who heartily endorsed it.[22]

Lincoln expressed concern that rebel disruptions and the virtual de-
population of communities would prevent the required 10-percent
participation at the polls. On March 12 he telegraphed Murphy and Fishback to "do your best to get out the largest vote possible; and, of course, as
much of it as possible on the right side."[23] Despite disruptions by Confederate raiders, Lincoln ultimately had no reason to worry. Arkansans, some
of whom defiantly crossed the line from "Dixie," voted in impressive numbers to approve the free-state constitution by a majority of 12,179 to 220;
they also elected Murphy governor by a similar result and sent three representatives to Congress. Edward W. Gantt claimed that three fourths of the
potential voters in the Federal-occupied area, augmented by Union stalwarts from rebel-held counties, cast ballots.[24]

The president hailed the election results. He told Murphy that he was
"much gratified to learn that you got out so large a vote, so nearly the right
way," and that the state government was already being put "in good working order."[25] Republican newspapers in the North proclaimed the dawning
of a new day in Arkansas and perhaps the South. The *New York Times* declared that, along with a free-state victory in Louisiana, the Arkansas
election demonstrated that emancipation "will come not simply by the military effect of the President's Proclamation. It will obtain a more important
sanction yet from the direct political action of the people. . . . The President's method of reconstruction may now be considered to be 'in full tide
of successful experiment.' It is progressing with every promise of complete
success."[26] Applauding the election of the "stout-hearted Unionist"
Murphy as governor, the *Washington Chronicle* declared that "a complete
State government will soon be in successful operation on the soil of
Arkansas, and thus her people will have the honor of heading that column

of regenerated States which, under the inspiration of free institutions, is to work a magic revolution in the land of the 'sunny South.'"[27]

On April 11 the new Arkansas legislature with representatives from a majority of the counties convened in Little Rock. Seven days later Isaac Murphy was inaugurated governor. Military units from General Steele's command and Arkansas Unionists marched to the state capitol, where a crowd estimated at between twelve and fifteen thousand witnessed the ceremony.[28] In his inaugural address, the soft-spoken Murphy declared that the "misery, desolation, and sorrow" produced by the war had taught the people of Arkansas that they should never again be divided by sectional passions. "I trust that we return [to the Union] purified by affliction, freed from some of the causes of our trouble, and our estimate of the value of law and order increased." The cause of the war and the main support of the rebellion, Murphy told his audience, was slavery. "Slavery became the enemy of the Government, endangering its very existence, and arraying itself in organized and armed rebellion against it. Then it became a right and an imperative duty" to destroy the institution. "Its very nature," Murphy said, was "hostile to democratic institutions, [and] the laws of nature and precepts of christianity are opposed to the enslaving of man by his fellow man. . . . Although individuals have suffered loss by the abolition of slavery, the public has and will benefit, and the prosperity of our nationality and the government of the people rendered more secure."[29]

Much of Murphy's inaugural address was a paean to education and its benefits for the state, including true liberty for whites and a complete rejection of slavery. Like other Unionists and many Northerners, Murphy believed that had the white population of the South "been educated and informed, a rebellion could not have taken place." Conversely, he claimed that "the vast energy and power displayed by the Government of the Union . . . to put down the rebellion of the several States, is the result of education and the general diffusion of knowledge among the masses of the free States." He maintained that an educated people "would be well informed as to the great interest of the State, and in their public acts would be guided by an enlarged and liberal policy, a policy that would elevate labor, confer honor on industry, and stamp idleness with dishonor." Education, Murphy declared, would also "create a taste for agricultural, mechanical and artistic pursuits."[30]

Finally, the new governor warned against permitting former rebels to share power with Arkansans who had never wavered in their loyalty to the United States. He also mildly criticized Lincoln for allowing disaffected Confederates to regain their rights without proper contrition and an appropriate waiting period. Murphy charged that these men "seek their own little selfish ends, rather than the prosperity of the people, who when the rebellion was strong, were rebels, and used the rebellion for their profit; but when the rebellion grows weak, encouraged by the President's too lenient amnesty proclamation, they become at once loyal, and use their loyalty in the same way. Such [persons] are not to be trusted, and should have no influence in the government." Murphy admonished Arkansans to "trust only those who are truly loyal and sincere friends of the government."[31]

Despite the fanfare of the inaugural ceremony, conditions in Arkansas in the spring and summer of 1864 were unpropitious for the success of Murphy's government and the complete restoration of the state to the Union. Since the framing of the new constitution, the military situation had rapidly deteriorated. Even before the inauguration, General Steele reluctantly, but under direct orders from General Grant, began his ill-advised movement to join General Banks on the Red River. He took more than half his army with him, leaving areas of occupied Arkansas exposed to guerrilla attacks and brigand depredations.[32] Steele's army, in fact, never reached the Red River. The repulse of Banks's forces and severe logistical problems ultimately forced Steele to abandon the campaign and retreat under enemy attack back to central Arkansas. Although Little Rock and other garrison towns remained secure, the Union cause in Arkansas suffered a severe setback in the aftermath of Steele's failure. Confederate guerrillas roamed the countryside, attacking Union activists and influencing many Arkansans who had taken Lincoln's oath to recant. Gen. C.C. Andrews lamented in a report to the president that "the serious reverses of the late campaign have caused some depression of union sentiment, so that the country seems to have degenerated into bushwhackers. It is hardly safe to go out of our lines a mile. I believe Union people are suffering more today in Arkansas than ever before since the war commenced." An excited Governor Murphy repeatedly asked Lincoln for more troops and more arms for Unionists or "all may be lost that has been gained by the election." The president answered that he would do his "best to protect [the] people and new State government, but can act with no better intentions than have always done." In the end he told Murphy: "You must do your utmost to protect yourselves."[33]

Governor Murphy had exaggerated the Confederate threat to his government in Little Rock. Overall Union control never was in jeopardy, though during the late summer a Confederate raid led by Gen. Sterling Price through western Arkansas and into Missouri again raised loyalist fears and produced new guerrilla activity in the state. A Little Rock newspaper, however, probably exaggerated when it claimed that there were fewer guerrillas in Arkansas than in either Kentucky or Missouri.[34] Arkansas's Confederate government, supported by Kirby Smith's troops, continued until the end of the war to occupy the southwest corner of the state.

Another serious challenge to Murphy's government occurred in Washington when Arkansas's representatives in Congress arrived to take their seats. In the March election, Arkansas voters had selected three men for the U.S. House of Representatives, and in early May the legislature chose Elisha Baxter and William M. Fishback for the Senate. Baxter, an unswerving loyalist of Batesville, had the support of both Unionist factions. Fishback, on the other hand, had exhibited questionable loyalty in the 1861 crisis. He was backed, however, by the self-styled "Unconditional Unionist" faction and legislators, who believed that the former Illinoisan's acquaintance with Lincoln would be useful in Washington.[35]

Fishback's election immediately spawned a controversy. Speaker H.B. Allis of the Arkansas House of Representatives refused to certify his election, an action supported by the *Little Rock National Democrat,* the organ of the faction opposed to the Unconditional Unionists. Referring to the senator-elect's supporters as "blackguards," the *National Democrat* declared that "true Union men" in Congress "will not sit in council with a traitor" like Fishback. When the Arkansas House removed Allis and selected a Speaker who immediately signed Fishback's election certificate, the deposed Speaker rushed to Washington, where he vigorously lobbied against Fishback.[36] General Steele meanwhile maintained a careful neutrality in the dispute, though he must have been deeply offended when Fishback, in a speech before the Arkansas legislature, referred to the editor of the *National Democrat* as a "pimp" for members of the general's staff.[37]

Lincoln feared that the division among the state's Unionists and the determination of each faction to take its case to Washington would work against the seating of Arkansas's senators and congressmen. On May 9 he wrote a note to William H. Seward suggesting that the secretary not be swayed by disloyalty charges brought by opponents of the state's representatives.[38] Seward evidently had been lobbied to use his influence against the Arkansas claimants. Though Seward followed Lincoln's advice, the factional warfare among Arkansas Unionists had a damaging effect when Congress, later in May, considered the right of the state to be represented in that body.

When Congress finally debated the question of seating the Arkansans, the focus of its attention was Fishback. On May 21 Republican Senator James H. Lane of Kansas presented Fishback's credentials to the Senate, but no action resulted. Three weeks later Lane introduced a resolution to recognize Arkansas's "free State government" and presented Baxter's credentials along with Fishback's. Lane's proposals were submitted to the Committee on the Judiciary, chaired by Lyman Trumbull of Illinois. The editor of the *Washington Chronicle* predicted that the presentation of the credentials and the resolution on Arkansas "will open up the whole question of the re-organization of 'seceded' State governments, and the discussion is expected to be a warm one."[39]

Even before the Trumbull committee made its report, debate flared in the Senate over Arkansas with the question of Fishback's loyalty dominating the debate. Supplied with information on his record by Allis and other Arkansas opponents, both Republicans and Democrats charged that as a member of the 1861 Arkansas state convention Fishback had advocated secession. Democratic Senator William A. Richardson of Illinois cited a resolution that Fishback had introduced in the convention calling for the state to resist "to the last extremity" any federal effort to coerce a seceded state. A prewar Illinois acquaintance informed Trumbull that Fishback had frequently proclaimed the right of secession before he moved to Arkansas during the late 1850s.[40] An Arkansas refugee made a similar charge, concluding that Fishback "has caused by his course of conduct the death of many Union men, and will turn traitor again whenever he finds it is his interest to do so."[41]

In addition to the question of Fishback's loyalty, the issue of whether the rebellion had been suppressed in Arkansas also received considerable attention in the congressional debate. Senator J.S. Ten Eyck, a New Jersey conservative Republican who had supported Lincoln's reconstruction plan, announced that before he voted to seat Fishback and Baxter he wanted a declaration from either the president or Congress that the insurrection had been suppressed in Arkansas and a republican form of government reestablished. Radical Republicans such as Benjamin F. Wade of Ohio and Charles Sumner of Massachusetts, with the passage of a congressional reconstruction plan imminent (the Wade-Davis bill), rejected out-of-hand the Senate's recognition of any Lincoln government in the South. Most Republicans and Democrats, even while they opposed both the seating of the Arkansans and Lane's resolution recognizing the Murphy government, denied that they sought to undermine the good work of Unionists in the state's reconstruction. They insisted, however, that they had not seen sufficient evidence indicating that the Arkansas government could stand on its own.[42]

On June 27 the Trumbull committee unanimously concluded that Fishback and Baxter "are not entitled to seats as senators from the State of Arkansas." The report indicated that rebels still controlled a portion of the state and other parts were dependent on Federal military power to maintain law and order; therefore no true civil government existed in the state. The committee concluded that the Murphy government, which had elected Fishback and Baxter, was not the republican form of government guaranteed by the Constitution. By a vote of 27 to 6 the Senate approved the committee's report. Of the six senators voting against the recommendation, four were Republicans.[43]

Criticism of Fishback and concern over political conditions in Arkansas contributed significantly to the Senate's decision. A more fundamental reason for the rejection, however, was Abraham Lincoln's weakening political position as the spring and summer military campaigns stalled, casualties increased, and war-weariness grew. Lincoln, not Fishback, was the real target in the Senate debate over Arkansas and the seating of its senators. The status of Arkansas and Louisiana served as a backdrop for the Wade-Davis bill, which passed Congress on July 2 only to be vetoed by the president. Contributing to the rejection of the Arkansans were Democrats who, though miles apart from Radical Republicans on reconstruction, sought by their opposition to embarrass the president as the fall election approached. Arkansas thus provided an opportunity to oppose Lincoln without rejecting the principle of state Unionist control of reconstruction. Democrats professed disapproval of the Arkansas government on the ground that the Murphy regime could not sustain itself. At the same time, they vehemently opposed the stringent Wade-Davis reconstruction plan proposed by Radical Republicans.

Some congressional Democrats repeatedly charged, as they did with his other reconstruction initiatives, that electoral considerations motivated Lincoln's effort to secure the restoration of Arkansas. Senator Willard Saulsbury of Delaware opposed seating the Arkansas claimants because "they come here as the government established by Abraham Lincoln" to advance his partisan purposes.[44] Reverdy Johnson of Maryland charged that the main reason behind Lincoln's reconstruction efforts in Arkansas and in other Southern states was simple: "A presidential election is near at hand; electoral votes are important."[45] In the House of Representatives, Samuel S. Cox, a Democratic leader from Ohio, indicated that "there is a fear upon the part of many members of the House that the State of Arkansas as at present organized may be used for some bad purpose at the next presidential election."[46]

Lincoln's Republican opponents expressed similar sentiments and privately used the debate on Arkansas to sound the political charge against him. Senator John P. Hale of New Hampshire told his colleagues that the Arkansas question, as well as the whole reconstruction issue, should be settled before the presidential election, since it was "pregnant with great danger to the peace of the country." The votes of the president's quasi-restored states, he said, could decide the election, which, by implication, would be in Lincoln's favor and contrary to the will of the Northern people.[47] Actually, those opposed to Lincoln's reconstruction efforts had greater election motives in mind than the president, who had consistently since the beginning of the war—and not just during political contests—sought the early restoration of the Southern states to their "proper practical relations" with the Union. Lincoln had not waited until the summer months preceding the election to launch his reconstruction effort. His opponents found it convenient in the debate over the Arkansas senators and representatives to charge Lincoln with seeking in 1864 to advance his re-election prospects by the early readmission of the Southern states to the Union. The *Little Rock Unconditional Union* exaggerated only slightly when it reported that "all opposed to the re-election of Abraham Lincoln were opposed to admitting our [representatives]."[48]

As soon as the Senate voted to reject the Arkansas senators, Fishback rushed to the Executive Mansion to report to Lincoln. The president reassured the crestfallen Arkansan that his reconstruction policy was still in place. According to Fishback, Lincoln said that he would protect the Murphy government regardless of Congress's action. Secretary of State Seward, who was present during the discussion, "heartily assented" to Lincoln's decision to sustain the Arkansas Unionists. On the same day the president directed General Steele to give the Arkansas government "the same support and protection that you would do if the members had been admitted" to Congress.[49] Lincoln's decision to sustain the Murphy administration occurred three days prior to the passage of the Wade-Davis bill and reflected the heightening tension between the president and Congress over reconstruction and the stalemated war.

Though disappointed by the Senate's refusal to seat Fishback and Baxter, Governor Murphy hailed Lincoln's determination to stand by his government. He wrote the president that the letter to General Steele "came in good time, as the rebels and rebel sympathizers were organizing for [the government's] overthrow." The governor still complained of insecurity in the state and asked for arms and provisions in order to organize a militia force in each Federal-occupied county.[50] He dispatched William D. Snow to Washington to lobby for the weapons. Snow found the president "deeply interested in the affairs of the loyal men of Arkansas" and anxious to provide them with the means to protect themselves, but on the specific matter of arms and material referred him to Secretary of War Stanton who, after some delay and without explanation, refused the request.[51]

Murphy also insisted that the War Department permit him to appoint officers for the seven to nine thousand Arkansas troops in the army. When Stanton ignored the request, the governor complained to Lincoln, comparing the War Department's treatment of him to Congress's rejection of the state's representatives. "We might as well be rebels," he bitterly told Lincoln, "as to be held in military subjection [subjugation?] by the Federals. The Federals ask us to form a state Government, and we have done it and now they refuse to recognize us." He pleaded with Lincoln: "For God's sake, Mr. President, and I say it out of the anguish of my despair, do not allow unnecessary obstacles to be thrown in the path of the State organization at this critical time, for I fear that if these things continue, Arkansas will be so lost that she can only be reclaimed as a barren wilderness."[52] Lincoln, in the month of his greatest despair as his war policy and his political future hung in the balance, did not respond.

Murphy and Arkansas Unionists soon had an additional reason to be upset. In November, General Steele was removed from command by Gen. Edward R.S. Canby, his superior in the Mississippi Valley. With few exceptions, Unionists of both state factions favored Steele's retention because of his assistance in the work of reconstruction. Earlier, when criticism of his military failures mounted in the North, Arkansas Unionists, including Governor Murphy, pleaded with Lincoln to sustain Steele. C.P. Bertrand, a transplanted New Englander and former Little Rock mayor, wrote Lincoln: "[Steele] has the confidence and respect of all parties, and has done more to restore Arkansas to her former relations to the Union than any other man."[53] The president repeated his earlier support for Steele, and even Stanton expressed confidence in the general. On November 22 Congressman John B. Steele wrote his brother that both Lincoln and Stanton "always speak of you in terms of the most unqualified praise, and I do not believe they will either of them go back on you now." However, neither Stanton nor Lincoln intervened a few days later when Steele was removed by Canby.[54]

Much to the relief of Murphy and associates, Steele's successor, Gen. Joseph J. Reynolds, continued to support the state's civil administration. At the same time Lincoln's reelection encouraged Arkansas Unionists to believe that their state would soon be fully recognized by Congress. In a move to improve the prospects for the seating of their representatives in Congress—the only important remaining barrier to the state's restoration to the Union—the legislature replaced the controversial senator-elect Fishback with William D. Snow. Congress, instead of rejecting the Arkansas representatives, as it had done earlier, in early 1865 postponed action on the matter until the next session.[55] When the Arkansas question was again raised in Congress, the war was over, Lincoln was dead, and political circumstances in Washington had dramatically swung against presidential reconstruction.

Despite congressional recalcitrance, Arkansas Unionists in early 1865 went forward with local elections and reorganization as Confederate resistance in the state crumbled. The legislature met in a regular session and enacted measures to meet the financial exigencies of the war-impoverished state. On April 3 Murphy called the legislature into special session to ratify the Thirteenth Amendment to the U.S. Constitution, declaring that its adoption "will be the great event of the age and will result in the restoration of peace and harmony among the States." This former small slaveholder also told legislators that "those whose names are connected with its adoption will obtain a high place in the history of political and moral progression." On April 13 members of the legislature unanimously ratified the amendment, thereby making Arkansas, along with Louisiana, one of the first states to do so. Four days later the same men assembled in a state of virtual shock to deplore "the sad and overwhelming depressing [news] of the foul assassination by the enemies of our country" of Abraham Lincoln.[56] Arkansas Unionists, like those elsewhere, had worked hard, and at no small risk to their lives and welfare to implement the president's reconstruction plan. The death of their national leader left these loyalists unsure of the postwar world that they had hoped to control. Without Lincoln's guidance and support the future would be marked by many uncertainties.[57]

10

Tennessee:
Unionists Divided

Tennessee moved at a slower pace than Arkansas and Louisiana to implement Lincoln's reconstruction plan. While the president's December 8, 1863, proclamation spurred Arkansas and Louisiana Unionists, with the aid of military authorities, to act quickly to abolish slavery and restore their states to the Union, radical loyalists in the Volunteer State led by Military Governor Andrew Johnson hesitated. These Unionists feared that a premature reorganization might permit rebels, in alliance with conservative Unionists, to regain their rights and power in the state. The conservative leadership consisted of old Union Whigs like William B. Campbell, Emerson Etheridge, and Thomas A.R. Nelson, who had been moderates on Southern rights before the war and ironically had been more vigorous than most Johnson Democrats in efforts to prevent the state's secession in 1860-61. Conservative Unionists believed that Johnson was determined to punish his old political enemies and impose a radical settlement upon the state, including the widespread confiscation of property and the permanent disfranchisement of anyone tainted with the rebellion. They feared that Johnson, in order to fulfill his vindictive agenda, would make good on his promise announced in a Nashville speech to be the Moses of black Tennesseans. Conservatives assumed that this meant black equality, which, from their perspective, would compound the social and economic ruin that war and emancipation had produced.[1]

Actually, Johnson had no such radical agenda. In the same speech in which he pledged to be the Moses of the black race, he denied that he was an "agrarian" and insisted that only the property of wealthy Confederates should be confiscated and "parcelled out among loyal, industrious farmers."[2] Even so, Johnson never proposed such a program, and as president in 1865 he ordered the restoration of confiscated property to their owners. It is reasonable to assume, however, that had Lincoln approved the confiscation of rebel estates, Military Governor Johnson would have acted and divided the state's "princely plantations" among white Unionists. Despite conservative concerns, Johnson's powerful racism, as historians have repeatedly demonstrated, prevented him from supporting black rights in Tennessee, much less the distribution of land to former slaves.

When Johnson visited Lincoln in late December 1863, he reminded the president that no statewide elections could be held until East Tennessee had been completely freed of Confederate forces and security from rebel armies and guerrillas had been achieved throughout the state. Louisiana and Arkansas faced the same problem of security for the loyal population. Nevertheless, military commanders and dominant Unionists in these two states, also prodded to action by Lincoln, knew that the risk of losing control of the reorganization process was not really great during the war because few rebel sympathizers would participate anyway in Union-held elections. Without rebel participation, reorganization elections would send ardent Unionists to the state houses where constitutional changes could be enacted insuring future loyal control. In Tennessee, Johnson's concern reflected not only his fear of returning Confederates but also his distrust of his old political foes in the Federal-occupied middle and western parts of the state.

Though opposed to state elections until Unionists were in firm control, Johnson was willing to approve local contests for county and municipal offices. The president's plan anticipated that the initial reorganization of the Southern states would occur at the state level, but Lincoln deferred to Johnson on how specifically it should begin in Tennessee. In mid-January 1864, Johnson supporters in Memphis, Nashville, and other Tennessee towns held "mass meetings" calling for the state's reconstruction under the provisions of Lincoln's December proclamation. Most of these meetings passed resolutions approving emancipation. At the Memphis meeting, reportedly attended by many large West-Tennessee slaveholders, an antislavery resolution was unanimously adopted. James B. Bingham, the editor of the *Bulletin* and Johnson's political lieutenant in Memphis, admitted that the conversion to emancipation by West Tennessee Unionists was primarily motivated by a desire to avoid greater evils that would occur if Lincoln's Radical opponents gained control of the federal government.[3]

At a Union rally in Nashville on January 21, Johnson outlined his plan for implementing the president's proclamation. He proposed to "begin at the foundation, elect the lower officers, and, step by step, put the government in motion." Johnson promised that he would require a more stringent test for voting than contained in Lincoln's "exceedingly lenient" amnesty oath. After the local governments had been reorganized, a state convention would be called to revise the constitution and arrange for elections to the new government. The convention would abolish slavery and, by implication, would proscribe rebels. Warming to an attack on the secessionists, Johnson shouted to the Nashville crowd words that would later become famous: "Treason must be made odious, traitors must be punished and impoverished. Their social power must be destroyed, and the effects that gave them power must be taken away." Rebel leaders, he exclaimed, "ought to be hung." The governor justified such harsh treatment on the ground that "sometimes we may do irregular things for the sake of returning to law and order." This was a most curious pronouncement by a man whose later reputation as president owed a great deal to his strict interpretation of the Constitution and the laws under it.[4]

A few days later Johnson authorized county elections for March 5 to choose local officials. As promised, he also prescribed a stringent oath for all prospective voters. Voters (only whites could register) had to pledge to support and defend the United States Constitution against all of its enemies and also swear that they "ardently desire the suppression of the insurrection" against the government.[5]

A fire-storm of protest from conservative Unionists and former rebels who already had taken Lincoln's oath greeted Johnson's proclamation. Protesters asserted that only the president's test was necessary to restore voter rights. Johnson's oath, they contended, was vindictive and designed to win control of the state for his radical faction.[6] When they appealed to Lincoln to invalidate the governor's requirement, the president refused to intervene. In a hurried reply to one protester, Lincoln in reference to the oath wired that "in county elections you had better stand by Governor Johnson's plan. Otherwise you will have conflict and confusion."[7] A few days later Lincoln provided a more extended explanation for his refusal to intervene. In the process, he exaggerated the similarity between the two oaths, writing that he could see no difference between Johnson's oath and the one that he had set forth in his December 8 proclamation. "[I] am entirely satisfied with [Johnson's] plan, which is to restore the State government and place it under the control of citizens truly loyal to the Government of the United States."[8]

The *Washington Chronicle,* Lincoln's organ in the national capital, attempted to forestall controversy by drawing a clear distinction between the purposes of the two proclamations. "The President's Proclamation," the editor explained, "is a declaration of the terms in which amnesty will be granted; while that of Governor Johnson was intended to call the people together to vote for various offices, and to exclude the enemies of the country from the polls." Repentant rebels, he said, could be granted amnesty under Lincoln's terms "without conferring upon them the right to re-organize the State government. None but true [Union] men should be able to vote, while amnesty may be granted to all who will honestly pledge themselves to be faithful in the future to the laws and Constitution."[9]

Actually, this position did not conform to what Lincoln had in mind when he issued his proclamation. The president intended for his amnesty oath to be a sufficient test for voting, a policy that was followed in Louisiana and Arkansas. Still, he was willing, in keeping with his concept of self-government as a guiding principle in reconstruction, to permit Unionists to determine voter requirements for their states. For this reason, Lincoln went along with Johnson's stringent oath.

The voter turnout in the March 5 county elections in Tennessee was mixed. In some districts, Confederate guerrillas, as before, prevented the opening of the polls. The presence of Gen. James Longstreet's troops in upper East Tennessee kept pro-Union officials from holding local elections. In areas of West and Middle Tennessee, where Confederate sympathizers were still relatively strong, voting was light. For example, in Clarksville, a town on the Cumberland River that Federal forces had occupied since early 1862, only eighty-four voters went to the polls. The local Union leader there expressed his frustration with the results in his report to Governor Johnson. "Public opinion is truly a Despotism; men were afraid to commit themselves," he lamented. Still others simply refused to take Johnson's stringent oath in order to vote.[10]

In other areas, however, the voter turnout was impressive. The election in Shelby County (Memphis) "was warmly contested" between the radical or Unconditional Union ticket and the conservative or National Union party, resulting in a disputed victory by the latter. In Davidson County (Nashville) a hard-fought contest between the Johnson radicals and the conservatives led to the opposite result. In Maury County (Columbia), two-thirds of the prewar vote was reported.[11] Altogether, between forty thousand and fifty thousand votes were cast in the state, with two-thirds of the counties electing officials. With varying degrees of enthusiasm, most successful candidates supported the Lincoln-Johnson plan, including emancipation.[12]

Encouraged by these election returns, Governor Johnson promised in a three-hour speech at Shelbyville on April 2 that a state convention soon would be held.[13] Meanwhile, Thomas A.R. Nelson, the conservative president of the 1861 Greeneville convention of Unionists, called for delegates of this body to reassemble in Knoxville on April 12. Warned that "indiscreet men" might seek to repudiate his leadership, Johnson rushed to Knoxville to prevent a serious embarrassment in the convention.[14] He arrived while the convention was in session.

As expected, Johnson immediately encountered trouble from conservative Unionists, most of whom were former Whigs of East and Middle Tennessee. Conservatives in the Knoxville convention objected to Lincoln's reconstruction plan, to a considerable extent because it would be implemented by Johnson, their old political adversary. They feared that the convention would frame a new constitution reflecting the military governor's radicalism and setting the stage for his election as governor by disfranchising opponents, whether loyal or not. They also opposed Lincoln's emancipation policy but expressed willingness to accept gradual freedom for blacks provided slaveholders were compensated, as required by Tennessee law. For the immediate future, they wanted Lincoln to honor his exemption of Tennessee from the Emancipation Proclamation. Some delegates—both conservative and radical—reopened the issue of separate statehood for East Tennessee, a position, however, that received little support in the convention.[15] A conservative credentials committee recommended the restoration of the status quo antebellum and rejected Johnson's rigid test oath for voting. The governor's forces in the convention condemned the report and proposed that the delegates adopt resolutions supporting immediate emancipation, the enlistment of black troops, and the reelection of Lincoln. A furious debate ensued. In the end, neither conservatives nor radicals prevailed. After four days of wrangling, both sides agreed to adjourn with their differences unresolved.[16]

Suddenly, with East Tennessee Union leaders seemingly intractably divided, the Lincoln reconstruction program in the state stood in grave danger of failure. To remedy the situation, Johnson and his friends organized a "grand mass meeting" in Knoxville to rally support for an early assembling of a convention to amend the state constitution, including the abolition of slavery, and also support for the administration of the president and the governor. After rousing speeches by Johnson and Brownlow, the convention adopted resolutions to this effect. Johnson reportedly wrote the resolutions. One resolution attempted to reassure white East Tennesseans that emancipation would not lead to black equality. It declared that, though slavery, "the disturbing element by which designing and wicked men were enabled to combine and delude the people into the highest crime known to civilization," would soon be destroyed, the federal and state governments were *"the Governments of the free white man."* A black man in freedom, this resolution proclaimed, "must assume that status to which the laws of an enlightened, moral, and high-toned civilization shall assign him."[17] Such a racist resolution by a so-called radical Union meeting did not bode well for the future of Tennessee blacks in freedom.

Meanwhile, newly elected county officials in the state began to restore local governments. A number of county administrations, particularly in Middle Tennessee, were functioning by the summer of 1864. By the late spring, the federal court, presided over by Connally F. Trigg, a conservative East Tennessee Unionist appointed judge by Lincoln in 1862, was adjudicating cases in Memphis. Later in the year Trigg opened his court in Knoxville.[18]

Despite such apparent progress, problems soon arose. In August 1864, Confederate Gen. Nathan Bedford Forrest made a daring raid into Memphis, shattering security and inspiring Confederate sympathizers to defy local Union governments. In Middle Tennessee, a similar raid by Gen. Joseph Wheeler's cavalry penetrated almost to Nashville. Later in the year a major thrust by Gen. John B. Hood's army reached the outskirts of the state capital before being repulsed.[19] These military incursions retarded Johnson's efforts in 1864 to reestablish local governments as the first step toward civil reorganization in Tennessee. Significantly, the setbacks occurred in West and Middle Tennessee, areas that had been nominally occupied by Federal forces since 1862.

East Tennessee also continued to pose problems for Johnson's efforts to restore local civil authority. By the spring of 1864 major armies had campaigned in the area for almost a year, disrupting society and leaving the people impoverished. Deplorable conditions continued, even after General Longstreet's forces withdrew from upper East Tennessee in May. Thousands of East Tennesseans were forced to flee the area, creating heart-rending scenes of suffering as they moved into Nashville and farther north. Relief societies in the North sent aid to desperate citizens remaining in East Tennessee, but recovery did not occur until after the war. The Georgians left in the wake of Sherman's march to the sea later in the year were no worse off than residents of East Tennessee in 1864. Compounding their difficulties was the presence of guerrillas or "bushwhackers" who continued to operate for months after the armies had left the area.[20]

Though by the summer of 1864 East Tennessee was free of Confederate forces, the precarious Union position in many areas of the state and other serious concerns caused Johnson again to hesitate in calling a state convention. Critical military operations in Georgia, Louisiana, and Virginia during mid-1864, in addition to the beginning of the 1864 presidential

campaign, diverted the attention of Johnson and Lincoln from reconstruction. In June Johnson had been nominated for vice president on the
National Union (Republican) ticket headed by Lincoln. A major political
canvass loomed on the horizon.

Johnson's selection as Lincoln's running mate was designed to marshal important Northern Democratic support to the Lincoln ticket.
Johnson was also popular among Northern Republicans, even though some
Radicals like Thaddeus Stevens and Benjamin F. Wade objected to his
nomination because of the legitimacy they feared it would give to the president's reconstruction policy. Historians remain divided on whether Lincoln
dictated the choice. Regardless of the president's role in the selection, he favored the Tennessean because of Johnson's popularity, his crucial role in
presidential reconstruction, and the recognition that his nomination would
give to the administration's Southern policy.[21]

Ironically, the presidential contest exacerbated political divisions in
Tennessee among Unionists and complicated further the Lincoln-Johnson
program of reconstruction. After the Republican convention, conservative
Unionists, already disgruntled with Lincoln's emancipation policy, charged
that the president and his party in adopting an abolition platform had violated their promises and succumbed to radicalism. They asserted that the
war had been transformed into a conflict to subjugate the South and feared
that this turnabout inevitably would cause the rebels to fight harder,
thereby postponing the collapse of the Confederacy. Conservative Unionists directed their main fire at vice presidential candidate Johnson. They
charged that Johnson sought to delay Tennessee's restoration to the Union
in order to give him time to consolidate his power in the state and to
punish his political enemies. "That Tennessee is not to-day in the full enjoyment of all her rights as a State of the Union," the *Memphis Argus*
declared, "is not the fault of the people of Tennessee, but of Governor
Johnson and the radical clique, who [are] opposed to reorganization" under
Lincoln's Proclamation of Amnesty and Reconstruction.[22]

Tennessee conservative Unionists soon organized a state party to
oppose the Republican ticket. They also joined with like-minded conservatives in the North and the border states to form the Conservative Union
party. Consisting overwhelmingly of former Whigs, many of whom prior
to emancipation had supported Lincoln, the new party sought an alliance
with their old Democratic opponents in order to defeat the Republicans in
1864 and conclude the war on the basis of reunion alone, leaving the question of emancipation to the states. The new party proposed a conservative
ticket of Gen. George B. McClellan, a war Democrat, for president and
William B. Campbell of Tennessee for vice president. Campbell subse-

quently declined to be a candidate, and conservative Unionists sought another old Whig for second place on their proposed ticket.[23]

Military events of the summer, however, worked against the success of the conservative Unionists and their coalition plan to continue the war until reunion had been achieved and the status quo antebellum restored. The war had stalemated, causing peace sentiment to flourish in the Democratic party. The demand for peace among Democrats culminated in the triumph of the "Copperhead" faction in the national convention that met in Chicago in August. Led by Clement Vallandigham of Ohio, Democrats adopted a platform that labeled the war a failure and proposed a cease-fire leading to a national convention of states to restore the Union. Despite uneasiness among many peace delegates, the convention nominated General McClellan for president. The convention, however, rejected the Whig claim for a place on the ticket and chose a Copperhead favorite, George Pendleton, a peace Democrat of Ohio, as the vice presidential candidate.[24]

Although McClellan repudiated the war-failure and peace plank, many conservative Unionists who wanted the Chicago convention to adopt a platform clearly affirming support for the war until the rebellion had been crushed reacted in dismay to the Democratic action. The national Conservative Union party immediately collapsed. In Tennessee, where political lines over reconstruction and emancipation had hardened, conservative Unionists ignored the platform and proclaimed their support for McClellan. Calling themselves the Constitutional Union party—an obvious reference to John Bell's 1860 party—they formed a McClellan electoral slate for the campaign. All ten electors were old Whigs and former Bell supporters, including William B. Campbell and Thomas A.R. Nelson. Ironically, conservative Unionists labeled Bell, a Tennessean who had cast his lot with the Confederacy, a traitor.[25] In raising McClellan's standard, Tennessee conservatives hoped to rid themselves of the Johnson regime, restore civil government under their control, obtain the support of former Confederates, and reverse emancipation, or at least gain federal compensation for their slaves. They preferred to believe that McClellan, despite his party's peace platform and Federal military successes in Georgia and Virginia in September and October, 1864, would win the election because of the Lincoln administration's perceived failure in the conduct of the war and its violation of civil liberties in Tennessee and elsewhere.[26]

Johnson, of course, had allies in Tennessee. His party's preparations for the presidential campaign, however, began in an unorthodox way. On August 2 a group of nine Johnson men met at Nashville and issued a call for a Union convention for the purpose of devising "some plan for the restoration of Tennessee to the rights and privileges to which her loyal population is entitled . . . and to take such action as may be necessary to entitle the qualified voters of the State to vote in the ensuing presidential election." Despite disruptions in some areas by Confederate cavalry, on September 5 delegates from fifty counties convened in Nashville. A number of conservative Unionists appeared, believing that the convention had been assembled to establish a nonpartisan procedure for the reorganization of the state government and for the fall presidential election.[27] They soon were disappointed, however, and quickly discovered that the Johnson "radicals" planned to use the convention to launch the Lincoln-Johnson campaign in the state. Johnson forces, angered by the Chicago platform and fearful of a Democratic victory in November, hooted down conservative speakers who proposed that Tennessee's antebellum state constitution remain the authority for the conduct of elections and for the reorganization of the state government. The convention also defeated a conservative suggestion that all who could take Lincoln's liberal amnesty oath should be permitted to vote.[28]

After suffering numerous taunts, the conservative Unionists walked out of the convention. The convention then resolved that Tennessee should participate in the presidential election, though it had not been restored to the Union. It also outlined a rigid requirement for voting that even exceeded the stringency of Johnson's earlier oath. A prospective voter must swear that he was "an active friend of the Government of the United States"; that he will "sincerely rejoice in the triumph of its armies and navies" over the Confederacy; that he "will cordially oppose all armistices or negotiations for peace with rebels in arms"; and that he "will heartily aid and assist the loyal people in whatever measures may be adopted for the attainment of these ends." Even having taken this oath, a voter's legitimacy still could be challenged or rejected at the polls by an election official. In addition, the convention provided that only unstinting Unionists should hold office and that Johnson or Lincoln should remove officials who could not meet this test. Finally, the convention endorsed Johnson's administration as military governor, Lincoln's candidacy for reelection, and slavery's abolition "by all suitable and proper amendments" to the fundamental law of the state and nation.[29]

On September 30 Governor Johnson announced that Tennessee would participate in the presidential election. He approved, with one modification, the voter test oath proposed by the Union convention. In communities where registration was impractical because of the brief enrollment period before the election, a person of "established loyalty" could vote simply by appearing at the polls. The governor also appointed election officials for the counties, none of whom was a known member of the conservative Unionist faction.[30] In authorizing a stringent voter requirement for the election, Johnson, as he had done previously in his March election order, clearly violated the spirit of Lincoln's amnesty proclamation. The president intended that all rights should be restored once an individual had taken a simple oath of loyalty to the Union. He assumed that persons who subscribed to the oath would feel morally bound to support the Union and sustain loyal candidates at the polls. Johnson had no such faith in the intentions of most Tennesseans who took Lincoln's oath. Furthermore, Johnson easily persuaded himself and his followers that conservative Unionists who supported the McClellan ticket were lukewarm in their loyalty and at the first opportunity would join with perjured rebels for the purpose of overturning a true Union settlement in Tennessee. The military governor probably believed that Lincoln, who might need Tennessee's electoral votes to win, would not intervene and require him to rescind the test oath. Johnson also knew that Lincoln could ill afford to revoke an order of his vice presidential running mate on the eve of the election.

Hoping to gain political mileage, conservatives rushed a long document to the president protesting Johnson's actions. The document, signed by ten McClellan electors and delivered to Lincoln by one of them, John Lellyett, "solemnly protest[ed] against the interference of the Military Governor with the freedom of the elective franchise in Tennessee." The protesters reminded Lincoln that "many of our citizens have complied in good faith with the terms of amnesty proposed in your Proclamation, . . . and are, therefore, by reason of the full pardon granted them, fully entitled to vote and exercise all other rights belonging to loyal citizens." They appealed to the president "to make good your promise of pardon to these citizens" by revoking Johnson's test oath and removing "all other and further hindrance to their exercise of the elective franchise," including military interference at McClellan rallies.[31]

The conservative protesters, according to Lellyett, received a stinging rebuke from Lincoln. When Lellyett read the protest to him, Lincoln reacted angrily: "May I inquire how long it took you and the New York [Democratic] politicians to concoct that paper?" When Lellyett answered that no one outside of Tennessee had a hand in the protest, Lincoln reportedly concluded the interview by declaring: "I expect to let the friends of George B. McClellan manage their side of this contest in their own way; and I will manage my side of it in my way." Whether Lincoln spoke these words or not, he clearly was provoked by Lellyett and the conservative demands. The president's ire was raised in part because the protesters cited Tennessee law in denying his and Johnson's authority to interfere with state elections, despite their contradictory pleas elsewhere in the document for

Lincoln to intervene and permit voting by citizens who had taken his amnesty oath. Lellyett's account of the interview was published in the national Democratic press and created considerable grist for McClellan's campaign mill.[32]

A few days after the appearance of Lellyett's account, Lincoln sent a sharply worded letter to the Tennessee protesters. He indicated that he could not "perceive any military reason for . . . interference in the matter" of the election. The president, Lincoln said, "is charged with no duty in the conduct of a presidential election in any State" except "to give protection against violence," which, he contended, Governor Johnson could provide in Tennessee. Lincoln informed the Tennessee conservatives that despite their insinuation of a high-level political conspiracy in the matter, "up to the present moment nothing whatever upon the subject has passed between Governor Johnson or anyone else connected with the [election] proclamation and myself." Lincoln, however, admitted that because "of so many pressing public duties" he had not given a careful consideration to their complaint.[33]

The Tennessee conservatives were determined to have the last word in the controversy, thereby providing additional propaganda for the Democratic campaign. Campbell, Lellyett, and another McClellan elector indignantly wrote Lincoln professing shock that he was unaware of Johnson's actions. "It is an evil of no small magnitude, connected with your administration," they lectured the president,

> that military subordinates assume despotic powers without asking the sanction of their superiors—even presuming to give law to the people by proclamation and to repeal and modify our laws at will. The idea that the President himself can make, or repeal, or modify a law of the land, state or national, constitutional or statutory, though freely practiced upon by yourself, is a doctrine of despotism in 'irrepressible conflict' with the principles of public liberty. And when these things are done by subordinates, the evil becomes intolerably oppressive, and calls for the firmest and most active lawful resistance which a people deserving to be free can offer.

These conservatives told Lincoln that, "in view of the fact that our people are overawed by military power [and] the laws set aside and violated with impunity," they were withdrawing the McClellan ticket in the state.[34]

Despite their public defiance, conservative Union leaders worried privately that their alliance with Northern Copperheads would tar them with the brush of disloyalty and lead to their suppression by Johnson and the Federal military. Already the government had suspended their party newspaper organs in Nashville and Memphis, and Tennessee troops under Johnson's command had dispersed a McClellan rally at the Nashville courthouse.[35] The dispatch in the fall of state troops under Gen. Alvan C. Gillem to expel rebel forces from upper East Tennessee was motivated partly by Johnson's desire to open the polls for a large, sympathetic Unionist vote. Anxious also for the complete liberation of East Tennessee, conservative Unionists made no complaint regarding the military operation.[36] By October, with a Lincoln victory virtually assured, conservatives realized that a continued challenge to the Republicans could only further delay Tennessee's restoration to the Union, leaving the state in the hands of the radical faction. Some conservatives then switched their support to the Lincoln ticket. On the eve of the election, Parson Brownlow jubilantly reported from East Tennessee that "the McClelland [sic] party is [now] a mere faction, led on by a set of sore-headed Union men, some of them old Democrats, but most of them old Whigs, who had a bad Union record. They have played out."[37]

Nonetheless, an election of sorts occurred in Tennessee. Despite the official withdrawal of the McClellan ticket, problems of communications and security prevented the information from reaching many communities. Approximately thirty-five thousand voters went to the polls, five thousand of whom cast ballots for McClellan. About half of Lincoln's thirty thousand votes came from East Tennessee, though Knoxville, the unofficial capital of the region, was a hotbed of conservative Unionist activity. Ironically, Nashville and Memphis, centers of secessionist strength early in the war, went overwhelmingly for Lincoln.[38] Congress considered neither Tennessee's nor Louisiana's electoral votes to be legitimate (loyal governments in Arkansas and Virginia offered no electoral slate) on the premise that no bona fide election had been held in these states.[39]

Victory over the "Copperheads" in the fall election spurred Johnson radicals, or self-styled "Unconditional Unionists," to undertake the central task of reorganizing Tennessee's government preparatory to the state's restoration to the Union. The new vice president-elect was determined, according to an associate, "to carry to Washington his own State, as a reconstructed member of the Union, and present it as a rich jewel of the nation."[40] To fulfill this goal, on November 12 East Tennessee radicals with Johnson's approval called for Union delegates to assemble in Nashville on December 19 to initiate the process of civil reorganization. Gen. John B. Hood's last-gasp invasion of Tennessee during the late fall, however, caused a postponement of the meeting. When the delegates finally met on Jan. 9, 1865, at the state capital, Hood's army had been destroyed, and the end of the war was imminent. Almost half of the more than five hundred delegates hailed from fourteen counties in East Tennessee. A debate immediately ensued over the nature of the convention itself. A large number of radical members wanted the convention to function as a constituent assembly empowered to propose constitutional amendments for ratification by the voters. Other members, including several radicals, argued that the body had no authority to act as an official state convention but only could nominate candidates for election as delegates to a constitutional convention that Military Governor Johnson presumably would call.[41]

After three days of debate on this issue, Johnson broke the deadlock by urging the delegates to draft constitutional amendments for approval by the people. He specifically proposed an amendment abolishing slavery but recommended no provision protecting the legal status of the freed people. Johnson suggested to the delegates that they should "control and punish the negro . . . by the same laws that you have to punish white criminals." He also told them that, as Lincoln's policy provided, "it will not hurt the negro to be an apprentice," citing his own youthful experience as justification but ignoring the fact that he had been raised in a benign white society sharply in contrast with the uncertain existence that blacks faced in freedom. For loyal conservatives who continued to hope that they could retain their slaves, Johnson declared: "It is easy to talk flippantly of radicals, and negro-lovers, but if Abraham Lincoln and Jeff. Davis were to unite, they could not force the negro back to slavery." It was impossible, he said, "to reverse this great movement."[42] Johnson also encouraged the delegates to invalidate the secession ordinance. He was willing to leave other matters, including suffrage qualifications, to the legislature. "I will wager my head," Johnson promised the delegates, "that if the people will go to the polls and ratify the amendments" to the state constitution proposed by him, and then elect their representatives in Congress, their action would be accepted in Washington, and the people of Tennessee "will stand once more as members of the great family" in the American Union.[43]

The next day the Union convention approved the proposed constitutional amendments abolishing slavery and invalidating the secession ordinance and laws relating to it. The convention provided for two elections, one to be held on Washington's birthday for the purpose of ratifying the amendments, and the other on Lincoln and Johnson's inauguration day for the election of a governor and legislature. Only Tennesseans who had qualified to vote in the fall presidential contest could participate in these elections, a requirement that effectively prevented many former Confederates from voting. The delegates also nominated William G. "Parson" Brownlow for governor and chose a slate of candidates for the legislature.[44]

Before adjourning, the Union convention appointed a three-member commission "to induce the President to issue a proclamation declaring Tennessee no longer in insurrection against the Government of the United States." The commission, which immediately left for Washington, also was directed "to secure the payment of claims for property taken by the United States army from loyal citizens" of the state and to seek the completion of a railroad from the Ohio Valley to Knoxville, a project that Lincoln earlier had supported.[45] Meeting with the delegation in early February, the president agreed that the state of insurrection should be officially lifted for Tennessee, but he believed that "present trade regulations" might create "some grave legal considerations" if he immediately issued a proclamation. Lincoln told the Tennesseans that he would consider the question, suggesting that a decision could be made in a few days. The president, however, never responded, probably because he wanted to wait until the war was over to announce the end of the rebellion throughout the South. His failure to act did not, however, indicate a reluctance on his part to recognize loyal governments in individual Southern states. The president expected civil reorganization to occur simultaneously with the suppression of the rebellion. On the issue of paying Unionist property claims, Lincoln informed the delegation that these would be honored after the war. Regarding the completion of the Ohio to Knoxville railroad, the president told the Tennessee commissioners that though he had previously supported its construction, he could not do so now because the military necessity justifying the expenditure had passed.[46]

Meanwhile, Governor Johnson had wired the president, informing him of the convention's action on slavery. "Thank God that the tyrants [sic] rod has been broken," Johnson exclaimed. The vice president-elect informed Lincoln that when the amendment was ratified by the people, which he confidently expected, "the state will be redeemed and the foul blot of Slavery erased from her escutcheon." Johnson pointedly remarked to Lincoln that he hoped "Tennessee will not be included in the bill now before Congress," because it would undercut the work of reorganization in the state. This bill, introduced by Representative James M. Ashley of Ohio, reflected the desire of Radical Republicans to impose a congressional plan of reconstruction upon the South (except for Louisiana and Arkansas) that would include black civil and political rights. The measure did not pass, but Johnson expressed uneasiness about the future course of reconstruction in the South if Congress interfered. "All is now working well," he informed the president, "and if Tennessee is now let alone [it] will soon resume all functions of a state."[47]

Lincoln immediately sent a message to Johnson expressing his "thanks to the convention and to you" for the action on emancipation.[48] He also asked Johnson to recommend a replacement as military governor. The Tennessean replied that he preferred to remain in Nashville until after the new civil administration had taken office in April and the state's reorganization completed. "I would rather have the pleasure and honor of turning over the State, organized, to the people properly Constituted, than be Vice President of the United States." He informed the president that a precedent existed "for qualifying Vice Presidents after the Fourth of March."[49] Lincoln did not agree and sent a message to Johnson indicating that he "fully appreciated" the governor's wish to remain in Tennessee until the new government had been inaugurated, but it was the "unanimous conclusion" of the Cabinet "that it is unsafe for you to not be here on the fourth of March. Be sure to reach here by that time," he told Johnson. Nevertheless, Johnson waited until late February to leave Nashville for Washington. When he did arrive a few days before the inauguration, he was suffering from a debilitating illness.[50] To strengthen himself for the ceremony, Johnson took a "sovereign remedy" for his illness and was inebriated at the inauguration. Johnson's tipsy behavior caused Lincoln a great deal of silent grief, so much so that, despite his earlier practice of holding frequent conferences with the Tennessean, he did not meet with him again until April 14—the day of the assassination.[51] They then met only briefly, and what they discussed never was revealed.[52]

Back in Tennessee, conservative Unionists denounced the work of the Union state convention. They repeatedly charged that the convention had no authority to act as a constituent assembly; therefore its action in drafting and submitting constitutional amendments to the people for ratification was illegal. Conservatives declared that the vindictive tone of the convention, especially its nomination of the vengeful Brownlow for governor, undercut President Lincoln's policy of reconciliation. The conservative press in Nashville and Memphis carried numerous excerpts from national Republican newspapers advocating a peace based on Lincoln's lenient plan of reconstruction and advising Tennesseans to ignore the February 22 and March 4 elections.[53] On the other hand, radical Unionists vigorously campaigned, particularly in East and Middle Tennessee, for ratification of the amendments and their slate of candidates. "The moral effect of a heavy poll will be great," the *Daily Union,* the Nashville organ of the radicals declared. "The more numerous the votes, the more readily will the State government go into peaceful operation."[54] This editor could have added that a large vote would enhance the likelihood of the new government and its representatives gaining recognition in Washington. Not surprisingly because of conservative opposition and the stringent voter qualification, the turnout at the polls was light, even falling short of the vote in the fall presidential election.

In the February election, the constitutional amendments were ratified easily—by a vote of 25,293 to 48. This ratification ended slavery officially in Tennessee. The next month Brownlow won the governorship and radical Unionists captured control of the new legislature. The polls for both elections were open in most East and Middle Tennessee counties, but not in West Tennessee, where armed bands of Confederates still operated.[55] More than 10 percent of Tennessee's 1860 electorate participated in the ratification campaign, thereby fulfilling Lincoln's requirement for recognition.

On April 3 the new legislature assembled in Nashville, and two days later Brownlow took the oath of office as governor. Brownlow, whose stock-in-trade as editor of the *Knoxville Whig* (which had become the *Whig and Rebel Ventilator*) was invective, demonstrated remarkable restraint in his first message to the General Assembly. Though describing in graphic language the ruin that the "abomination" of secession had caused, the new governor exhibited little recrimination and had little to recommend in the way of punishment for rebels. He simply asked the legislature "to guard the ballot box faithfully and effectively against treason," but made no specific recommendations regarding suffrage or officeholding.[56] After Lincoln's assassination and the end of the war, the radical-controlled legislature, in a more vengeful mood and probably egged on by Brownlow, disfranchised almost all former Confederates. President Johnson, who later would turn on his radical Tennessee friends, applauded the action and admonished Governor Brownlow to enforce the new voting law.[57] In his message to the General Assembly, Brownlow urged the legislators to ratify the proposed Thirteenth Amendment and provide "for the protection, government and control of the emancipated slaves among us." Unlike Governor Murphy in neighboring Arkansas, Brownlow only dealt briefly, and without mention of race, with the need for public education in the war-torn state. Not until the fall session of the General Assembly did the governor make a specific recommendation regarding the status of blacks in postwar Tennessee. He then asked the legislature to allow black testimony in court but warned that the enfranchisement of the freedmen would be a "bad policy," a position that the lawmakers approved. Finally, in his April message Brownlow told the legislators that if they elected U.S. senators he was confident that Congress would accept them.[58]

In early May the General Assembly elected David T. Patterson (Johnson's son-in-law) and Joseph S. Fowler as Tennessee's U.S. senators.[59] For Brownlow and Tennessee Unionists, the reorganization of the state under Lincoln's plan had been completed. Ironically, Andrew Johnson, the man who had initiated the reconstruction process in the state, now held the key to Tennessee's restoration to the Union. As the new president, he had inherited the issue of reconstruction policy, not just for Tennessee and other occupied states, but for all of the former Confederacy as well. But first, the final act in Lincoln's reconstruction efforts was to be played out in Washington in late 1864 and early 1865. The history of wartime reconstruction during the few months between Lincoln's triumphant fall election and his tragic death reveals much about the martyred president's postwar intentions for the South, both in states where loyal governments already existed and in those where reorganization and emancipation awaited the Confederacy's demise.

11

The Final Months

Lincoln's election in the fall of 1864, accompanied by important military successes, strengthened the president's hand and set the stage for the final act in wartime reconstruction. Despite the election's significance for the history of reconstruction, historians have indicated that the 1864 political contest focused not on the future of the South when the war was over, but on whether the war could be won at all, particularly with Lincoln at the helm. The fact that the national Republican platform ignored the reconstruction issue has suggested to historians that either it was unimportant in the presidential contest or too controversial to be raised. According to some historians, when the Wade-Davis bill in July and the later manifesto by the bill's sponsors failed to replace Lincoln with a Radical candidate, the reconstruction issue was virtually ignored during the campaign.[1]

Such an assessment of the 1864 election, however, fails to recognize that reconstruction issues, including Lincoln's emancipation requirement for Southern restoration, punctuated much of the debate over war and peace in the campaign. In fact all political elements touched upon reconstruction questions. Although Republicans failed specifically to mention reconstruction in their platform, they did not ignore it in the election. For example, of the nineteen speeches listed by the Union (Republican) Congressional Committee for the 1864 campaign, five dealt directly and primarily with Southern restoration and the remainder concerned related issues such as slavery and the confiscation of rebel property.[2] In addition, Republican pamphlets issued during the campaign generally supported Lincoln's lenient reconstruction policy while demanding harsh treatment for rebel leaders.[3] Also prominent Southern Unionists, including Francis

H. Pierpont, Edward W. Gantt, and vice presidential candidate Andrew Johnson, went north to campaign for Lincoln. At numerous Republican rallies they praised the president for his success in restoring loyal self-government in their states and ending slavery.[4]

During the campaign opposition Democrats and ultraconservatives insisted that a liberal reconstruction policy, including a general amnesty for Confederates, was central to the return of peace and the restoration of the South to the Union. They faulted Lincoln for a reconstruction plan that violated constitutional principles in its insistence on exacting terms, especially emancipation, on states that legally had never been out of the Union. These critics claimed that the Union could not be restored as long as the Emancipation Proclamation stood.[5] E.C. Seaman, editor of the *Ann Arbor Journal,* who had previously supported the Republican party, wrote that Lincoln's emancipation requirement in his reconstruction plan had united white Southerners and "given them a fanatical zeal and energy, as persecuted patriots, fighting for the defense of their property, their families, and their firesides." He declared that the president's policy "in effect disfranchises all the Southern people who will not . . . swear to abide by his emancipation proclamation."[6]

Robert C. Winthrop, scion of a distinguished Massachusetts family and a former speaker of the U.S. House of Representatives, expressed the most effective campaign criticisms of Lincoln and his policies toward the South. At large McClellan rallies in New York, Boston, and New London, Winthrop, who once supported the Wilmot Proviso, exclaimed that Lincoln's emancipation policy "has been calculated to extinguish every spark of Union sentiment in the Southern states. . . . [It] tended to breathe a spirit of defiance and desperation into the breasts of every southern man and woman and child." Emancipation, he charged, had become the pretext for Republicans to continue the war "until the whole social structure of the South has been re-organized." Such a policy was "utterly unconstitutional, and as much in the spirit of rebellion as almost anything which has been attempted by the Southern States." A McClellan presidency, Winthrop contended, would take advantage of recent military successes at Atlanta and elsewhere in the South by "opening the way for a wise, conciliatory, healing policy to come in and settle the questions" produced by the war.[7]

While Lincoln's conservative critics faulted him for emancipation, abolitionists like Wendell Phillips attacked the president during the campaign for the failure of his reconstruction plan to insure black rights and require rebel disfranchisement. Phillips excoriated "Mr. Lincoln's model of reconstruction" in Louisiana, "which puts all power into the hands of the unchanged white race, soured by defeat, hating the laboring classes, plotting constantly for aristocratic institutions." "Such reconstruction," Phillips averred, "makes the freedom of the negro a sham, and perpetuates slavery under a softer name." It also left "the seeds of discontent and division in the South in the places of power, [and] tempts and facilitates another rebellion," with the aid of the French in Mexico. "If Mr. Lincoln is re-elected, I do not expect to see the Union reconstructed in my day, unless on terms more disastrous to liberty than even disunion would be."[8]

The American Anti-Slavery Society, the most influential abolitionist organization in the United States, supported Phillips's position on reconstruction but rejected his condemnation of Lincoln. In a meeting on May 11, the society went on record endorsing only candidates who "will secure the immediate abolition of slavery . . . and the equal enfranchisement of the Negro." Significantly, William Lloyd Garrison dissembled, insisting that abolitionists should actively support Lincoln because no one had done more for black freedom than he had. Garrison suggested that reconstruction issues could be resolved later to the satisfaction of antislavery zealots.[9] The collapse in September of the Radical Republican movement to replace Lincoln on the party's ticket and the threat of a Copperhead victory led most abolitionists, but not Phillips, to rally behind the president in the election.[10] Aided by military successes in Georgia and the Shenandoah Valley in the fall, Lincoln defeated Democrat George B. McClellan by a surprisingly wide margin of 212 to 21 electoral votes.

After his triumph at the polls Lincoln turned his thoughts to ending the war and restoring the Union without slavery.[11] In his annual message to Congress on December 6, he outlined the progress toward restoration that had been made in the South. "Important movements have . . . occurred during the year to the effect of moulding society for durability in the Union," Lincoln told Congress and the nation. "Although short of complete success, it is much in the right direction, that twelve thousand citizens in each of the States of Arkansas and Louisiana have organized loyal State governments with free constitutions, and are earnestly struggling to maintain and administer them." The president tied these developments with progress toward emancipation and Union success in Tennessee and the border states. "The movements in the same direction, more extensive, though less definite in Missouri, Kentucky and Tennessee, should not be overlooked." Maryland, he happily announced, "is secure to Liberty and Union for all the future. The genius of rebellion will no more claim Maryland."[12]

To insure the eradication of slavery in the United States, Lincoln called on Congress to pass the Thirteenth Amendment and send it to the states for ratification. "The voice of the people" had spoken in the election, he declared. "The common end is the maintenance of the Union; and, among the means to secure that end," the people had "most clearly declared in favor of [a] constitutional amendment" to abolish slavery.[13] The ratification of the amendment, Lincoln knew, finally would put to rest the issue of the legality of his emancipation edicts.

The president concluded his annual message with an appeal to the Southern people to end the rebellion. He announced that the military resources of the Union were "inexhaustible" and the Union people determined "to re-establish and maintain the national authority." Southerners should defy Jefferson Davis, who "cannot voluntarily accept the Union," and resume their allegiance to the United States. Southern rebels "can, at any moment, have peace simply by laying down their arms and submitting to the national authority under the Constitution. After so much [conflict], the government could not, if it would, maintain war against them. The loyal people would not sustain or allow it. If questions should remain, we would adjust them by the peaceful means of legislation, conference, courts, and votes, operating only in constitutional and lawful channels." Lincoln admitted that "some certain, and other possible, questions are, and would be, beyond the Executive power, to adjust; as, for instance, the admission of members into Congress, and whatever might require the appropriation of money." However, he would put no barriers in the way to the immediate restoration of Southern rights and equality in the Union.[14]

Lincoln reminded Southerners, as well as Northerners, that his power "would be greatly diminished by the cessation of actual war." "Pardons and remissions of [property] forfeitures, however, would still be within Executive control. In what spirit and temper this control would be exercised can be fairly judged of by the past," he said. Lincoln indicated that many Southerners "had availed themselves of the general provision" of his amnesty proclamation, "and many more would, only that the signs of bad faith in some led to such precautionary measures as rendered the practical process less easy and certain." At the same time, he said, not a single application for pardon by Southerners in the excepted class had been denied. Clemency "is still open to all" the president informed Southerners. "But the time may come—probably will come—when public duty shall demand that it be closed; and that, in lieu, more vigorous measures than heretofore shall be adopted."[15]

Based on this last sentence, some historians have concluded that by late 1864 Lincoln was reconsidering his reconstruction policy and threatening Southerners with a harsher plan unless they acted soon to end the rebellion and restore their states to the Union.[16] The president, however, addressed only the issues of pardon and amnesty for individual rebels, not the mode of state reorganization. Only one comment—that "if questions should remain" after reunion, "we would adjust them by the peaceful means of legislation, conference, courts, and votes"—suggests a larger issue than clemency. But Lincoln promised that these matters would be handled "only in constitutional and lawful channels," meaning those institutions created by loyal governments organized under his Proclamation of Amnesty and Reconstruction and providing for emancipation. He saw no reason why Congress should refuse to seat senators and representatives from Louisiana and Arkansas who had been elected under his restoration plan. Lincoln stated the case plainly to Senator Lyman Trumbull, chair of the Senate Judiciary Committee. "Can Louisiana be brought into proper practical relations with the Union, sooner, by *admitting* or by *rejecting* the proposed Senators?" he asked. Lincoln's answer obviously was the former.[17]

Even so, the president realized that Radical Republicans in Congress, joined by Democrats along the other extreme of the political spectrum, would seek to block the seating of the Louisiana and Arkansas representatives and, perhaps, even challenge his reconstruction plan. Tempered by his Whiggish reluctance to interfere with the business of the legislative branch, Lincoln called on General Banks to lobby for acceptance of the Southern representatives and, specifically, the Louisianans. The president earlier had ordered Banks, who had been in Washington since the fall building support for the Hahn government, to return to his command in New Orleans and to repair the damage that Generals Canby and Hurlbut had done to Louisiana's new civil government. But Lincoln soon changed his mind, directing Banks to remain in the Northeast and assist in "harmoniz[ing] matters between Congress and the Executive."[18]

Banks employed all of his considerable persuasive skills and prewar political connections on behalf of the Louisiana government, its representatives in Washington, and, generally, Lincoln's Southern policy. He provided Senate and House committees with voluminous information on Louisiana's reconstruction history and his own controversial free-labor program, as well as a twenty-three page letter that he had written to Senator James H. Lane on Louisiana affairs. In a speech at Faneuil Hall, Boston, Banks, with typical exaggeration, declared that "no better Constitution has ever been presented to any people on the face of the earth" than the new Louisiana document.[19] As part of a letter writing campaign to support the president's plan, Banks sent a lengthy letter to William Lloyd Garrison's *Liberator* explaining what he had done in Louisiana for black freedom and progress. Banks also told the abolitionist community that, while he and

Lincoln favored conferring the ballot on some Louisiana blacks, the federal government could not impose suffrage upon a state. However, "my belief is that the question of suffrage will be settled sooner in Louisiana than in any other State." He warned that a premature movement in that direction could prevent the incorporation of a black suffrage provision in the Louisiana constitution.[20] Lincoln closely followed Banks's lobbying efforts and conferred with the general on numerous occasions, even stopping him in a reception line at the White House to talk "business" while other guests waited.[21]

Radical Republicans launched a counterattack against Banks's lobbying campaign. Wendell Phillips, whose dislike for the president had become obsessive, stumped the Northeast denouncing Lincoln and Banks for "sacrificing the very essence of the negro's liberty to the desire for a prompt reconstruction."[22] At Cooper Institute, before an audience including many hecklers, Phillips declared that the president in his "imperious anxiety . . . to force upon us the sham State of Louisiana" had misinterpreted the radical results of the 1864 election. Black leaders in New Orleans and in the North, though not as harsh in their criticism of Lincoln, also voiced opposition to the president's Southern policy. A black Boston correspondent to the *New Orleans Tribune* regretted that Lincoln would permit rebel states like Louisiana to return to the Union without insuring "Equality of Rights and Franchises" for the freedmen. The future liberty of the race, he declared, depended upon the extension of these rights to blacks prior to the readmission of the Southern states to the Union.[23]

While sympathizing with the position of Phillips and African-American spokesmen, most Radicals in Congress realized that during the winter of 1864-65 the question of black rights was not the central issue for Northerners. Practical-minded Radicals understood that complete emancipation and the establishment of loyal Southern governments were the only reconstruction guarantees that most Northerners and border-state men wanted at this time, a settlement coinciding with Lincoln's position and requiring little in the way of federal intervention in the affairs of the states. Though most Radicals favored some form of black suffrage, they refrained from any outright demand for full black political and civil rights. Even Charles Sumner soft-pedaled black political equality after the election. In a letter to Lincoln, he endorsed a reconstruction policy based on steadfast white loyalty and bona fide freedom for blacks. "Next to Rebellion itself, I most dread a premature State Government in a rebel State, placing at hazard, as it must, those two things which we so much desire, Peace and Liberty."[24]

Fundamentally, Radicals were appalled by Lincoln's conservatism.[25] They were convinced that his reconstruction policy would not insure black freedom and white loyalty in the postwar South. Some Radicals like Benjamin F. Wade and Henry Winter Davis simply did not trust Lincoln. Radicals publicly targeted the "military character" of the president's Southern governments, arguing that military control of reconstruction in Louisiana and elsewhere under Lincoln's plan violated republican and constitutional principles of government and prevented a true expression of the loyal people on the reconstruction issue. Only Congress, they declared, had the authority to establish procedures for the reorganization of civil governments in the South. The president's role should be limited to the implementation of the congressional mandate.[26]

When Congress convened in December, Radicals put forth a mild challenge to Lincoln's reconstruction plan. On December 15 James M. Ashley of the House Select Committee on the Rebellious States introduced a bill "to guarantee to certain States whose governments have been usurped or overthrown, a republican form of government." The bill, similar to the Wade-Davis bill in most of its features, outlined a procedure for the reorganization of loyal governments in the South and their recognition by the president and Congress. Emancipation would be required of the restored states and criminal penalties attached to persons attempting to restrain the liberty of blacks. A provision that only "loyal male citizens" were eligible to vote in the reconstruction elections was generally viewed as a circuitous attempt to enfranchise male black adults. The bill, however, did not define citizenship. The Ashley bill did indicate that only those "loyal male citizens" who could subscribe to the iron-clad oath (i.e., affirm that they had never aided the rebellion) were eligible to vote in the first elections or serve as jurors. Except for these vaguely worded concessions to black equality, the bill, like the earlier Wade-Davis measure, ignored the issue of African-American rights in the South. Because Lincoln's support was necessary for its enactment, the Ashley measure recognized the Louisiana and Arkansas governments without the above guarantees. The bill also authorized the president to appoint provisional governors to oversee the work of framing acceptable constitutions for each state (except Louisiana and Arkansas).[27]

Historians have concluded that Lincoln initially was willing to endorse the Ashley bill in order to obtain congressional approval of his Louisiana and Arkansas governments. Their argument mainly rests on marginal notations that the president made on a printed copy of the bill.[28] But close reading of the holograph document in Lincoln's Papers reveals that the emendations were only for quick reference to the bill's provisions, not indicators of his position on the bill itself. In the margin of the section outlining voter qualifications, Lincoln simply wrote, "Qualification of voters for delegates to convention." Adjacent to a long section in the bill on reconstruction procedure, he made this notation: "How proceed, and how State may come in." A Lincoln emendation by the section establishing a provisional governor for each state read, "temporary governor." Even the notation in the margin of the section on emancipation contained only the reference note "Emancipation." These marginal notations, as well as others on the Ashley bill, provide no evidence of Lincoln's support for the measure.[29] Historians also cite a December 27 letter from Senator Charles Sumner to Francis Lieber as further evidence that the president had accepted the Ashley compromise. The letter, however, indicated only that Lincoln, in a meeting with Sumner, agreed that there should be "harmony between Congress and the Executive." Sumner never explicitly wrote Lieber that the president had endorsed the Ashley bill.[30]

Historians also have claimed that Lincoln's appointment in December of a special commission to investigate conditions west of the Mississippi River, mainly around New Orleans, was clear evidence of the president's uneasiness "over the manner in which reconstruction was working out in practice," particularly in Louisiana.[31] These historians suggest that Lincoln was inclined to accept significant changes in his reconstruction policy, perhaps agreeing to the Radical demand for federal-imposed black suffrage upon the Southern states. The War Department's instructions to the commission, headed by William F. Smith, however, contained no reference to reconstruction or the civil government of Louisiana. The investigation was to "embrace the condition, discipline, and supplies of [the military] division, the operations of the quartermasters and other staff departments, and all matters connected with contraband trade."[32] In other words, the commission was to ferret out corruption in the military, especially illicit commerce in the lower Mississippi Valley. By late 1864 this commerce had assumed gigantic dimensions and created serious concern in Washington.

After beginning its work in the spring, the Smith-Brady Commission, as it was called, expanded the scope of its investigation to include civil affairs. In its report to Secretary of War Stanton in September 1865, the commission faulted the military command for "gross misconduct" and also criticized the way Louisiana's civil government had been organized in 1864.[33] By the time the report was made, however, President Lincoln was dead, Union Governor J. Madison Wells was appointing returning Confederates to office, and General Banks, the architect of the 1864 reorganization, was at odds with President Johnson's administration and no longer was involved in the state's reconstruction.

Despite Lincoln's reluctance to support a congressional initiative on reconstruction, he and General Banks had met on December 18, 1864, to consider the Ashley bill. According to John Hay, who was present at the meeting and wrote an account of it in his diary, Lincoln opposed the provision that made blacks "jurors and voters under the temporary governments." Banks, though like Lincoln supportive of limited black enfranchisement by state action, replied that "what you refer to would be a fatal objection to the Bill." At the same time the president wanted a stronger statement on emancipation than the bill provided. Concerned about the legality of his emancipation edicts, Lincoln sought explicit congressional approval of his actions in ending slavery.[34]

Banks, exceedingly anxious to obtain congressional recognition for the Louisiana government, urged the president to support a modified Ashley bill. He told Lincoln that if the bill, without the suffrage provision, became law it would not undercut his liberal, Unionist-based reconstruction policy. Nor would it preclude congressional approval of Southern states with differing political conditions and constitutions. The bill, Banks argued, provided only for "concurrence with the executive action" regarding reconstruction, particularly in the matter of "the prerogative of Congress to decide as to qualifications of its own members." In other words, the Ashley bill, shorn of federal dictation on suffrage, would not violate Lincoln's commitment to the self-reconstruction of the Southern states. The president seemed to agree with Banks's assessment, but Hay does not indicate in his diary what Lincoln proposed to do on the issue.[35] In the end, Lincoln did nothing; the requirement that only loyal male citizens who could subscribe to the iron-clad oath were eligible to vote in the first elections was too similar to the Wade-Davis bill for him to support.

Nonetheless, in apparent deference to Lincoln's reservations and those of most Republicans, Ashley altered his bill by striking out the provisions that would allow black voting and jury duty. Radicals like Henry Winter Davis, however, were dissatisfied with the watered-down version and, joined by Democrats who opposed any reconstruction requirement, particularly emancipation, forced Ashley repeatedly to revise his bill, to the point that it was unacceptable to a majority of the members. Finally, on February 21 it was tabled by an overwhelming vote in the House. Other congressional efforts to pass reconstruction legislation met a similar fate.[36] The *Springfield Republican* issued an epitaph for congressional efforts to override Lincoln's policy: "Thus the president's reconstruction policy stands, and the readmission of the recovered states will be obstructed by no inflexible rule, but each case can be determined according to circumstances existing when it comes up."[37]

Lincoln's deep concern for the legitimacy of his Emancipation Proclamation reinforced his conservatism on reconstruction. Though he favored the emancipation provision in the Ashley bill, the president did not believe that congressional legislation abolishing slavery would provide the necessary legal authority for his Emancipation Proclamation once the war had ended. He held the view that only a constitutional amendment could provide the permanent legal foundation for his Emancipation Proclamation and also abolish slavery in loyal states like Kentucky. Lincoln desperately wanted the passage and ratification of the Thirteenth Amendment under consideration by Congress in January 1865. As the new year began, prospects for the amendment's success in Congress appeared dim.[38] Concerned that this cornerstone of his emancipation policy would fail, Lincoln actively sought the support of Democrats and conservatives. In a meeting with Congressman Samuel S. Cox, a prominent Ohio Democrat, and John T. Stuart (Lincoln's first law partner but a leading Illinois conservative opponent during the war), the president expressed his anxiety regarding the amendment. In return for Democratic support for the amendment, Lincoln promised to press for peace on the basis of his liberal amnesty and reconstruction plan. Congressman John Hogan, a Missouri Democrat and another old Illinois friend of Lincoln's despite their political differences, later wrote that the president also sought his support for emancipation, which the president tied to his reconstruction policy.[39]

On January 31 a sufficient number of Democrats and conservatives in Congress voted with the Republicans to send the proposed amendment to the states for ratification. The next day, an exuberant Lincoln told a crowd at the White House that "this amendment is a King's cure for all the evils" created by slavery, suggesting that after the cessation of hostilities nothing more would be required of the South.[40]

With his emancipation policy secure, the president met with three Confederate peace emissaries or commissioners at Hampton Roads on February 3. Confederate Vice President Alexander H. Stephens, one of the commissioners, provided the only detailed account of the four-hour meeting. The Confederates came seeking an armistice, not the reestablishment of ties with the United States. Lincoln, of course, could not accept a peace without reunion; thus no agreement was reached at Hampton Roads. Nevertheless, Lincoln, with the backing of Seward, tried to reassure the Confederates that the federal government would not pursue a policy of subjugation or suppression of traditional liberties after Southerners laid down their arms. He repeatedly declared that once "the National Authority was recognized, the States would be immediately restored to their practical relations to the Union," and personal and political rights would be respected. The president, according to Stephens, even said that he would be willing to be taxed to compensate the Southern people for their slaves if they disbanded their armies, renewed their allegiance to the Union, and ratified the Thirteenth Amendment. Though he could not force the admission of Southern representatives in Congress, Lincoln indicated to Stephens that "they ought to be" seated.[41]

Historians have questioned Stephens's account, which appears in his postwar memoirs. The former Confederate vice president's improbable story that Lincoln urged him to go home and have the Thirteenth Amendment ratified prospectively, to take effect in five years, has served to cast doubt on much of his account of the conference.[42] Stephens was obviously in error on this point. Lincoln was committed to the immediate ratification of the amendment and, as his reconstruction plan indicated, would not approve the restoration of states to the Union until they had abolished slavery. Still, Stephens's account generally conforms to Lincoln's position on reconstruction and his conservative concerns regarding the disruptions that could occur with emancipation. A succinct report of the Confederate commissioners to President Davis immediately after their return to Richmond indicates that Lincoln anticipated no change in his reconstruction plan, set forth in December 1863. According to the commissioners, Lincoln reiterated the provisions of his reconstruction proclamation, explaining "distinctly his sentiments as to the terms, conditions, and method of proceeding by which peace can be secured."[43]

Furthermore, when Lincoln returned to Washington, he made good on his promise to Stephens to seek compensation for slaveholders forced to free their slaves. He drafted a proposal asking Congress to issue $400 million in bonds to distribute to the Southern states, including the border states, in proportion to their slave population. Half of the bonds were to be distributed if by April 1 resistance to national authority had ceased. The remaining half would be paid only if the Thirteenth Amendment became "valid law" by July 1.[44] Lincoln's proposal "did not meet with favor" when he presented it to the Cabinet for consideration. Secretary of Navy Gideon Welles noted after the meeting: "The earnest desire of the President to conciliate and effect peace was manifest, but there may be such a thing as so overdoing as to cause a distrust or adverse feeling." Faced with the unanimous opposition of his Cabinet and the virtual certainly of a congressional rejection, Lincoln abandoned the scheme and did not again raise the issue of compensating slaveholders.[45] Biographer David Donald has aptly concluded that the compensation proposal "told much of Lincoln's generosity of spirit and of his understanding of the problems the South faced in making the transition from a slave society to a free society." It also revealed "his almost desperate sense of urgency to bring the war to a speedy end."[46]

Though his compensation scheme had failed, Lincoln was determined to fulfill his promise, expressed in his reconstruction proclamation and reaffirmed at Hampton Roads, that the rights of the states and individuals would be fully restored once fighting ceased and Southerners had taken the oath of allegiance to the Union. In this policy, which included the restoration of self-government in the South, Lincoln was influenced by his fear that unless a conciliatory hand was extended, diehard rebels would resort to guerrilla tactics after the surrender of the Confederate armies. Anarchy in many areas of the South, the president believed, would be the inevitable result of a harsh policy. As early as 1863 he manifested this concern when he wrote Gens. William Rosecrans and Henry W. Halleck and Secretary of War Edwin M. Stanton that as the rebellion weakened brigands would infest the Southern states.[47] The rampant lawlessness in Kentucky and Missouri in 1864 and early 1865, even where no organized rebel force existed, confirmed Lincoln's fears that guerrilla activity would follow the disbandment of the Confederate military forces. He told Governor Thomas C. Fletcher of Missouri in February 1865 that the cure for such disturbances could only be found in a policy of pacification and mutual respect for the security and rights of others.[48] Secretary of Navy Gideon Welles later reported that in the early months of 1865 Lincoln "frequently expressed his opinion that the condition of affairs in the rebel States was deplorable, and [he] did not conceal his apprehension that, unless immediately attended to, . . . civil, social, and industrial relations [would] be worse after the rebellion was suppressed."[49]

Lincoln's new appointments to office also reflected his unwillingness to compromise on his conservative Southern policy. His selection of Salmon P. Chase as chief justice in November 1864 was the only significant concession to party Radicals made by the president after his reelection. Though bombarded with petitions from Radicals to appoint Massachusetts Governor John A. Andrew as attorney general, Lincoln refused to select such a powerful Radical to a position that would have an important hand in reconstruction, particularly the implementation of his amnesty and pardon policy. Instead, after first offering the position to Judge Advocate Gen. Joseph Holt, a War Democrat of Kentucky, the president chose fellow Kentuckian James Speed, the brother of his closest prewar friend and a supporter of the president's Southern program.[50] Within the Bluegrass State, Lincoln also tilted to the conservative Unionist faction of Governor William E. Bramlette, which had opposed his reelection. In February the president removed Gen. Stephen G. Burbridge from command of U.S. troops there. Burbridge had been acting in a highhanded manner in suppressing Confederate sympathizers and anti-Republican dissidents. The removal of Burbridge, along with other indications of Lincoln's commitment to a conservative course, brought him the support of the *Louisville Journal* and the *Frankfort Commonwealth,* both influential border-state newspapers that also had opposed Lincoln in 1864. Conversely, Radicals found cause for despair in Lincoln's border-state policy.[51] Further south, in Louisiana and Arkansas, the president upon the recommendation of state Unionists appointed conservatives to federal positions. Lincoln's replacement of Louisiana radicals with Cuthbert Bullitt, a leading Southern conservative, and Charles A. Peabody as United States marshal and United States district attorney respectively sent a clear signal that he would not change his conciliatory reconstruction policy.[52]

Even Lincoln's Northern appointments suggested a conservative course for his new administration. The president's selection of Indianan Richard W. Thompson, "an old pro-slavery fossil," to the federal Court of Claims outraged Radicals. Despite Radical proddings, Indiana Republicans in Congress refused to protest the Thompson appointment because, as Radical George W. Julian lamented, "they don't want any quarrel with Lincoln," who "through his patronage is the virtual dictator of the country." The president's appointment of Daniel S. Dickinson as United States attorney for the Southern District of New York would have created Radical concern, but Lincoln's death two days later stilled the opposition to it. Though his office would not be involved in Southern affairs, Dickinson, a Democrat who had reluctantly supported Lincoln in 1864, had been an outspoken supporter of a conciliatory reconstruction policy. In other important New York appointments, Lincoln replaced Chase men with supporters of William H. Seward and his alter ego, the conservative Thurlow Weed.[53]

An important indicator of Lincoln's success was the fact that the major Republican press in early 1865 threw its support behind the president's conservative policy for the South as the war entered its final phase. Like the president, Republican editors believed that his course would lead to a quick termination of the war and the restoration of a harmonious Union. The *Washington Chronicle* and the *Philadelphia Press,* both controlled by John W. Forney, a Lincoln confidant, repeatedly reminded Southerners of the president's good will and his determination to restore all of their rights except slavery. "No military force will be necessary except for a short period, if the States shall be promptly readmitted as soon as they reorganize on the basis of freedom," the *Chronicle* declared. When Southerners "return to their allegiance," this editor wrote, "they will be equals in everything of those who defeated their attempt to break up the Union. As to the question of negro suffrage, that is a matter of purely State concern."[54]

The *New York Times,* whose editor, Henry J. Raymond, chaired the Republican national committee, also praised Lincoln's Southern policy and attacked those Radicals in Congress who sought vengeance on the South. "The great end and aim of our policy in dealing with the population of the revolted States ought to be the removal of all traces of the struggle from their memory," the *Times* declared. "Nothing that serves to remind them of their defeat, and is not absolutely necessary for the safety of the Government, ought to be retained either in our legislation or our policy." Raymond decried those Radicals who clamored for the punishment of Confederate leaders. "It may be laid down as a rule, dictated not simply by humanity and Christianity, but by sound policy, that no punishments whatever ought to be inflicted on anybody, except such as are plainly called for by a prudent regard for our own safety." Slavery, which had been the cause of the sectional division, was gone forever, "so that, as far as this is concerned, there is no further need of repressive measures."[55] The timing of the removal of military control and the revival of civil rule should "depend upon the disposition cherished by the Southern people after active hostilities are over."[56] Raymond did not expect the process to be prolonged. Though Raymond's *Times* admitted that temporary protection for blacks might be necessary, in a series of editorials in February and March it almost completely avoided this question, stressing instead the importance of returning white loyalty and political restoration.

Even Horace Greeley's *New York Tribune,* which had earlier allied with the Radicals and opposed Lincoln's renomination, in March 1865 announced its support for the president's lenient reconstruction policy. It attacked the Ashley bill and similar measures in Congress that would "fetter and hedge about the action of our Government with conditions and limitations that are likely—nay, are calculated—to embarrass the President" and postpone the ending of the war. "The country confides in the President, and would to-morrow decide unhesitatingly to leave the matter [of reconstruction] to his uncontrolled discretion." Insisting that "the Nation needs peace, not vengeance," the *Tribune* maintained that "a great majority of the Southern people have taken no further part in the Rebellion than such as was imposed on them by falsehood and terrorism." It agreed with the *Chronicle* and the *Times* that Southerners "need but due assurance that they will be treated with magnanimity to induce them to flock in thousands to the National standard."[57]

The independent *New York Herald* also expressed approval of the president's policy. On January 10 the *Herald,* whose editor James Gordon Bennett repeatedly had criticized Lincoln until offered the position of minister to France in 1864 (which he declined), reported "a powerful reaction throughout the South in favor of submission to the Union." According to Bennett, Union sentiment could even be found in Charleston, South Carolina, and Wilmington, North Carolina, former centers of secession, proving that the rebellion was "manifestly not a revolt of the Southern masses, so much as of the Southern politicians." Like Lincoln, Bennett believed that the rebellion had been sustained by military coercion. "The masses of the people and of the armies of the rebellious States are not only ready but anxious to end the war on the simple basis of submission," he declared.[58]

A *Herald* correspondent in Washington reported in January that both Lincoln and Congress had been moved by such reports toward a policy of conciliation and a desire for an easy transition of the rebel states back into the Union. "The signs of the times plainly indicate," this correspondent wrote, "that the administration has determined to pursue a more conservative and conciliatory course from this time onward. In other words it is believed that the so-called Southern confederacy has reached that point in its downward career when the true policy of our government is to temper justice with mercy." Other indicators of the growing conservatism in the national capital included the removal of Ben Butler from command of the Army of the James, the House Committee on Elections' recommendation to seat the Louisiana representatives, and the defeat of the Ashley reconstruction bill. Lincoln finally had emerged as the master of affairs, the *Herald* asserted. Its Washington correspondent reported that "the President was bored and hampered by the [Radical] faction of his party, and forced to yield to them during his first term [on the slavery question]; but the indications now are that he intends to have his own way during his second term."[59]

Lincoln was especially upset with Senator Charles Sumner's obstructionism. On January 18, John G. Nicolay, one of the president's secretaries, recorded an incident that revealed Lincoln's frustration with the Radical senator. Sumner repeatedly had refused to support in Congress a local railroad concession to New Jersey's Democratic congressmen in order to secure their support for the Thirteenth Amendment. This, according to Nicolay, raised the president's ire. When Nicolay indicated that practical-minded Republicans in Congress suggested that the president intercede with the senator, Lincoln responded sharply. "I can do nothing with Mr. Sumner in these matters. While Mr. Sumner is very cordial with me, he is making his history in an issue with me on this very point. He hopes to succeed in beating the President *so as to change this Government from its original form and make it a strong centralized power.*"[60]

Though Lincoln and Sumner's personal relationship continued to be cordial, their differences over reconstruction in early 1865 widened.

Sumner refused an invitation by Mrs. Lincoln to attend a reconstruction address by Lincoln on April 11 at the White House because, as he wrote Salmon P. Chase, his presence would give symbolic approval to the president's conservative course toward the South. At the same time, Sumner informed Francis Lieber that Lincoln's policy augured ominous "confusion and uncertainty in the future, with hot controversy."[61]

On the eve of Lincoln's second inaugural, and one week after the defeat of the Ashley bill, Congress stunned the president by adjourning without seating his Louisiana and Arkansas delegations. Throughout January and February 1865, while committees in both houses studied the credentials of the claimants and prepared their reports, prospects appeared bright for congressional acceptance of these senators and representatives.[62] On February 11 Henry L. Dawes for the Committee on Elections reported that M.F. Bonzano of Louisiana was entitled to a seat in Congress. Six days later the committee made similar recommendations for A.P. Field and William D. Mann of Louisiana, and T.M. Jacks and J.M. Johnson of Arkansas. The House, however, agreed informally before acting to await the decision of the Senate on the seating of the senators from these two states.[63]

The wait was brief. On February 18 the Senate Committee on the Judiciary made its report regarding the Louisiana claimants. This committee sought a middle ground in the lingering jurisdictional dispute between the president and many members of Congress over reconstruction. Speaking for the committee, Senator Lyman Trumbull, who earlier, in June 1864 had recommended the rejection of Arkansas's senators on the ground that no real civil government existed in the state, now declared that Charles Smith and R. King Cutler, the Louisiana claimants, had been "duly elected" by a majority of the state's loyal voters under Lincoln's plan of reconstruction. But, as a sop to those senators who wanted to retain the right of congressional authority in reconstruction and perhaps also in order to avoid a bruising debate, the committee concluded that the Louisianans should not be seated "till by some joint action of both Houses there shall be some recognition of an existing State government acting in harmony with the government of the United States." It therefore proposed a resolution recognizing the Louisiana government, which, when adopted by both houses of Congress, would immediately entitle Smith and Cutler to seats in the Senate.[64]

Ironically, Radicals and proslavery senators, like Garret Davis of Kentucky and John S. Carlile of the Restored Government of Virginia, joined forces to block the seating of the Louisianans and thereby stymie Lincoln's efforts to obtain congressional recognition for the Southern governments.

Davis, Carlile, and other ultraconservatives opposed recognition of the Louisiana government because they feared that if restored the state's vote on the Thirteenth Amendment would be cast in its favor. Members of this strange coalition of Radicals and proslavery men concluded that the report of the Trumbull committee, introduced near the end of the session, might be defeated or postponed by a filibuster. With that in mind, Sumner and other Radicals sought by debate to prolong consideration of the committee's report. Then, on February 25, Radical Senator Benjamin F. Wade moved postponement of the issue until the next regular session of Congress in December. The motion, however, failed by a vote of twelve to seventeen, suggesting to observers that had the Trumbull committee recommendation come to a vote in the Senate, it would have passed.[65]

After the failure of the Wade motion, Radicals intensified their efforts on the floor of the Senate to prevent the seating of Louisiana's delegation. As the session wound down, Senator John Sherman indicated that appropriation bills necessary for the operation of the government would be lost if the debate on the Trumbull report continued. A number of Republicans who had supported Lincoln's Southern governments but were leery of acting in haste to seat the Louisianans, now joined the Radicals and ultraconservatives in a successful effort to postpone the issue. Their opposition to the immediate seating of the Louisianans was partly inspired by an incident in which Louisiana congressman-elect A.P. Field assaulted Republican representative William D. Kelley with a pocket knife in the lobby of Willard's Hotel in Washington. Inflamed by this violent act, many Republicans concluded that Field and other Louisiana claimants were unfit to serve in Congress.[66]

Middle-of-the road Republicans probably did not believe the postponement action would be a serious blow to Lincoln's plan or to his governments in the South. Along with some Radical and ultraconservative opponents of the president, they expected the president to have a free hand in reconstruction affairs at least until Congress reconvened in December. It seemed logical that at that time Congress would seat the Southern senators and representatives, including those from states still to be occupied and reorganized under Lincoln's plan.

The Louisiana claimants for seats, as well as those from Virginia and Arkansas who were waiting in the wings for congressional approval, were stunned by the postponement. The Louisianans rushed to the White House to determine what they should do. Lincoln, in "a long and very satisfactory interview" with the delegation, reaffirmed his support for them, the Louisiana government, and by implication other Union governments in the South. Senator-elect Cutler quoted the president as saying all

Louisianans should "stand firmly by the acts of the late Constitutional Convention and the Constitution of 1864." He had given similar advice to the rejected Arkansas representatives in 1864. Lincoln expressed confidence that Congress would admit the Louisiana members at its next session. Before leaving, the delegation, aware of Lincoln's intense concern for the Louisiana government's success, reminded the president of the further need to remove Chase men, particularly Benjamin F. Flanders, who still held federal positions in Louisiana and were frustrating efforts to restore the civil administration there.[67] Having recently satisfied Louisiana conservatives with the appointment of Cuthbert Bullitt as U.S. marshal, Lincoln did not feel compelled to make additional federal patronage changes in Louisiana. He probably understood that the dismissal of Flanders, a former congressman who was popular among Radicals in Washington, could unnecessarily arouse opposition in Congress.

A few days later Lincoln directed General Banks to return to New Orleans and resume command of the Department of the Gulf. Prior to leaving for New Orleans in early April, Banks telegraphed the president at City Point, Virginia, for instructions. Lincoln tersely replied: "I really have no directions to give you. . . . You and I will correspond when desired by either."[68] In general, Banks was expected to sustain the civil government and, perhaps, lobby the legislature for the enfranchisement of blacks, a major task because the Louisiana lawmakers were mainly conservative Unionists who had already indicated their opposition to black political rights. No evidence exists that Lincoln authorized Banks to interfere with political authorities in Louisiana.

Events, however, had taken a disturbing turn in Louisiana. On March 3 Michael Hahn, one of Lincoln's favorites, had resigned as governor to accept a seat in the U.S. Senate. Lieutenant Governor J. Madison Wells, a conservative Unionist, replaced him and immediately removed Banks's friend Stephen Hoyt as mayor of New Orleans, replacing him with ultraconservative Hugh Kennedy. The appointment of conservatives and former Confederates to judicial and municipal offices soon followed and were confirmed by the state senate.[69] Both Wells and Kennedy insisted that they were acting to end corruption and extravagance in the affairs of the state and in New Orleans. Although unsaid, they hoped to form a coalition with contrite returning Confederates to preserve conservative control after the war. Gen. Stephen A. Hurlbut, whom Banks replaced, supported Governor Wells, believing that he was following the president's policy of reconciliation. General Edward R.S. Canby, Hurlbut's superior, who had earlier clashed with Banks, gave tacit approval to what soon became an ultraconservative course by the governor and the mayor in the appointment of former Confederates to office and resistance to rights for blacks. Durant radicals and members of the Hahn-Banks faction were furious at Wells's apostasy, but only after Lincoln's death and Banks's subsequent arrival in New Orleans did a strong challenge to the governor develop.[70] Lincoln never knew of the bitter new political divisions that were developing in Louisiana as peace became a reality and Confederates returned home.

A few days after Congress rejected the Louisiana claimants for seats, Lincoln took the oath of office for his second term. The president devoted most of his brief inaugural address to what he believed was a divine purpose in the war on slavery. In a rhetorical flourish to emphasize the significance of emancipation, the president exclaimed:

> Fondly do we hope—fervently do we pray—that this mighty scourge of war may speedily pass away. Yet, if God wills that it continue, until all the wealth piled by the bond-man's two hundred and fifty years of unrequited toil shall be sunk, and until every drop of blood drawn with the lash, shall be paid by another drawn with the sword, as was said three thousand years ago, so still it must be said 'the judgments of the Lord, are true and righteous altogether.'

Lincoln concluded his address with the now famous appeal for a just peace and for national reconciliation:

> With malice toward none; with charity for all; with firmness in the right, as God gives us to see the right, let us strive on to finish the work we are in; to bind up the nation's wounds; to care for him who shall have borne the battle, and for his widow, and his orphan—to do all which may achieve and cherish a just, and a lasting peace, among ourselves, and with all nations.[71]

Lincoln spoke these words with Union victory clearly in sight. Sherman was completing his march through South Carolina and stood poised to invade North Carolina. Fort Fisher and Wilmington, North Carolina, had fallen to General Alfred Terry's forces, eliminating Lee's last hope as he faced an encircling Federal army at Petersburg. Throughout the Southland the Confederacy was coming unglued and daily thousands of war-weary, impoverished Southerners were abandoning the cause.

Mindful of conditions in the South, Lincoln increasingly turned his thoughts toward ending the war and restoring the Southern states to their "proper practical relations with the Union." On March 2 General Lee proposed a meeting with General Grant to arrange a "military convention" for the purpose of concluding the war. Grant immediately wired the War Department for instructions. Stanton showed Grant's message to Lincoln, who at first was willing to authorize the meeting, perhaps not realizing that Lee also had a political settlement in mind. But Lincoln changed his mind, according to the president's friend and bodyguard, Ward H. Lamon, when Stanton angrily reminded him that peace terms should be decided by the president and not by generals in the field. Lincoln then dictated a message for Stanton to send Grant. It read: "The President directs me to say to you that he wishes you to have no conference with General Lee unless it be for the capitulation of Gen. Lee's army, or on some minor, and purely, military matter. He instructs me to say that you are not to decide, discuss, or confer upon any political question. Such questions the President holds in his own hands; and will submit them to no military conferences or conventions."[72]

Lincoln, Secretary of Navy Gideon Welles recorded in his diary, also expressed concern that "the military men are not very solicitous to close hostilities,—fears our generals will exact severe terms."[73] The president had little reason to fear that either Grant or Sherman would continue the war for the sole purpose of exacting severe terms. Actually, both generals during the fall and winter of 1864-65, though unsuccessful, explored opportunities for an early end of the war before the final defeat of the Confederate armies. Neither, however, sought to circumvent Lincoln's authority in political and civil matters regarding the rebellion.[74]

On March 23 the president, anxious to be with the army and eager to press his generals for an early end to the bloodshed, joined Grant in Virginia. He remained with him for two weeks until news of a serious injury to Secretary of State William H. Seward caused him to return to Washington. On March 27-28 Lincoln met with Grant and Sherman on board the *River Queen* at the City Point dock in an effort to encourage the two generals to end the war quickly and humanely. According to Sherman, "Mr. Lincoln exclaimed, more than once, that there had been blood enough shed, and asked us if another battle could not be avoided." Sherman told the president that he expected the Confederates "to fight one more desperate and bloody battle."[75]

During the conference Sherman asked Lincoln if he had plans for the disbandment of the defeated rebel armies and the treatment of their political leaders. Lincoln replied that all he wanted was the defeat of the rebel army and the return of the men to their homes and work. The president assured Sherman that "in his mind he was ready for the civil reorganization of affairs at the South as soon as the war was over"; and, according to the general, "he distinctly authorized me to assure Governor [Zebulon B.] Vance and the people of North Carolina that, as soon as the rebel armies laid down their arms, and resumed their civil pursuits, they would at once be guaranteed all their rights as citizens of a common country; and that to avoid anarchy the State government, with their civil functionaries, would be recognized by him."[76]

Sherman's recollections of this conference became important when, after Lincoln's death, the general offered peace terms to Gen. Joseph E. Johnston in North Carolina. Meeting Johnston near Durham Station on April 17-18, and following what he believed were the deceased president's instructions (he had been informed April 17 of Lincoln's assassination), Sherman went beyond military terms to provide the Southern states with what amounted to a peace treaty. This extraordinary agreement, which a surprised Johnston signed, provided for "the recognition, by the Executive of the United States, of the several State governments, [upon] their officers and Legislatures taking the oaths prescribed by the Constitution of the United States." The document indicated that "where conflicting State governments have resulted from the war, the legitimacy of all shall be submitted to the Supreme Court of the United States." In this provision, Sherman obviously had in mind states such as Louisiana, where Union governments had been formed and would contest the holdover rebel regimes for control. The "treaty" provided for the reestablishment of federal courts in the South and the restoration, "so far as the Executive can" guarantee, all political rights and rights of person and property, "as defined by the Constitution of the United States and of the States respectively." Such a provision, had it stood, conceivably could have led to the restoration of slave property as long as the Thirteenth Amendment remained unratified. The amendment's ratification by the requisite three-fourths of the states would have been problematical if the slavery-based Southern governments had been restored under Sherman's plan.[77]

Sherman's terms, however, exceeded Lincoln's intentions and stunned authorities in Washington and Republicans throughout the nation. Southern Unionists, who would be left in the lurch if the treaty stood, vehemently protested against it.[78] As a result President Johnson and his cabinet promptly repudiated the agreement and sent General Grant to Raleigh with instructions to order Sherman to dictate to Johnston the same surrender terms that Grant had given Lee, which he did on April 26.[79]

Chagrined by his treatment at Washington, particularly by Stanton's public disapproval, Sherman then and later denied that he had exceeded

Lincoln's instructions. In addition to what he understood to be the president's directives to him aboard the *River Queen,* the general also was influenced by national newspaper reports of Lincoln's efforts, which were subsequently withdrawn, to arrange for the reassembling of Virginia's Confederate legislature. For example, on April 14, the *New York Herald* reported that the president had invited "the leading rebels of Virginia, from the Governor down, . . . to meet in council in Richmond, to deliberate upon the ways and means for the restoration of the State to the blessings of the Union. . . . The assemblage thus convened cannot fail to be influenced by the generous spirit of President Lincoln." In his meeting with Grant in Raleigh, Sherman told the general-in-chief that he had been "guided in his negotiations with Johnston by what he thought was prescendents [*sic*] authorized by the President," including the call for the rebel legislature of Virginia to reconvene in Richmond. At the time of his April 18 agreement with Johnston, Sherman said that he did not know of Lincoln's withdrawal of the authority for the Virginia legislature to meet.[80]

Few actions of Lincoln were more misinterpreted or created as much opposition within his administration than his proffer to the rebel Virginia legislature to meet during the waning days of the war. The Virginia plan developed when the president visited Richmond on April 4-5, immediately after its capture, and met with the Confederate assistant secretary of war, John A. Campbell, a former U.S. Supreme Court justice and a participant in the Hampton Roads conference. General Godfrey Weitzel, the Federal commander in the city, also was present. Lincoln, in response to an inquiry by Campbell, which the president put in writing, indicated that "three things are indispensable" to peace. These were "the restoration of national authority," emancipation, and "no cessation of hostilities short of an end of the war, and the disbanding of all force hostile to the government." The president told Campbell that "if the war be now further persisted in, by those opposing the government," the confiscation and sale of rebel property to support the Federal forces "will be insisted on." He promised, however, that property confiscations, except for slave property, "will be remitted to the people of any State which shall now promptly, and in good faith, withdraw it's [*sic*] troops and other support, from further resistance to the government."[81]

To facilitate the withdrawal of Virginia's troops and end support for the Confederacy, Lincoln, at Campbell's suggestion, directed General Weitzel to permit "the gentlemen who have acted as the Legislature of Virginia" to assemble in Richmond. He told Weitzel that if "they attempt some action hostile to the United States," he was to "give them reasonable time to leave; & at the end of which time, arrest any who may remain."

The president instructed the general to show Campbell the message, but, anticipating opposition in Washington and in the army, he directed that it not be made public.[82] Lincoln later declared, according to Virginia Governor Pierpont, that the drafting of the order to Weitzel, "though short, gave me more perplexity than any other paper I ever drew up. I went to the boat at 7 o'clock, and worked at that proclamation [order] until 1 o'clock before I got it to suit me."[83]

Lincoln also informed Grant of his instructions to Weitzel. He indicated to the commanding general, who was chasing Lee's rag-tag army westward, that "I do not think it probable that anything will come" of the effort to recall the Virginia legislature; "but I have thought best to notify you, so that if you should see signs, you may understand them. From your recent despatches it seems that you are pretty effectually withdrawing the Virginia troops from opposition to the government. Nothing I have done, or probably shall do, is to delay, hinder, or interfere with you in your work."[84]

Despite the president's order to avoid public disclosure of the scheme, Weitzel directed his chief of staff, Gen. George F. Shepley, to publish the call for the legislature to assemble. As Weitzel later wrote, Shepley "looked at me with surprise and asked me was I doing this on my own responsibility. I informed him that I was not, but that I had an order" to call the legislature into session. Weitzel permitted his subordinate to read Lincoln's order, after which Shepley turned to him and remarked: "General, this is a political mistake. Don't you lose that letter, for if you do, your Major General's commission may not be worth a straw." The next day Shepley dutifully published in the Richmond press the call for the legislature to meet.[85]

On April 9, the day that Lee surrendered to Grant at Appomattox Court House, Lincoln returned to Washington. He found members of his Cabinet and Republicans in Congress—conservatives as well as Radicals—disturbed by his decision to permit the assembling of the rebel Virginia legislature. Members of the congressional Committee on the Conduct of the War, who were visiting Richmond on the day that Weitzel's call appeared in the local newspaper, were "thunderstruck" and "disgusted by the display of misguided magnanimity" on the part of the president.[86] Critics vehemently complained that his action recognized rebel authority and repudiated Pierpont's Union government. They also expressed fear that once the rebels were in control of the Virginia government, they would continue their hostility toward the Union. If his decision stood, it would create a dangerous precedent for reconstruction in all of the defeated South. Already five or six members of the old legislature had returned to Richmond, and a few days later they were joined by a half dozen more members.[87]

On the defensive, Lincoln explained to Secretary of Navy Welles that the rebels were too badly beaten to embarrass the government. "His idea was," according to Welles, "that the members of the legislature, comprising the prominent and influential men of their respective counties, had better come together and undo their own work." Lincoln, Welles wrote, "felt assured" that the Virginia legislators would act responsibly. He told the Navy Secretary that civil governments must be reestablished as soon as possible; "there must be courts, and law, and order, or society would be broken up, the disbanded armies would turn into robber bands and guerrillas."[88]

Faced with criticism from his party, Lincoln reconsidered his decision regarding the Virginia legislature. On April 10 he summoned Pierpont to Washington for a conference. During a three and one-half hour meeting, the president reassured the apprehensive governor that his intention in permitting the recall of the rebel legislature was not to repudiate the Restored Government: "Your government at Alexandria was fully in my mind" when drawing up the plan for the assembling of members of the rebel legislature. These men were "to do a single act—that was to withdraw the army of Virginia . . . from the field; and with this act I expected their powers as legislators to cease." Lincoln assured Pierpont that his object in drafting the order to General Weitzel "was so to draw [it] as to give no authority to do anything except to take the rebel soldiers out of the field, and at the same time, in no way compromise your position as Governor of the Restored Government of Virginia." Lincoln admitted that "if I had known that General Lee would surrender so soon I would not have issued the proclamation [order]."[89]

Still, the president hesitated in revoking his order to Weitzel. On the morning of April 12 he sent a telegram to the general inquiring, "Is there any sign of the rebel Legislature coming together . . . ? If there is any such sign, inform me what it is; if there is no such sign you may as [well] withdraw the offer." Later that day Lincoln received from Weitzel a letter that John A. Campbell had written him. Campbell, who had suggested the convening of the Old Dominion legislature, coolly informed Weitzel that the president intended for the Virginia assembly to negotiate with Federal authorities "the questions that are supposed to require adjustment." Campbell also recommended that the same arrangement should be offered to the South Carolina legislature, which was scheduled to meet in its regular session in May. He even implied that the Emancipation Proclamation might not be constitutionally valid.[90]

That same day Lincoln, angered by Campbell's effrontery, wired Weitzel to revoke his order for the Virginia legislature to meet. Campbell, the president indignantly declared, assumes . . . that I have called the insurgent Legislature of Virginia together, as the rightful Legislature of the State, to settle all differences with the United States. I have done no such thing. I spoke of them not as a Legislature, but as 'the gentlemen who have *acted* as the Legislature of Virginia in support of the rebellion.' I did this on purpose to exclude the assumption that I was recognizing them as a *rightful* body. I dealt with them as men having power *de facto* to do a specific thing, to wit, 'to withdraw the Virginia troops, and other support from resistance to the General Government.'

General Grant, the president said, "has since captured the Virginia troops, so that giving a consideration for their withdrawal is no longer applicable, let my letter [order] to you, and the paper to Judge Campbell both be withdrawn. . . . Do not now allow the [Virginians] to assemble; but if any have come, allow them safe-return to their homes."[91] Sherman in Raleigh never received a similar message from Lincoln clarifying the status of North Carolina's rebel government as the war ended, a failure that caused confusion over surrender terms and humiliation for the conqueror of Georgia and the Carolinas.

With the war rushing to a close, Lincoln knew that in order to avoid anarchy he had to arrange for the quick resumption of Federal authority in Southern states where no loyal governments existed. Even in those states with reorganized governments—Louisiana, Arkansas, Tennessee, and Virginia—he realized that Federal forces were still necessary to suppress guerrillas and restore law and order to the countryside. Lincoln understood that his Proclamation of Amnesty and Reconstruction, though its spirit of conciliation and principle of self-government should be retained, no longer might fit the urgent need for federal action to reestablish authority in the defeated South.

Along with many members of Congress, Lincoln had become increasingly concerned about the poverty and insecurity of uprooted whites and newly freed blacks in the South. Social order and loyalty to the Union could not be easily restored as long as such conditions existed. On March 3 he had signed into law a bill establishing the Bureau of Refugees, Freedmen, and Abandoned Lands in the War Department for the purpose of aiding displaced Southerners, both black and white. The Freedmen's Bureau, as it became known, also could assign and rent for three years abandoned lands to loyal refugees and former slaves. The bill provided that at the end of the three-year period "the occupants of any parcels so assigned may purchase the land and receive such title thereto as the United States can convey."[92] Despite his deep reservations regarding the extension of federal power, Lincoln approved the bill because of the tremendous human problems created by the war. Emancipation, which the president had justified on grounds of military necessity to suppress the rebellion, produced unprecedented social problems that needed the immediate attention of federal authorities. The bill met Lincoln's constitutional concerns, since the Bureau would have a temporary existence (for one year after the war) with no political authority; in addition, its tenuous land provision would not conflict with his opposition to the permanent confiscation of property.

As Confederate resistance collapsed, Lincoln received no end of advice regarding reconstruction. In early April he was visited by a number of prominent men, evidently of his party, who recommended that he continue his conciliatory policy and arrange for the quick restoration of the Southern states to the Union. They were pleased with his response. "He makes no secret of his disposition to waive everything but the Union and emancipation for the sake of restoring tranquility," a Washington correspondent reported.[93] Powerful Republican newspapers also urged the president to maintain his lenient course toward the South. The Southern surrender, the *New York Times* declared, should be "unconditional" only "so far as the maintenance of the National authority is concerned" and the abolition of slavery. Otherwise, as Lincoln "has repeatedly assured the people of the South," the defeated section should be a full partner in the postwar adjustment. The *Times* recommended that the president issue a proclamation announcing the rebellion at an end and, reflecting New York's keen commercial interest in the South, declaring the reopening of the channels of trade in the region.[94] The *Baltimore American and Commercial Advertiser,* which had supported Lincoln in 1864, strongly argued that a policy of sectional reconciliation was essential for "the speedy restoration of our national unity."[95]

The *Washington Chronicle* warned that a proscriptive policy toward former Confederates as some Radicals advocated "will nurse the seeds of discontent, and necessitate the maintenance of a large standing army to prevent future revolts."[96] Likewise, Horace Greeley's *New York Tribune* demanded "a speedy and thorough reestablishment of Peace and return to the ways of Industry and Thrift under the aegis of the Union," free of the source of sectional passion—slavery. The *Tribune* apparently assumed that with the end of slavery and the suppression of the rebellion no further federal action was required to make black freedom a reality.[97]

The *Chicago Tribune,* arguably the leading Republican newspaper in the Midwest, joined the chorus supporting a conciliatory policy toward the defeated South by recommending that Lincoln extend amnesty to all rebels except for "miscreants who, by violating the laws of war, have merited the punishment due to the common enemies of mankind." The *Tribune* indicated that "the spirit of the loyal States will not call for further vengeance than the Almighty [had already] visited in full measure upon the authors and promoters of the rebellion." Though their freedom and property (except for slaves) should be returned to them, rebel leaders should never again be permitted to hold state or federal office, the *Tribune* declared. The question of black suffrage should be left to the restored state governments.[98]

With growing support for Lincoln's inaugural plea of malice toward none and charity for all, many Radicals and abolitionists feared that leading rebels would be returned to power and black rights would be ignored after the war. On the day after Appomattox, Ben Butler, who had been removed from military command by Lincoln in January after the botched Fort Fisher campaign, made an impromptu speech from the balcony of Willard's Hotel in Washington in which he urged the disfranchisement of rebel leaders and "equal rights for the black man under the law."[99] At a meeting with the president, an unnamed Radical senator reportedly became so upset with Lincoln's talk of clemency for rebel leaders that when he left the room he indignantly exclaimed to all who could hear: "Lincoln is a damned fool. He has no spirit, and [is] as weak as an old woman." This senator declared that he would not be surprised if Lincoln after the war "filled the public offices with a horde of these infernal rebels."[100] On April 11 Chief Justice Salmon P. Chase met in Baltimore with Henry Winter Davis and other Maryland Radicals.[101] Later that day he wrote the president insisting that it would be "a crime & a folly if the colored loyalists of the rebel states shall be left to the control of restored rebels" who would perpetuate "new calamities" upon them and upon white Unionists. Significantly, Chief Justice Chase, whose radicalism was well-established, did not recommend that Lincoln impose black suffrage upon the Southern states. He argued instead that black rights could be achieved if the president impressed upon the restored Southern legislatures—and Louisiana's in particular—that the extension of such rights to blacks was "essential to the future tranquility of the country" as well as to their own security.[102]

Before receiving Chase's letter, on the evening of April 11, Lincoln, from the balcony of the White House, made his last public statement regarding reconstruction. As it turned out, this would be his last public address of any kind. In the audience that day was John Wilkes Booth, who, according to Lewis Paine, one of the conspirators against the president, muttered as he walked away: "That is the last speech he will ever make."[103] After announcing that he soon would call for a period of thanksgiving to

God for the wonderful success of Union arms, the president told the crowd that reconstruction was now "pressed much more closely upon our attention." He warned that the issue "is fraught with great difficulty," because "there is no authorized organ for us to treat with" in the rebel states. "We simply must begin with, and mould from, disorganized and discordant elements. Nor is it a small additional embarrassment that we, the loyal people, differ among ourselves as to the mode, manner, and means of reconstruction."[104]

Lincoln blamed these disagreements on the Radicals who criticized his reconstruction plan and specifically his Louisiana government. "As a general rule," he declared, "I abstain from reading the reports of attacks upon myself, wishing not to be provoked by that which I cannot properly offer an answer. . . . However, it comes to my knowledge that I am much censured" for setting up and sustaining the Louisiana government. Lincoln reminded his audience that in December 1863, he had announced a reconstruction plan that, if adopted by a Southern state, would be recognized by him. "I distinctly stated that this was not the only plan which might possibly be acceptable; and I also distinctly protested that the Executive claimed no right to say when, or whether members should be admitted to seats in Congress from such States." The president indicated that all members of his Cabinet, including Chase, had "approved every part and parcel of the plan." He would change his policy "whenever I shall be convinced that keeping it is adverse to the public interest. But I have not yet been so convinced."[105] The debate over whether the so-called seceded states were in or out of the Union was "good for nothing at all—a merely pernicious abstraction." All loyal men agreed that the Southern states, as Lincoln had said many times, "are out of their proper practical relation with the Union; and that the sole object of the government, civil and military, in regard to those States is to again get them into that proper practical relation. . . . Finding themselves safely at home, it would be utterly immaterial whether they had ever been abroad."[106]

The president then launched into a long defense of reconstruction in Louisiana. He began by conceding that

> the amount of constituency . . . on which the new Louisiana government rests, would be more satisfactory to all, if it contained fifty, thirty, or even twenty thousand, instead of only twelve thousand, as it does. It is also unsatisfactory to some that the elective franchise is not given to the colored man. I would myself prefer that it were now conferred on the very intelligent, and on those who serve our cause as soldiers. Still the question

is not whether the Louisiana government, as it stands, is quite all that is desirable. The question is 'Will it be wiser to take it as it is, and help to improve it; or to reject, and disperse it?' Can Louisiana be brought into proper practical relation with the Union *sooner* by *sustaining*, or by *discarding* her new State Government?

Twelve thousand Louisiana voters, Lincoln continued, representing "the rightful political power of the State," had done "nearly all the things the nation wants—and they ask the nations [*sic*] recognition, and it's [*sic*] assistance to make good their committal." They had "held elections, organized a State government, adopted a free-state constitution, giving the benefit of public schools equally to black and white, and empowering the Legislature to confer the elective franchise upon the colored man. Their Legislature has already voted to ratify the constitutional amendment recently passed by Congress, abolishing slavery throughout the nation." Lincoln contended that "if we reject, and spurn them, we do our utmost to disorganize and disperse them." Such a course would also say to black Louisianans: "This cup of liberty which these, your old masters, hold to your lips, we will dash from you, and leave you to the chances of gathering the spilled and scattered contents in some vague and undefined when, where, and how. . . . If, on the contrary, we recognize, and sustain the new government of Louisiana the converse of all this is made true." Both whites and blacks, the president argued, would be "inspired with vigilance, and energy, and daring, to the same end" after the war. It was at this point in his April 11 address that Lincoln used the frequently quoted chicken-egg metaphor, in the form of a question, to indicate his support for Louisiana's reconstruction government. "Concede that the new government of Louisiana is only to what it should be as the egg is to the fowl, we shall sooner have the fowl by hatching the egg than by smashing it?"[107]

The president announced that "what has been said of Louisiana will apply generally" to Southern states where reorganization had not begun. "Yet so great peculiarities pertain to each state; and such important and sudden changes occur in the same state; and withal, so new and unprecedented is the whole case, that no exclusive, and inflexible plan can safely be prescribed as to details and collatterals [*sic*]." For these reasons, the policy for each state must be flexible while the "important principles"—emancipation and loyalty—"may, and must, be inflexible." In conclusion, he indicated that "it may be my duty to make some new announcement to the people of the South."[108] Lincoln probably had in mind a declaration extending temporary military control to states where no loyal governments existed, a purpose that became clearer when he met with his Cabinet three days later. Once military pacification had been completed, political reorganization, as was occurring in Louisiana, Arkansas, Tennessee, and Virginia, would be initiated by Southern Unionists who had never faltered in their loyalty and who now promised to abolish slavery.

The ending of the war had not changed Lincoln's fundamental approach to the restoration of the Southern states to the Union. The president's wartime reconstruction policy was based on his conviction that rebel leaders had subverted the state governments, thus making it his constitutional responsibility, not that of Congress, to provide for the restoration of a republican form of government in each state. His definition of republicanism was broad, requiring in the beginning of the war only the organization of loyal civil governments. These governments would be formed by a "tangible nucleus" of Southern Unionists and would meet the president's important test for self-government in the South. Civil reorganization, according to Lincoln, should occur as soon as possible after the suppression of rebel arms. Federal military commanders were to aid local Unionists and jump-start the process of reconstruction. However, they were not to interfere in the actual work of reorganization nor with the elections of delegates to state conventions or offices in the new governments. Lincoln frequently became annoyed with Southern Unionists and military commanders, particularly in Louisiana and Tennessee, when factional disputes, confusion regarding authority, and fears of a rebel resurgence forestalled action on reconstruction. At first, in 1862, Lincoln, using the threat of black freedom contained in his preliminary Emancipation Proclamation, urged Unionists in Federal-controlled districts to hold elections for seats in Congress even before their state governments had been reorganized. This policy, in effect, put the cart before the horse in the reconstruction process and resulted in sham elections in several occupied areas. Congress rejected most of these newly elected Southern congressmen; a notable exception was the seating of Michael Hahn and Benjamin F. Flanders after 60 percent of the 1860 electorate in two Louisiana districts voted in an 1862 congressional election. After Lincoln issued his Emancipation Proclamation, he wisely ceased to advocate congressional elections before civil governments had been formed.

Disappointed with the slow pace of reorganization in the South and persuaded that the time was ripe for a new presidential initiative, in late 1863 Lincoln issued his Proclamation of Amnesty and Reconstruction. Lincoln indicated to Thomas Cottman of Louisiana, as well as to others, that, though he found certain points "indispensible" to reunion, he did not put forth his reconstruction plan expecting "exact conformity." Moreover, he wanted "to avoid the substance and the appearance of dictation" in the reorganization of the state governments.[109] In outlining his new plan, Lincoln added emancipation to Union as an indispensable point for the reestablishment of republican forms of government in the Southern states. The president insisted on the antislavery requirement, as he said, to give his Emancipation Proclamation its "fullest effect." He declared that to abandon the liberated blacks, including thousands serving in the Union army, "would be not only to relinquish a lever of power but would also be a cruel and an astounding breach of faith."[110] Lincoln's antislavery sentiments, however tempered by his constitutional and political conservatism, had grown during the war, impelling him by late 1863 to work for the complete eradication of the slave institution, which "somehow," he declared, had caused the sectional conflict and would continue to be a threat to the Union if it were not destroyed. Still, Lincoln's actions against slavery were war measures that, he greatly feared, might be later declared unconstitutional by federal courts. This explains in part his almost desperate proposal in February 1865 to compensate Southerners for their slaves if their states would ratify the Thirteenth Amendment. Lincoln calculated that the requisite three-fourths of the states for ratification might not be found unless restored Southern states approved the amendment. The compensation scheme, which his Cabinet unanimously opposed and which he immediately dropped, also was designed to make emancipation palatable to white Southerners, thereby reducing their will to continue the war.

Though committed to freedom in his reconstruction plan, Lincoln announced that in order to cushion the social impact of emancipation he would accept any state provision establishing a "temporary arrangement," or apprenticeship system, for freed blacks. He also stipulated in his 1863 reconstruction plan that the reorganized states should provide for the education of blacks, a vague requirement that all of his Southern governments failed to fulfill. Lincoln recommended but did not require the enfranchisement of the "very intelligent" blacks and those who had served in the army. This suggestion, which was made only to Louisiana Unionists and reaffirmed in his April 11, 1865, address defending his Louisiana policy, was ignored. Before the end of the war, all four reorganized states (Virginia, Louisiana, Tennessee, and Arkansas) had abolished slavery in their fundamental law but at the same time were moving toward the creation of halfway stations between slavery and freedom for blacks, a direction that Lincoln made no real effort to check. However much he might have preferred civil and political rights for blacks, as far as Lincoln was concerned, the position of African Americans in freedom should be determined by loyal state and local authorities. The president's deference to the reorganized governments on this issue of black rights in the postwar South can clearly be seen in his response to the Radical Republican demand that he reject the Louisiana constitution because it did not enfranchise blacks or provide for equal rights. Lincoln refused to interfere; indeed, he vigorously defended the new constitution, observing that it was "better for the poor black man than we have in Illinois."[111] Furthermore, when the Louisiana legislature met in late 1864, Lincoln did not ask the lawmakers to extend the ballot to blacks, though the state constitution had granted them the authority to do so.

The fact that former rebels under his liberal amnesty and pardon policy would become a majority soon after the war, and thus might threaten local Unionist control, did not seem unduly to concern Lincoln. In 1863 the president, before announcing his reconstruction plan, had briefly raised the issue with John Hay, his secretary, when he asked: how could "the rebellious populations" be prevented "from overwhelming and outvoting the loyal minority" in the South?[112] Lincoln provided no answer to this question. Neither did he address the problem in his Proclamation of Amnesty and Reconstruction nor in his April 11, 1865, speech on reconstruction. With Unionists like Hahn, Pierpont, Hamilton, Murphy, and Brownlow in control in their states and supported by his administration, Lincoln evidently expected little trouble from rank-and-file Southerners after the war. Despite his comment to Hay, Lincoln thought that most white Southerners had been reluctant participants in secession and, having suffered from a rebel tyranny and its devastating results, would accept, if not welcome, the restoration of the Union and the self-government that his reconstruction plan provided. He believed that the "good sense" of the Southern people would prevail once they were free from the passions of the war and the coercive power of Davis's army. Southerners would take the loyalty oath in good faith, accept emancipation, and follow the lead of Union authorities. Furthermore, Lincoln reasoned, his liberal amnesty policy, guaranteeing the rights of citizens, including property except for slaves, and the early restoration of self-government would prevent die-hard rebel resistance and violence, the kind that plagued Missouri where a draconian state policy of denying rights to Confederates had been imposed.

Nevertheless, Lincoln, in the implementation of his amnesty and reconstruction policy during the war, permitted Southern Union authorities, if they found it necessary, to require a more stringent loyalty oath for voting than he prescribed. The reorganized governments in Louisiana and Arkansas, following Lincoln's wishes, adopted the president's loyalty oath for political participation. During his brief tenure, North Carolina Military Governor Stanly required no formal voting test. On the other hand, the Virginia state constitutional convention of 1864 and Military Governor Johnson of Tennessee imposed stringent oaths for voting designed to disfranchise many former rebels, despite the fact that they had taken Lincoln's oath. When conservative Unionists of Tennessee demanded that he disapprove Johnson's oath, Lincoln refused, explaining that it did not "deviate from my views . . . to any ruinous extent."[113] Except for Louisiana, where it failed, no movement was launched during the war in any of the Federal-occupied areas to permit black loyalists to vote.

Though Lincoln expressed his willingness to pardon freely those classes of high-ranking Confederates who were excluded from his general amnesty, he expected Southern Unionists to reorganize their governments in such a way as to prevent rebel leaders from regaining power in the South. As he told Johnson in 1863, the reestablishment of civil government in Tennessee "must not be such as to give control of the State . . . to the enemies of the Union. The whole struggle for Tennessee will have been profitless to both State and nation, if it so ends that Gov. Johnson is put down, and [rebel] Governor Harris is put up."[114] Still, Lincoln established no formal policy requiring the reorganized governments to prohibit former Confederate leaders from holding public office.

As the war came to an end, Radicals like Charles Sumner and George W. Julian became increasingly alarmed by Lincoln's reconstruction policy. They knew that it had broad support in the North.[115] The president's let-alone approach flew in the face of what Radicals believed was a federal responsibility for black freedom. Radicals vehemently objected to Lincoln's willingness to leave the issues of rights and racial adjustment to the restored state and local governments. They sought the disfranchisement of many former Confederates, and the enfranchisement of blacks as a matter of equal justice for the freedmen and security for the Union. Radicals wanted federal protection for black civil rights in the defeated South; only a few advocated the confiscation of rebel property and its division among blacks and white Unionists. In early 1865 they vainly focused their attention on the extension of the ballot to the freedmen, hoping that political rights would provide the lever for the enactment of state legislation to guarantee other fundamental rights. However, at the time of Lee's surrender at Appomattox, Radicals understood that as long as Lincoln controlled reconstruction policy their objectives in the South would be thwarted.

Many historians have indicated that Lincoln's Emancipation Proclamation represented a radical change for the South and the nation. In broad historical perspective this is true. But in the context of the Civil War's virtually unlimited potential for revolutionary change in the Southern racial and social structure, Lincoln's emancipation and reconstruction policies were conservative. While eliminating the cause of the sectional conflict (slavery), the president's policies acted in a major way to restrain the unsettling forces released by the destructive war and to maintain almost intact the antebellum federal system. Even when the Radicals, along with other aroused Republicans, triumphed over the inept President Andrew Johnson in 1866 and 1867, their changes in reconstruction policy did not revolutionize the South or its race relations, though many white Southerners thought otherwise. It is reasonable to conclude that Lincoln's conservative leadership prevented a truly radical reordering of the South when it was most vulnerable to revolutionary changes—during the war and in the moment of defeat.

Radical Republican anger toward Lincoln was due to his failure to understand the need for thoroughgoing changes in the South before it was too late. Black freedom, as well as a true and lasting Union settlement, was at stake in the direction that reconstruction would follow immediately after the war. Radicals like Sumner and Julian believed that with the return of the rebel majority white Southern Unionists would find it impossible to protect blacks or themselves if Lincoln's policy prevailed.

Julian later wrote that "aside from Mr. Lincoln's known policy of tenderness to the Rebels . . . his well-known views on the subject of reconstruction were as distasteful as possible to radical Republicans." The president's April 11, 1865, address, Julian lamented, reaffirmed "his adherence to the plan of reconstruction announced by him in December, 1863," which provided that "reconstruction in the rebel States was to be inaugurated and carried on by those only who were qualified to vote under the Constitution and laws of these States as they existed prior to the Rebellion. Of course the negroes of the South would have no voice in framing the institutions under which they were to live." Julian regretfully concluded that Lincoln, in essence, had settled the question of black political rights, leaving the matter to the reorganized state governments.[116]

Black spokesmen deplored the president's leniency toward returning rebels and vainly appealed to the Republican Congress to assume control of reconstruction policy. The *New Orleans Tribune*, though admitting that "magnanimity and amnesty are noble things," admonished Congress to "retain the power in your hands. Do not allow yourselves to be deceived by wolves in sheep's clothing. Look at Louisiana and Arkansas [where] the perjured rebels, the persecutors of negroes, the slave-drivers, the Confederate officers (their hands still dripping with the blood of your sons and brothers) [have been] intrusted with the important legislative, civil and judicial offices of the State government. The old spirit of slaveocracy is still alive."

Former rebels, the *Tribune* charged, were determined under the current policy "to perpetuate slavery in disguise or to maintain an apprenticeship [that was] repugnant to our republican institutions." This newspaper advocated black suffrage as a protection for freedom and loyalty in the South. It also urged the enforcement of the Confiscation laws against wealthy rebels, insisting that Lincoln's amnesty policy should not prevent the seizure of Southern property.[117]

Three days after his April 11 reconstruction address, Lincoln met with his Cabinet to begin planning for the transition from war to peace. An extended discussion developed regarding the restoration of communications and trade with the Southern states. When nothing could be resolved, the president referred the matter to the secretaries of Treasury, War, and Navy, and told them that he would be satisfied with any decisions that they made.[118]

Secretary of War Stanton then presented to the Cabinet a "rough plan" for the appointment of a military governor for Virginia and North Carolina, whose responsibility would be to restore order and initiate the return of civil rule. According to Secretary of Navy Welles, who provided the only first-hand account of the meeting, Stanton reminded the Cabinet of the president's "frequent recurrence to the necessity of establishing civil governments and preserving order in the rebel States" as soon as possible. For the purpose of having something practical to discuss, Stanton said that he had drawn up his plan and given it to the president the day before the meeting.[119]

Lincoln informed the Cabinet that he had not had time to give much attention to Stanton's proposal, but he believed that it was substantially the plan discussed in earlier Cabinet meetings, although "some modifications" in Stanton's draft were probably necessary. When several members protested the inclusion of Virginia in the plan, since it would undermine the authority of the Pierpont government, Lincoln remarked that this objection had already occurred to him. "We must not," Welles recalled Lincoln as saying, "stultify ourselves as regards Virginia, but we must help her." The Cabinet agreed that in North Carolina, presumably after a military or provisional governor had restored order, a loyal government was to be organized and the state reestablished in its proper relations to the Union.[120] The North Carolina model evidently could be applied to other Southern states where reorganized governments did not exist.

The president directed Stanton to revise his plan to exclude Virginia and also make other changes that might be necessary. He asked the Secretary of War to have a draft ready for discussion and action at the regular meeting of the Cabinet on April 18. In a pointed aside, Lincoln remarked that it was providential that Congress was not in session to embarrass the work of restoration. Citing the criticism in Congress of the Louisiana government, the president, according to Welles, declared that "there was too much of a desire on the part of some of our very good friends to be masters, to interfere with and dictate to those States, to treat the people not as fellow citizens; there was too little respect for their rights." Lincoln repeated what he had said in his April 11 address regarding black suffrage in Louisiana. He "wished" that the Louisiana government "had permitted negroes who had property, or could read, to vote"; but this was a question that they must decide for themselves.[121] In what would be his last meeting with his Cabinet, Lincoln gave no indication that he was prepared to change his reconstruction policy.

One hour after the Cabinet meeting, Lincoln met for twenty minutes with Vice President Johnson.[122] No record of their discussion exists, though it is reasonable to assume that they talked about the restoration of Tennessee to the Union now that the Brownlow government had been inaugurated. On the same day he responded to a letter from James H. Van Alen of New York, a former general, who evidently had warned the president against attempts on his life and indicated that Northern conservatives supported his reconstruction policy. "I intend to adopt the advice of my friends and use due precaution" to avoid assassination, Lincoln wrote. He thanked Van Alen "for the assurance you give me that I shall be supported by conservative men like yourself, in the efforts I make to restore the Union, so as to make it, to use your language, a *Union of hearts and hands as well as of States.*"[123] The Van Alen letter may have been the last letter Lincoln ever wrote. That evening an assassin's bullet ended the life of "the good and gentle, as well as truly great, man," who had led the Union through its most difficult days and had labored hard for a rapid restoration of the wayward South.

Epilogue

The spirit of conciliation that Lincoln had successfully cultivated during the closing days of the war was shattered by the bullet from John Wilkes Booth's derringer. Two days after Lincoln's death, the *Washington Chronicle* discerned that "the indignation and horror created by this foul murder will serve, more than anything else could possibly do, to destroy the feeling of commiseration and brotherly love for the misguided people of the South, and the policy of magnanimity toward the leaders of the rebellion, which had taken root in the North."[1] The spirit of vengeance that swept the North following Lincoln's murder greatly complicated postwar reconstruction. Most Northerners believed that the assassination and simultaneous attempt on the life of William H. Seward were part of a vast rebel conspiracy to avenge Confederate defeat. A foreign observer summed up the impact of the assassination when he wrote: "Vengeance on the rebel leaders is the universal cry heard from one end of the country to the other. Lincoln's recommendations are forgotten."[2]

The new president, Andrew Johnson, during the first days after the assassination further inflamed passions by echoing the cry for vengeance. On several occasions he exclaimed that "treason is a crime" and rebel leaders should be hanged. Northern conservatives, and even a few Radicals like Sumner, who had supported a stringent reconstruction policy, cringed when they heard Johnson's rhetorical call for rebel blood.[3] As Orville Browning, a close conservative friend of Lincoln wrote, the assassination "must, necessarily, greatly inflame and exasperate the minds of the people," bringing down their wrath not only upon Southerners but also upon "those among us who have been suspected of sympathy with the rebellion, and hostility to our government. This would be followed by anarchy and the wildest scenes of confusion and blood-shed, ending in military Despotism."[4] Conservatives who had opposed Lincoln now proclaimed his "sterling excellencies" and expressed their fears that worse would occur at the hands of Johnson and a vengeful Congress. Robert C. Winthrop, the Boston Brahmin who had made the most effective McClellan speeches in the 1864 campaign, wrote a friend that "Lincoln had displayed great moderation and magnanimity since his re-election" and had clearly set a conservative course for postwar reconstruction, but the assassination had so inflamed the victorious North that it would be impossible for the new administration to continue Lincoln's Southern policy.[5]

In Washington, Republican Henry L. Dawes, a Lincoln leader in the House of Representatives, was appalled to hear some Radicals express pleasure that Lincoln no longer was president. On the morning of Lincoln's death, Senator Benjamin F. Wade, according to Dawes, clasped Johnson's hand and exclaimed: "I thank God you are here. Mr. Lincoln had too much of human kindness in him to deal with these infamous traitors, and I am glad that it has fallen into your hands to deal out justice to them."[6] Still later in the day, George W. Julian, an Indiana congressman, attended a meeting of members of his Radical faction in which "hostility toward Lincoln's policy of conciliation and contempt for his weakness were undisguised; and the universal feeling among radical men here is that his death is a godsend." Julian concluded that the "dastardly attack upon Lincoln and Seward, the great leaders in the policy of mercy, puts to flight utterly every vestige of humanitarian weakness, and makes it seem that justice shall be done and the righteous ends of the war made sure."[7]

Many Republicans who had earlier endorsed Lincoln's conciliatory policy now demanded strong federal action to insure the preservation of Union victory in the South. George Templeton Strong, a prominent eastern Republican and an official in the U.S. Sanitary Commission, recorded in his diary that the mood toward the South in New York had been dramatically reversed by the assassination. On the day of Lincoln's death he attended a large meeting "at which there was no talk of concession and conciliation." The sentiment of the meeting was: "Let us henceforth deal with rebels as they deserved. The rose-water treatment does not meet their case." Strong further wrote: "I have heard it said fifty times today: 'These madmen have murdered the two best friends [New Yorkers assumed that Seward had been killed] that they had in the world.'"[8]

Three days after the president's death, the *Chicago Tribune* declared that Lincoln "had sought to conquer" the rebel leaders "by kindness and clemency, and to effect peace and reconcilement at the expense of justice and retribution. . . . They murdered their friend and intercessor who stood between them and the just wrath of the people." The *Tribune* predicted that, while Lincoln "whipped them gently with cords," Johnson "will scourge them with a whip of scorpions." This newspaper demanded that all authority in the rebel states be placed in the hands of Unionists and suggested that Congress at its next session pass a stringent law to provide for the permanent confiscation of the property of Confederate leaders. In addition, it suggested that Southern Unionists meet in state conventions and extend the ballot to blacks as an additional protection for their governments.[9] The *Washington Chronicle* also urged Southern Unionists to adopt black suffrage as a means to protect the truly loyal people in the South.[10]

Unlike the Radicals who had demanded federally imposed black suffrage, the *Tribune* and the *Chronicle* still insisted that the states should decide the question of political and civil rights for the freedmen. These Republican newspapers abandoned their preassassination position that former Confederates who took Lincoln's loyalty oath could immediately participate in their state's political reorganization. Now they insisted that Confederates be required to wait until loyal authority clearly had been reestablished before regaining their political rights. At least one departmental commander, Gen. George H. Thomas at Nashville, with the support of local Unionists, revoked Lincoln's amnesty proclamation in his district and required that all who sought to take the loyalty oath must be approved by his headquarters.[11]

Lincoln's tragic death stunned Southern blacks and white Unionists as much as it did their compatriots in the North. Like Northerners, many Southern loyalists believed that "the bloody minds of the rebel leaders concocted and procured the murder of the President."[12] The *Little Rock Unconditional Union* passionately exclaimed: "In this barbarous and inhumane act, we behold the culmination of that fiendish and malignant hate which has characterized the leaders of the rebellion from its inception to the present time. . . . Rebels have slain the greatest and best friend they had in the Republic." This newspaper's sister journal, the *Little Rock National Democrat,* denounced the assassination as "the most desperate act ever committed in the United States," and like Northern conservatives feared that it "may be the harbinger of awful scenes to follow."[13]

On the other hand, black spokesmen, though deploring the death of the man who had issued the Emancipation Proclamation, confidently predicted that the assassination would produce a more realistic and radical reconstruction policy. The *New Orleans Tribune* declared that "Abraham Lincoln, the honest, the good, the religious man, who did not understand . . . duplicity and trickery, believed in the protestations and solemn oaths of rebels. He was too confident, too lenient, and too mild." Just when "a generous and liberal peace" for the South was being agreed upon, the *Tribune* announced, "this great catastrophe" occurred, opening the eyes of Union men throughout the land. With the elevation of Andrew

Johnson, a radical Unionist, to the presidency, backed by an aroused Congress, "a new era, a radical era, for our glorious nation" will begin. Under Johnson, the Southern states will be readmitted to the Union only after they had adopted "a radical republican form of government," the central feature of which would be "universal suffrage."[14]

Southern towns that had been under Federal occupation were draped in mourning and businesses closed in honor of the fallen leader. As church bells tolled throughout the day, citizens in New Orleans, Natchez, Nashville, Little Rock, Memphis, and New Bern held memorial services for Lincoln. Union mourners respectfully referred to the martyred president as "our second Washington." Even small towns like Columbia, Shelbyville, and Fayetteville in Middle Tennessee, and Huntsville in Alabama held Unionist-sponsored meetings deploring the assassination.[15] Many former Confederates turned out for these rallies, motivated in part by concern for their future in the hands of an embittered Andrew Johnson and a vengeful Northern people. Confederates belatedly seemed to realize that Lincoln was not quite the villain they had believed. In Richmond a prominent Virginia Unionist reported that news of the assassination "has caused deep feeling of regret on all sides, more particularly on the part of those unfriendly to the Government heretofore, but now were satisfied to return and be loyal to the Government. I have never known such expressions of regret on all sides, and fears expressed that by the accession of President Johnston [*sic*] they will have a harder time of it."[16]

Southern white loyalists especially had lost a friend and a champion. Their future as well as that of reconstruction was now filled with great uncertainties. Though Johnson was a fellow Southerner, Unionists sensed that he possessed neither Lincoln's political stature nor his broad understanding of reconstruction.[17] Furthermore, many Unionists who were familiar with Johnson's history in Civil War Tennessee knew that the new president lacked the temperament to provide wise leadership for the difficult work ahead. More troubling for them was the fact that wartime Northern passions, which Lincoln had deftly held in check during the conflict's final phase, were released by the assassination. They feared loss of control of reconstruction, along with the control of the former slaves to unfriendly Radicals in Congress, an eventuality that Lincoln had prevented.

Most Unionists expected their reorganized state governments to provide for the political proscription of Confederate leaders, freedom but not equal rights for blacks, and an early restoration of the Southern states to the Union accompanied by the immediate seating of their representatives in Congress. At the time of his death, Lincoln differed with them in his support for limited black suffrage, particularly for Louisiana, and the early restoration of rights for ex-rebels who would take his loyalty oath. But Southern Unionists had little reason to believe that Lincoln, based on his policy during the war, would go beyond the bounds of persuasion and impose his views upon them after the conflict.

Lincoln's unwillingness to dictate to the restored loyal governments in the South does not mean that had he lived he would have been a negligible influence on reconstruction in those states. The Illinoisan's exalted standing with Southern Unionists and his experience in dealing with them to achieve his purposes (for example, the rather dramatic acceptance of emancipation by many formerly proslavery Unionists) would have produced changes in the South different from those that occurred under Johnson's administration. Lincoln, free of the heavy demands of the war, would have paid closer attention than Johnson to the postwar plight of the freed blacks and white Unionists. His influence on the side of bona fide freedom for blacks would have prevented the kind of racially discriminatory laws, or Black Codes, enacted by several of the Southern state governments after the war—laws that Johnson implicitly endorsed. Union leaders, who owed their success to the war president, could hardly have ignored his strong recommendations regarding state policies of national concern. Except for some Tennessee Unionists, Southern loyalists had no such bond with Johnson. Furthermore, as the victorious war leader, Lincoln's support of Unionists in positions of authority would have carried far more weight than Johnson's weak efforts to sustain them in the face of returning Confederates. Indeed, Lincoln would have exercised more influence over former Confederates, particularly ex-Whigs of his old party who had the support of the Southern masses immediately after the war, than Johnson, a former Democrat.[18] Though Lincoln had demonstrated his willingness to let bygones be bygones, he would have made clear his opposition to an early return of rebel leaders to political power, a position he had expressed during the war. Such a stance would have prevented the kind of rash pardoning that occurred under Johnson during the summer and fall of 1865, arousing the Republican majority in Congress against the new president. Lincoln thus would have avoided a major source of conflict with his party in Congress as well as with ardent Southern Unionists. This president's deft handling of the pardon issue would have virtually assured congressional acceptance of the Southern governments and their representatives, thus fulfilling his plan for the self-reconstruction of the Southern states.

The postwar history of the four states reorganized under Lincoln's tutelage demonstrates how reconstruction failed to achieve the promise of the war president. It also suggests what might have been had Booth's bullet gone astray. All four of the reorganized governments survived the war and maintained an existence, albeit a shaky one, until overturned (except for Tennessee) by congressional or military reconstruction in 1867 and 1868. The failure of presidential leadership in the postwar reconstruction of these states, particularly Louisiana, contributed significantly to the defeat of the Lincoln-initiated policy of self-reconstruction controlled by Southern Unionists.

Andrew Johnson, after a brief flirtation with the Radical Republicans, abandoned his fire and brimstone pronouncements against "traitors" and essentially adopted Lincoln's plan of reconstruction. The first step in this direction was the new president's executive order of May 9, 1865, recognizing the Restored Government of Virginia and directing that Governor Pierpont go to Richmond and assume control. Pierpont immediately stunned Virginia Unionists by seeking the advice of two former Confederate governors and having a rump legislative session repeal the 1864 provisions disfranchising rebels. When President Johnson did not respond to his inquiries regarding pardons for Confederate leaders, the governor simply endorsed all applications and sent them to Washington for approval. Despite his strong support for black freedom in 1863 and 1864 (but not black rights), Pierpont in 1865 rejected an African-American appeal for protection from violence and intimidation. The governor's flirtation with ex-Confederate Virginians was brief. When the General Assembly met in December 1865, it ignored his advice and adopted numerous reactionary measures, including the removal from office of Unionists who had served with Pierpont during the war. The governor soon realized that his faith in former rebels had been misplaced. The damage to the cause of postwar Unionism and black civil equality, however, had been done. Ironically in view of the Republican Congress's wartime recognition of the governor, in 1868 conservative Gen. John M. Schofield removed Pierpont from office under the authority of congressional or Republican reconstruction.[19]

Unlike Lincoln, President Johnson largely ignored reconstruction affairs in Arkansas. On July 8, 1865, Governor Isaac Murphy and other Unionists, having heard nothing from the new president, pleaded with Johnson to issue a proclamation declaring Arkansas "no longer in insurrection and counselling obedience to constitutions, laws and civil authorities." These Arkansans reported that peace had been restored to the state and local governments reorganized in almost all of the counties. They wrote Johnson that a want of confidence in the civil government, however, remained because the president had not officially recognized an end to the rebellion in Arkansas and Congress had not seated the state's senators and representatives. At the same time, these Unionists asked Johnson to retain Federal troops in the state in case they were needed "to suppress sporadic cases of violence and to aid the state & U S Civil authorities in the reestablishment of civil law."[20]

Johnson did not respond until October 30, informing Murphy then that "there will be no interference with your present organization of State Government." By this time the effort to seat the state's congressional delegation, which had been elected during the war, had become ensnared in the national debate over the president's reconstruction policy. When Congress met in December, the Arkansas claimants, along with those from the other former Confederate states, were denied seats. In August 1866, Arkansas conservatives, with Johnson's encouragement and with former rebels voting, swept Murphy's supporters from the legislature. Lacking any real authority, Murphy continued in office until April 1868, when he was replaced by Powell Clayton, the first governor elected under congressional reconstruction.[21]

Though Tennessee was the last of the Lincoln state governments to be organized, it proved to be the most durable. The Brownlow administration, which took office two weeks before Lincoln's assassination, survived the struggle over reconstruction policy in Washington by aligning with dominant Republicans in Congress. Brownlow and the Tennessee legislature adopted a radical policy of political proscription toward former rebels, one similar to what Johnson as military governor had supported but, ironically, as president had rejected. Old political wounds between Union Whigs and Democrats, which had not completely healed during the war, remained in 1865 and by 1866 had led to a bitter division between the Brownlow and Johnson forces. A further irony was the fact that after the war conservative Whigs, who generally had opposed Johnson's radical policies during the war, now supported by pardoned secession Democrats, provided most of the leadership for the president's faction in the state. Nevertheless, Brownlow radicals were on the winning side in the struggle for power in Washington, and when the legislature ratified the Fourteenth Amendment in 1866, Tennessee was readmitted to the Union by Congress and its representatives seated. It was the only state under presidential reconstruction to approve the amendment and thus to escape military reconstruction. In 1867 the Brownlow government, in order to satisfy its patrons in Congress and provide a counterweight to the restoration of former Confederates and conservatives to power, enfranchised blacks but provided few other rights for them.[22] The radical regime continued in control until 1869, when Brownlow resigned to take a seat in the U.S. Senate.

As throughout the war, national attention focused on Louisiana during Reconstruction. Sarcastically referred to as "Lincoln's model of reconstruction" by Wendell Phillips of Massachusetts, in March 1865, the reorganized Louisiana and New Orleans governments fell into the hands of ultraconservative Unionists led by J. Madison Wells, who became governor when Michael Hahn was elected to the U.S. Senate. Lincoln probably never knew of Wells's determination to undercut both the Hahn-Banks party in Louisiana and the radical Durant faction. Hardly had General Banks arrived in the state on April 21 to resume command of the military forces when he discovered that Wells was busy appointing "copperheads and returning rebels" to public office.[23] Banks, believing that he still had military authority in New Orleans, immediately removed Mayor Hugh Kennedy, a Wells appointee. Much to Banks's dismay, Gen. Edward R.S. Canby, overall commander in the Mississippi Valley and a foe of the Massachusetts general, reinstated Kennedy and on May 17 removed Banks from command.[24] Governor Wells now authorized elections in thirty-five Northern parishes that heretofore had been controlled by Confederate officers. Neither Wells nor the Federal military intervened to insure the legitimacy of the elections or the loyalty of the elected officials.[25]

Banks remained in New Orleans during the summer in an effort to rally opposition to the Wells regime. However, he approved of Johnson's proclamations establishing provisional governments in the South, believing that this action followed Lincoln's plan. "If we had urged [Johnson] to adhere to [Lincoln's policy], we should be all right now," Banks wrote on July 26, 1865. But congressional Radicals drove Johnson over to the Democratic side, according to the general, and Louisiana Unionists failed to urge Johnson to sustain his postwar proclamations by insisting on the exclusion of rebels from power.[26] Banks's efforts to organize an opposition to the Louisiana government was complicated by his rejection of an alliance with his old foes in the Durant faction and by the tacit support of Johnson for Governor Wells. A trip to Washington by Wells satisfied the governor that the president neither would interfere with his administration nor allow the military to intervene in civil affairs.[27] Still, reports from Banks, Michael Hahn, and other old Lincoln stalwarts that Wells not only was permitting ex-rebels to return to power, but also was violating provisions of the 1864 state constitution, caused concern at the White House. Instead of insisting that Wells abide by the Louisiana constitution and prevent a restoration of Confederates to positions of influence, on September 18 Johnson informed the governor that he should "act with promptness and decision and cause the work of reorganization to go forward without delay or hindrance." The president considered appointing a provisional governor for the state who would have extensive authority until a new civil government could be elected. But when senator-elect Hahn, fearing that Wells would be selected, took "decided grounds against the appointment," Johnson failed to act.[28]

Three days after receiving Johnson's message, Wells, who seemed genuinely to believe that former rebels were anxious to renew their allegiance and abide by the results of the war, called for a state election on November 6.[29] He followed his election proclamation with the organization of the state National Democratic party on a platform pledging "unqualified adhesion to the National Democracy, . . . the only agent by which Radicalism can be successfully met," and "emphatically" endorsing Johnson's policy toward the South. The platform also condemned the 1864 constitution as a fraud, but gave it *de facto* recognition pending the promulgation of a legitimate document. Wells was nominated for governor. The Conservative Union party, consisting of many former delegates to the 1864 state convention, endorsed Wells but proclaimed support for the wartime constitution. Durant radicals met, declared the election illegal, and announced that they would hold a "voluntary election" for a "territorial delegate" to be sent to Washington. A neo-Confederate party nominated former Governor Henry Watkins Allen, then in exile, to head their ticket.[30]

Wells easily won the election, and ultraconservatives gained control of the legislature. Congress, however, refused to seat either the newly elected representatives and senators from Louisiana or those from other former Confederate states.[31] The new Louisiana legislature adopted laws discriminating against blacks and took other actions that infuriated Republicans in Congress and their friends in Louisiana. Belatedly, Governor Wells, like Pierpont in Virginia, realized that he had been betrayed by former rebels and ultraconservatives. In early 1866, when Wells attempted with the support of General Canby to check neo-Confederate designs, the president sided with the governor's reactionary opponents who vigorously supported Johnson's war against congressional Radicals and his hostility to black rights. By the summer Wells and many conservative Unionists had joined with Louisiana radicals in a movement to reconvene the state convention of 1864 for the purpose of adopting black suffrage and disfranchising former Confederates in order to thwart reactionary control. The attempt of the convention to reassemble triggered the bloody New Orleans race riot of July 30, 1866, culminating in the deaths of three or four white Unionists and forty-six blacks.[32] The failure of presidential leadership in postwar Louisiana clearly had contributed to the political and racial setting for the riot as well as other brutal acts against blacks and Unionists.

The New Orleans disturbance and the suppression of Louisiana Unionists, along with the failure of Johnson's reconstruction program

elsewhere, led to the triumph of congressional Republicans and the imposition of military reconstruction upon the former Confederate states with
the exception of Tennessee. The new plan required black suffrage and the
temporary disfranchisement of former Confederate leaders. Presidential
reconstruction, based on an early reorganization of loyal governments and
a quick restoration of the states to the Union, had failed. The primary
causes of the failure were Johnson's unrealistic assessment of the political
situation in the South, his ineptitude and neglect of Southern affairs, and
his blind racism.

It is inconceivable that Abraham Lincoln, despite his wartime reluctance to dictate to loyal Southern governments, would have permitted
events to take the calamitous course that followed under Johnson. This
war president's confidence in the returning loyalty of Southerners would
have been sorely tested after the war by reports of defiance coming from the
South and repeated by many Northern Democrats. Lincoln, with his pulse
on conditions in the South and on the political mood in the North, would
have grasped the danger posed by former Confederates and, despite his
early willingness to pardon freely, would have warned Pierpont, Wells, and
other Southern governors of the deleterious consequences of hasty efforts
to secure pardons for defiant former rebel leaders who sought to undercut
the Union cause. He probably would have urged his Southern governments, while exercising clemency toward the masses, to withhold political
rights to leading insurgents until loyalty had been firmly established. Fearful of losing their property and other rights, former state and Confederate
leaders would have more quickly ceased their defiance, accepted postwar
realities, and adopted a low political profile until Southern Unionists and
Northerners were satisfied that they no longer posed a threat to loyal governments in the South or to the republic. Lincoln's position thus would
have made a difference in the Southern Unionist effort to maintain control
of the restored governments after the war and protect the fruits of Union
victory.

After a brief military occupation to restore order, Lincoln, whose
commitment to self-government within the traditional federal system was
strong, would have been reluctant to use national power in the South
unless appealed to by loyal officials to suppress disorders and threats against
their authority. Nevertheless, he would have clearly indicated to Southern
Union authorities, including leaders in state conventions and legislatures,
that he expected them to protect the fundamental civil rights of blacks and
their white supporters. Because Louisiana, unlike the other Southern states,
had a large literate and relatively affluent black middle class, Lincoln probably would have pressed the state's lawmakers to provide limited suffrage

for them. He might even have urged other reorganized governments to enfranchise blacks in order to safeguard the results of the war. Though Southern Unionists had demonstrated no important support for black rights, particularly political equality, they could hardly have failed to follow Lincoln's entreaties on fundamental rights for blacks. The consequences of losing this strong president's support would have been too great for Southern loyalists to risk defying his wishes.

Such a scenario suggests that the planned quick restoration of the Southern states to their "proper practical relation with the Union" would have been delayed. Nevertheless, Lincoln's conservative reconstruction policy, launched during the war first with the Restored Government of Virginia, then, in 1862, with the appointment of military governors in Federal-occupied states, and finally in late 1863 with his Proclamation of Amnesty and Reconstruction, would have remained essentially unchanged. This scenario also begs the question: if Lincoln had succeeded after the war in his self-reconstruction plan, would sufficient national support have existed to secure congressional legislation and constitutional amendments for the federal protection of black rights? Probably not. As did occur after the war and as Professor Kenneth M. Stampp has written, the Fourteenth and Fifteenth amendments, providing blacks with the ultimate promise of equal rights, "could have been adopted only under the conditions of radical reconstruction." These conditions were produced largely by the blunders of President Johnson and his Confederate-style governments in the South.[33] It is unlikely that Lincoln would have so blundered in his conduct of postwar affairs.

Lincoln, of course, did not survive Booth's attack, and historians can only speculate as to what postwar reconstruction would have been like under this great president's careful stewardship. Even if Lincoln had lived and set in motion a coherent, integrated program of self-reconstruction, unforeseeable contingencies, such as terror campaigns to undermine black freedom and loyal control, might have compelled him to adjust his Southern policy to meet new realities. Under the circumstances and with great reluctance he might have abandoned his aversion to the use of federal power to insure a true and lasting Union settlement in the South. Whatever the postwar exigencies might have been, it is still reasonable to assume that Abraham Lincoln would have been far more successful than Andrew Johnson in managing Southern affairs and gaining widespread support for his efforts to establish and sustain a loyal political reconstruction in the South, insure, at least for a time, bona fide freedom for blacks, and restore a nation where "the mystic chords of memory . . . will yet swell the chorus of Union."[34]

Notes

Introduction

1. Eric Foner, *Reconstruction: America's Unfinished Revolution, 1863-1877* (New York: Harper & Row, 1988), 36; David Donald, *Lincoln* (New York: Simon & Schuster, 1995), 561. See also Ted Tunnell, *Crucible of Reconstruction: War, Radicalism, and Race in Louisiana, 1862-1877* (Baton Rouge: Louisiana State Univ. Press, 1984), 4, for the view that Lincoln's Ten Percent Plan was "a war policy, not . . . a prescription for the postwar South."

2. William B. Hesseltine, *Lincoln's Plan of Reconstruction* (Tuscaloosa: Confederate, 1960), 46-47, 141 (quotation).

3. Kenneth M. Stampp, *The Era of Reconstruction, 1865-1877* (New York: Alfred A. Knopf, 1965), 48.

4. Herman Belz, *Reconstructing the Union: Theory and Policy during the Civil War* (Ithaca: Cornell Univ. Press, 1969); Hans L. Trefousse, *The Radical Republicans: Lincoln's Vanguard for Racial Justice* (New York: Alfred A. Knopf, 1969); Michael Les Benedict, *A Compromise of Principle: Congressional Republicans and Reconstruction, 1863-1869* (New York: W.W. Norton, 1974); LaWanda Cox, *Lincoln and Black Freedom: A Study in Presidential Leadership* (Columbia: Univ. of South Carolina Press, 1981); Peyton McCrary, *Abraham Lincoln and Reconstruction: The Louisiana Experiment* (Princeton: Princeton Univ. Press, 1978).

5. James M. McPherson, *Battle Cry of Freedom: The Civil War Era* (New York and Oxford: Oxford Univ. Press, 1988), 500 (quotation), 563, 565; Stephen B. Oates, *Abraham Lincoln: The Man Behind the Myths* (New York: Harper & Row, 1984), 136-37. See also James M. McPherson, "Lincoln and the Strategy of Unconditional Surrender," in *Lincoln, the War President: The Gettysburg Lectures,* ed. Gabor S. Boritt (New York and Oxford: Oxford Univ. Press, 1992), 47-48.

6. Harold M. Hyman, *A More Perfect Union: The Impact of the Civil War and Reconstruction on the Constitution* (New York: Alfred A. Knopf, 1973), 210-11, 281.

7. Second Inaugural Address, March 4, 1865, in *The Collected Works of Abraham Lincoln,* Roy P. Basler, ed. (Brunswick, N.J.: Rutgers Univ. Press, 1953-1955), 8:332, hereinafter cited as Basler, *CWL.*

8. Early in the war, Lincoln hoped that the formation of the Restored Government of Virginia at Wheeling would become a model for the restoration of

loyal governments in Tennessee and elsewhere. No other Southern states followed such a reconstruction formula.

9. Historians customarily use the uppercase when referring to Federal military forces during the Civil War and the lowercase for the federal government or its officials. I have followed this practice.

10. Most Southern blacks, of course, were loyal to the Union, especially after the Emancipation Proclamation, but they did not have political standing as did Southern whites.

11. Frank W. Klingberg, *The Southern Claims Commission* (Berkeley and Los Angeles: Univ. of California Press, 1955); Carl N. Degler, *The Other South: Southern Dissenters in the Nineteenth Century* (New York: Harper & Row, 1974; Richard N. Current, *Lincoln's Loyalists: Union Soldiers from the Confederacy* (Boston: Northeastern Univ. Press, 1992). See also my article "The Southern Unionist Critique of the Civil War," *Civil War History* 31 (March 1985): 39-56. Professor Current calculates that 104,000 Southerners from Confederate states joined the Union army. His figures include thirty thousand from Unionist western Virginia, which early in the war separated from Confederate Virginia and was controlled by Federal forces. Current probably also slightly overcounted the number of Union troops from Tennessee and Arkansas.

12. I also have chosen to refer to these loyalists as *conservatives,* though in the context of national politics they could be described as ultraconservatives. They differed, however, from the Northern Copperheads in that they favored no peace short of the suppression of the rebellion.

1. 1861: An Early Start

1. First Inaugural Address, final text, March 4, 1861, Basler, *CWL,* 4:264-65, 268. For an insightful account and analysis of Lincoln's inaugural address, see David M. Potter, *The Impending Crisis, 1848-1861,* completed and edited by Don E. Fehrenbacher (New York: Harper & Row, 1976), 566-70.

2. Daniel W. Crofts, *Reluctant Confederates: Upper South Unionists in the Secession Crisis* (Chapel Hill: Univ. of North Carolina Press, 1989), is an especially revealing account of Southern Unionism when Lincoln took office.

3. Basler, *CWL,* 4:262-64.

4. Ibid., 265-66, 270.

5. Ibid., 270-71.

6. Crofts, *Reluctant Confederates,* 34-36, 221-24, 245. Crofts attributes Lincoln's decision to appoint Gilmer to the lobbying efforts of William H. Seward and his alter ego Thurlow Weed.

7. Proclamation Calling Militia and Convening Congress, April 15, 1861, Basler, *CWL,* 4:331-32.

8. Delaware's decision to remain in the Union was never in doubt. Though a slaveholding state and hostile to Lincoln and the Republicans, its economy was oriented toward Pennsylvania. On January 3, 1861, the Delaware legislature unanimously rejected secession.

9. Abraham Lincoln to Winfield Scott, April 25, 27, 1861, Basler, *CWL,* 4:344, 347; William B. Hesseltine, *Lincoln and the War Governors* (Gloucester, Mass.: Peter Smith, 1972), 154-56; Mark E. Neely Jr., *The Fate of Liberty: Abraham Lincoln and Civil Liberties* (New York and Oxford: Oxford Univ. Press, 1991), 6-9.

10. Basler, *CWL*, 4:429-31.

11. The standard account of Missouri during the war is William E. Parrish, *Turbulent Partnership: Missouri and the Union, 1861-1865* (Columbia: Univ. of Missouri Press, 1963). For a survey of the events in Missouri in 1861, see J.M. McPherson, *Battle Cry of Freedom*, 290-93.

12. Message to Congress in Special Session, July 4, 1861; Lincoln to Orville H. Browning, Sept. 22, 1861, both in Basler, *CWL*, 4:428, 532; J.M. McPherson, *Battle Cry of Freedom*, 294-95; Ross A. Webb, "Kentucky: Pariah among the Elect," in *Radicalism, Racism, and Party Realignment: The Border States during Reconstruction*, ed. Richard O. Curry (Baltimore: The Johns Hopkins Press, 1969), 108-9.

13. Message to Congress in Special Session, July 4, 1861, Basler, *CWL*, 4:432-33, 437.

14. Ibid., 426, 439-40. On this point, Lincoln referred Congress to his inaugural address. As indicated above, the president in this address was explicit in assuring Southerners that he would not interfere with their laws and institutions.

15. Ibid., 5:48-49.

16. Henry Steele Commager, ed., *Documents of American History*, 8th ed. (New York: Appleton-Century-Crofts, 1968), 395-96.

17. George H. Reese, ed., *Proceedings of the Virginia State Convention of 1861, February 13-May 1*, 4 vols. (Richmond: Virginia State Library, 1965), 1:468, 474, 477; 3:168-69.

18. Francis H. Pierpont, "History of the Reorganization of the Restored Government of Virginia and the Formation of the State of West Virginia," in Papers of Francis H. Pierpont and the Restored Government of Virginia, Virginia State Library, Richmond, hereinafter cited as Pierpont Papers; a version of Pierpont's "History" was printed in the *New York Times,* June 26, 1864; Richard O. Curry, *A House Divided: A Study of Statehood Politics and the Copperhead Movement in West Virginia* (Pittsburgh: Univ. of Pittsburgh Press, 1964), 34; Virgil A. Lewis, ed., *How West Virginia Was Made: Proceedings of the First Convention of the People of Northwestern Virginia at Wheeling, May 13, 14, and 15, 1861, and the Journal of the Second Convention of the People of Northwestern Virginia at Wheeling* (Charleston: State of West Virginia, 1909), 34.

19. For the administration's opposition at this time to the division of Virginia, see Attorney General Edward Bates to A.F. Ritchie, Aug. 12, 1861, in Lewis, *How West Virginia Was Made*, 219.

20. Ibid., 35n, 63-64. Delegates to the Wheeling convention were selected by local mass meetings of Unionists. Pro-Confederates, a majority in some counties, boycotted the meetings.

21. Pierpont, "A History of the Restored Government of Virginia," Pierpont Papers; Curry, *House Divided*, 69-72.

22. Francis H. Pierpont to Abraham Lincoln, June 21, 1861, *Calendar of Virginia State Papers, and Other Manuscripts, 1836-1869*, 11 vols.(Richmond: Virginia State Library, 1893), 11:353-54. For an excellent biographical sketch of Pierpont (sometimes spelled Peirpoint) and a description of his physical features, see Richard G. Lowe, "Francis Harrison Pierpont: Wartime Unionist, Reconstruction Moderate," in *The Governors of Virginia, 1860-1978*, ed. Edward Younger and James Tice Moore (Charlottesville: Univ. Press of Virginia, 1982), 33-45. See also Charles H. Ambler's now dated biography of Pierpont (*Francis H. Pierpont: Union*

War Governor of Virginia and Father of West Virginia [Chapel Hill: Univ. of North Carolina Press, 1937]).

23. Simon Cameron to Francis H. Pierpont, June 25, 1861, *Calendar of Virginia State Papers,* 11:354; James E. Wharton to Pierpont, June 26, 1861, Pierpont Papers.

24. Pierpont, "A History of the Restored Government of Virginia," Pierpont Papers; Ambler, *Pierpont,* 109-10; James C. McGregor, *The Disruption of Virginia* (New York: Macmillan, 1922), 219-23.

25. Message to Congress in Special Session, July 4, 1861, Basler, *CWL,* 4:427-28.

26. *Congressional Globe,* 37th Cong., 1st sess. (July 4, 1861), 6; (July 13, 1861), 103-6; McGregor, *Disruption of Virginia,* 224-28.

27. Belz, *Reconstructing the Union,* 31-32; *Congressional Globe,* 37th Cong., 1st sess. (July 13, 1861), 104-5.

28. Richard G. Lowe, *Republicans and Reconstruction in Virginia, 1856-70* (Charlottesville: Univ. of Virginia Press, 1991), 15. *Congressional Globe,* 37th Cong., 1st sess. (July 16, 1861), 144 (Lane quotation). See also Wisconsin Senator James Doolittle's comments, ibid. (July 25, 1861), 263.

29. James W. Patton, *Unionism and Reconstruction in Tennessee, 1860-1869* (Chapel Hill: Univ. of North Carolina Press, 1934), 17-18; Thomas B. Alexander, *Thomas A.R. Nelson of East Tennessee* (Nashville: Tennessee Historical Commission, 1956), 75.

30. Patton, *Unionism and Reconstruction in Tennessee,* 51-53; Alexander, *Nelson,* 76, 79; Jeptha Fowlkes to Andrew Johnson, May 29, 1861, in *The Papers of Andrew Johnson,* vol. 4, *1860-1861,* ed. Leroy P. Graf and Ralph W. Haskins (Knoxville: Univ. of Tennessee Press, 1976), 482, hereinafter cited as Johnson, *JP,* with volume designation.

31. Speech of Andrew Johnson at Lexington, Kentucky, June 18, 1861, Johnson, *JP,* 4:487-88, 489n; Alexander, *Nelson,* 84.

32. Oliver P. Temple, *East Tennessee and the Civil War* (1899; Freeport, New York: Books for Libraries Press, 1971), 345-49, 357-58, 565-69; Proceedings of the East Tennessee convention, held at Greeneville on the 17th day of June, 1861, and succeeding days, in *The War of the Rebellion: A Compilation of the Official Records of the Union and Confederate Armies,* 73 vols., 128 parts (Washington, D.C.: GPO, 1880-1901), ser. 1, vol. 52, pt. 1, 168-79, hereinafter cited as *OR;* Thomas W. Humes, *The Loyal Mountaineers of Tennessee* (Knoxville: Ogden Brothers, 1888), 115-19. Senator Johnson returned to Washington after the June 8 election and was not a member of the convention.

33. The Greeneville convention's "Declaration of Grievances and Resolutions" are found in Temple, *East Tennessee and the Civil War,* 565-69. For the conclusion that the declaration was probably read by Lincoln, see William R. Hurley to Johnson, July 4, 1861, Johnson, *JP,* 4:540.

34. Vernon M. Queener, "The Origin of the Republican Party in East Tennessee," *East Tennessee Historical Society Publications* 13 (1941): 72-74; Patton, *Unionism and Reconstruction in Tennessee,* 26-30.

35. Patton, *Unionism and Reconstruction in Tennessee,* 28-29; Alexander, *Nelson,* 87-93; Oliver P. Temple, *Notable Men of Tennessee, from 1833 to 1875: Their Times and Their Contemporaries* (New York: Cosmopolitan Press, 1912), 137, 140.

36. Charles Faulkner Bryan, "The Civil War in East Tennessee: A Social, Political, and Economic Study" (Ph.D. diss., University of Tennessee, 1978), 71, 78-80; Patton, *Unionism and Reconstruction in Tennessee,* 60; Johnson, *JP,* 4:690n; Humes, *Loyal Mountaineers of Tennessee,* 122-23; *Knoxville Brownlow's Weekly Whig,* Sept. 14, 21, 1861.

37. Salmon P. Chase to Andrew Johnson, June 29, 1861; William Nelson to Johnson, July 16, 1861; Bill Appropriating Arms to Loyal Citizens, July 20, 1861, all in Johnson, *JP,* 4:522-23, 586-88, 592-93.

38. Judah P. Benjamin to William B. Wood, Nov. 25, 1861; Proclamation of Gen. William H. Carroll, Dec. 13, 1861, both in *OR,* ser. 1, vol. 4, 848, 855. General Zollicoffer, who was on a military campaign at the time of the bridge burnings, believed that his conciliatory policy was succeeding and warned against abandoning it, but Secretary of War Judah P. Benjamin ordered the suppression of the Unionists. Temple, *East Tennessee and the Civil War,* 369-71, 388-91, 404-06.

39. Temple, *East Tennessee and the Civil War,* chap. 19; Report of state Adjutant General Edward S. Richards, Jan. 10, 1865, in *The Papers of Andrew Johnson,* vol. 7, *1864-1865,* ed. Leroy P. Graf (Knoxville: University of Tennessee Press, 1986), 385-88, hereinafter cited as Johnson, *JP,* with volume designation.

40. William G. Brownlow, *Sketches of the Rise, Progress, and Decline of Secession; with a Narrative of Personal Adventures among the Rebels* (Philadelphia: George W. Childs, 1862). Within a few months one hundred thousand copies of the book had been sold in the North. E. Merton Coulter, *William G. Brownlow: Fighting Parson of the Southern Highlands* (Chapel Hill: Univ. of North Carolina Press, 1937), 236-39. Other popular accounts of East Tennessee Unionists and their struggle published in the North are Herman Bokum, *The Testimony of a Refugee from East Tennessee* (Philadelphia, 1863); and James R. Gilmore, *Down in Tennessee, and Back by Way of Richmond* (New York: Carleton, 1864).

41. Louis Austin Warren, *Lincoln's Parentage and Childhood* (New York and London: Century, 1926), 43-44; Victor Searcher, *Lincoln Today: An Introduction to Modern Lincolniana* (New York: Thomas Yoseloff, 1969), 110-12; James G. Randall, *Lincoln and the South* (Baton Rouge: Louisiana State Univ. Press, 1946), 3, 9.

42. For a good description of East Tennessee at the time of the war, see Bryan, "Civil War in East Tennessee," 8-17. My conclusions, however, differ regarding the relative isolation of the region.

43. Temple, *East Tennessee and the Civil War,* chaps. 1-2 and 174-75. This quotation appears in Lincoln's Annual Message to Congress, Dec. 1, 1862, Basler, *CWL,* 5:537.

44. *New York World,* March 25, 1862.

45. Entry for Oct. 21, 1863, in *Lincoln and the Civil War in the Diaries and Letters of John Hay,* ed. Tyler Dennett (New York: Dodd, Mead, 1939), 104-5.

46. Andrew Johnson to Gideon Welles, Sept. 30, 1861; Johnson to Gen. William Tecumseh Sherman, Oct. 30, 1861, in *The Papers of Andrew Johnson,* vol. 5, *1861-1862* ed. Leroy P. Graf and Ralph W. Haskins (Knoxville: Univ. of Tennessee Press, 1979), 12-13, 29, hereinafter cited as Johnson, *JP,* with volume designation; Memorandum for a Plan of Campaign, ca. Oct. 1, 1861, Basler, *CWL,* 4:544-45. See also Gen. Lorenzo Thomas to Gen. W.T. Sherman, Oct. 12, 1861; Thomas to Simon Cameron, Oct. 21, 1861, Gen.George B. McClellan to Gen. D.C. Buell, Nov. 12, 1861, *OR,* ser. 1, vol. 4,299, 313-14, 355.

47. Gen. George H. Thomas to Andrew Johnson, Nov. 7, 1861, Johnson, *JP,* 5:31-32; Gen. William Tecumseh Sherman to Gen. George H. Thomas, Oct. 22, 25, Nov. 8, 1861, *OR,* ser. 1, vol. 4, 315-16, 318, 347.

48. Robert L. Stanford to Andrew Johnson, Dec. 13, 1861, Johnson, *JP,* 5:48-49. See also L.C. Houk to Johnson, Dec. 7, 1861, and Abner A. Steele to Johnson, Dec. 14, 1861, ibid., 41, 57-59.

49. Andrew Johnson and Horace Maynard to Gen. Don Carlos Buell, Dec. 7, 1861, ibid., 43-44; President Lincoln's Annual Message to Congress, Dec. 3, 1861, Basler, *CWL,* 5:37.

50. Johnson and Maynard to General Buell, Dec. 7, 1861, Johnson, *JP,* 5:43-44; Lincoln to Don Carlos Buell, Jan. 4, 1862, Basler, *CWL,* 5:90. Buell's reply may be found in ibid., 90n.

51. Lincoln to Gen. Don Carlos Buell, Jan. 6, 1862, Basler, *CWL,* 5:91. In declaring that East Tennesseans "are thinking of taking rebel arms," Lincoln meant that they would join Confederate units in order to obtain security for their families and communities.

52. Gen. George B. McClellan to Gen. Don Carlos Buell, Jan. 6, 1862, *OR,* ser. 1, vol. 4, 531; Henry W. Halleck to Lincoln, Jan. 6, 1862, Lincoln Papers; Lincoln to Simon Cameron, Jan. 10, 1862, Basler, *CWL,* 5:95 and n.

53. Annual Message to Congress, Dec. 3, 1861, Basler, *CWL,* 5:50.

54. The quotation is from his Peoria speech, Oct. 16, 1854, ibid., 2:276.

2. A Presidential Initiative

1. William C. Harris, "Lincoln and Wartime Reconstruction in North Carolina, 1861-1863," *North Carolina Historical Review,* 63 (April 1986): 153-54.

2. Joseph Segar to Francis H. Pierpont, Feb. 12, 1862, *Calendar of Virginia State Papers,* 11:367; Susie M. Ames, "Federal Policy toward the Eastern Shore of Virginia in 1861," *Virginia Magazine of History and Biography* 69 (Oct. 1961): 456; *Congressional Globe,* 37th Cong., 2d sess. (Feb. 10, 11, 1862), 728, 755; U.S. Congress, 37th Cong., 2d sess., *House Report No. 70,* 2-3. Complicating the political situation on the Eastern Shore was a movement among "men of property, respectability and influence" to have the area annexed to Maryland. A. Watson to Francis H. Pierpont, Dec. 12, 1861, Pierpont Papers.

3. For a detailed account of the territorialization bills in Congress, see Belz, *Reconstructing the Union,* chap. 3. For Sumner's resolutions, see the *Congressional Globe,* 37th Cong., 2d sess. (Feb. 11, 1862), 736-37.

4. *Congressional Globe,* 37th Cong., 2d sess. (Feb. 13, 1862), 786. See also comments of Senator John Carlile of Virginia, ibid. (March 11, 1862), 1157-62.

5. *Washington National Intelligencer,* March 1, 1862.

6. As reported in ibid., March 8, 1862; *New York Times,* Feb. 26, March 6, 1862.

7. Basler, *CWL,* 5:48-49.

8. Commager, ed., *Documents of American History,* 395-96.

9. *Congressional Globe,* 37th Cong., 2d sess. (Feb. 11, 1862), 736-37.

10. Basler, *CWL,* 5:144-46. Lincoln's support for a plan of gradual, compensated emancipation predates the Civil War. As a congressman in 1849, Lincoln announced that he would offer a bill for the gradual emancipation of slaves in the District of Columbia. The plan would require the ratification by District voters

before it would take effect. When resistance developed to the projected bill, he never introduced it in the House of Representatives. Stephen B. Oates, *With Malice toward None: The Life of Abraham Lincoln* (New York: Harper & Row, 1977), 93-94.

11. Basler, *CWL*, 5:145; *Washington National Intelligencer*, March 11, 1862.

12. Basler, *CWL*, 5:146n.

13. David Donald, *Charles Sumner and the Rights of Man* (New York: Alfred A. Knopf, 1970), 51-52, 57.

14. Basler, *CWL*, 5:153n.

15. *New York World*, March 7, 1862.

16. Ibid., March 8, 1862.

17. Abraham Lincoln to Henry J. Raymond, March 9, 1862, Basler, *CWL*, 5:152-53, and Raymond's reply, ibid., 153n. See *Times* editorials of March 8, 12, 1862.

18. Basler, *CWL*, 5:145. The December 1, 1862, plan is included in the president's Annual Message to Congress, Basler, *CWL*, 5:530-37.

19. *Washington National Intelligencer*, March 8, 1862.

20. Basler, *CWL*, 5:169n; Benjamin Quarles, *The Negro in the Civil War*, 2d. ed. (Boston: Little, Brown, 1969), 138; *New York Tribune*, March 7, 8, 11, 1862.

21. *Washington National Intelligencer*, March 13, 1862; Quarles, *Negro in the Civil War*, 144-45.

22. Edwin M. Stanton to Andrew Johnson, March 3, 1862, Johnson, *JP*, 5:177 and n; *Washington National Intelligencer*, March 8, 1862.

23. *New York World*, March 4, 1862. See also editorial in *New York World*, March 5, 1862.

24. *New York Times*, March 6, 1862.

25. *Washington National Intelligencer*, March 22, 1862; Montgomery Blair to Andrew Johnson, April 29, 1862, Johnson, *JP*, 5:347-48.

26. William C. Harris, "Andrew Johnson's First 'Swing around the Circle': His Northern Campaign of 1863," *Civil War History*, 35 (June 1989): 155-56, 155n.

27. Middle Tennessee Whigs had supported John Bell, the Constitutional Union candidate for president and a resident of the area. Johnson and Bell had crossed swords repeatedly in Tennessee and, as the state's U.S. senators before the war, in Washington.

28. William Nelson to Salmon P. Chase, Feb. 28, 1862, quoted in Hans L. Trefousse, *Andrew Johnson: A Biography* (New York and London: W.W. Norton, 1989), 153.

29. Peter Maslowski, *Treason Must Be Made Odious: Military Occupation and Wartime Reconstruction in Nashville, Tennessee, 1862-65* (Millwood, N.Y.: KTO Press, 1978), 21.

30. Harris, "Unionist Critique," 42-43.

31. Cf. Johnson's speech to Davidson County Citizens, March 22, 1862, Johnson, *JP*, 5:22-37, which was made only four days after the issuance of the Appeal.

32. Johnson, *JP*, 5:210-11. The republican guarantee clause in Article IV of the Constitution provides that "The United States shall guarantee to every State in this Union a Republican Form of Government."

33. Ibid., 211.

34. Maslowski, *Treason Must Be Made Odious*, 77-78; Clifton R. Hall, *Andrew Johnson, Military Governor of Tennessee* (Princeton: Princeton Univ. Press, 1916), 42.

35. Walter T. Durham, *Nashville, the Occupied City: The First Seventeen Months—February 16, 1862, to June 30, 1863* (Nashville: Tennessee Historical Society, 1985), 63-64; Andrew Johnson to Stanley Matthews, March 29, 1862; Proclamation re Nashville City Council, April 7, 1862, both in Johnson, *JP,* 5:253, 278-79.

36. *Appleton's Annual Cyclopedia and Register of Important Events*, 15 vols. (New York: Appleton, 1861-1875), *1862,* 766; Johnson, *JP,* 5:418n, 577n; *Washington National Intelligencer,* May 27, 1862.

37. Andrew Johnson to William H. Polk, May 22, 1862; Johnson to Marcellus Mundy, June 23, 1862, both in Johnson, *JP,* 5:411-12, 504.

38. Horace Maynard to Andrew Johnson, Dec. 1, 1862, Johnson, *JP,* 6:79.

39. Andrew Johnson to Stanley Matthews, March 17, 1862; Johnson to General James S. Negley, April 29, 1862, both in Johnson, *JP, 5:*208-9, 349, and 349-50n; Durham, *Nashville,* 75.

40. Andrew Johnson to Abraham Lincoln, April 9, 1862, Johnson, *JP,* 5:289, 634n; Maslowski, *Treason Must Be Made Odious,* 54.

41. Speech at Nashville, July 4, 1862; Andrew Johnson to Jeremiah T. Boyle, Aug. 4, 1862, both in Johnson, *JP,* 5:537, 595-96; *Appleton's Annual Cyclopedia, 1862,* 766.

42. Memorandum about Churches, March 4, 1864; Endorsement Concerning Churches in New Orleans, March 15, 1864, both in Basler, *CWL,* 7:223, 247.

43. *New York World,* March 20, 1862.

44. Andrew Johnson to William H. Seward, April 19, 1862, Johnson, *JP,* 5:314. For other optimistic reports of Unionist sentiment, see General Ormsby M. Mitchel to Johnson, March 30, 1862, and Alvan C. Gillem to Johnson, April 27, 1862, ibid., 257, 337.

45. Andrew Johnson to William H. Seward, April 19, 1862, ibid., 314, 314-15n.

46. *Appleton's Annual Cyclopedia, 1862,* 765.

47. Speech at Nashville, May 12, 1862, Johnson, *JP,* 5:379-85.

48. Johnson, *JP,* 5:xlii-xliii; *Washington National Intelligencer,* June 10, 1862.

49. Colonel Marcellus Mundy to Johnson, June 22, 1862, Johnson, *JP,* 5:496.

50. Ernest Walter Hooper, "Memphis, Tennessee: Federal Occupation and Reconstruction, 1862-1870" (Ph.D. diss., University of North Carolina at Chapel Hill, 1957), 60-61; Absalom H. Markland to Andrew Johnson, June 21, 1862, Johnson, *JP,* 5:494-95.

51. *Washington National Intelligencer,* Oct. 23, 1862.

52. Ibid, Aug. 2, 1862 (excerpt from the *St. Louis Missouri Republican*); Lewis C. Norvell to Andrew Johnson, June 10, 1862, Johnson, *JP,* 5:462-63; *Appleton's Annual Cyclopedia, 1862,* 567.

53. Approximately thirty newspapers were published in the Federal-occupied South during the war.

54. General Orders No. 67, Headquarters, Fifth Division, Army of the Tennessee, Aug. 8, 1862, *OR,* ser. 1, vol. 17, pt. 2, 158-60; William Tecumseh Sherman, *Memoirs of Gen. W.T. Sherman, Written by Himself* (New York: Charles L. Webster, 1891), 293-94, 297-98.

55. Lew Wallace to Andrew Johnson, June 22, 1862; Johnson to Wallace, June 30, 1862; Absalom H. Markland to Johnson, June 21, 1862, all in Johnson, *JP,* 5:494-95, 498, 523; James B. Bingham to Johnson, Aug. 11, 1863, Johnson, *JP,* 6:324-25.

56. William Tecumseh Sherman to Mayor John Park, July 27, 1862, in Sherman, *Memoirs,* 298-99; *Washington National Intelligencer,* July 31, Aug. 2, 1862; Joseph H. Parks, "Memphis under Military Rule, 1862 to 1865," *East Tennessee Historical Society Publications* 14 (1942): 33-34.

57. "Alvin Hawkins," 37th Cong., 3d sess., *House Report No. 46,* 1-3.

58. *Washington Daily Chronicle,* Dec. 20, 1862; General Stephen A. Hurlbut to Johnson, Nov. 12, 1862; Pitser Miller to Andrew Johnson, Nov. 29, 1862; Certification of Congressional Election, Jan. 10, 1863; U.S. Grant to Johnson, Jan. 16, 1863; James B. Bingham to Johnson, Nov. 4, 1863, all in Johnson, *JP,* 6:51, 78, 112, 121, 453-55.

59. Abraham Lincoln to Andrew Johnson, July 3, 1862, Basler, *CWL,* 5:302-3; Johnson to Lincoln, July 10, 1862, Johnson, *JP,* 5:549-50.

60. See below, 105.

61. Don Carlos Buell to Andrew Johnson, March 19, 1862, Johnson, *JP,* 5:213.

62. Edwin M. Stanton to Andrew Johnson, March 22, 1862, Johnson, *JP,* 5:222.

63. Andrew Johnson to Abraham Lincoln, April 12, 1862, ibid., 5:301; Maslowski, *Treason Must Be Made Odious,* 39.

64. Andrew Johnson to Horace Maynard, April 24, 1862; Maynard to Johnson, April 25, 1862; Maynard to Johnson, April 26, 1862, all in Johnson, *JP,* 5:331, 332, 335; Henry W. Halleck to Edwin M. Stanton, April 25, 1862; Don Carlos Buell to Halleck, April 26, 1862, both in *OR,* ser. 1, vol. 10, pt. 2, 128-29.

65. Andrew Johnson to Abraham Lincoln, April 26, 1862; Lincoln to Johnson, April 27, 1862, both in Johnson, *JP,* 5:336-37, 338.

66. Andrew Johnson to Henry W. Halleck, April 27, 1862, ibid., 340.

67. See, for example, Andrew Johnson to Edwin M. Stanton, May 11, 1862, ibid., 378.

68. Andrew Johnson to Abraham Lincoln, July 10, 1862; Edwin M. Stanton to Johnson, July 12, 1862, both in Johnson, *JP,* 5:549-50, 555; Lincoln to Johnson, July 11, 1862; Lincoln to Henry W. Halleck, July 11, 1862, both in Basler, *CWL,* 5:313.

69. When Nashville was virtually besieged during the summer and early fall of 1862 by Confederate cavalry under Nathan Bedford Forrest and John Hunt Morgan, Johnson assumed direction of the town's defense. He shocked many residents when he threatened to destroy the state capital before surrendering it to the rebels. Nashville, however, was saved, largely due to the military defenses organized by the governor.

70. Horace Maynard to Andrew Johnson, June 17, 1862; Johnson to Abraham Lincoln, July 10, 1862, both in Johnson, *JP,* 5:484, 549-50; Lincoln to Henry W. Halleck, June 30, 1862; Lincoln to Johnson, Oct. 31, 1862, both in Basler, *CWL,* 5:295, 295n, 483-84.

71. Johnson to Lincoln, Sept. 1, 1862, Johnson, *JP,* 6:4-5 and 5n.

72. Most historians have probably exaggerated the finality of Lincoln's mid-1862 decision to move directly against slavery in the South. For the view that

Lincoln's mind was not entirely made up on the issue at the time, despite his July 22 announcement to his Cabinet that he intended to act, see Herman Belz, *Emancipation and Equal Rights: Politics and Constitutionalism in the Civil War Era* (New York: W.W. Norton, 1978), 40-41, and Donald, *Lincoln,* 373-74.

73. Preliminary Emancipation Proclamation, Sept. 22, 1862, Basler, *CWL,* 5:433-34.

74. General Sam Jones to Confederate Secretary of War George W. Randolph, Oct. 14, 1862; Address of Hon. T.A.R. Nelson to the People of East Tennessee, Oct. 3, 1862; Gen. Sam Jones to Thomas A.R. Nelson, Oct. 17, 1862, all in *OR,* ser. 1, vol. 16, pt. 2, 945-46, 909-11, 957-58.

75. Petition to the President, Dec. 4, 1862, Johnson, *JP,* 6:85-86. This petition was signed by forty Tennessee Union leaders, including Johnson and William B. Campbell. Lincoln received it on December 23, eight days before issuing his Emancipation Proclamation.

76. Horace Maynard to Abraham Lincoln, Oct. 1, 1862, Abraham Lincoln Papers, Library of Congress (microfilm).

77. Horace Maynard to Henry W. Halleck, Dec. 13, 1862; statement of Maynard, Dec. 13, 1862, both in *OR,* ser. 1, vol. 20, pt. 2, 167-71. Halleck was now general-in-chief of the army.

78. East Tennessee representatives elected in 1861 would not hold seats in the new Congress.

79. Andrew Johnson to Abraham Lincoln, Jan. 11, 1863, Johnson, *JP,* 6:114.

80. Annual Message to Congress, Dec. 1, 1862, Basler, *CWL,* 5:530-31.

81. Don E. Fehrenbacher, *Prelude to Greatness: Lincoln in the 1850s* (Stanford: Stanford University Press, 1962), 110-11.

82. Basler, *CWL,* 6:29-30.

3. North Carolina: The Stanly Experiment

1. William C. Harris, *North Carolina and the Coming of the Civil War* (Raleigh: Division of Archives and History, North Carolina Department of Cultural Resources, 1988), 54-56.

2. James M. McPherson, *Abraham Lincoln and the Second American Revolution* (New York: Oxford Univ. Press, 1991), 48.

3. Abraham Lincoln, Annual Message to Congress, Dec. 3, 1861, Basler, *CWL,* 5:50; *New York Times,* May 15, 1862.

4. *Biographical Directory of the American Congress, 1774-1971* (Washington: GPO, 1971), 1743. For an account of Stanly's life, see Norman D. Brown, *Edward Stanly: Whiggery's Tar Heel "Conqueror"* (University: Univ. of Alabama Press, 1974). The quotation is found on p. 1.

5. Edward Stanly, *Letter from Hon. Edward Stanly, Military Governor of North Carolina, to Colonel Henry Gilliam, refuting certain charges and insinuations made by Hon. George E. Badger, in behalf of the Southern Confederacy* (New Bern, N.C., 1862), 3-4; Harris, "Lincoln and Wartime Reconstruction in North Carolina," 156.

6. Edward Stanly, *A Military Governor among Abolitionists: A Letter from Edward Stanly, to Charles Sumner* (New York, 1865), 28.

7. Edwin M. Stanton to Edward Stanly, May 19, 20, 1862; Stanton to Gen. Ambrose E. Burnside, May 20, 1862, both in *OR,* ser. 1, vol. 9, 391, 396-97.

8. Ambrose E. Burnside to Edwin M. Stanton, May 19, 1862, *OR*, ser. 1, vol. 9, 390.

9. Report of Lt. C.W. Flusser, May 18, 1862; Flusser to S.C. Rowan, May 18, 1862, both in *Official Records of the Union and Confederate Navies in the War of the Rebellion*, series I, (Washington, D.C.: GPO, 1894-1917), 7:385, 386. For an in-depth study of the war and the Federal occupation in one of these northeastern North Carolina counties, see Wayne K. Durrill, *War of Another Kind: A Southern Community in the Great Rebellion* (New York and Oxford: Oxford Univ. Press, 1990).

10. See, for example, entries for Dec. 14, 1862, Jan. 4, May 23, Dec. 11, 1863, in Beth G. Crabtree and James W. Patton, eds., *"Journal of a Secesh Lady": The Diary of Catherine Ann Devereux Edmondston, 1860-1866* (Raleigh: North Carolina Division of Archives and History, 1979), 316, 336, 393, 506-7.

11. *New Bern Daily Progress,* March 22, 26, April 2, May 22, 26, 1862.

12. Ambrose E. Burnside to Edwin M. Stanton, May 28, 1862, *OR*, ser. 1, vol. 9, 393-94.

13. Oliver S. Coolidge to (?), May 15, 1862, Oliver S. Coolidge Papers, Manuscript Department, Duke University Library, Durham; Z.T. Haines, *Letters from the Forty-Fourth Regiment M.V.M.: A Record of the Experiences of a Nine Months' Regiment in the Department of North Carolina in 1862-3, by "Corporal"* (Boston: Herald Job Office, 1863), 37-38, 45, 51, 112; Joe A. Mobley, *James City: A Black Community in North Carolina, 1863-1900* (Raleigh: North Carolina Division of Archives and History, Department of Cultural Resources, 1981), 5-6.

14. Stanly, *Military Governor,* 16, 26; Stanly, *Letter to Gilliam,* 4; Edward Stanly to Edwin M. Stanton, June 12, 1862, *OR*, ser. 1, vol. 9, 400-401 (quotation).

15. Stanly's speech may be found in the *New Bern Daily Progress,* June 30, 1862, and the *New York Times,* June 25, 1862.

16. Edward Stanly to Abraham Lincoln, July 7, 1862, Lincoln Papers.

17. Entry for May 30, 1862, in Thomas Bragg Diary, Southern Historical Collection, University of North Carolina, Chapel Hill; *New York Tribune,* May 23, 1862; *New York Times,* Aug. 19, 1862; William C. Harris, *William Woods Holden: Firebrand of North Carolina Politics* (Baton Rouge: Louisiana State Univ. Press, 1987), 118; *New Bern Daily Progress,* May 22, 1862.

18. Abraham Lincoln to Edward Stanly, Aug. 4 (21?), 1862, in Stanly, *Mili-tary Governor,* 44. In a Sept. 2, 1862, letter to President Lincoln (Lincoln Papers), Stanly refers to an Aug. 21, 1862, message from Lincoln inviting him to the White House. In his pamphlet, printed in 1865, Stanly may have incorrectly given the August 4 date, which was the date of the North Carolina election. Historians evidently are not aware of the letter. No copy of the original has been found, and it is not printed in Roy Basler's comprehensive edition of Lincoln's correspondence.

19. Abraham Lincoln to Edward Stanly, Sept. 29, 1862, Basler, *CWL,* 5:445.

20. *Raleigh North Carolina Standard,* May 28, June 25, 1862.

21. Edward Stanly to Edwin M. Stanton, June 12, 1862, *OR*, ser. 1, vol. 9, 400-401; *New York Tribune,* June 18, 1862; Charles Sumner, *The Works of Charles Sumner,* 15 vols. (Boston: Lee and Shepard, 1875-83), 7:113.

22. Ambrose E. Burnside to Edwin M. Stanton, May 23, 1862, *OR*, ser. 1, vol. 9, 390; *New York Times,* June 4, 1862; Stanly, *Military Governor,* 12.

23. Sumner, *Works of Charles Sumner,* 7:112; Vincent Colyer, *Report of the Services Rendered by the Freed People to the United States Army, in North Carolina, in the Spring of 1862, after the Battle of Newbern* (New York: Vincent Colyer, 1864), 5.

24. Stanly, *Military Governor,* 12.

25. Belz, *Reconstructing the Union,* 85-87; Sumner, *Works of Charles Sumner,* 7:119-20; *New York Times,* June 6, 1862.

26. For an account of the differences between Radicals and other Republicans over slavery and reconstruction, see Belz, *Reconstructing the Union,* 88-89, 96. Although Congress passed a series of antislavery acts in 1862, including a law abolishing slavery in the District of Columbia, the majority of congressmen refused to act against the institution in the Southern states.

27. Edwin M. Stanton to President Lincoln, June 4, 1862, *OR,* ser. 1, vol. 9, 396; Abraham Lincoln to the House of Representatives, June 4, 1862, Basler, *CWL,* 5:259; U.S. Congress, "Letter of Secretary of War in Answer to a Resolution of the Senate . . . Transmitting a Copy of Appointment Constituting Hon. Edward Stanly Military Governor of North Carolina," *Senate Executive Document No. 54,* 37th Cong., 2d sess., 1-2.

28. Edwin M. Stanton to Edward Stanly, June 3, 1862; Edward Stanly to Edwin M. Stanton, June 12, 1862, both in *OR,* ser. 1, vol. 9, 395-96, 399-402. See also *New York Tribune,* June 18, 1862.

29. Ambrose E. Burnside to Edwin M. Stanton, June 9, 1862; Ambrose E. Burnside to Edwin M. Stanton, June 24, 1862, both in *OR,* ser. 1, vol. 9, 398, 403; Edward Stanly to Abraham Lincoln, July 7, 1862, Lincoln Papers.

30. Colyer, *Report of the Services Rendered by the Freed People,* 52.

31. For the failure of the congressional challenge, see Belz, *Reconstructing the Union,* 100.

32. Edward Stanly to Edwin M. Stanton, June 12, 1862, *OR,* ser. 1, vol. 9, 401-2; Stanly to Abraham Lincoln, July 7, 1862, Lincoln Papers.

33. C.C. Howard to "Cousin Harry," Aug. 21, 1862, Edwin Ruffin Beckwith Papers, Southern Historical Collection, University of North Carolina Library, Chapel Hill; Edward Stanly to Gen. John G. Foster, Dec. 29, 1862, *OR,* ser. 1, vol. 14, 498; Stanly, *Military Governor,* 32-35.

34. *New Bern Semi-Weekly Progress,* Jan. 31, 1863.

35. Immediately after the interview, Stanly reported the president's comments to Welling, who recorded its substance in his diary. This part of Welling's diary may be found in Allen Thorndike Rice, ed., *Reminiscences of Abraham Lincoln by Distinguished Men of His Time* (New York: North American Review, 1888), 533. Lincoln's explanation for his proclamation, if reported correctly, may have reflected his practice of dissembling, as revealed by Professor LaWanda Cox, in order to obtain support for his plans. In this case, Lincoln probably knew that the Radicals would not withhold supplies for the army. Such an argument, however, could influence a conservative Unionist like Stanly to agree to the practical necessity for the proclamation. *Lincoln and Black Freedom: A Study in Presidential Leadership* (Columbia: Univ. of South Carolina Press, 1981), 10, 43.

36. Abraham Lincoln to Edward Stanly, Sept. 29, 1862; Stanly to Lincoln, Sept. 29, 1862, both in Basler, *CWL,* 5:445 and 445n.

37. *New Bern Daily Progress,* Nov. 28, 1862.

38. Ibid., Dec. 1862 issues; *New York Times,* Nov. 14, 1862; Brown, *Stanly,* 245.

39. "Protest from Charles Henry Foster in Relation to the Election of Jennings Pigott to Congress from the Second District of North Carolina," *House Miscellaneous Document No. 14,* 37th Cong., 3d sess., 1-3; *New York Times,* Jan. 15, 1863.

40. Stanly, *Military Governor,* 51.

41. Petition of members of the House of Representatives, Feb. 23, 1863, Lincoln Papers; Brown, *Stanly,* 252-53.

4. The Southwest: An Uncertain Beginning

1. William Reed Mills to Michael Hahn, Dec. 20, 1862, Lincoln Papers; Ted Tunnell, *Crucible of Reconstruction: War, Radicalism and Race in Louisiana, 1862-1877* (Baton Rouge: Louisiana State Univ. Press, 1984), 10-11; James Parton, *General Butler in New Orleans* (New York: Mason Brothers, 1864), 121; *Congressional Globe,* 37th Cong., 3d sess. (Feb. 9, 1863), 832.

2. Edwin M. Stanton to Col. George S. Shepley, June 10, 1862, *OR,* ser. 3, vol. 2, 141; Stanton to Gen. Benjamin F. Butler, June 10, 1862; Stanton to Butler, June 23, 1862, both in *OR,* ser. 1, vol. 15, 471, 493.

3. McCrary, *Lincoln and Reconstruction,* 83-84; Stanley W. Campbell, *The Slave Catchers: Enforcement of the Fugitive Slave Law, 1850-1860* (Chapel Hill: Univ. of North Carolina Press, 1968), 191-92 (quotation); Ira Berlin, et al., eds., *The Destruction of Slavery,* series 1, vol. 1 of *Freedom: A Documentary History of Emancipation, 1861-1867* (Cambridge: Cambridge Univ. Press, 1985), 193-95; Parton, *Butler,* 132-33.

4. Abraham Lincoln to Reverdy Johnson, July 26, 1862, Basler, *CWL,* 5:342-43. Less than a month later, Phelps resigned his command.

5. Abraham Lincoln to Cuthbert Bullitt, July 28, 1862, ibid., 344-46.

6. Ibid., 346.

7. Abraham Lincoln to August Belmont, July 31, 1862, ibid., 350-51 and 351n. August Belmont, a prominent New York banker and Democrat, had sent extracts of the Louisiana Unionist's letter to Lincoln. Belmont identified his Louisiana correspondent as a "very wealthy and influential planter."

8. Though the president's party suffered significant election losses in the conservative lower North, partly due to his emancipation policy, his reconstruction efforts probably had little influence on the outcome.

9. Abraham Lincoln to Benjamin F. Butler, George Shepley, and Others, Oct. 14, 1862, Basler, *CWL,* 5:462-63. Lincoln sent a similar letter to Union authorities in Tennessee and Arkansas. Although he continued in Congress after secession, Bouligny's term had expired by late 1862.

10. Abraham Lincoln to George F. Shepley, Nov. 21, 1862, ibid., 504-5. Both letters were written on the same day.

11. McCrary, *Lincoln and Reconstruction,* 98-99; *Congressional Globe,* 37th Cong., 3d sess. (Feb. 9, 1863), 832; John G. Nicolay and John Hay, *Abraham Lincoln: A History* (New York: Century, 1890), 6:352-53; Benjamin F. Butler to the President of the U.S.A., Nov. 28, 1862, *Private and Official Correspondence of Gen. Benjamin F. Butler during the Period of the Civil War* (Norwood, Mass.: Plimpton Press, 1917), 2:449.

12. *Congressional Globe,* 37th Cong., 3d sess. (Feb. 9, 1863), 832. It should be remembered, as Peyton McCrary has noted, that New Orleans,

whose population overlapped both congressional districts, had had an appallingly low voter turnout before the war. McCrary, *Lincoln and Reconstruction,* 100-101.

13. See elsewhere in this book for congressional elections in Virginia, North Carolina, and Arkansas.

14. Belz, *Reconstructing the Union,* 108-9; Abraham Lincoln to George F. Shepley, Nov. 21, 1862, Basler, *CWL,* 5:504; *Congressional Globe,* 37th Cong., 3d sess. (Feb. 9, 1863), 833.

15. Abraham Lincoln to George F. Shepley, Nov. 21, 1862, Basler, *CWL,* 5:504.

16. *Congressional Globe,* 37th Cong., 3d sess. (Feb. 9, 1863), 831-33, (Feb. 11, 1863), 855-67.

17. Ibid. (Feb. 17, 1863), 1036. A few days before the vote, Dawes, who had his finger on the pulse of congressional opinion, wrote his wife that Flanders and Hahn would be rejected by the House, a defeat that, he declared, "would be a sad thing for the future of the Union cause in these rebel states." Henry L. Dawes to Electra Dawes, Feb. 11, 1863, Henry L. Dawes Papers, Manuscript Division, Library of Congress.

18. Harris, "Andrew Johnson's First Swing around the Circle," 153-71; *New York Tribune,* Oct. 4, 1862, March 21, 1863; *Speech of Hon. Andrew Jackson Hamilton, of Texas, Late Representative of Texas, in the 36th Congress, on the Condition of the South under Rebel Rule, and the Necessity of Early Relief to the Union Men of Western Texas* (1862); *Washington Daily Chronicle,* Jan. 27, 1864; *Nashville Daily Union,* March 29, Oct. 11, 1863.

19. *Congressional Globe,* 37th Cong., 3d sess., (Feb. 17, 1863), 1030-32.

20. James G. Blaine, *Twenty Years of Congress: From Lincoln to Garfield with a Review of the Events Which Led to the Political Revolution of 1860* (Norwich, Conn.: Henry Bill, 1884-86), 2:37.

21. Michael B. Dougan, *Confederate Arkansas: The People and Policies of a Frontier State in Wartime* (University: Univ. of Alabama Press, 1976), 88-90.

22. Gen. E.B. Brown to Gen. John M. Schofield, June 22, 1862; John S. Phelps to Edwin M. Stanton, Oct. 20, 1862, both in *OR,* ser. 1, vol. 13, 444-45, 751; U.S. Congress, "Report of the Adjutant General of the State of Arkansas, for the period of the late rebellion, and to November 1, 1866," *Senate Miscellaneous Document No. 53,* 39th Cong., 2d sess., 2.

23. "Report of the Adjutant General of Arkansas," 1-3; Albert W. Bishop, *Loyalty on the Frontier, or Sketches of Union Men of the South-West; With Incidents and Adventures in Rebellion on the Border* (St. Louis: R.P. Studley, 1863), 12-13; *St. Louis Missouri Republican,* June 11, 1864; *Little Rock National Democrat,* Aug. 13, 1864 (quotation).

24. Edwin M. Stanton to John S. Phelps, July 19, 1862, *OR,* ser. 3, vol. 2, 233. Phelps's appointment as a general was never confirmed by the Senate.

25. *Washington National Intelligencer,* July 19, 22, 1862; John S. Phelps to Edwin M. Stanton, Oct. 20, 1862, *OR,* ser. 1, vol. 13, 751.

26. John S. Phelps to Edwin M. Stanton, Oct. 20, 1862, *OR,* ser. 1, vol. 13, 751-53; William M. McPherson to Abraham Lincoln, Dec. 25, 1862, Lincoln Papers; "Report of the Adjutant General of Arkansas," 4. Before his appointment was revoked, Phelps raised an Arkansas regiment and commissioned officers in other Federal state units. Although his talents and temperament were unequal to

the task in Civil-War Arkansas, Phelps was not politically inept. He later served ably as governor of Missouri. Ezra J. Warner, *Generals in Blue: Lives of the Union Commanders* (Baton Rouge: Louisiana State Univ. Press, 1964), 367-68.

27. Abraham Lincoln to Frederick Steele, John S. Phelps and Others, Nov. 18, 1862, Basler, *CWL*, 5:500.

28. William M. McPherson to Abraham Lincoln, Nov. 28, Dec. 25, 1862, Lincoln Papers.

29. Abraham Lincoln to Stephen A. Hurlbut, July 31, 1863, Basler, *CWL*, 6:358, 359n.

30. L. Pierce Jr., U.S. Consul at Matamoros, to William H. Seward, May 5, 1862; C.B.H. Blood, U.S. Consul at Monterey, to Seward, May 23, 1862, both in *OR*, ser. 1, vol. 9, 684-86; *Washington National Intelligencer*, Oct. 2, 1862; Robert L. Kerby, *Kirby Smith's Confederacy: The Trans-Mississippi South, 1863-1865* (New York: Columbia Univ. Press, 1972), 93-94. According to one student of wartime Texas, one third of its citizens were Unionists or neutrals during the war. Nannie M. Tilley, ed., *Federals on the Frontier: The Diary of Benjamin F. McIntyre, 1862-1864* (Austin: Univ. of Texas Press, 1963), 258n.

31. *Speech of Hamilton on the Condition of the South under Rebel Rule*, 8-9. This address may also be found in the *New York Tribune*, Oct. 4, 1862. For a brief biography of Hamilton, see John L. Waller, *Colossal Hamilton of Texas: A Biography of Andrew Jackson Hamilton* (El Paso: Texas Western Press, 1968). See also James Marten, *Texas Divided: Loyalty and Dissent in the Lone Star State, 1856-1874* (Lexington: Univ. Press of Kentucky, 1988), 66-67.

32. *Washington National Intelligencer*, Oct. 2, 1862; *New York Tribune*, Oct. 4, 1862.

33. *New York Tribune*, Feb. 7, 1863.

34. *Speech of Hamilton on Condition of the South under Rebel Rule;* New York *Tribune*, Oct. 4, 1862.

35. Comments of Mayor George Opdyke and resolution of support by the New York war committee in *Speech of Hamilton on Condition of the South under Rebel Rule*, 2, 18; *New York Tribune*, Feb. 7, 1863; entries for Oct. 5, 10, 1862, Diary and Correspondence of Salmon P. Chase, American Historical Association, *Annual Report for the Year 1902* (Washington, D.C., 1903), 2:101-2, 104.

36. *Washington National Intelligencer*, Oct. 18, 1862.

37. *New York Tribune*, Feb. 7, 1863. In 1862 France, Spain, and Britain dispatched troops to Mexico to collect debts owed Europeans. Spain and Britain soon withdrew. Napoleon III's French forces remained and soon became involved in a major imperial adventure. In 1863 Napoleon III's army overthrew Mexican President Benito Juarez and installed Archduke Ferdinand Maximilian of Austria as emperor of Mexico. The Confederate government proposed to ignore this flagrant violation of the Monroe Doctrine in exchange for French recognition. Fearful of United States retaliation, Napoleon, however, never approved such an agreement.

38. *New York Tribune,* Feb. 7, 1863; *Report of the Committee Who Visited Washington on the Affairs of Western Texas* (New York: National War Committee of the Citizens of New York, 1862).

39. Abraham Lincoln to William H. Seward, Nov. 8, 1862, Basler, *CWL*, 5:492; Edwin M. Stanton to Andrew Jackson Hamilton, Nov. 14, 1862; Stanton to Nathaniel P. Banks, Nov. 14, 1862, both in *OR*, ser. 3, vol. 2, 782-83; A.J.

Hamilton to Salmon P. Chase, Nov. 30, 1862, Salmon P. Chase Papers, Historical Society of Pennsylvania, Philadelphia.

40. John A. Andrew to Gustavus V. Fox, Nov. 27, 1861, *OR,* ser. 1, vol. 15, 412-13; Ludwell Johnson, *Red River Campaign: Politics and Cotton in the Civil War* (Baltimore: Johns Hopkins Univ. Press, 1958), 9-10; William Schouler, *A History of Massachusetts in the Civil War* (Boston: E.P. Dutton, 1868), 237-38.

41. *New York Times,* Oct. 30, 1862.

42. Thomas H. O'Connor, "Lincoln and the Cotton Trade," *Civil War History* 7 (March 1961), 20-35; Maurice G. Baxter, *Orville H. Browning: Lincoln's Friend and Critic* (Bloomington: Indiana Univ. Press, 1957), 169-71.

43. Michael Hahn to Abraham Lincoln, Jan. 29, 1864; Crafts J. Wright and Charles K. Hawks to Lincoln, Jan. 4, 1864, both in Lincoln Papers. See also the *Washington National Intelligencer,* Jan. 19, 1864.

44. Abraham Lincoln to General Edward R.S. Canby, Dec. 12, 1864, Basler, *CWL,* 8:164 (quotation); Nathaniel P. Banks to Edwin M. Stanton, Feb. 2, 1864, Nathaniel P. Banks Papers, Manuscript Division, Library of Congress.

45. Gabor S. Boritt, *Lincoln and the Economics of the American Dream* (Memphis: Memphis State Univ. Press, 1978), 243-44, 247-48.

46. *New York Tribune,* Feb. 7, 1863; Henry G. Pearson, *Life of John A. Andrew* (Boston: Houghton, Mifflin, 1904), 2:124-25.

47. Fred Harvey Harrington, *Fighting Politician: Major General N.P. Banks* (1948; Westport, Conn.: Greenwood Press, 1970): 86; *New York Tribune,* Feb. 7, 1863; Salmon P. Chase to Benjamin F. Butler, Dec. 14, 1862, *Correspondence of Butler,* 2:541-42; Nathaniel P. Banks to Edwin M. Stanton, Jan. 7, 1863, *OR,* ser. 1, vol. 15, 643. The Texas regiment, consisting mainly of Lone Star State refugees, was organized in 1862 at New Orleans by Col. Edmund J. Davis, a district judge before the war and a future Republican governor. After the Galveston debacle, the regiment served along the Rio Grande. Frank H. Smyrl, "Texans in the Union Army, 1861-1865," *Southwestern Historical Quarterly* 65 (Oct. 1961), 235-37.

48. Nathaniel P. Banks to Edwin M. Stanton, Jan. 7, 1863; Banks to Henry W. Halleck, Jan. 7, 1863, both in *OR,* ser. 1, vol. 15, 642-43.

49. George S. Denison to Salmon P. Chase, Jan. 2, 1863, in Diary and Correspondence of Chase; *New York Tribune,* Jan. 31, March 21, 1863; *New York Times,* April 10, 1863; *Speech of Gen. A.J. Hamilton, of Texas, at the War Meeting at Faneuil Hall, Saturday Evening, April 18, 1863* (Boston: T.R. Marvin & Son, 1863); William Alexander to Benjamin F. Butler, March 24, 1863, *Correspondence of Butler,* 3:40-41.

50. For a brief account of the French intervention in Mexico and the Union reaction to the threat, see Kerby, *Kirby Smith's Confederacy,* 186-87.

51. *Letter of Gen. A.J. Hamilton of Texas, to the President of the United States* (New York: Loyal Publication Society, 1863). The quotation is from pp. 16-17. In a private letter to Secretary of Treasury Salmon P. Chase, the military governor bitterly wrote of Secretary of State Seward's indifference toward the French threat and complained of General Banks's "unalterable dislike of Texas men and Texas interests." He suggested that Banks should be replaced as commander of the forces to redeem Texas from rebel rule. A.J. Hamilton to Salmon P. Chase, Aug. 31, 1863, Chase Papers, The Historical Society of Pennsylvania.

52. Abraham Lincoln to Edwin M. Stanton, July 29, 1863, Basler, *CWL,* 6:354-55. Hamilton's July 28 letter to Lincoln, though printed for distribution, cannot be found in the Lincoln Papers.

53. Lincoln to Nathaniel P. Banks, Aug. 5, 1863; Lincoln to Ulysses S. Grant, Aug. 9, 1863, both in Basler, *CWL,* 6:364, 374; entry for Aug. 9, 1863, Dennett, *Hay Diaries,* 77.

54. Henry W. Halleck to Nathaniel P. Banks, Aug. 10, 1863, *OR,* ser. 1, vol. 26, pt. 1, 673; Banks to Abraham Lincoln, Sept. 5, 1863, Lincoln Papers; Lincoln to Banks, Sept. 19, 1863, Basler, *CWL,* 6:465-66.

55. A.J. Hamilton to Salmon P. Chase, Dec. 19, 1863, Chase Papers, The Historical Society of Pennsylvania. For similar reports of Confederate defeatism in Texas at this time, see the *New Orleans Daily True Delta,* Jan. 3, 1864, and M.M. Kinney, United States consul at Monterrey, to Nathaniel P. Banks, Nov. 18, 1863, Banks Papers. Kinney claimed that one third of the Texas state troops would desert to the Union if an invasion were launched.

56. Gen. N.J.T. Dana to Gen. Charles P. Stone, Dec. 11, 1863; Banks to A.J. Hamilton, Dec. 29, 1863, both in Banks Papers. Seward later asked Hamilton for an explanation of his toast at Matamoros in order to reassure the French that the governor did not speak for the Washington administration. William H. Seward to A.J. Hamilton, May 9, 1864, Andrew Jackson Hamilton Collection, Eugene C. Barker Texas History Center, University of Texas at Austin.

5. Stalemate

1. Abraham Lincoln to Salmon P. Chase, Sept. 2, 1863, Basler, *CWL,* 6:428-29.

2. Montgomery Blair to John L. Scripps, Aug. 4, 1863, Blair Family Papers, Manuscript Division, Library of Congress; Speech of Andrew Johnson at Nashville, Aug. 29, 1863; Johnson to Abraham Lincoln, Sept. 17, 1863, both in Johnson, *JP,* 6:344; Abraham Lincoln to Andrew Johnson, Sept. 11, 1863, Basler, *CWL,* 6:440; Governor's Message, Dec. 4, 1862, Virginia, *Journal of the House of Delegates, of the Commonwealth of Virginia, Extra Session, Held in the City of Wheeling, on Thursday, December the 4th, 1862* (Wheeling: A.S. Trowbridge, 1862), 10-11.

3. For these quotations, see William C. Harris, "Abraham Lincoln and Southern White Unionism," in *Abraham Lincoln: Sources and Style of Leadership,* ed. Frank J. Williams, William D. Pederson, and Vincent J. Marsala (Westport, Conn.: Greenwood Press, 1994), 132-33.

4. Abraham Lincoln to Andrew Johnson, Sept. 11, 1863, Basler, *CWL,* 6:440.

5. Abraham Lincoln to Francis H. Pierpont, March 20, 1862, Basler, *CWL,* 5:166.

6. Hesseltine, *Lincoln and the War Governors,* 253-62; Address to the President, Sept. 30, 1862, Lincoln Papers; *Washington National Intelligencer,* Oct. 4, 1862.

7. As reported in the *Baltimore American,* Aug. 29, 1863. Pierpont was never governor of the state of West Virginia. He gave up his authority over this area when the new state was formed.

8. *St. Louis Missouri Republican,* Dec. 11, 1863; Lowe, *Republicans and Reconstruction in Virginia,* 17, 19. Pierpont brought with him from western Virginia

sufficient funds to meet the small budget required by the Alexandria government. Virginia, *Journal of the House of Delegates, Extra Session, 1862,* 15.

9. *New York Times,* June 26, 1864; Ambler, *Pierpont,* 177-78. Letcher continued in office as governor of Confederate Virginia.

10. Abraham Lincoln to Francis H. Pierpont, March 20, 1862, Basler, *CWL,* 5:166 and n.

11. K.V. Whaley to Francis H. Pierpont, May 12, 1862; Jonathan Roberts to S.A. Higgins(?), May 29, 1862; Roberts to Pierpont, June 19, 1862, all in Pierpont Papers; *Calendar of Virginia State Papers,* 11:409.

12. *Alexandria Gazette,* Nov. 14, Dec. 10, 1862; *Washington Daily Chronicle,* Sept. 16, 1863, Jan. 14, 1864; Joseph Segar to Abraham Lincoln, Sept. 6, 7, 1863, Lincoln Papers.

13. Abraham Lincoln to George S. Boutwell, Nov. 24, 1862, Basler, *CWL,* 5:507-8.

14. Lemuel Bowden to Abraham Lincoln, July 31, 1863; L.H. Chandler to Lincoln, Aug. 1, 1863, both in Lincoln Papers; Lincoln to General John G. Foster, Aug. 3, 28, 1863; Lincoln to John P. Gray, Sept. 10, 1863; Approval of Sentence in Case of David M. Wright, Oct. 7, 1863, all in Basler, *CWL,* 6:362, 419, 437-38, 505.

15. Butler had commanded at nearby Fort Monroe in 1861 before his Louisiana assignment.

16. Mayor Daniel Collins of Portsmouth to Francis H. Pierpont, July 15, 1863, *Calendar of Virginia State Papers,* 11:412 Abraham Lincoln to Gen. John G. Foster, Aug. 8, 1863, Basler, *CWL,* 6:371; General Foster to Edwin M. Stanton, Aug. 16, 1863; Henry M. Naglee to General Foster, Aug. 15, 1863, both in *OR,* ser. 1, vol. 29, pt. 2, 54-58.

17. Virginia, *Journal of House of Delegates, Extra Session, 1862,* 9-14; *Washington Daily Chronicle,* Dec. 10, 1863. See below, 162-63, for the actions of the 1864 constitutional convention. Both the General Assembly and the constitutional convention met in Alexandria.

18. Abraham Lincoln to John A. Dix, Oct. 26, 1862, Basler, *CWL,* 5:476-77; Lincoln to Dix, Dec. 31, 1862, ibid., 6:26. Dix's reply is included in the note on p. 26. For Lincoln's affirmation of his late 1862 assurance that occupied Virginia would be exempted from emancipation if they elected congressmen, see Lincoln to Joseph Segar, April 23, 1863, ibid., 6:186-87.

19. Warren W. Wing to Francis H. Pierpont, Dec. 23, 1862; James H. Clements to Pierpont, Dec. 23, 1862; John C. Underwood to Pierpont, Dec. 29, 1862, all in Pierpont Papers; U.S. Congress, 38th Cong., 1st sess., *House Report No. 9,* 1-3; ibid., *House Report No. 14,* 1-5, 10-11.

20. Though Federal armies had taken possession of West and Middle Tennessee, their control at times was precarious, with the likes of rebel Gen. Nathan Bedford Forrest operating in the region and some communities subject to temporary Confederate control.

21. Abraham Lincoln to Andrew Johnson, Jan. 8, 10, 1863, Basler, *CWL,* 6:48, 53.

22. Andrew Johnson to Abraham Lincoln, Jan. 11, 1863, Johnson, *JP,* 6:114.

23. Johnson, *JP,* 6:l-li.

24. Andrew Johnson to William S. Rosecrans, Jan. 14, 1863, ibid., 118-19; Rosecrans to Henry W. Halleck, April 4, 1863, *OR,* ser. 1, vol. 23, pt. 2, 208.

25. Henry W. Halleck to William S. Rosecrans, March 20, 1863, *OR*, ser. 3, vol. 3, 77-78.

26. William S. Rosecrans to Henry W. Halleck, March 26, 1863, *OR*, ser. 1, vol. 23, pt. 2, 174; Halleck to Rosecrans, March 30, 1863, ibid., 191; Andrew Johnson to Rosecrans, April 8, 1863, Johnson, *JP,* 6:209 and n.

27. Andrew Johnson to William S. Rosecrans, April 8, 1863; Rosecrans to Johnson, April 12, 1863, both in Johnson, *JP,* 6:209, 211.

28. Benjamin W. Sharp to Andrew Johnson, June 28, 1863, *JP,* 6:278; Ernest Walter Hooper, "Memphis, Tennessee: Federal Occupation and Reconstruction, 1862-1870" (Ph.D. diss., Univ. of North Carolina, Chapel Hill, 1957), 69-70.

29. Resolutions from Union State Convention, July 13, 1863, Johnson, *JP,* 6:289n.

30. Ibid., 288-89, 289n. For the conservative Unionists' purposes in the convention, see John Lellyett to William B. Campbell, June 29, 1863, Campbell Family Papers, Manuscript Department, Duke University Library, Durham.

31. James B. Bingham to Andrew Johnson, Aug. 11, 1863, Johnson, *JP,* 6:324-25; *Nashville Daily Press,* Oct. 3, 1863.

32. Speech at Franklin, Aug. 22, 1863, Johnson, *JP,* 6:335-38.

33. Johnson, *JP,* 6:404n; *Nashville Daily Press,* Oct. 3, 1863, Oct. 12, 1864; Emerson Etheridge to Abraham Lincoln, Sept. 28, 1863, Lincoln Papers.

34. For an account of the Etheridge plot in the House, see Herman Belz, "The Etheridge Conspiracy of 1863: A Projected Conservative Coup," *Journal of Southern History* 36 (Nov. 1970), 549-67.

35. The quotation can be found in Lonnie E. Maness, "Emerson Etheridge and the Union," *Tennessee Historical Quarterly* 48 (Summer 1989), 103.

36. Abraham Lincoln to Andrew Johnson, Sept. 11, 1863, Basler, *CWL,* 6:440. Harris was the Confederate governor of Tennessee.

37. C.A. Dana to Edwin M. Stanton, Sept. 8, 1863, *OR,* ser. 2, vol. 30, pt. 1, 182-83; *Nashville Daily Union,* Oct. 9, 1863.

38. Abraham Lincoln to John M. Fleming and Robert Morrow, Aug. 9, 1863, Basler, *CWL,* 6:373.

39. Abraham Lincoln to William S. Rosecrans, Oct. 4, 1863, ibid., 6:498.

40. Andrew Johnson to Montgomery Blair, Nov. 24, 1863, Johnson, *JP,* 6:492.

41. Abraham Lincoln to Andrew Johnson, Oct. 28, 1863, Basler, *CWL,* 6:543; Johnson to Lincoln, Nov. 2, 1863, Johnson, *JP,* 6:448; Lincoln to Johnson, Dec. 10, 1863, Basler, *CWL,* 7:59.

42. *Louisville Journal,* Oct. 30, 1863, as quoted in Johnson, *JP,* 6:448n. Johnson called this editorial to Lincoln's attention as a prime example of the "violent attack" he was subjected to from "disloyal" elements. Whiting was a legal counsel in the War Department whose theories supporting the territorialization of the rebel states Radicals found attractive.

43. Announcement of Union Success in Tennessee, Dec. 7, 1863, Basler, *CWL,* 7:35.

44. William C. Harris, "East Tennessee's Civil War Refugees and the Impact of the War on Civilians," *Journal of East Tennessee History* 64 (1992): 3.

45. Nathaniel P. Banks to Mary Banks, Jan. 15 (quotation), 27, 1863, Banks Papers.

46. Joseph G. Dawson III, *Army Generals and Reconstruction: Louisiana, 1862-1877* (Baton Rouge and London: Louisiana State Univ. Press, 1982), 9, 11.

47. *Appleton's Annual Cyclopedia, 1862,* 585-86; Citizens of New Orleans to Abraham Lincoln, Dec. 16, 1862, Lincoln Papers; Gen. Nathaniel P. Banks to Gen. Henry W. Halleck, Jan. 7, 1863; Banks to Edwin M. Stanton, Feb. 2, 1864, both in Banks Papers.

48. As quoted in McCrary, *Lincoln and Reconstruction,* 111n.

49. Ibid., 115-20; Cox, *Lincoln and Black Freedom,* 131.

50. *New York Tribune,* March 4, 1863.

51. *New York Times,* March 5, 1863; *Boston Liberator,* Feb. 24, 1865.

52. Executive Order Establishing a Provisional Court in Louisiana, Oct. 20, 1862, Basler, *CWL,* 5:467-68; Charles A. Peabody, "The United States Provisional Court for the State of Louisiana, 1862-1865," *Annual Report of the American Historical Association for the Year 1892* (Washington, D.C.: GPO, 1893), 202-5. Peabody was also empowered to select officers for his court. In Tennessee and Virginia, Lincoln in 1862 and 1863, without resort to a provisional court arrangement, appointed federal court officers. Earlier, in 1861, Lincoln appointed a district judge for North Alabama, but the court was not organized during the war.

53. *Appleton's Annual Cyclopedia, 1863,* 770-72; Michael Hahn to Abraham Lincoln, May 9, 1863, Lincoln Papers. The relationship of military provost courts to civilian courts in the occupied South is a rather murky one. See Hyman, *A More Perfect Union,* 199-202, for an account.

54. Abraham Lincoln to Edward Bates, May 20, 1863, Basler, *CWL,* 6:223, and n.

55. Nathaniel P. Banks to Mary Banks, Feb. 26, 1863, Banks Papers; Rush Pumly to Salmon P. Chase, March 23, 1863; Crofts J. Wright to Chase, April 8, 1864, both in Chase Papers, Library of Congress.

56. George F. Shepley to Benjamin F. Butler, Feb. 20, 1863; Salmon P. Chase to Butler, Feb. 24, 1864, both in *Correspondence of Butler,* 3:14-15; George S. Denison to Salmon P. Chase, March 29, April 13, 1863, Chase Papers, Library of Congress.

57. Thomas J. Durant and James Graham to George F. Shepley, May 23, 1863, *OR,* ser. 3, vol. 3, 231-33.

58. Ibid., 232.

59. Abraham Lincoln to E.E. Malhiot, Bradish Johnson, and Thomas Cottman, June 19, 1863, Basler, *CWL,* 6:287-88, 288n; Michael Hahn to Lincoln, May 9, 1863; J.Q.A. Fellows, Plan for Re-establishing a Union Government in Rebel States, June 26(?), 1863, both in Lincoln Papers.

60. Thomas Cottman to Abraham Lincoln, June 18, 1863, Lincoln Papers; Lincoln to E.E. Malhiot, Bradish Johnson, and Thomas Cottman, June 19, 1863, Basler, *CWL,* 6:288.

61. Abraham Lincoln to Nathaniel P. Banks, Aug. 5, 1863, Basler, *CWL,* 6:364-65.

62. Edwin M. Stanton to George F. Shepley, Aug. 24, 1863, *OR,* ser. 3, vol. 3, 711. Herman Belz (*Reconstructing the Union,* 145) and LaWanda Cox (*Lincoln and Black Freedom,* 52-53, 56-57) contend that Lincoln's rejection of the conservative proposals for reconstruction, along with his and Stanton's letters to Banks and Shepley, indicated that the president had allied himself with

the radical Durant faction. Although Lincoln believed that a convention, which would end slavery, was highly desirable, he did not require it. The president understood that such action at this time would alienate moderate Unionists, such as Michael Hahn, and establish a precedent for intervention that he did not want. Lincoln was prepared to go either way, with or without a constitutional convention, provided a loyal government was soon established in Louisiana. For Hahn's important advice to Lincoln on this issue, see Hahn to Lincoln, Aug. 11, 1863, Lincoln Papers.

63. Nathaniel P. Banks to Abraham Lincoln, Sept. 5, 1863; Thomas J. Durant to Lincoln, Oct. 1, 1863, both in Lincoln Papers.

64. McCrary, *Lincoln and Reconstruction,* 173; *Appleton's Annual Cyclopedia, 1863,* 591.

65. Nathaniel P. Banks to Mary Banks, Sept. 15, 1863, Banks Papers; clipping from *New Orleans Era,* Nov. 15, 1863; Michael Hahn to Abraham Lincoln, Nov. 20, 1863, both in Lincoln Papers; *New York Times,* Nov. 19, 1863.

66. McCrary, *Lincoln and Reconstruction,* 174, 182.

67. In his correspondence warning Republican senators and representatives against the Etheridge scheme, Lincoln made no mention of the effort to seat Southern Unionists. He alerted them to the attempt "to shut out proper" members from the North. Basler, *CWL,* 6:546-50. For the view that Lincoln linked the Etheridge plot with Louisiana conservatives, see Cox, *Lincoln and Black Freedom,* 63, McCrary, *Lincoln and Reconstruction,* 179-80, and Belz, "Etheridge Conspiracy," 556, 561. For the Lincoln-Cottman relationship, which continued after the failure of the Etheridge conspiracy, see Lincoln to Cottman, Dec. 15, 1863, Basler, *CWL,* 7:66-67.

68. *Appleton's Annual Cyclopedia, 1863,* 591.

69. Lincoln to Nathaniel P. Banks, Nov. 5, 1863, Basler, *CWL,* 7:1-2.

70. Nathaniel P. Banks to Abraham Lincoln, Dec. 6, 1863, ibid., 7:90-91n. Banks in a Dec. 11, 1864, letter to Lincoln (Banks Papers) repeated his complaint to the president.

71. Abraham Lincoln to Nathaniel P. Banks, Dec. 24, 1863, Basler, *CWL,* 7:89-90.

72. For Lincoln's strong support of Banks and his belief that the general would quickly succeed as "master" of Louisiana reconstruction, see George W. Boutwell to Nathaniel P. Banks, Dec. 21, 1863; H.W. Osborn to Banks, Dec. 26, 1863, both in Banks Papers.

6. A New Presidential Initiative

1. Edmund Fowler to Abraham Lincoln, Oct. 27, 1863, Lincoln Papers. Fowler had clearly misled Lincoln. Though some new legislators, particularly from North Alabama, had campaigned on a peace platform, the majority of the new General Assembly were anti-Davis, not anti-Confederate. No resolution favoring reconstruction was introduced.

2. Armistead Burwell to Abraham Lincoln, Aug. 28, 1863, Lincoln Papers. See also Gen. Stephen A. Hurlbut to Abraham Lincoln, Aug. 11, 1863, *OR,* ser. 1, vol. 24, pt. 3, 588-89; *Washington Daily Chronicle,* Dec. 1, 1863; *Washington National Intelligencer,* Aug. 1863 issues; and entry for Oct. 23, 1863, Dennett, ed., *Hay Diaries,* 106.

3. Lorenzo Thomas to Edwin M. Stanton, Oct. 24, 1863, *OR,* ser. 3, vol. 3, 916-17.

4. To the editors of the *Washington National Intelligencer,* Aug. 26, 1863, as reported in the *Nashville Daily Union,* Sept. 7, 1863.

5. *Little Rock National Democrat,* Oct. 20, 1863; *New York Tribune,* Nov. 19, 1863; *Nashville Daily Union,* Dec. 8, 1863; *Washington National Intelligencer,* Dec. 9, 1863; Message of Governor Isaac Murphy, April 16, 1864, Arkansas, *Journal of the Convention of Delegates of the People of Arkansas, Assembled at the Capitol, January 4, 1864; Also, Journals of the House of Representatives of the Sessions 1864, 1864-65, and 1865* (Little Rock: Price and Barton, 1870), 17-18, hereinafter cited as Arkansas, *Convention Journal, 1864.*

6. As reported in the *Washington National Intelligencer,* Dec. 9, 1863.

7. Ibid. See also C.P. Bartrand to Abraham Lincoln, Oct. 19, 1863, Lincoln Papers.

8. E.W. Gantt to Abraham Lincoln, July 15, 1863, Lincoln Papers; *Address of Brig. Gen. E.W. Gantt, C.S.A., First Published October 7, 1863, at Little Rock, Arkansas* (1863). Gantt's address was also printed and distributed by the Loyal Publications Society in New York. For a biographical sketch of Gantt, see Bruce S. Allardice, *More Generals in Gray* (Baton Rouge: Louisiana State Univ. Press, 1995), 96.

9. E.W. Gantt to Abraham Lincoln, Jan. 29, 1864, Lincoln Papers; *New York Times,* Jan. 20, 1864; *New Orleans Daily True Delta,* Jan. 27, 1864; Gen. J.W. Davidson to S.H. Boyd, Dec. 23, 1863, *OR,* ser. 1, vol. 34, pt. 2, 105 (quotation).

10. C.C. Bliss to Abraham Lincoln, Nov. 9, 1863, with two newspaper clippings, Lincoln Papers; *Washington Sunday Chronicle,* Dec. 27, 1863; Message of Governor Isaac Murphy, April 16, 1864, Arkansas, *Convention Journal, 1864,* 18; U.S. Congress, *Senate Report No. 94,* 38th Cong., 1st sess.

11. William C. Harris, *William Woods Holden: Firebrand of North Carolina Politics* (Baton Rouge: Louisiana State Univ. Press, 1987), 131-36; Basler, *CWL,* 6:330-31n; *Washington Daily Chronicle,* July 16, Aug. 3, 14, 20, 21, 1863; *Washington National Intelligencer,* Aug. 3, 13, 1863; Citizens of Second Congressional District (North Carolina) to Abraham Lincoln, Sept. 30, 1863, Lincoln Papers; *Appleton's Annual Cyclopedia, 1863,* 217-18.

12. Entry for Aug. 22, 1863, Howard K. Beale, ed., "The Diary of Edward Bates," in *Annual Report of the American Historical Association for the Year 1930* (Washington, D.C.: American Historical Association, 1930), 4:410.

13. Endorsement on Letter of James R. Gilmore to Zebulon B. Vance, n.d., Basler, *CWL,* 6:330, 330-31n. The editor of Lincoln's *Collected Works* believes that this endorsement was written in mid-July 1863. A more probable date would be late August 1863, at the height of the North Carolina peace movement.

14. Allan Nevins, *The War for the Union: The Organized War, 1863-1864* (New York: Charles Scribner's Sons, 1971), 466-67. The designation old Union Whigs refers to those prewar Whigs who resisted secession until their states left the Union. During the war they frequently became critics of the Davis administration and the secession Democrats in their states. Some of them, but not a majority, became early supporters of reunion.

15. *Appleton's Annual Cyclopedia, 1863,* 569, 731, 740; entry for Aug. 9, 1863, Dennett, *Hay Diaries,* 77.

16. Harris, *Holden,* 131-32, 142-43.

17. Thomas B. Alexander, "Persistent Whiggery in the Confederate South, 1860-1877," *Journal of Southern History* 27 (Aug. 1961): 308-9.

18. Abraham Lincoln to William S. Rosecrans, Oct. 4, 1863, Basler, *CWL,* 6:498.

19. *New York Tribune,* Nov. 21, 1863; Salmon P. Chase to Abraham Lincoln, Nov. 25, 1863; James Dixon to Lincoln, Nov. 14, 1863, both in Lincoln Papers.

20. Abraham Lincoln to John A. McClernand, Jan. 8, 1863, Basler, *CWL,* 6:48-49; Salmon P. Chase to Abraham Lincoln, Nov. 25, 1863, Lincoln Papers.

21. William E. Smith, *The Francis Preston Blair Family in Politics* (New York: Macmillan, 1933), 2:237-38.

22. Belz, *Reconstructing the Union,* 173-75, 185n.

23. Charles Sumner to Montgomery Blair, Oct. 21, 1863, Blair Family Papers.

24. [Charles Sumner], "Our Domestic Relations; Or, How to Treat the Rebel States," *Atlantic Monthly* 12 (Oct. 1863): 507-29; Donald, *Sumner and the Rights of Man,* 120-21, 178-79.

25. This speech was subsequently published as *The Administration and the War: Remarks of Mr. H.J. Raymond, of New York, at Wilmington, Delaware, November 6, 1863* (1863). Professor Belz asserts that Lincoln "tended toward a more radical position" at this time, perhaps influenced by William Whiting's theories outlined in his book *The War Powers of the President and the Legislative Powers of Congress in Relation to Rebellion, Treason, and Slavery* (Boston: J.L. Shorey, 1862). Belz, *Reconstructing the Union,* 132 and n; Herman Belz, *Emancipation and Equal Rights: Politics and Constitutionalism in the Civil War Era* (New York: W.W. Norton, 1978), 82-83. Belz cites an 1864 conversation George Julian, a Radical Republican, had with Lincoln in which the president indicated that after reading Whiting's legal argument he had changed his mind on the issue of permanent confiscation of rebel estates. Julian's report of the conversation occurred many years after the war and probably reflected his attempt to get Lincoln right with the Radicals. Rice, *Reminiscences of Lincoln,* 58-59. I doubt that Whiting, a legal adviser in the War Department, whom Lincoln reportedly was fond of, had much influence with the president in reconstruction matters. Whiting's radical theory that the seceded states had committed suicide and thus reverted to a territorial status stood diametrically opposite of Lincoln's concept that the states had never left the Union.

26. See, for example, J.W. Denver to Montgomery Blair, Oct. 9, 1863; J.L. Scripps, editor of the *Chicago Tribune,* to Montgomery Blair, Oct. 26, 1863, both in Blair Family Papers.

27. Proclamation of Amnesty and Reconstruction, Dec. 8, 1863, Basler, *CWL,* 7:53-55. Prior to issuing the proclamation, Lincoln read it to his Cabinet, which, according to a report, unanimously approved it. *Boston Daily Advertiser,* Dec. 5, 1863.

28. Lincoln's Annual Message to Congress, Dec. 8, 1863, Basler, *CWL,* 7:51.

29. Proclamation of Amnesty and Reconstruction, Dec. 8, 1863, Basler, *CWL,* 7:55.

30. Jonathan T. Dorris, *Pardon and Amnesty under Lincoln and Johnson: The Restoration of the Confederates to Their Rights and Privileges, 1861-1898* (Chapel Hill: Univ. of North Carolina Press, 1953), 67-68; entry for Dec. 19, 1863, Dennett, *Hay Diaries,* 139; Lincoln's Annual Message to Congress, Dec. 6, 1864, Basler, *CWL,* 8:152.

31. Proclamation of Amnesty and Reconstruction, Dec. 8, 1863, Basler, CWL, 7:55-56.

32. Annual Message to Congress, Dec. 8, 1863, ibid., 7:52.

33. Remarks to Arkansas Delegation, Jan. 22, 1864, ibid., 144. Andrew Jackson Hamilton continued as military governor of Texas, but he had little territory to reconstruct. Francis H. Pierpont was never a military governor; from the beginning he was recognized by both Lincoln and Congress as the civil governor of Virginia.

34. Noah Brooks, *Washington in Lincoln's Time* (New York: Century, 1895), 271-72.

35. Entry for Dec. 11, 1863, *The Diary of George Templeton Strong* (New York: Macmillan, 1952), 3:379.

36. *Chicago Tribune,* Dec. 10, 1863.

37. As reported in the *New York Tribune,* Dec. 11, 1863.

38. Edward L. Pierce, *Memoirs and Letters of Charles Sumner* (Boston: Roberts Brothers, 1878-1894), 4:216; *Congressional Globe,* 38th Cong., 1st sess. (Jan. 22, 1864), 317.

39. *National Anti-Slavery Standard,* Dec. 19, 1863.

40. *New York Times,* Dec. 10, 1863.

41. *Washington Daily Chronicle,* Dec. 10, 1863, Jan. 23, 1864; *Boston Daily Advertiser,* Dec. 10, 1863.

42. *St. Louis Missouri Republican,* Dec. 11, 1863. Despite its name, this was not a Republican party newspaper.

43. Lincoln's commitment to emancipation was even stronger in his annual message to Congress. For Republican delight with this message, see entry for Dec. 9, 1863, Dennett, *Hay Diaries,* 131-32.

44. *Washington Daily Chronicle,* March 18, 1864.

45. As reported in the *Washington National Intelligencer,* Jan. 7, 1864.

46. As quoted in James M. McPherson, *The Struggle for Equality: Abolitionists and the Negro in the Civil War and Reconstruction* (Princeton: Princeton Univ. Press, 1964), 243.

47. William S. McFeely, *Frederick Douglass* (New York: W.W. Norton, 1991), 234-35; Philip S. Foner, *The Civil War, 1861-1865,* vol. 3 of *The Life and Writings of Frederick Douglass* (New York: International, 1952), 42-43. Douglass also protested Lincoln's tolerance of unequal treatment of black soldiers.

48. *New Bern North Carolina Times,* May 21, 1864. As will be described in chapter 8, Lincoln followed the visit from the Louisiana delegation with a "private" message to Michael Hahn, Louisiana's new loyal governor, that the state might consider enfranchising "the very intelligent" blacks and "those who have fought gallantly in our ranks." But Lincoln made it clear that this was only a suggestion, not a change in his policy of noninterference in the work of reorganization.

49. *New York News* as quoted in the *New York Tribune,* Dec. 11, 1863; New York, *Journal of the Senate of the State of New York: At Their Eighty-Seventh Session, Begun and Held at the Capitol, in the City of Albany, on the Fifth Day of January, 1864* (Albany: Comstock & Cassidy, 1864), 24-25. Seymour insisted that "there is but one course that will save us from national ruin. We must adhere to the solemn pledges made by our Government at the outset of the war" (26).

50. *New York Tribune,* Dec. 11, 1863, contains these and other newspaper comments on Lincoln's proclamation. *Alexandria Gazette,* Dec. 12, 1863, also reported synopses of the Northern press reaction to it.

51. *Washington Constitutional Union,* Dec. 11, 31, 1863, Jan. 9, 16, 1864; *Alexandria Gazette,* Dec. 12, 1863. The *Constitutional Union* proposed its own plan for the restoration of the Union: an armistice followed by a national convention of all the states, including the Southern states. This would become the "Copperhead" platform in 1864.

52. Brooks Simpson, *Let Us Have Peace: Ulysses S. Grant and the Politics of War and Reconstruction, 1861-1868* (Chapel Hill and London: Univ. of North Carolina Press, 1991), 50.

53. James H. Wilson to U.S. Grant, Feb. 25, 1864, in John Y. Simon, ed., *The Papers of Ulysses S. Grant* (Carbondale and Edwardsville: Southern Illinois Univ. Press, 1982), 10:142n.

54. Simpson, *Let Us Have Peace,* 50-51.

55. Entry for Dec. 20, 1863, Crabtree and Patton, *Journal of a Secesh Lady,* 508-9.

56. *Richmond Sentinel,* Dec. 14, 1863.

57. Ibid.; *Lynchburg Virginian,* Dec. 12, 15 (quotation), 1863; entry for Dec. 20, 1863, Crabtree and Patton, *Journal of a Secesh Lady,* 508.

58. *Raleigh Weekly North Carolina Standard,* Dec. 23, 1863.

59. *Journal of the Congress of the Confederate States of America, 1861-1865* (Washington, D.C.: GPO, 1904-1905), 6:536-38. Though less strident, President Davis had a similar reaction to the proclamation. Jefferson Davis to Zebulon B. Vance, Jan. 8, 1864, Letterbook of Governor Zebulon B. Vance, North Carolina Division of Archives and History, Raleigh.

60. *New Orleans Daily True Delta,* Feb. 2, 11, 1864.

61. J.L. Riddell to Abraham Lincoln, Dec. 15, 1863, *Lincoln Papers;* Lincoln to Thomas Cottman, Dec. 15, 1863, Basler, *CWL,* 7:66-67.

62. Andrew Johnson, Speech on the Restoration of State Government, Jan. 21, 1864; William Young to Johnson, ca. Feb. 20, 1864; Samuel C. Mercer to Johnson, Feb. 28, 1864; Johnson, *Speech on Vice-Presidential Nomination,* June 9, 1864, all in Johnson, *JP,* 6:588, 626-27, 629, 726; J.D. Hale to Horace Maynard, June 25, 1864; Maynard to Abraham Lincoln, July 1, 1864, both in Lincoln Papers.

63. Abraham Lincoln to Horace Maynard, Feb. 13, 1864, Basler, *CWL,* 7:183 and n. For Johnson's oath, see Johnson, *JP,* 6:595. A fuller account of Johnson's voting oath and its application can be found in chapter 10.

64. Andrew Johnson to Abraham Lincoln, May 17, 1864, Johnson, *JP,* 6:699, 701n.

65. Nathaniel P. Banks to Abraham Lincoln, Jan. 22, 1864, Lincoln Papers; *New Orleans Bee,* Jan. 14, 1864; J.S. Whitaker to Salmon P. Chase, April 14, 1864, Chase Papers, Library of Congress; *Nashville Daily Union,* Feb. 5, 1864; Abraham Lincoln to Edwin M. Stanton, Feb. 5, 1864, all in Basler, *CWL,* 7:169 and n.

66. Abraham Lincoln to Andrew Johnson, Jan. 25, 1864; Lincoln to Nathaniel P. Banks, Jan. 31, 1864; Lincoln to Horace Maynard, Feb. 13, 1864, all in Basler, *CWL,* 7:149-50, 161-62, 183.

67. *Congressional Globe,* 39th Cong., 1st sess. (Jan. 5, 1864), 97-99.

68. Ibid., (Dec. 16, 1863), 37; Belz, *Reconstructing the Union,* 173-75.

69. *Congressional Globe,* 38th Cong., 1st sess. (Dec. 21, 1863), 70.

70. Professor Herman Belz, who has studied the interaction of Congress and president over reconstruction policy, reaches a different conclusion regarding

Ashley's bill. He writes that "Ashley's bill seemed to implement the President's plan," since it incorporated the Ten Percent concept and provided for state governments based on new constitutions prohibiting slavery. The provision for black suffrage, Belz says, was premature and not really an issue for House members. Furthermore, according to Belz, Ashley's provisional military-governor arrangement was the same as Lincoln's and involved "a great assertion of federal power" over the South. "The possibility that southern Unionists might organize state governments on their own initiative had long since disappeared," Belz asserts. Belz, *Reconstructing the Union*, 183-85, 185n.

71. *Congressional Globe*, 38th Cong., 1st sess. (Jan. 18, 1864), 259; ibid., (Jan. 20, 1864), 288.

7. A Flurry of Activity

1. The evidence of increased war-weariness and disarray in the South as the winter progressed is extensive. See the *Washington Daily Chronicle*, Dec. 28, 1863, Jan. 23, Feb. 3, 1864, and the *Little Rock National Democrat*, Feb. 13, 1864. See also Emory M. Thomas, *The Confederate Nation, 1861-1865* (New York: Harper & Row, 1979), 284-85.

2. Entry for Dec. 25, 1863, Dennett, *Hay Diaries*, 144.

3. *New Bern North Carolina Times*, Jan. 2, 1864; *Nashville Daily Union*, Jan. 26, 1864; Abraham Lincoln to Frederick Steele, Jan. 5, 1864; Lincoln to Andrew Johnson, ca. Jan. 15, 1864, both in Basler, *CWL*, 7:108-9, 130 and n.

4. *New Orleans Daily True Delta*, March 31, 1864; *New Bern North Carolina Times*, Jan. 2, March 30, 1864; *Nashville Daily Union*, Jan. 26, 1864.

5. Colonel R. A. Alger to Benjamin F. Butler, Feb. 23, 1864, *Correspondence of Butler*, 3:463-64.

6. *New Orleans Daily True Delta*, March 31, 1864.

7. Abraham Lincoln to Gen. John G. Foster, Jan. 27, 1864, Basler, *CWL*, 7:153. The Longstreet-Foster correspondence can be conveniently found in ibid., 153-54n. In an equally bizarre incident regarding the circulation of Lincoln's proclamation, Gen. John B. Margruder, commanding Confederate forces on the Texas coast, actually printed and distributed copies of it among his troops, though he left out the amnesty provision. *Louisville Daily Journal*, Feb. 26, 1864.

8. Entries for Dec. 28, 1863, Jan. 2, 1864, Dennett, *Hay Diaries*, 145, 148-52; Abraham Lincoln to Benjamin F. Butler, Jan. 2, 1864, Basler, *CWL*, 7:103 and 95n. According to Butler's interpretation, Lincoln's definition of "service" for released Confederates included labor on public works in the North. At least 150 prisoners at Point Lookout chose this option. Benjamin F. Butler to Gen. Gilman Marston, Jan. 9, 1864, *OR*, ser. 2, vol. 6, 823; Butler to Col. William Hoffman, March 11, 1864, ibid., 1033-34; Gen. Lew Wallace to Col. E.D. Townsend, April 15, 1864, *OR*, ser. 2, vol. 7, 56.

9. J.T Clifton to William Campbell, Feb. 2, 1864, Campbell Family Papers.

10. Abraham Lincoln to Edwin M. Stanton, March 18, 1864; Proclamation About Amnesty, March 26, 1864, both in Basler, *CWL*, 7:254-55, 269-70; Col. William Hoffman to Col. A.G. Draper, May 29, 1864, *OR*, ser. 2, vol. 7, 177.

11. To the Senate and House of Representatives, July 17, 1862, Basler, *CWL*, 7:328-31 and 329n; John Syrett, "The Confiscation Acts: Efforts at Reconstruction during the Civil War" (Ph.D. diss., University of Wisconsin, 1971), 85-86.

Although the president under the 1862 law could not restore condemned property to its former owners, the measure did authorize him to extend executive clemency to persons engaged in rebellion, a power that Lincoln already thought he possessed.

12. Syrett, "Confiscation Acts," 93, 95; *Washington National Intelligencer,* Nov. 29, 1862.

13. Abner A. Steele to Andrew Johnson, Dec. 14, 1861; Emerson Etheridge to Johnson, Dec. 19, 1861, both in Johnson, JP, 5:58, 66; *Nashville Daily Union,* April 4, 23, 1863.

14. Syrett, "Confiscation Acts," 101.

15. *Nashville Daily Union,* April 4, 1863; *Washington Daily Chronicle,* Jan. 28, 1864; Syrett, "Confiscation Acts," 50. For most of the war, even Radicals like Charles Sumner did not propose the redistribution of lands to blacks. Ibid., 52.

16. Edward Bates to John C. Underwood, March 28, 1863; sundry newspaper clippings, no dates; *Speech of John C. Underwood of Alexandria, Va., July 4, 1863* (printed), all in Underwood Papers. Since the mid 1850s, Underwood had supported the Republican party. Because of his outspoken antislavery views, he was driven from the state in 1856.

17. Newspaper clippings, no dates, in Underwood Papers.

18. Ibid.

19. Ibid.; Lowe, *Republicans and Reconstruction in Virginia,* 207-8n; *U.S. Supreme Court Reports,* John R. Bigelow v. Douglas F. Forrest, 9 Wallace (1870), 339-53.

20. *Washington National Intelligencer,* Jan. 26, 1864, which opposed Underwood's seizures, reported that Lincoln still maintained the view that rebel property could not be alienated in perpetuity. Republican congressman George W. Julian, however, later remembered that the president in 1864 told him that he would not object to a repeal of the explanatory resolution in the Confiscation Act of 1862 denying the government's right to seize property in fee simple. In mid 1864, Congress rescinded the resolution. After the war the Johnson administration, influenced in part by Pierpont's conversion to conservatism, ended the confiscation proceedings in Virginia. Rice, *Reminiscences of Lincoln,* 58-59; clipping from *Alexandria State Journal,* July 6, 1864, in Underwood Papers.

21. William A. Sorrels to Andrew Johnson, June 23, 1864, Johnson, *JP,* 6:753-54; *New York Times,* Jan. 21, 1864.

22. General Order No. 10, Headquarters, Department of Arkansas, March 3, 1864, Steele Papers. For evidence of women taking the oath to avoid confiscation, see Lou B. Green to General Frederick Steele, n.d. [1864], ibid.

23. *Washington Daily Chronicle,* Feb. 22, 1864; *Little Rock Unconditional Union,* March 25, 1864; *St. Louis Missouri Republican,* Feb. 24, 1864. Coffey's circular letter can be found in the *New York Times,* Feb. 22, 1864.

24. *Washington Daily Chronicle,* Jan. 1, 26, 1864; L.D. Stickney to Salmon P. Chase, Jan. 26, 1864, Chase Papers, Libary of Congress.

25. John E. Johns, *Florida during the Civil War* (Gainesville: Univ. of Florida Press, 1963), 154; Jerrell H. Shofner, *Nor Is It Over Yet: Florida in the Era of Reconstruction, 1863-1877* (Gainesville: Univ. Presses of Florida, 1974), 2-3.

26. *Washington National Intelligencer,* March 20, April 1, 1862; To the People of East Florida, March 20, 1862, *OR,* ser. 1, vol. 6, 251-52.

27. Report of General Horatio G. Wright, April 13, 1862, *OR,* ser. 1, vol. 6, 124-25; *Washington National Intelligencer,* April 22, 1862. About one hundred

Union families left Jacksonville with the Union troops. Having lost everything, they went to New York and joined the growing Southern refugee colony there.

28. *Washington Daily Chronicle,* Jan. 1, 26, 1864.

29. John Hay indicated to Lyman D. Stickney, a Northerner in Florida, that Lincoln "was highly pleased with the result of the meeting at St. Augustine." L.D. Stickney to Salmon P. Chase, Jan. 26, 1864, Chase Papers, Library of Congress.

30. Entry for Jan. 13, 1864, Dennett, *Hay Diaries,* 154.

31. Abraham Lincoln to Gen. Quincy A. Gillmore, Jan. 13, 1864, Basler, *CWL,* 7:126.

32. Quincy A. Gillmore to Abraham Lincoln, Jan. 21, 1864, Basler, *CWL,* 7:126n; Gillmore to Lincoln, [Jan. 30, 1864], *OR,* ser. 1, vol. 35, pt. 1, 295 (quotation). After the failure of the Florida campaign, which he blamed on Gen. Truman Seymour, Gillmore told Hay that he only added the reconstruction purpose to please President Lincoln. Entry of March 1, 1864, Dennett, *Hay Diaries,* 166.

33. Report of Brigadier Gen. Truman Seymour, Feb. 17, 1864, *OR,* ser. 1, vol. 35, pt. 1, 295.

34. John Hay to Abraham Lincoln, Feb. 8, 1864, Lincoln Papers; entries for Feb. 9, 10, 1864, Dennett, *Hay Diaries,* 159.

35. Lyman Stickney to Salmon P. Chase, Feb. 16, March 2, 1864, Chase Papers, Library of Congress; entry for March 1, 1864, Dennett, *Hay Diaries,* 165.

36. *New York World,* as quoted in the *Alexandria Gazette,* Feb. 16, 1864; L.D. Stickney to Salmon P. Chase, March 2, 1864, Chase Papers, Library of Congress.

37. As quoted in Shofner, *Nor Is It Over Yet,* 11.

38. *Washington Daily Chronicle,* March 2, 1864; *Washington Daily National Republican,* March 2, 1864; *New York Times,* March 15, 1864.

39. Entry for March 24, 1864, Dennett, *Hay Diaries,* 166.

40. The Florida Unionists told Lincoln that, though the loyal cause had suffered a setback with the Olustee defeat of the army, Floridians continued to take the oath of allegiance. They reported that the numbers now enrolled exceeded the required one-tenth of the 1860 voters. They also sent a delegation to Washington to plead for Lincoln's support. It was unsuccessful. Loyal citizens of Florida to Abraham Lincoln, May 20, 1864; Loyal Citizens of Florida Committee to Lincoln July 9, 1864, both in Lincoln Papers.

41. For a fuller account of the state convention movement and its objectives, see Harris, *Holden,* 141-49.

42. *Washington Daily Chronicle,* Jan. 19, 30, 1864; *Nashville Daily Union,* March 22, 1864; *New Bern North Carolina Times,* Jan. 9 (quotations), 16, 23, 1864.

43. *New Bern North Carolina Times,* Jan. 16, 1864.

44. Edward Stanly to Abraham Lincoln, Jan. 27, 1864, *OR,* ser. 1, vol. 33, 430; Lincoln to Stanly, Jan. 28, 1864, Basler, *CWL,* 7:158. Stanly, in expressing his willingness to assist in North Carolina's reconstruction, informed Lincoln that he would not serve as governor.

45. Harris, *Holden,* 150-51, 154.

46. Notable exceptions to this pattern were the fertile river counties of Madison (Huntsville) and Limestone (Athens), both of which contained a more than 50 percent slave population. These counties, consisting of a mixed planter-yeoman

society, were similar to the Alabama River counties of Monroe (Mt. Pleasant) and Clarke (Grove Hill) in the Southern part of the state.

47. As quoted in J. Mills Thornton III, *Politics and Power in a Slave Society, 1800-1860* (Baton Rouge: Louisiana State Univ. Press, 1978), 439.

48. Jeremiah Clemens to Leroy Pope Walker, April 4, 1861, *OR,* ser. 1, vol. 52, pt. 2, 35; O.M. Mitchel to Edwin M. Stanton, May 4, 1862, *OR,* ser. 1, vol. 10, pt. 2, 162-63; Walter Lynwood Fleming, *Civil War and Reconstruction in Alabama* (New York: Columbia Univ. Press, 1905), 125; Johnson, *JP,* 5:582n.

49. *Washington National Intelligencer,* Feb. 22, 1862. See also report of Lt. William Gwin, Feb. 23, 1862, *OR,* ser. 1, vol. 7, 421.

50. Robert M. Patton to Andrew Johnson, July 1, 1865, Johnson, *JP,* 8:337. Patton, president of the state senate at the time of secession, like other North Alabama cooperationists claimed later that he "was always an ardent and faithful supporter of the Union [and] exercised all his influence to prevent [the] fatal step" of secession. Also similar to many fellow cooperationists, he ceased to support the Confederacy when Federal forces in 1862 occupied his home county.

51. O.M. Mitchel to Edwin M. Stanton, May 4, 1862 *OR,* ser. 1, vol. 10, pt. 2, 163.

52. Basler, *CWL,* 7:15 and n. Busteed, a former Democrat who had raised Irish-American troops for the Union and in 1862 was appointed a brigadier general, became a controversial judge in postwar Alabama. Faced with impeachment for malfeasance in office, Busteed resigned in 1874 and returned to New York. *Appleton's Cyclopedia of American Biography* (New York: D. Appleton, 1887-1901), 1:476. See chapter 5 for Peabody and the Louisiana "provisional court."

53. Report of Col. Abel D. Streight, July 16, 1862, *OR,* ser. 1, vol. 16, pt. 1, 785-86, 789-90; James E. Saunders to General Joseph Wheeler, Jan. 30, 1864, *OR,* ser. 1, vol. 52, pt. 2, 613-14; *Louisville Daily Journal,* April 16, 1864.

54. Fleming, *Civil War and Reconstruction in Alabama,* 125; P.H. Watson to O.M. Mitchel, May 8, 1862, *OR,* ser. 1, vol. 10, pt. 2, 175; Current, *Lincoln's Loyalists,* 104-6, 218. The First Alabama Cavalry later distinguished itself in Sherman's army in Georgia and the Carolinas.

55. Clement C. Clay Jr. to George W. Randolph, Oct. 24, 1862, *OR,* ser. 4, vol. 2, 141-42.

56. Gov. John Gill Shorter, Watts's secession-Democratic opponent, carried only four counties in North Alabama, formerly a Democratic stronghold. Malcolm C. McMillan, *The Disintegration of a Confederate State: Three Governors and Alabama's Wartime Home Front, 1861-1865* (Macon, Ga.: Mercer Univ. Press, 1986), 68, 70; Walter L. Fleming, "The Peace Movement in Alabama during the Civil War—II, The Peace Society, 1863-1865," *South Atlantic Quarterly* 2 (1903): 250-51; Edmund Fowler to Abraham Lincoln, Oct. 27, 1863, Lincoln Papers.

57. *New York Times,* Feb. 14, 1864; *Nashville Daily Union,* Feb. 4, 1864; *Louisville Daily Journal,* March 4, 1864; *Washington Daily Chronicle,* Feb. 27, 1864.

58. *Nashville Daily Union,* Feb. 4, 26, 1864; *New York Times,* Feb. 14 (quotation), March 11, 1864; *Washington Daily National Republican,* March 25, 1864; *Washington Daily Chronicle,* March 26, 1864.

59. *Address to the People of Alabama, by D.C. Humphreys* (1864), 2.

60. *Nashville Daily Union,* March 26, 1864.

61. Jeremiah Clemens to William H. Seward, May 5, 1864; Seward to Clemens, May 6, 1864, both in Lincoln Papers. Clemens had written his letter from Philadelphia, where he had just arrived for medical treatment.

62. *New York Times,* Oct. 29, 1864; McMillan, *Disintegration of a Confederate State,* 105; *Appleton's Annual Cyclopedia, 1864,* 10-11.

63. *Letter from the Hon. Jere. Clemens* (1864), 15; Jeremiah Clemens to Benjamin F. Butler, Nov. 16, 1864; Clemens to William H. Seward, Nov. 17, 1864; Clemens to Abraham Lincoln, Jan. 21, 1865, all in Lincoln Papers; Clemens to Andrew Johnson, Nov. 19, 1864, Johnson, *JP,* 7:303-4. Clemens sent the same letter to Charles Sumner, Johnson, *JP,* 7:305n. For other Alabamians in Washington, see William C. Bibb to Lincoln, April 12, 1865, Lincoln Papers.

64. Jeremiah Clemens to Andrew Johnson, April 21, 1865, Johnson, *JP,* 7:598-600.

65. T. Conn Bryan, *Confederate Georgia* (Athens: Univ. of Georgia Press, 1953), 144-45, 147, 150-52; Steven Hahn, *The Roots of Southern Populism: Yeoman Farmers and the Transformation of the Georgia Upcountry, 1850-1890* (New York and Oxford: Oxford Univ. Press, 1983), 130-32; *Appleton's Annual Cyclopedia, 1863,* 449.

66. William T. Sherman to Abraham Lincoln, Sept. 17, 28, 1864; Lincoln to Augustus R. Wright, Nov. 21, 1864, Basler, *CWL,* 8:9-10n, 27n, 119-20; *Testimony Taken by the Joint Select Committee to Inquire into the Condition of Affairs in the Late Insurrectionary States. Georgia.* (Washington, D.C.: GPO, 1872), 1:90-91.

67. *Savannah Daily Republican,* April 3, 1865; Bryan, *Confederate Georgia,* 172-73. Only a handful of Unionists could be found at any time during the war in South Carolina, precluding any movement toward reconstruction under Lincoln's plan.

68. Carl N. Degler, *The Other South: Southern Dissenters in the Nineteenth Century* (New York: Harper & Row, 1974), 177-78; John F.H. Claiborne to Nathaniel P. Banks, Dec. 27, 1863, Banks Papers; *Washington Daily Chronicle,* Nov. 30, 1863.

69. Lorenzo Thomas to Edwin M. Stanton, Oct. 24, 1863, *OR,* ser. 3, vol. 3, 916-17. See also Armstead Burwell to Abraham Lincoln, Aug. 28, 1863, Lincoln Papers.

70. William T. Sherman to U.S. Grant, July 21, 1863, *OR,* ser. 3, vol. 3, pt. 2, 530-31; William C. Harris, *Presidential Reconstruction in Mississippi* (Baton Rouge: Louisiana State Univ. Press, 1967), 12-13.

71. For Lincoln's concern regarding the continuing diminutive size of the Restored Government, see Lincoln to Benjamin F. Butler, Jan. 9, 1864, Basler, *CWL,* 7:487-88.

72. *Alexandria Gazette,* Jan. 4, 1864; *Washington National Intelligencer,* Jan. 4, 1864. Bowden had earlier replaced Waitman T. Willey in the Senate.

73. Henry Dawes, who chaired the House Committee on Elections throughout the war, reaffirmed the principle held by Lincoln and expressed in the seating of Hahn and Flanders of Louisiana in early 1863 that Unionists, though constituting a minority of the voters, could be recognized as the political body of a district or state. U.S. Congress, 39th Cong., 1st sess., *House Report No. 9,* 3-4.

74. Francis H. Pierpont to Abraham Lincoln, Sept. 3, 1863, Lincoln Papers.

75. A contemporary account of these events, probably written by Pierpont, can be found in the *New York Times,* June 26, 1864. See also the *Washington Daily Chronicle,* Dec. 29, 1863, and the *Alexandria Gazette,* Jan. 6, 1864.

76. Lowe, *Republicans and Reconstruction in Virginia,* 22; *Alexandria Gazette,* Jan. 21, 23, 1864.

77. Virginia, *Journal of the Constitutional Convention Which Convened at Alexandria on the 13th of February, 1864* (Alexandria: D. Turner, 1864), 30, 37-38; Virginia, *Constitution of the State of Virginia and the Ordinances Adopted by the Convention Which Assembled at Alexandria on the 13th Day of February, 1864* (Alexandria: D. Turner, 1864), 8-9.

78. Virginia, *Convention Journal, 1864,* 16-19.

79. Virginia, *Constitution of Virginia, 1864,* 14.

80. The above account disagrees with Professor Richard Lowe's assessment of the work of the Virginia convention of 1864. Lowe concludes that the convention "legally destroyed much of what was old Virginia and laid the constitutional groundwork for a new society. [It] substituted a more democratic political system" for the old one. Lowe, *Republicans and Reconstruction in Virginia,* 22.

81. Virginia, *Constitution of Virginia, 1864,* 26-27; J.A. Winston to Francis H. Pierpont, May 18, 1864; reports of commissioners of elections, May 1864, passim, all in Pierpont Papers; Gen. John Echols to Confederate Secretary of War J.A. Seddon, Nov. 4, 1864, *OR,* ser. 4, vol. 33, 812-14. The commissioners of elections reported the winners in the contests but not the voter returns.

82. A. Watson to Francis H. Pierpont, April 24, 1864; John Hawxhurst to Pierpont, June 2, 1864; G.F. Watson to Pierpont, June 6, 1864, all in Pierpont Papers.

83. *Alexandria Gazette,* Jan. 6, 13, Feb. 17, March 2, 1864; *Washington National Intelligencer,* Aug. 27, 1864.

84. Francis H. Pierpont to Benjamin F. Butler, Jan. 11, 1864, *Correspondence of Butler,* 3:282-84; Ambler, *Pierpont,* 232-33.

85. Secretary of War Edwin M. Stanton to Benjamin F. Butler, Jan. 18, 1864, Basler, *CWL,* 7:135-36. This directive was written by Lincoln but signed by Stanton. See also Francis H. Pierpont to Edwin M. Stanton, Jan. 20, 1864, *Correspondence of Butler,* 3:321-24.

86. Benjamin F. Butler to the President of the United States, Feb. 23, 1864, *Correspondence of Butler,* 3:450-60.

87. Memorandum Concerning Benjamin F. Butler, Feb. 26, 1864, Basler, *CWL,* 7:207 and n.

88. Francis H. Pierpont to Abraham Lincoln, June 25, 1864, Lincoln Papers; George Gordon, *War Diary of Events in the War of the Great Rebellion, 1863-1865* (Boston: James R. Osgood, 1882), 379-80.

89. *Letter of Governor Pierpont, to His Excellency the President and the Honorable Congress of the United States, on the Subject of Abuse of Military Power in the Command of General Butler in Virginia and North Carolina* (Washington, D.C.: McGill & Witherow, 1864). The quotations are on pp. 9, 52. J.K. Herbert to Benjamin F. Butler, May 2, 1864, *Correspondence of Butler,* 4:150-51; Francis H. Pierpont to William R. Jones, March 16, 1864, Governor Francis H. Pierpont Letterbook, 1861-64, Virginia State Library, Richmond.

90. *Washington Daily Chronicle,* May 7, 13, 1864.

91. Charles H. Porter to Edward K. Sneed, June 18, 1864; Sneed to Francis H. Pierpont, June 18, 1864; Pierpont to Abraham Lincoln, June 25, 1864, all in Lincoln Papers; Virginia Attorney General Thomas R. Bowden to U.S. Attorney General Edward Bates, June 20, 1864, *Calendar of Virginia State Papers,* 11:429-30. As early as May, a report reached Pierpont that whiskey dealers in Norfolk were scheming to have Butler set aside the civil government so they would not have to pay state and municipal taxes. J.T. Daniels to Francis H. Pierpont, May 14, 1864; William H. Brooks to Pierpont, May 16, 1864, William R. Jones to Pierpont, May 17, 1864, all in Pierpont Papers.

92. Francis H. Pierpont to Abraham Lincoln, June 25, 1864, Lincoln Papers.

93. Francis H. Pierpont to Edward Bates, June 28, 1864, ibid.; entry for June 25, 1864, Beale, *Bates Diary,* 378.

94. Entry for June 25, 1864, Beale, *Bates Diary,* 378.

95. This is not to suggest that Lincoln's reluctance to intervene in the conflict between Butler and the Restored Government was motivated mainly by personal ambition. Lincoln, as well as most Republicans, strongly believed that the cause of Union and freedom hinged on his victory in November. Support for the war itself was at stake.

96. Entries for July 20, Aug. 4, 1864, Beale, *Bates Diary,* 386-87, 393.

97. Entry for Aug. 4, 1864, ibid., 393-94.

98. Entry for Aug. 5, 1864, ibid., 394.

99. Francis H. Pierpont to Abraham Lincoln, July 8, 1864, Lincoln Papers. For Butler's account of the election, see Benjamin F. Butler to the President of the United States, Aug. 1, 1864, *Correspondence of Butler,* 4:580-81.

100. Benjamin F. Butler to the President of the United States, Aug. 1, 1864, *Correspondence of Butler,* 4:581-82; Edward R. Snead to Francis H. Pierpont, Aug. 1, 1864, *Virginia Calendar of State Papers,* 11:431-32.

101. Francis H. Pierpont to Abraham Lincoln, Aug. 4, 1864 (telegram), Lincoln Papers; Lincoln to Pierpont, Aug. 5, 1864; Lincoln to Benjamin F. Butler, Aug. 20, 1864 (quotation), Basler, *CWL,* 7:481, 508. Porter was subsequently released.

102. Abraham Lincoln to Benjamin F. Butler, Aug. 6, 1864, Basler *CWL,* 7:487-88.

103. Gordon, *War Diary,* 376-80; Gen. Edward O.C. Ord to Gen. U.S. Grant, Jan. 19, 1865, *OR,* ser. 1, vol. 46, pt. 2, 181.

104. Francis H. Pierpont to Abraham Lincoln, Aug. 24, 1864, Lincoln Papers; entry for Aug. 20, 1864, Beale, *Bates Diary,* 400.

105. Col. Frank White to Benjamin F. Butler, Nov. 15, 1864; White to Butler, Dec. 20, 1864, both in *Correspondence of Butler,* 5:351-52, 444.

106. Abraham Lincoln to Benjamin F. Butler, Dec. 21, 1864, Basler, *CWL,* 7:174.

107. Ibid., 174n.

108. Abraham Lincoln to Benjamin F. Butler, Dec. 28, 1864, ibid., 186 and n; Col. Frank White to Benjamin F. Butler, Dec. 20, 1864, *Correspondence of Butler,* 5:444.

109. Basler, *CWL,* 8:207n; *Reorganization of Civil Government, Speech of Governor Pierpont, Delivered at Mechanics' Hall in the City of Norfolk on Thursday Evening, February 16, 1865* (Norfolk?, 1865).

8. Louisiana: A Tangled Skein of Reconstruction

1. Belz, *Reconstructing the Union,* 145-46, 151.
2. McCrary, *Lincoln and Reconstruction,* xi-xii.
3. Joseph G. Tregle Jr., "Thomas J. Durant, Utopian Socialism, and the Failure of Presidential Reconstruction in Louisiana," *Journal of Southern History* 45 (Nov. 1979): 509, 511-12.
4. Cox, *Lincoln and Black Freedom,* chap. 3 and 112-13. See also Tunnell, *Crucible of Reconstruction,* chap. 2.
5. *New York Times,* Nov. 19, 1863; Cuthbert Bullitt to Orville Browning, Feb. 25, 1864, Lincoln Papers; McCrary, *Lincoln and Reconstruction,* 181-82.
6. Abraham Lincoln to Nathaniel P. Banks, Dec. 24, 1863, Basler, *CWL,* 7:89-90.
7. Nathaniel P. Banks to C.C. Washburne, Jan. 13, 1864, Banks Papers.
8. Nathaniel P. Banks to Abraham Lincoln, Dec. 30, 1863, Lincoln Papers. Most of this letter can be found in Basler, *CWL,* 7:124-25n.
9. Abraham Lincoln to Nathaniel P. Banks, Jan. 13, 1864, ibid., 123-24.
10. Proclamation of General Nathaniel P. Banks, Jan. 11, 1864, *OR,* ser. 3, vol. 4, 22-23; U.S. Congress, *Senate Miscellaneous Document No. 9,* 38th Cong. 2d sess., 2-3. Only 808 soldiers and sailors voted in the February election.
11. U.S. Congress, *Senate Miscellaneous Document No. 9,* 38th Cong., 2d sess., 23; Thomas J. Durant to Henry L. Dawes, Feb. 8, 1864, Dawes Papers; Durant to Salmon P. Chase, Feb. 21, March 5, 1864, Chase Papers, Library of Congress.
12. George S. Shepley to Abraham Lincoln, Dec. 31, 1863; Shepley to Edwin M. Stanton, Dec. 31, 1863; Thomas J. Durant to Lincoln, Feb. 26, 1864, all in Lincoln Papers.
13. McCrary, *Lincoln and Reconstruction,* 218-19; *New Orleans Daily Picayune,* Feb. 3, 1864; Denison to Salmon P. Chase, Jan. 29, Feb. 5, 1864, Chase Papers, Library of Congress.
14. *New Orleans Daily True Delta,* Feb. 13, 1864; *New Orleans Daily Picayune,* Feb. 11, 19, 1864; Thomas J. Durant to Salmon P. Chase, Feb. 21, 1864; John Hutchins to Chase, Feb. 12, 24, 1864; George Denison to Chase, Feb. 19, 1864, all in Chase Papers, Library of Congress.
15. *New Orleans Daily True Delta,* Feb. 15, 17, 20, 1864; Nathaniel P. Banks to Abraham Lincoln, Jan. 22, 1864, Lincoln Papers.
16. Nathaniel P. Banks to Abraham Lincoln, Jan. 22, Feb. 25, 1864, Lincoln Papers; Banks to Frank E. Howe, March 6, 1864, Chase Papers, Library of Congress.
17. Cuthbert Bullitt to Abraham Lincoln, Jan. 2, 1864, Lincoln Papers. See the issues of the *New Orleans Daily True Delta,* the *New Orleans Bee,* and the *New Orleans Daily Picayune* for Jan.-Feb., 1864. The political positions of the *New Orleans Tribune* and the other two city newspapers are noted in McCrary, *Lincoln and Reconstruction,* 166-67, 208, 294-95.
18. John Hutchens to Salmon P. Chase, Feb. 12, 1864, Chase Papers, Library of Congress; *New Orleans Daily True Delta,* Feb., 1864, issues; *New Orleans Bee,* Feb. 18, 1864.
19. B. Rush Plumly to Salmon P. Chase, Feb. 26, March 5, 1864; Thomas J. Durant to Chase, Feb. 21, 1864, all in Chase Papers, Library of Congress; *Politi-*

cal Position of Thomas J. Durant: A Letter from Hon. A.P. Dostie to Hon. Henry L. Dawes (New Orleans: Office of the True Delta, 1865), 4, 6. Durant had gone to Washington during the winter to see Lincoln, but was unable to arrange a meeting.

20. Nathaniel P. Banks to Frank E. Howe, March 6, 1864, Chase Papers, Library of Congress.

21. For Chase's patronage strategy, see Frederick J. Blue, *Salmon P. Chase: A Life of Politics* (Kent, Ohio: Kent State University Press, 1987), 214.

22. Salmon P. Chase to Frank E. Howe, Feb. 20, 1864; George S. Denison to Chase, Feb. 5, March 6, April 13, 19, 1864; B. Rush Plumly to Chase, Feb. 26, 1864, all in Chase Papers, Library of Congress.

23. *New Orleans Daily True Delta,* Jan. 1, 1864.

24. Ibid., Feb. 26, 1864; Cuthbert Bullitt to Abraham Lincoln, Jan. 2, 1864; Bullitt to Orville Browning, Feb. 23, 1864, both in Lincoln Papers.

25. Resolutions of the New Orleans Lincoln Pioneer Club [Feb. 22, 1864], reported in *New Orleans Daily True Delta,* Feb. 23, 1864.

26. For example, Cuthbert Bullitt, a friend of long-time Lincoln confidant Orville Browning, as well as the president's, repeatedly informed Lincoln of the Free State party's support of the president and his policies. He also sent the president newspaper clippings from Hahn's *True Delta* reporting strong support for him. Cuthbert Bullitt to Abraham Lincoln, Feb. 23, March 5, 1864; Bullitt to Orville Browning, Feb. 23, 1864, all in Lincoln Papers.

27. Michael Hahn to Abraham Lincoln, Feb. 6, 1864; Cuthbert Bullitt to Lincoln, March 5, 1864, both in Lincoln Papers.

28. *New Orleans Daily Picayune,* Feb. 19, 1864; George S. Denison to Salmon P. Chase, Feb. 5, 1864, R. Rush Plumly to Chase, March 5, 1864, both in Chase Papers, Library of Congress; *Letter from Dostie to Dawes,* 7-8.

29. I have used Professor Peyton McCrary's figures, which were compiled from the manuscript returns of the election and differ slightly from those reported in the newspapers. McCrary, *Lincoln and Reconstruction,* 235 and n. Banks reported that 11,414 ballots were cast. U.S. Congress, *Senate Miscellaneous Document No. 9,* 38th Cong., 2d sess., 2.

30. For the city-rural returns, see John Hutchins to Salmon P. Chase, Feb. 24, 1864, Chase Papers, Library of Congress.

31. Nathaniel P. Banks to Abraham Lincoln, Feb. 25, 1864, Lincoln Papers.

32. General Order No. 23, Feb. 3, 1864, *OR,* ser. 1, vol. 34, pt. 2, 231.

33. U.S. Congress, *Senate Miscellaneous Document No. 9,* 38th Cong., 2d sess., 3.

34. Nathaniel P. Banks to Abraham Lincoln, Feb. 25, 1864, Banks Papers.

35. *New Orleans Daily True Delta,* Feb. 24, 1864; *New York Times,* March 4, 1864.

36. *Nashville Daily Union,* March 5, 1864.

37. Thomas J. Durant to Abraham Lincoln, Feb. 26, 1864, Lincoln Papers.

38. John Hutchins to Salmon P. Chase, Feb. 24, 1864; Thomas J. Durant to Chase, March 5, 1864; R. Rush Plumly to Chase, March 5, 1864, all in Chase Papers, Library of Congress; *St. Louis Democrat,* March 16, 1864, clipping in Banks Papers; *National Anti-Slavery Standard,* March 19, 1864.

39. As quoted in Cox, *Lincoln and Black Freedom,* 93.

40. *New York Times,* March 14, 1864; *Inaugural Address of Michael Hahn, Governor of the State of Louisiana, Delivered at New Orleans, March 4, 1864,* in

Warmoth Pamphlets, vol. 2 [a collection of printed documents in Davis Library, University of North Carolina, Chapel Hill]. Lincoln strengthened Hahn's position by investing him "with the powers exercised hitherto by the Military Governor of Louisiana." Lincoln thereby officially ended the military governorship of the state. However, he dodged the question of whether the military commander still had the authority to supersede the civil government. Abraham Lincoln to Michael Hahn, March 15, 1864, Basler, *CWL*, 7:248.

41. *New York Times,* April 11, 1864; Michael Hahn to Abraham Lincoln, April 2, 1864, Lincoln Papers.

42. McCrary, *Lincoln and Reconstruction,* 245. A heavy rain on election day, in addition to the fact that there was no important opposition to the Hahn party, contributed to the light turnout. Some Flanders adherents organized the "Citizens Free State" party for the election, but it garnered few votes. *New York Times,* April 5, 1864.

43. Michael Hahn to Abraham Lincoln, April 2, 1864, Lincoln Papers.

44. Nathaniel P. Banks to John Hay, March 28, 1864, ibid.

45. Abraham Lincoln to Michael Hahn, March 13, 1864, Basler, *CWL,* 7:243.

46. The substance of Lincoln's interview with Bertonneau and Roudanez has been pieced together from the *New York Principia,* March 10, 1864, and the *New Orleans Era,* as quoted by Cox, *Lincoln and Black Freedom,* 95. The petition of "Colored Citizens of Louisiana" is found in the *Washington Chronicle,* March 22, 1864, and in the *Boston Liberator,* April 1, 1864. Twenty-seven of the free-black signatures on the petition were veterans of the war of 1812, while twenty-one white radicals signed it. The date of the delegation's meeting with Lincoln has been erroneously reported as March 10.

47. Michael Hahn to William D. Kelley, June 21, 1865, in *New York Times,* June 23, 1865.

48. Cox, *Lincoln and Black Freedom,* 98; T.B. Thorpe to Nathaniel P. Banks, April 12, 1864, Banks Papers.

49. Nathaniel P. Banks to J. M. McKaye, March 28, 1864, rough draft in Banks Papers.

50. Michael Hahn to Abraham Lincoln, May 11, 1864, Lincoln Papers; McCrary, *Lincoln and Reconstruction,* 260, 262; Cox, *Lincoln and Black Freedom,* 99.

51. Michael Hahn to William D. Kelley, June 21, 1865, printed in *New York Times,* June 23, 1865.

52. *The Reconstruction of States: Letter of Major-General Banks to Senator Lane* (New York: Harper & Brothers, 1865), 18. The 1864 Louisiana constitution may be found in Francis H. Thorpe, ed., *The Federal and State Constitutions, Colonial Charters, and Other Organic Laws of the States, Territories, and Colonies Now or Heretofore Forming the United States of America* (Washington, D.C.: GPO, 1909), 3:1429-48. In a temporary apportionment of legislative seats made by the convention, New Orleans received 42 of the 112 seats in the House of Representatives and 9 in the Senate. Ibid., 3:1430-31.

53. Thorpe, *Federal and State Constitutions,* 3:1430, 1443; Michael Hahn to Abraham Lincoln, Aug. 31, 1864, Lincoln Papers.

54. Thorpe, *Federal and State Conventions,* 3:1447-48; Michael Hahn to Abraham Lincoln, Aug. 13, 1864, Lincoln Papers.

55. Nathaniel P. Banks to Abraham Lincoln, July 25, 1864, Lincoln Papers.

56. Although in 1864 it had officially assumed the name National Union party, the Republican party was still referred to by its old name. Democrats and conservatives, however, routinely called it the Radical party despite the fact that a majority of its supporters could not be so classified. To avoid confusion, I have used the name Republican throughout this book.

57. Although somewhat dated, James G. Randall and Richard N. Current's account in *Lincoln the President: Last Full Measure* (New York: Dodd, Mead, 1955), chap. 10, is still an excellent summary of the political events of the summer. For an account of the conservative Whig movement to collaborate with the Democrats in 1864, see William C. Harris, "Conservative Unionists and the Presidential Election of 1864," *Civil War History* 38 (Dec. 1992), 298-318.

58. As reported in Randall and Current, *Lincoln the President,* 192.

59. Belz, *Reconstructing the Union,* 215-21.

60. The complete bill can be found in Harold M. Hyman, ed., *The Radical Republicans and Reconstruction, 1861-1870* (Indianapolis: Bobbs-Merrill, 1967), 128-34. Interestingly, in view of earlier Radical support of confiscation, the Wade-Davis bill made no mention of confiscation.

61. Belz, *Reconstructing the Union,* 225-26.

62. Hay recorded these words in his diary. Entry for July 4, 1864, Dennett, *Hay Diaries,* 205-6.

63. Proclamation Concerning Reconstruction, July 8, 1864, Basler, *CWL,* 7:433-34.

64. Thaddeus Stevens to Edward McPherson, July 10, 1864, Thaddeus Stevens Papers, Manuscript Division, Library of Congress. Davis's opposition to Lincoln predated the events of the summer. In 1863 he had emerged as a leader of Lincoln critics in the House of Representatives after the president had extended patronage to the Montgomery Blair faction in Maryland. Montgomery Blair to Thomas Swann, Oct. 17, 1863, Blair Family Papers.

65. The Wade-Davis Manifesto may be found in Hyman, *Radical Republicans and Reconstruction,* 137-47. Cuthbert Bullitt, Lincoln's conservative Louisiana friend, wrote the president (Aug. 20, 1864, Lincoln Papers) that Thomas J. Durant collaborated with Davis in writing the manifesto. He probably exaggerated, though a comparison of the data on Louisiana contained in the manifesto and a subsequent Durant letter to Davis is evidence that the New Orleans radical provided the information on that state. *Letter of Thomas J. Durant to the Hon. Henry Winter Davis* (New Orleans: H.P. Lathrop, 1864).

66. A staunch supporter of Ben Butler for president declared that the Wade-Davis Manifesto was "one of the greatest documents of the age," increasing Butler's chances of replacing Lincoln as the Republican candidate. J.K. Herbert to Benjamin F. Butler, Aug. 6, 1864, *Correspondence of Butler,* 5:9.

67. Belz, *Reconstructing the Union,* 230-31.

68. J.K. Herbert to Benjamin F. Butler, Aug. 6, 1864, *Correspondence of Butler,* 5:8.

69. Ibid.

70. As quoted in Cox, *Lincoln and Black Freedom,* 128.

71. Michael Hahn to Abraham Lincoln, Aug. 12, 1864, Lincoln Papers; Lincoln to Nathaniel P. Banks, Aug. 9, 1864, Basler, *CWL,* 7:486 and n.

72. Cuthbert Bullitt to Abraham Lincoln, Sept. 6, 1864, Lincoln Papers.

73. Randall Terry to Michael Hahn, Nov. 23, 1864, ibid., giving the official election returns.

74. Nathaniel P. Banks to Abraham Lincoln, Sept. 6, 1864; Cuthbert Bullitt to Lincoln, Sept. 6, 1864, both in Lincoln Papers; *Letter of Banks to Senator Lane,* 16-17.

75. Nathaniel P. Banks to Abraham Lincoln, Sept. 6, 1864, Lincoln Papers. Excerpts from this letter can be found in Basler, *CWL,* 7:486-87n.

76. Nathaniel P. Banks to "My Dear Wife," Sept. 6, 1864, Banks Papers.

77. Michael Hahn to Abraham Lincoln, Sept. 24, 1864; Cuthbert Bullitt to Lincoln, Sept. 12, 17, 1864, all in Lincoln Papers.

78. Notation by John Hay, Sept. 28, 1864; Michael Hahn to Abraham Lincoln, Nov. 11, 1864, both in Lincoln Papers.

79. Michael Hahn to Abraham Lincoln, Sept. 24, 1864, Lincoln Papers.

80. Nathaniel P. Banks to his wife, Dec. 22, 1864, Jan. 8, 1865, Banks Papers.

81. *New York Times,* Oct. 17, 1864; U.S. Senate, 38th Cong., 2d sess., *Senate Miscellaneous Document No. 1,* 2; *Senate Miscellaneous Document no. 2,* 4; Michael Hahn to Abraham Lincoln, Nov. 11, 1864, Lincoln Papers.

82. Louisiana, *Journal of the House of Representatives of the State of Louisiana* [1864-1865] (New Orleans: W.R. Fish, 1865), 10-13.

83. Michael Hahn to Abraham Lincoln, Nov. 11, 1864, Lincoln Papers; Hahn to William D. Kelley, June 21, 1865, printed in *New York Times,* June 23, 1865.

84. Gerald M. Capers, *Occupied City: New Orleans under the Federals, 1862-1865* (Lexington: University of Kentucky Press, 1965), 230; *New Orleans Tribune,* Jan. 17, 22, 1865; Cox, *Lincoln and Black Freedom,* 124, 125 (quotation), 127-28.

85. Louisiana, *Journal of the House of Representatives* [1864-65], 179.

86. Harrington, *Fighting Politician,* 148-49, 159-60.

87. Stephen A. Hurlbut to Edward R.S. Canby, Oct. 22, 1864, *OR,* ser. 1, vol. 41, pt. 4, 412-13.

88. Edward R.S. Canby to Stephen A. Hurlbut, Oct. 29, 1864, ibid., 413.

89. Michael Hahn to Abraham Lincoln, Oct. 29, 1864, Lincoln Papers.

90. Abraham Lincoln to Stephen A. Hurlbut, Nov. 14, 1864, Basler, *CWL,* 7:106-07. Lincoln also expressed to Orville Browning a similar outrage regarding Canby and Hurlbut's obstructionism. Entry for Nov. 14, 1864, in *The Diary of Orville Hickman Browning,* ed. Theodore C. Pease and James G. Randall (Springfield: Illinois State Historical Library, 1925), 1:692. John Slidell, a Louisianan, was the Confederate minister in France.

91. Abraham Lincoln to Stephen A. Hurlbut, Nov. 14, 1864, Basler, *CWL,* 8:107.

92. Ibid., 164-65n.

93. Abraham Lincoln to Edward R.S. Canby, Dec. 12, 1864, ibid., 163-64.

94. Michael Hahn to Stephen A. Hurlbut, Dec. 1, 5, 1864; Hahn to Abraham Lincoln, Dec. 2, 1864, all in Lincoln Papers.

9. Arkansas: An Unfilfilled Promise

1. William D. Snow to Abraham Lincoln, Dec. 25, 1863, Lincoln Papers.

2. A report of the Little Rock rally appeared in the *Washington Daily Chron-*

icle, Jan. 20, 1864. Union rallies in Benton and Fort Smith adopted similar resolutions. *Washington Sunday Chronicle,* Dec. 27, 1863.

3. Frederick Steele to General John M. Schofield, Dec. 12, 1863, *OR,* ser. 1, vol. 22, pt. 2, 741; Frederick Steele to R.J. White, Nov. 30, 1864, Steele Papers, part II, folder 6, Department of Special Collections and University Archives, Stanford University Libraries.

4. "Little Rock" in Steele Papers, part II, folder 2; "Steele" broadside [1864], in C.C. Bliss Papers, Arkansas History Commission, Little Rock; *Little Rock Unconditional Union,* Sept. 8, 1864; Isaac Murphy to Frederick Steele, Jan.21, 1864, Steele Papers, part II, folder 4.

5. Arkansas, *Convention Journal, 1864,* 3, 11, 28, 31-32; Thomas S. Staples, *Reconstruction in Arkansas, 1862-1874* (New York: Columbia University, 1923), 28. No delegates were seated without a certificate of election from their district.

6. Arkansas, *Convention Journal, 1864,* 31-35; Thorpe, *Federal and State Constitutions,* 1:291, 295-96.

7. Arkansas, *Convention Journal, 1864,* 32, 40.

8. As reported in the *Nashville Daily Union,* Feb. 14, 1864. For Murphy's role in the 1861 secession convention, see James M. Woods, *Rebellion and Realignment: Arkansas's Road to Secession* (Fayetteville: Univ. of Arkansas Press, 1987), 160.

9. Staples, *Reconstruction in Arkansas,* 39.

10. Abraham Lincoln to Frederick Steele, Jan. 20, 1864; Remarks to Arkansas Delegation, Jan. 22, 1864, both in Basler, *CWL,* 7:141-42, 144; John B. Steele to Frederick Steele, Jan. 20, 1864; Joseph Snow to Frederick Steele, Jan. 20, 1864, both in Steele Papers, part II, folder 2. For Gantt's high standing with Lincoln, see Gen. J.W. Davidson to S.H. Boyd, Dec. 28, 1863, *OR,* ser. 1, vol. 34, pt. 2, 105.

11. Abraham Lincoln to Frederick Steele, Jan. 20, 1864, Basler, *CWL,* 7:141-42.

12. Abraham Lincoln to Frederick Steele, Jan. 27, 1864, ibid., 154-55.

13. Abraham Lincoln to Frederick Steele, Jan. 20, 1864, ibid., 161.

14. J.N. Johnson to Isaac Murphy, Feb. 8, 1864, Steele Papers, part II, folder 4; *Little Rock Unconditional Union,* Feb. 5, 1864.

15. Frederick Steele to Abraham Lincoln, Feb. 2, 1864, Steele Papers, part II, folder 4; Isaac Murphy to Lincoln, Feb. 8, 1864, Lincoln Papers.

16. Abraham Lincoln to William M. Fishback, Feb. 17, 1864; Lincoln to John M. Thayer, Feb. 15, 1864, both in Basler, *CWL,* 7:185, 189.

17. Abraham Lincoln to Frederick Steele, Jan. 5, 1864, ibid., 7:108-9.

18. General Orders Number 2, Feb. 2, 1864, Headquarters, Department of Arkansas, Steele Papers, part II, folder 4; Frederick Steele to Nathaniel P. Banks, Feb. 28, March 10, 1864, Banks Papers.

19. William D. Snow to Abraham Lincoln, Feb. 27, 1864, Lincoln Papers; *Little Rock National Democrat,* Feb. 27, March 12, 1864; *Little Rock Unconditional Union,* March 11, 14, 26, 1864.

20. Lieutenant E. Cunningham to Gen. T.H. Holmes, March 4, 1864, *OR,* ser. 1, vol. 34, pt. 2, 1020.

21. Frederick Steele to Nathaniel P. Banks, Feb. 28, 1864, Banks Papers; William Tecumseh Sherman to Frederick Steele, March 6, 1864, *OR,* ser. 1, vol. 34, pt. 2, 516. In his reply to Sherman, Steele cited other reasons, in addition to

the election, for the delay of his military movement. Steele to Sherman, March 10, 1864, ibid., 547.

22. To the People of Arkansas, Feb. 29, 1864, Steele Papers, pt. 2, folder 4; Frederick Steele to Abraham Lincoln, March 2, 1864; Lincoln to Steele, March 3, 1864, both in Basler, *CWL*, 7:221, 221-22n.

23. Abraham Lincoln to William M. Fishback, March 12, 1864; Lincoln to Isaac Murphy, March 12, 1864, both in Basler, *CWL*, 7:239, 240.

24. Isaac Murphy to Abraham Lincoln, April 15, 1864, Lincoln Papers; E.W. Gantt to Salmon P. Chase, March 19, 1864, Chase Papers, Library of Congress.

25. Abraham Lincoln to Isaac Murphy, April 27, 1864, Basler, *CWL*, 7:318.

26. *New York Times,* March 21, 1864.

27. *Washington Daily Chronicle,* March 22, 1864.

28. Forty-five of the fifty-four counties had elected legislators; however, only fifteen members of the state Senate and forty-two House members attended the session. Arkansas, *Journal of the House of Representatives, Session of 1864-65* (in *Convention Journal, 1864*), 1-3, 16-17, 30; Arkansas, *Journal of the Senate of Arkansas, Sessions of 1864, 1864-65 and 1865* (Little Rock: Price and Barton, 1870), 1-2; Staples, *Reconstruction in Arkansas,* 45.

29. Arkansas, *Journal of the House of Representatives, Session of 1864-65* (in *Convention Journal, 1864*), 30-31, 33-34.

30. Ibid., 31-33.

31. Ibid., 35.

32. Frederick Steele to Henry Halleck, March 12, 1864; U.S. Grant to Steele, March 15, 1864, both in *OR,* ser. 1, vol. 34, pt. 2, 547, 616.

33. C.C. Andrews to Abraham Lincoln, June 5, 1864; Isaac Murphy to Lincoln, March 17, March 22, April 15, 1864, all in Lincoln Papers; Lincoln to Murphy, March 18, April 27, 1864, Basler, *CWL*, 7:253, 318. Despite Steele's failure, the president continued to express confidence in him, probably because too much was at stake in Arkansas's reconstruction to dismiss the general who had become identified with it. Francis H. Manter to Frederick Steele, May 13, 1864; John B. Steele to Frederick Steele, May 14, 1864, both in Steele Papers, pt. 2, folder 6.

34. Isaac Murphy to Abraham Lincoln, Aug. 6, 1864, Lincoln Papers; *Little Rock National Democrat,* Aug. 27, 1864; *Washington National Intelligencer,* Sept. 20, 1864; Frederick Steele to Abraham Lincoln, Nov. 30, 1864, *OR,* ser. 1, vol. 41, pt. 4, 723.

35. William Fishback to Frederick Steele, May 3, 1864, Steele Papers, pt. 4, folder 4; *Little Rock National Democrat,* May 7, 21, 1864.

36. *Little Rock National Democrat,* May 28, 1864; *Louisville Daily Journal,* May 28, 1864; *Washington National Intelligencer,* June 14, 1864; Henry L. Dawes to Electra Dawes, June 13, 1864, Dawes Papers.

37. William Fishback to Frederick Steele, May 3, 1864, Steele Papers, pt. 2, folder 4. Fishback's comment led to fisticuffs between the would-be senator and a member of Steele's staff.

38. Abraham Lincoln to William H. Seward, May 8, 1864, Basler, *CWL*, 7:334.

39. *Congressional Globe,* 38th Cong., 1st sess., 2842, 2895; *Washington Daily Chronicle,* May 23, 1864.

40. *Congressional Globe,* 38th Cong., 1 sess., 2900-2901; Warren Munroe to Lyman Trumbull, June 18, 1864, Lyman Trumbull Papers, Library of Congress; *Washington Daily Chronicle,* June 21, 1864.

41. Loyal Case to J.W. Forney, June 13, 1864, Stevens Papers.

42. *Congressional Globe,* 38th Cong., 1st sess., 3361-68; *New York Tribune,* June 30, 1864.

43. *Congressional Globe,* 38th Cong., 1st sess., 3360, 3368; U.S. Congress, *Senate Report No. 94,* 38th Cong., 1st sess. Following the lead of the Senate, the House of Representatives rejected Arkansas's claimants to seats in that body.

44. *Congressional Globe,* 38 Cong., 1 sess., 2903.

45. Ibid., 2900.

46. Ibid., 3389.

47. Thaddeus Stevens to Edward McPherson, July 10, 1864, Stevens Papers; *Congressional Globe,* 30th Cong., 1st sess., 3361 (quotation); *New York Tribune,* June 14, 1864.

48. *Little Rock Unconditional Union,* July 28, 1864.

49. William M. Fishback to Frederick Steele, June 29, 1864, Steele Papers, part II, folder 6; Abraham Lincoln to Frederick Steele, June 29, 1864, Basler, *CWL,* 7:418.

50. Isaac Murphy to Abraham Lincoln, July 23, 1864, Lincoln Papers.

51. William B. Snow to Isaac Murphy, Oct. 1, 1864, in Arkansas, *Journal of the House of Representatives, Session of 1864-65* (in *Convention Journal,* 1864), 203-8.

52. Isaac Murphy to Abraham Lincoln, Aug. 6, 1864, Lincoln Papers. On April 18, 1864, the War Department had given Murphy authority to appoint officers to some of its regiments, but it was withdrawn in July.

53. Clipping from *Chicago Tribune* [Dec. 1864?]; John B. Steele to Frederick Steele, Sept. 26, 1864, both in Steele Papers, pt. 2, folder 6; *Little Rock Unconditional Union,* Sept. 8, 1864; H.B. Allis to Abraham Lincoln, Oct. 13, 1864, Lincoln Papers; C.P. Bertrand to Lincoln, Dec. 12, 1864, *OR,* ser. 1, vol. 41, pt. 4, 835-38.

54. John B. Steele to Frederick Steele, Nov. 22, 1864, Steele Papers, pt. 2, folder 6; *Little Rock National Democrat,* Dec. 10, 1864.

55. *Little Rock National Democrat,* Feb. 25, 1865; *Little Rock Unconditional Union,* March 30, 1865. The division among Arkansas Unionists over the senator-elects continued, though it played a minor role in the congressional decision to postpone action on the seating of the state's representatives. *Little Rock National Democrat,* Jan. 21, March 11, 1865.

56. *New York Times,* Dec. 27, 1864; *Little Rock Unconditional Union,* March 30, 1865; Arkansas, *House Journal, 1864-65,* 179, 240; Arkansas, *House Journal, Special Session, 1865,* 12-13, 33-34.

57. *Little Rock National Democrat,* April 22, 1865; *Little Rock Unconditional Union,* April 20, 27, 1865.

10. Tennessee: Unionists Divided

1. John Lellyett to William B. Campbell, Sept. 15, Nov. 28, 1864, Campbell Family Papers; "The Moses of the Colored Men" Speech, Oct. 24, 1864, Johnson, *JP,* 7:252-53.

2. Ibid., 7:251.

3. *Nashville Daily Union*, Jan. 28, 1864.

4. Speech on the Restoration of State Government, Jan. 21, 1864, Johnson, *JP,* 6:574-88.

5. Proclamation Ordering Elections, Jan. 25, 1864, Johnson, *JP,* 6:594-95.

6. Edwin H. Ewing to Andrew Johnson, Feb. 1, 1864; James B. Bingham to Johnson, Feb. 11, 1864, both in Johnson, *JP,* 6:601, 612-13; Joseph Ramsey to Horace Maynard, Feb. 12, 1864, Lincoln Papers; *Nashville Daily Union,* Feb. 13, 1864.

7. Abraham Lincoln to Warren Jordan, Feb. 21, 1864, Basler, *CWL,* 7:196.

8. Abraham Lincoln to E.H. East, Feb. 27, 1864, Basler, *CWL,* 7:209.

9. *Washington Daily Chronicle,* Feb. 16, 1864.

10. *Nashville Daily Union,* March 23, 1864; James O. Shackleford to Andrew Johnson, March 6, 1864 (quotation); Alvan C. Gillem to Johnson, March 11, 1864, both in Johnson, *JP,* 6:638-39, 643-44.

11. *Nashville Daily Union,* March 11, 13, 1864; Robert Johnson to Andrew Johnson, March 5, 1864, Johnson, *JP,* 6:637-48 and n.

12. Alvan C. Gillem to Andrew Johnson, March 15, 1864, Johnson, *JP,* 6:646; *New York Times,* March 21, 1864. Soon after the elections, Johnson directed that in counties and districts where contests did not occur county courts could call elections when they "can be conveniently held." Proclamation re County Elections, April 4, 1864, Johnson, *JP,* 6:658-69.

13. *Nashville Daily Union,* March 16, 1864; Speech at Shelbyville, April 5, 1864; Andrew Johnson to Abraham Lincoln, April 5, 1864, both in Johnson, *JP,* 6:658 and n, 660.

14. Johnson, *JP,* 6:663n, 664n.

15. *Appleton's Annual Cyclopedia, 1864,* 764; *Louisville Daily Journal,* April 28, 1864; *Nashville Daily Union,* April 17, 19, 1864; Speech at Knoxville, April 16, 1864, Johnson, *JP,* 6:674. A notable exception to the Old Whigs who opposed Governor Johnson during the war was Parson Brownlow. Ironically, Brownlow became a bitter enemy of President Johnson after the war.

16. Temple, *Notable Men of Tennessee,* 407-8; *New York Tribune,* April 30, 1864; *Louisville Daily Journal,* April 28, 1864.

17. Johnson, *JP,* 6:lvii-lviii. The resolutions can be found in the *New York Tribune,* April 30, 1864.

18. D.A. Campbell to "My Dear Sister," Feb. 15, 1865, Campbell Family Papers; *Nashville Daily Union,* May 14, 1864; Horace Maynard to Andrew Johnson, May 30, 1864, Johnson, *JP,* 6:711; Hooper, "Memphis," 90-91.

19. Shelby Foote, *The Civil War, a Narrative: Red River to Appomattox* (New York: Random House, 1974), 516-17, 597, 601, 614.

20. Loyal Citizens of Upper East Tennessee to Andrew Johnson, June 12, 1864; Absalom A. Kyle to Johnson, June 13, 1864, both in Johnson, *JP,* 6:734, 735; William C. Harris, "The East Tennessee Relief Movement of 1864-1865," *Tennessee Historical Quarterly* 48 (summer 1989): 86-96.

21. For a good brief account of the Republican decision to nominate Johnson for vice president, see Richard H. Abbott, *The Republican Party and the South, 1855-1877* (Chapel Hill: Univ. of North Carolina Press, 1986), 35-37. Evidence of Johnson's popularity among Northern Republicans can be found in Johnson, *JP,* vol. 7. In a well-argued recent article, Don E. Fehrenbacher concludes that,

though the president did not have a direct hand in Johnson's selection, convention delegates "had little reason to doubt that broadening the national ticket would meet with Lincoln's approval; for the choice of a Southern Unionist, like the convention's admission of Southern delegates, fitted his reconciliatory vision of the future and could even be viewed as an endorsement of his approach to reconstruction." "The Making of a Myth: Lincoln and the Vice-Presidential Nomination in 1864," *Civil History* 41 (Dec. 1995): 290.

22. Edwin Paschall to William B. Campbell, Aug. 20, 1864, Campbell Family Papers; *Memphis Argus* as quoted in *Appleton's Annual Cyclopedia, 1864,* 764; *Nashville Daily Press,* June 13, 20, 29, 1864.

23. William C. Harris, "Conservative Unionists and the Presidential Election of 1864," *Civil War History* 38 (Dec. 1992): 303-5. Tennessee was the only occupied Southern state where a Union faction challenged the Lincoln-Johnson ticket.

24. Ibid., 308-11; J.M. McPherson, *Battle Cry of Freedom,* 772.

25. *Nashville Daily Press,* Oct. 24, 1864.

26. John Lellyett to William B. Campbell, Sept. 15, 1864; Jordan Stokes to Campbell, Sept. 24, 1864, both in Campbell Family Papers; *Nashville Daily Press,* Oct. 3, 14, 24, 1864.

27. *Appleton's Annual Cyclopedia, 1864,* 764; Johnson, *JP,* 7:xxxii (quotation), 120n.

28. Hall, *Johnson, Military Governor,* 141-44; *Chattanooga Daily Gazette,* Sept. 10, 1864.

29. The resolutions may be found in *Appleton's Annual Cyclopedia, 1864,* 764-65. For the proceedings of the convention, see the *Nashville Daily Press,* Sept. 10, 12, 1864. A committee of the Union convention later issued a lengthy address denouncing the Chicago platform, defending Lincoln's war policies—including emancipation—and encouraging people to vote for the Lincoln-Johnson ticket. Johnson, *JP,* 7:195-96.

30. Proclamation re Presidential Election, Sept. 30, 1864, Johnson, *JP,* 203-5. Johnson's list of election officials is found in Basler, *CWL,* 8:68-70.

31. The conservative protest is printed in Basler, *CWL,* 8:62-65n.

32. Ibid., 8:58-59n.

33. Abraham Lincoln to William B. Campbell and Others, Oct. 22, 1864, ibid., 8:58, 71-72.

34. William B. Campbell, Bailie Peyton, and John Lellyett to Abraham Lincoln, Oct. 29, 1864, ibid., 8:59-61n.

35. A.J. Fletcher to Oliver P. Temple, Oct. 17, 1864, Oliver P. Temple Papers, Manuscript Division, Library of Congress; Bailie Peyton to William B. Campbell, Oct. 25, 1864, Campbell Family Papers; *Nashville Daily Press,* Oct. 24, 1864.

36. A. C. Gillem to Joseph Fowler, Nov. 17, 1864, Joseph Fowler Papers, Southern Historical Collection, University of North Carolina Library, Chapel Hill; Leonidas C. Houk to Andrew Johnson, Johnson, *JP,* 7:262. The Gillem operation failed.

37. William G. Brownlow to Andrew Johnson, Nov. 5, 1864, Johnson, *JP,* 7:267.

38. No accurate record had been kept of the election returns. Brownlow's *Knoxville Whig and Rebel Ventilator* probably exaggerated when it reported that forty thousand votes had been cast. Johnson, *JP,* 7:301n. *New York Times,* Nov. 21, 1864, placed the number at thirty-five thousand, which represents a more

realistic figure. For the Nashville vote, see Maslowski, *Treason Must Be Made Odious,* 92, and for Memphis, see James B. Bingham to Andrew Johnson, Nov. 9, 1864, Johnson, *JP,* 7:273.

39. Thomas B. Alexander, *Political Reconstruction in Tennessee* (Nashville: Vanderbilt Univ. Press, 1950), 16.

40. Temple, *Notable Men of Tennessee,* 411.

41. Alexander, *Political Reconstruction in Tennessee,* 28-29; Johnson, *JP,* 7:398-99n.

42. Speech to Union State Convention, Jan. 12, 1865, Johnson *JP,* 7:396-97. Johnson as military governor had already taken an important step to end slavery in Tennessee. In September 1864, he suspended the slave code in the state and directed state courts to treat slaves as free blacks. David W. Bowen, *Andrew Johnson and the Negro* (Knoxville: Univ. of Tennessee Press, 1989), 111.

43. Johnson, *JP,* 7:396-98.

44. Alexander, *Political Reconstruction in Tennessee,* 30-31; Coulter, *Brownlow: Fighting Parson,* 261. Debate also erupted over voting in the convention. Some East Tennessee delegates argued that a county's vote should be based on the proportion of Union ballots cast in the June 1861 election. Middle and West Tennessee delegates, whose counties had supported secession, vehemently opposed such a rule, and the proposal was rejected by the convention. *Nashville Daily Press,* Jan. 11, 1865.

45. Union Free State Convention Commissioners to Andrew Johnson, Feb. 1865, Johnson, *JP,* 7:453; John R. Rogers and others to Abraham Lincoln, Jan. 14, 1865, Lincoln Papers.

46. Union Free State Convention Commissioners to Andrew Johnson, Feb. 1865, Johnson, *JP,* 7:453-55.

47. Andrew Johnson to Abraham Lincoln, Jan. 13, 1864, ibid., 7:404. See above, page 142, for an account of the Ashley bill.

48. Abraham Lincoln to Andrew Johnson, Jan. 14, 1865, Basler, *CWL,* 8:216.

49. Andrew Johnson to Lincoln, Jan. 17, 1865, Johnson, *JP,* 7:420-21.

50. Abraham Lincoln to Andrew Johnson, Jan. 24, 1865, Basler, *CWL,* 8:235. The use of the word unsafe in the telegram may not have been an accurate transposition. It hardly would have been unsafe for Johnson to arrive after March 4. More likely, Lincoln and Cabinet members believed that the absence of the new vice president at the inaugural would have created, as Secretary of Navy Gideon Welles later wrote, "an unfortunate influence and construction abroad." Johnson, *JP,* 7:427n. Edward H. East, Tennessee's secretary of state, was left in charge of the state's administration until the restored government was inaugurated in April.

51. Part of the reason for the failure of Lincoln to meet with his vice president was Johnson's continued sickness, at least for several days after the inauguration. Lincoln, too, was incapacitated for a few days in March. Andrew Johnson to Abraham Lincoln, March 8, 1865, Johnson, *JP,* 7:511-12, 515n. The rapid events leading to the surrender of the Confederate armies also intruded upon Lincoln's time to confer with Johnson and other political leaders. On one occasion Johnson went to City Point, Virginia, to see Lincoln, but evidently was unable to talk to him. Trefousse, *Johnson,* 192.

52. Trefousse, Johnson's most recent biographer, surmises that the vice president's purpose in visiting Lincoln on April 14 was to induce him not to be too lenient on traitors. Trefousse, *Johnson,* 192.

53. Thomas B. Alexander, "Political Reconstruction in Tennessee" in Curry, *Border States during Reconstruction*, 46-47.

54. As quoted in Alexander, *Political Reconstruction in Tennessee*, 34-35.

55. Patton, *Unionism and Reconstruction in Tennessee*, 49; Alexander, *Political Reconstruction in Tennessee*, 36-37.

56. Tennessee, *Senate Journal of the First Session of the General Assembly of the State of Tennessee, Which Convened at Nashville, Monday, April 3, [1865]* (Nashville: S.C. Mercer, 1865), 19, 28.

57. *Appleton's Annual Cyclopedia, 1865*, 778; Andrew Johnson to William G. Brownlow, July 16, 1865, Johnson, *JP*, 8:413.

58. Tennessee, *Senate Journal*, 20-22, 27, 30; *Appleton's Annual Cyclopedia, 1865*, 781. Brownlow even urged the removal of blacks from the state. After his break with President Johnson, he would change his mind and reluctantly support black suffrage.

59. Tennessee, *Senate Journal*, 93, 96.

11. The Final Months

1. Belz, *Reconstructing the Union*, 228, 230-31; J.M. McPherson, *Battle Cry of Freedom*, 717; Phillip S. Paludan, *"A People's Contest": The Union and the Civil War, 1861-1865* (New York: Harper & Row, 1988), 254-57; Randall and Current, *Lincoln the President*, 128, 210. David E. Long in his fine study of the 1864 presidential election indicates that "the infringements on civil liberties, the lack of military success, the possibility of a negotiated peace, the printing of paper money and inflation of the economy, and serious infighting in the Republican Party over Reconstruction" were issues raised by the Democrats during the campaign, "but [these] arguments were deflected by the race-baiting" of the Democratic speakers and propagandists. David E. Long, *The Jewel of Liberty: Abraham Lincoln's Re-Election and the End of Slavery* (Mechanicsburg, Pa.: Stackpole Books, 1994), 177.

2. Mark E. Neely Jr., "The Lincoln Theme since Randall's Call: The Promises and Perils of Professionalism," *Papers of the Abraham Lincoln Association* 1 (1979): 50-51. For example, a speech by Isaac N. Arnold was entitled "Reconstruction: Liberty the Cornerstone and Lincoln the Architect." See also *Washington Daily Chronicle*, Aug. 17, 22, 24, 1864.

3. Frank Freidel, ed., *Union Pamphlets of the Civil War, 1861-1865* (Cambridge: Harvard Univ. Press, 1967), 2:911-12, 938.

4. *Boston Daily Advertiser*, Sept. 14, 1864; *New Bern North Carolina Times*, July 20, 1864; Julia Pierpont to Will Robertson, Jan. 27, 1865, in *Calendar of Francis Harrison Pierpont Letters and Papers in West Virginia Depositories* (Charleston: West Virginia Historical Records Survey, Works Progress Administration, 1940), 251; Andrew Johnson, Speech at Logansport, Ind., Oct. 4, 1864, Johnson, *JP*, 7:224-30. Gen. Nathaniel P. Banks campaigned for Lincoln in the Northeast. He emphasized the success of presidential reconstruction in Louisiana. *Boston Daily Advertiser*, Oct. 31, Nov. 1, 1864.

5. See, for example, the *Louisville Journal*, Aug. 24, 1864, *Washington National Intelligencer*, Oct. 11, 1864, and *St. Louis Republican*, Aug. 1, 1864.

6. As quoted in the *Louisville Journal*, Aug. 24, 1864.

7. *Washington National Intelligencer*, Sept. 20, Oct. 25, 1864; Great Speech of Hon. Robert C. Winthrop, at New London, Conn., Oct. 18, in Freidel, *Union*

Pamphlets of the Civil War, 2:1080-81, 1098-100. All three of Winthrop's speeches were printed and distributed as Democratic campaign documents. Two hundred thousand copies of the New London address, which Lincoln judged to be the best Democratic speech of the campaign, were distributed in the Union states.

8. Edward McPherson, *Political History of the United States of America, during the Great Rebellion,* 2d ed. (Washington, D.C., Philp & Solomons, 1865), 412. Phillips was a leader in the John C. Frémont campaign for president. Supporters of Frémont met at Cleveland and adopted a far-ranging platform that attacked Lincoln, called for "absolute equality before the law" for all men, and declared that Congress, not the president, should have authority over reconstruction in the South. They also demanded the confiscation of rebel property and its distribution among "soldiers and settlers." Frémont repudiated the confiscation plank in the platform. *Appleton's Annual Cyclopedia,* 1864, 786-87.

9. *National Anti-Slavery Standard,* May 14, 21, 1864.

10. J.M.McPherson, *Struggle for Equality,* 281-85.

11. Montgomery Blair, asked by Lincoln to comment on the future of reconstruction, wrote Lincoln on the day that he sent his annual message to Congress that the president's policy "has stood the test" in the South and also the test of "sinister" Radical attacks. "And it has passed through the crucible of the late presidential election. It has the stamp of the popular sovereignty which alone has the right to decide authoritatively all fundamental contests." Montgomery Blair to Abraham Lincoln, Dec. 6, 1864, Lincoln Papers. The conservative Blair, though no longer a member of the administration, was still an important adviser of the president.

12. Annual Message to Congress, Dec. 6, 1864, Basler, *CWL,* 8:148. Lincoln could have added Virginia to the list of states that had made progress toward emancipation and reconstruction. Though limited in its authority to a handful of counties, the Pierpont government, as mentioned earlier, had abolished slavery in the state's constitution.

13. Ibid., 149.

14. Ibid., 151-52.

15. Ibid., 152.

16. Belz, *Reconstructing the Union,* 248-49; Stephen B. Oates, *Abraham Lincoln: The Man Behind the Myth* (New York: Harper & Row, 1984), 140; J.M. McPherson, *Battle Cry of Freedom,* 843.

17. Abraham Lincoln to Lyman Trumbull, Jan. 9, 1865, Basler, *CWL,* 8:207.

18. Abraham Lincoln to Nathaniel P. Banks, Nov. 26, Dec. 2, 1864, Basler, *CWL,* 8:121, 131; Banks to his wife, Dec. 22, 1864 (quotation), Jan. 8, 1865, Banks Papers.

19. *The Reconstruction of States: Letter of Major-General Banks to Senator Lane* (New York: Harper & Brothers, 1865); *Anti-Slavery Standard,* Dec. 17, 1864.

20. *Boston Liberator,* Feb. 24, 1865.

21. Nathaniel P. Banks to his wife, Dec. 29, 1864, Jan. 8, 11, 1865, Banks Papers; Henry W. Halleck to Edward R.S. Canby, Feb. 28, 1865, *OR,* ser. 1, vol. 48, pt. 1, 1001-2.

22. As quoted in Michael Les Benedict, *A Compromise of Principle: Congressional Republicans and Reconstruction, 1863-1869* (New York: W.W. Norton, 1974), 87.

23. *New York Times*, Dec. 28, 1864; *New Orleans Tribune*, Dec. 21, 1864, Jan. 3, 1865.

24. Charles Sumner to Abraham Lincoln, Nov. 20, 1864, Lincoln Papers.

25. Adolphe de Chambrun, *Impressions of Lincoln and the Civil War: A Foreigner's Account,* trans. by Aldebert de Chambrun (New York: Random House, 1952), 94; entry for April 15, 1865, "George W. Julian's Journal—Assassination of Lincoln," *Indiana Magazine of History* 11 (Dec. 1915): 335.

26. Most of the argument for the Radical attack on Lincoln's plan of reconstruction appeared in Thomas J. Durant of Louisiana to Henry Winter Davis, Oct. 27, 1864, subsequently published as a thirty-page pamphlet. Durant went to great pains to explain irregularities in the 1864 Louisiana elections and in the framing of the reconstruction constitution, but he only referred obliquely to the question of black rights. *Durant Letter to Davis;* U.S. Congress, 38th Cong., 2d sess., *Senate Miscellaneous Document No. 2.* See also the *New York Times,* Feb. 26, 1865.

27. The bill's provisions may be found in E. McPherson, *Political History of the Great Rebellion,* 576. The Arkansas exception was not included in the original bill but was added in the modified version of Dec. 20.

28. Trefousse, *Radical Republicans,* 302; LaWanda Cox, "From Emancipation to Segregation: National Policy and Southern Blacks," in *Interpreting Southern History: Historiographical Essays in Honor of Sanford W. Higginbotham,* ed. John B. Boles and Evelyn Thomas (Baton Rouge: Louisiana State Univ. Press, 1987), 222-23. Professor Herman Belz, the author of the standard account of the debate over wartime reconstruction policy, writes that Lincoln was "generally in favor" of the Ashley bill, "provided that it would be modified in certain respects." Belz suggests that Lincoln's marginal notations on the bill were evidence of his willingness to support the measure. Belz, *Reconstructing the Union,* 252.

29. Printed copy of a bill to guarantee to certain states whose governments have been usurped or overthrown a republican form of government, in Lincoln Papers. This document is undated but is listed as number 39293 in Lincoln's Papers.

30. Belz, *Reconstructing the Union,* 256; Charles Sumner to Francis Lieber, Dec. 27, 1864, in Pierce, *Sumner,* 4:205.

31. Benjamin F. Thomas and Harold M. Hyman, *Stanton: The Life and Times of Lincoln's Secretary of War* (New York: Alfred A. Knopf, 1962), 460-61; Phillip Shaw Paludan, *The Presidency of Abraham Lincoln* (Lawrence: Univ. of Kansas Press, 1994), 306.

32. Basler, *CWL,* 8:161-62; Assistant Adjutant General E.D. Townsend to W.F. Smith and Henry E. Stanberry, Dec. 12, 1864, *OR,* ser. 1, vol. 41, pt. 4, 818.

33. William F. Smith and James T. Brady to Edwin M. Stanton, Sept. 23, 1865, Smith-Brady Special Commission Report, entry 737, Records Group 94, National Archives, Washington, D.C.

34. Entry for Dec. 18, 1864, Dennett, *Hay Diaries,* 244-45.

35. Ibid. Present also in the White House meeting was Montgomery Blair, who, according to Hay, attacked the Radicals, accusing them of vile motives and bitter hostility to Lincoln. After patiently listening to Blair's tirade, the president admonished him: "It is much better not to be led from the region of reason into that of hot blood, by imputing to public men motives which they do not avow."

36. Benedict, *Compromise of Principle*, 91-92; E. McPherson, *Political History of the Great Rebellion*, 276-77. For a detailed account of the complicated congressional proceedings over reconstruction, see Belz, *Reconstructing the Union*, 250-65. Again, my interpretation of the conflict between Lincoln and the Radicals differs from Professor Belz, who maintains that a compromise between the president and Congress on the basis of black political equality and the congressional recognition of the Louisiana and Arkansas governments was the only reasonable solution to the impasse over reconstruction. Such a compromise, Belz maintains, was almost achieved. Belz writes that "although Lincoln's opinion of the amended bill is not known, his earlier recommendation of suffrage for educated blacks and Negro soldiers suggests that he probably would have accepted it." Herman Belz, "Origins of Negro Suffrage during the Civil War," *Southern Studies* 17 (summer 1978), 126. I contend that Lincoln would accept no compromise that imposed a suffrage requirement upon a state.

37. *Springfield Weekly Republican*, Feb. 25, 1865, as quoted in Belz, *Reconstructing the Union*, 267.

38. *New York Times*, Jan. 12, 1865; George W. Julian, *Political Recollections, 1840-1872* (Chicago: Jansen, McClurg, 1884), 250-51; Nicolay and Hay, *Lincoln*, 10:84.

39. Samuel S. Cox, *Three Decades of Federal Legislation, 1855-1885* (Freeport, N.Y.: Books for Libraries Press, 1970), 310; John Hogan to Andrew Johnson, June 19, 1865, Papers of Andrew Johnson, Manuscript Division, Library of Congress (microfilm). Cox based his account of his meeting with Lincoln on notes that he made at the time.

40. Response to a Serenade, Feb. 1, 1865, Basler, *CWL*, 8:254-55.

41. Alexander H. Stephens, *A Constitutional View of the Late War between the States; Its Causes, Character, Conduct and Results* (Philadelphia: National Publishing Co., 1870), 2:599-618; report of William H. Seward, Basler, *CWL*, 8:286-87n; *New York Times*, Feb. 6, 1865.

42. Richard N. Current, *The Lincoln Nobody Knows* (New York: Hill and Wang; 1963), 244-47; J.M. McPherson, *Battle Cry of Freedom*, 832 and n; Mark E. Neely Jr., *The Abraham Lincoln Encyclopedia* (New York: McGraw-Hill, 1982), 137.

43. Alex. H. Stephens, R.M.T. Hunter, and J.A. Campbell to the President of the Confederate States, Feb. 5, 1865, *OR*, ser. 1, vol. 46, pt. 2, 446.

44. To the Senate and House of Representatives, Feb. 5, 1865, Basler, *CWL*, 8:260-61.

45. Basler, *CWL*, 8:261n (Welles quotation); Francis Fessenden, *Life of William Pitt Fessenden* (Boston: Houghton, Mifflin, 1907), 2:8.

46. Donald, *Lincoln*, 560.

47. Abraham Lincoln to William Rosecrans, Feb. 17, 1863; Lincoln to Edwin M. Stanton and Henry W. Halleck, ca. June 27, 1863, both in Basler, *CWL*, 6:108, 352. In his 1861 inaugural address, Lincoln expressed the fear that if disunion was not checked it would lead eventually to anarchy in the North as well as in the South. Basler, *CWL*, 4:268.

48. Abraham Lincoln to Thomas C. Fletcher, Feb. 20, 27, 1865, Basler, *CWL*, 8:308, 319. Governor Fletcher told Lincoln that such a pacification policy would not end guerrilla warfare in Missouri. Nevertheless, the governor issued a proclamation designed to test the president's policy. Ibid., 8:319-20n. The procla-

mation, as Fletcher predicted, proved a dead letter. Disorganized guerrilla forces continued to plague Missouri, finally sputtering out during the summer of 1865. Michael Fellman, *Inside War: The Guerrilla Conflict in Missouri during the American Civil War* (New York and Oxford: Oxford Univ. Press, 1989), 231-34.

49. Gideon Welles, *Selected Essays by Gideon Welles: Civil War and Reconstruction,* Albert Mordell, comp. (New York: Twayne, 1959), 182-83. See also Gideon Welles, *Diary of Gideon Welles: Secretary of the Navy under Lincoln and Johnson* (Boston: Houghton Mifflin, 1911), 2:279.

50. George L. Stearns to Andrew Johnson, Jan. 16, 1865, Johnson, *JP,* 7:414-15, 415n; Sarah F. Hughes, ed., *Letters and Recollections of John Murray Forbes* (Boston: Houghton, Mifflin, 1899), 2:122-24. A proslavery man until Lincoln issued his Emancipation Proclamation, Holt had been a loyal supporter of the administration and was not considered a member of the Radical faction, though his sometimes vigorous prosecution of disloyal elements in the Union states led to conservative criticism. Allen Johnson and Dumas Malone, eds., *Dictionary of American Biography* (New York: Charles Scribner's Sons, 1928-), 9:182. Historians have assumed erroneously that James Speed was a Radical. Though an early supporter of emancipation, as late as 1863 Speed argued that it should come by means of state initiative, not federal action. Like Lincoln, he also supported a lenient restoration policy. Later, after Lincoln's death and President Johnson's failed reconstruction policy, Speed cooperated with the Radicals. Gary Lee Williams, "James and Joshua Speed: Lincoln's Kentucky Friends" (Ph.D. diss., Duke University, 1971), 127, 138, 181. For the view that Speed was a Radical, though appointed to balance the Cabinet on the conservative side, see Randall and Current, *Lincoln the President,* 277, 279. Lincoln also attempted to appoint Senator Edwin D. Morgan, a non-Radical, as secretary of treasury, but the New Yorker refused the office. *Welles Diary,* 2:240, 244. He then offered the position to Hugh McCulloch, a strong conservative, who accepted the appointment. Donald, *Lincoln,* 551.

51. For the Bramlette-Burbridge affair, see E. Merton Coulter, *The Civil War and Readjustment in Kentucky* (Chapel Hill: Univ. of North Carolina Press, 1926), 211-13, and Lowell H. Harrison, *The Civil War in Kentucky* (Lexington: Univ. Press of Kentucky, 1975), 77-78.

52. Basler, *CWL,* 8:242n; Thomas Cottman to Abraham Lincoln, March 15, 1865, Lincoln Papers; *New York Herald,* Jan. 22, 1865.

53. "Julian's Journal," 328; Daniel S. Dickinson to Lewis Cass, Sept. 26, 1864, in *Speeches, Correspondence, etc., of the late Daniel S. Dickinson of New York* (New York: G.P. Putnam & Sons, 1867), 2:658. Despite his state rights orientation, Dickinson supported federal emancipation. Harry J. Carman and Reinhard H. Luthin, *Lincoln and the Patronage* (New York: Columbia Univ. Press, 1943), 314-15.

54. *Washington Daily Morning Chronicle,* Jan. 4, 11, 12, Feb. 13, 1865.

55. *New York Times,* Feb. 24, 1865.

56. Ibid., Feb. 28, 1865.

57. *New York Tribune,* Feb. 23 (quotations), March 24, 27, 1865.

58. *New York Herald,* Jan. 10, Feb. 28, March 25, 1865. Though not reported in the North, Professor Samuel F. Phillips of the University of North Carolina expressed a growing Southern view that the South should accept Lincoln's terms as outlined in his reconstruction proclamation and in the Hampton Roads

conference. Immediate reunion, Phillips wrote a friend, would mean amnesty for all and gradual black emancipation "under the name of apprenticeship." Samuel F. Phillips to R. L. Patterson, March 1, 1865, Rufus L. Patterson Papers, North Carolina Division of Archives and History, Raleigh.

59. *New York Herald,* Jan. 22 (quotation), March 4, 1865. During the early weeks of 1865, the *Herald* devoted as much space in its editorial columns to the French threat on the Southern border and to former California Senator William M. Gwin's fanciful effort to carve out a "dukedom" in northwest Mexico as it did to the ending of the Civil War. This newspaper argued that the North and South should reunite immediately and send forces to counter the French designs and restore American influence in the area. The *Herald's* effort coincided with the failed mission of Francis Preston Blair, Sr., to Richmond to gain a restoration of the Union on that basis.

60. Nicolay and Hay, *Lincoln,* 10:84-85, quoting from Nicolay's Personal Memoranda. The italics are mine.

61. Donald, *Sumner,* 215; Edward L. Pierce, *Memoir and Letters of Charles Sumner* (Boston: Roberts Brothers, 1894), 4:236.

62. Nathaniel P. Banks to his wife, Feb. 24, 1865, Banks Papers; *Address of Hon. R. King Cutler, United States Senator of Louisiana to the Citizens of the State of Louisiana,* in Warmoth Pamphlets.

63. E. McPherson, *Political History of the Great Rebellion,* 581, 586.

64. U.S. Congress, 38th Cong., 2d sess., *Senate Report No. 127,* 2-3; Belz, *Reconstructing the Union,* 270.

65. *Address of Cutler,* 3, in Warmoth Pamphlets; E. McPherson, *Political History of the Great Rebellion,* 580-81.

66. Belz, *Reconstructing the Union,* 271-72; U.S. Congress, 38th Cong., 2d sess., *House Report No. 10.* The brief special session that convened in early March 1865 postponed seating a senator-elect from Arkansas and two newly elected Virginia senators, one of whom was the radical John C. Underwood who had been chosen for the six-year term vacated by Carlile. This action created division among Radicals in Congress, who had recognized the Restored Government of Virginia and wanted Underwood to augment their ranks in the Senate. Contributing to their dilemma, however, was the fact that the other Virginia senator-elect, Joseph E. Segar, was a conservative supporter of Lincoln's Southern policy, and had been selected to complete the unexpired term of Lemuel J. Bowden. Clippings from *Alexandria State Gazette,* Dec. 9, 1864, March 1865, in Underwood Papers; E. McPherson, *Political History of the Great Rebellion,* 588.

67. A.P. Field to Lincoln, March 16, 1865, Lincoln Papers; *Address of Cutler,* 5, in Warmoth Pamphlets.

68. Abraham Lincoln to Nathaniel P. Banks, April 5, 1865, Basler, *CWL,* 8:386 and n. For several weeks, Banks had been seeking Lincoln's approval to return to New Orleans and resume his old command. Nathaniel P. Banks to his wife, Feb. 14, 1865, Banks Papers.

69. *Resignation of Governor Hahn: His Farewell Message* (New Orleans: William H. Moore, 1865); McCrary, *Lincoln and Reconstruction,* 308; Nathaniel P. Banks to Montgomery Blair, May 6, 1865, Blair Family Papers. Hahn was selected to replace Charles Smith, whose Senate term expired on March 3.

70. Hugh Kennedy to Andrew Johnson, April 27, 1865; J. Madison Wells to Johnson, April 27, 1865, both in Johnson, *JP,* 8:647, 648-49; Stephen A. Hurlbut

to Abraham Lincoln, March 15, 1865, Lincoln Papers; Walter M. Lowrey, "The Political Career of James Madison Wells," *Louisiana Historical Quarterly* 31 (Oct. 1948): 1026, 1028; Nathaniel P. Banks to his wife, July 7, Aug. 2, 1865, Banks Papers.

71. Second Inaugural Address, March 4, 1865, Basler, *CWL,* 8:332-33.

72. Edwin M. Stanton to Ulysses S. Grant, March 3, 1865, *CWL,* 8:330-31 and 331n; Ward Hill Lamon, *Recollections of Abraham Lincoln, 1847-1865* (Chicago: A.C. McClurg, 1895), 245-46.

73. Entry for March 30, 1865, *Welles Diary,* 2:269.

74. Simpson, *Let Us Have Peace,* 69-74

75. *Memoirs of General William T. Sherman,* rev. ed. (New York: D. Appleton, 1913), 2:326.

76. *Sherman Memoirs,* rev. ed., 2:326-31 (quotation on 327). Admiral David D. Porter, who was present and made notes on the discussions, later confirmed Sherman's account regarding the president's instructions. Porter reported that General Grant remained silent through most of the conference, which suggested to him that the general agreed with Lincoln's position.

77. The Sherman-Johnston agreement is printed in *Sherman Memoirs,* rev. ed., 2:356-57.

78. *Nashville Daily Union,* April 25, 1865; Sam Milligan to Andrew Johnson, April 29, 1865, Johnson, *JP,* 7:664-65; *Chicago Tribune,* April 27, 1865.

79. John F. Marszalek, *Sherman: A Soldier's Passion for Order* (New York: Free Press, 1993), 347.

80. *New York Herald,* April 14, 1865; U.S. Grant to Edwin M. Stanton, April 24, 1865, Simon, ed., *Papers of Grant,* 14:432.

81. Abraham Lincoln to John A. Campbell, April 5, 1865, Basler, *CWL,* 8:386-87 and 387n.

82. Abraham Lincoln to Godfrey Weitzel, April 6, 1865, ibid., 8:389.

83. As quoted in Ambler, *Pierpont,* 256.

84. Abraham Lincoln to U.S. Grant, April 6, 1865, Basler, *CWL,* 8:388.

85. Godfrey Weitzel, *Richmond Occupied,* ed. and introduced by Louis H. Manarin (Richmond: Richmond Civil War Centennial Committee, n.d.), 57. Weitzel later wrote that "one of these papers came into the possession of General Sherman and led him into some difficulty with General Johnston in North Carolina." Ibid.

86. Julian, *Political Recollections,* 253-54.

87. *Alexandria Gazette,* April 10, 1865; *New York Herald,* April 14, 1865; Salmon P. Chase to Abraham Lincoln, April 11, 1865, in Jacob W. Schuckers, *Life and Public Services of Salmon Portland Chase* (New York: D. Appleton, 1874), 515.

88. Entry for April 13, 1865, *Welles Diary,* 2:279-80.

89. Abraham Lincoln to Francis H. Pierpont, April 10, 1865, Basler, *CWL,* 8:392. Pierpont's account of this conference appears in Ambler, *Pierpont,* 255-57, and Anna P. Siviter, *Recollections of War and Peace, 1861-1868,* ed. Charles H. Ambler (New York: G.P. Putnam's Sons, 1938), 136-42.

90. Abraham Lincoln to Godfrey Weitzel, April 12, 1862, Basler, *CWL,* 8:405; John A. Campbell to Godfrey Weitzel, April 7, 1865, *OR,* ser. 1, vol. 46, pt. 3, 657.

91. Abraham Lincoln to Godfrey Weitzel, April 12, 1862, Basler, *CWL,* 8:406-7.

92. Commager, *Documents of American History*, 1:451-52. For a revealing account of the Republican purposes behind the bill and the conditional nature of the land provision, see Herman Belz, "The Freedmen's Bureau Act of 1865 and the Principle of No Discrimination according to Color," *Civil War History* 21 (Sept. 1975): 197-217. The Bureau's operations in the South did not begin until the summer and fall of 1865. Though the Bureau provided important aid to impoverished former slaves and whites, it failed to shield blacks from discriminating laws and prejudiced officials, mainly because of the obstructionism of Lincoln's successor, Andrew Johnson. Donald G. Nieman, "Andrew Johnson, the Freedmen's Bureau, and the Problem of Equal Rights, 1865-1866," *Journal of Southern History* 44 (Aug. 1978): 399, 420.

93. As reported in the *Alexandria Gazette*, April 13, 1865. Adolphe de Chambrun, a French lawyer-journalist who was in Lincoln's company on several occasions in April, also reported that the president during this period was preoccupied with a desire "to recall the Southern States into the Union as soon as possible." Lincoln frequently "declared his firm resolution to stand for clemency against all opposition." Chambrun, *Impressions of Lincoln and the Civil War*, 84, 93.

94. *New York Times*, March 31, April 7, 1865.

95. *Baltimore American and Commercial Advertiser*, April 13, 1865.

96. *Washington Daily Morning Chronicle*, April 6, 1865.

97. *New York Tribune*, April 11, 1865.

98. *Chicago Tribune*, April 2 (quotation), 14, 1865.

99. *National Anti-Slavery Standard*, April 15, 1865.

100. Lamon, *Recollections of Lincoln*, 240-41.

101. J.M. McPherson, *Struggle for Equality*, 311; entry for April 11, 1865, David Donald, ed., *Inside Lincoln's Cabinet: The Civil War Diaries of Salmon P. Chase* (New York: Longmans, Green, 1954), 265.

102. Salmon P. Chase to the President, April 11, 1865, in Schuckers, *Chase*, 514-15.

103. William Hanchett, *The Lincoln Murder Conspiracies* (Urbana: Univ. of Illinois Press, 1983), 37.

104. Last Public Address, April 11, 1865, Basler, *CWL*, 8:399-400.

105. Ibid., 401-2.

106. Ibid., 402-3.

107. Ibid., 403-4.

108. Ibid., 404-5.

109. Abraham Lincoln to Thomas Cottman, Dec. 15, 1863, Basler, *CWL*, 7:66-67.

110. Lincoln's Annual Message to Congress, Dec. 8, 1863, Basler *CWL*, 7:51.

111. Abraham Lincoln to Stephen A. Hurlbut, Nov. 14, 1864, Basler, *CWL*, 8:106-7.

112. Entry for Nov. 1, 1863, Dennett, *Hay Diaries*, 113.

113. Abraham Lincoln to Horace Maynard, Feb. 13, 1864, Basler, *CWL*, 7:183 and n. Soon after the war, the legislature of the Restored Government of Virginia removed that state's stringent oath for voting.

114. Abraham Lincoln to Andrew Johnson, Sept. 11, 1863; Basler, *CWL*, 6:440.

115. *New York Times*, April 13, 1865. Chambrun, the French journalist-lawyer, reported that Lincoln's April 11 speech "called forth violent reactions" from

Radicals. Chambrun, *Impressions of Lincoln,* 94. Attorney General James Speed reportedly dissented from the view that the president had reaffirmed his conservative reconstruction policy. According to Salmon P. Chase, Speed on the day of Lincoln's death indicated that the president "never seemed so near our views" as he did earlier in the week at a Cabinet meeting. Speed, however, only cited Lincoln's withdrawal of his controversial offer for the Virginia legislature to reconvene as evidence for this change. Entry for April 15, 1865, Donald, *Chase Diaries,* 268.

116. Julian, *Political Recollections,* 255-56. Sumner was deeply depressed after reading Lincoln's speech. Pierce, *Sumner,* 4:236 and n.

117. *New Orleans Tribune,* April 6 (quotation), 19, 1865.

118. Entry for April 14, 1865, *Welles Diary,* 2:280-81.

119. Ibid., 281-82; Welles, *Selected Essays,* 190.

120. Entry for April 14, 1865, *Welles Diary,* 2:282; Welles, *Selected Essays,* 193.

121. Welles, *Selected Essays,* 191. Lincoln had not referred to a property qualification for voting in his April 11 address, as Welles suggests.

122. Earl Schenck Miers, ed., *Lincoln Day by Day: A Chronology, 1809-1865* (Washington, D.C.: Lincoln Sesquicentennial Commission, 1960), 3:329. This was only the first time that the president met with his new vice president after the inauguration, when Johnson was inebriated. Johnson, *JP,* 7:lxii.

123. Abraham Lincoln to James H. Van Alen, April 14, 1865, Basler, *CWL,* 8:413. Van Alen's letter to Lincoln has not been found. The italics are mine.

Epilogue

1. *Washington Daily Morning Chronicle,* April 17, 1865; John Ganson to Montgomery Blair, April 17, 1865, Blair Family Papers.

2. Chambrun, *Impressions of Lincoln,* 106.

3. Remarks to Illinois's Delegation, April 18, 1865; Speech to Indiana Delegation, April 21, 1865; Address to Loyal Southerners, April 24, 1865, all in Johnson, *JP,* 7:582-84, 610-15, 630-32; Charles Sumner to John Bright, April 18, 1865, in Pierce, *Sumner,* 4:239.

4. Entry for April 15?, 1865, in Pease and Randall, *Browning Diary,* 2:19.

5. Robert C. Winthrop to Count Circourt(?), May 18, 1865; John H. Clifford to Winthrop, May 28, 1865, both in Robert C. Winthrop Papers, Massachusetts Historical Society, Boston (microfilm).

6. Henry L. Dawes to Electra Dawes, April 16, 1865; "The Reconstruction Period, 1865-1869," unpublished manuscript in Dawes Papers.

7. Entry for April 15, 1865, "Julian's Journal," 335. Julian was also present in the meeting of Radical leaders with President Johnson on April 16. He is the source for the much-cited comment by Senator Wade: "Johnson, we have faith in you. By the gods, there will be no trouble now in running the government." Entry for April 16, 1865, ibid.

8. Entry for April 15, 1865, *Strong Diary,* 3:583-84.

9. *Chicago Tribune,* April 18 (quotation), 26, 27, 1865. The *Tribune* did not propose how the confiscated property should be distributed.

10. *Washington Daily Morning Chronicle,* May 15, 19, 1865. The *Chronicle* later retreated from its support for black suffrage.

11. *Nashville Daily Union,* April 29, 1865.

12. Ibid., May 17, 1865.

13. *Little Rock Unconditional Union,* April 20, 1865; *Little Rock National Democrat,* April 22, 1865.

14. *New Orleans Tribune,* April 22, 28, 1865.

15. Entry for April 17, 1865, in Nimrod Porter Books, 1819-1871, Southern Historical Collection, University of North Carolina, Chapel Hill; Thomas Cottman to Montgomery Blair, April 21, 1865, Blair Family Papers; *Nashville Daily Union,* April 16, 25, May 2, 1865; *Alexandria Gazette,* April 27, 28, 1865; *Little Rock Unconditional Union,* April 20, 1865.

16. Louis McKenzie to Francis H. Pierpont, April 17, 1865, *Calendar of Virginia State Papers,* 11:433. Of course, not all Confederates regretted Lincoln's assassination. Many expressed joy and wished that his death had occurred earlier. Emma LeConte of Columbia, South Carolina, reflected the bitterness of many defeated Confederates when she confided to her diary upon hearing the news of Lincoln's murder: "Sic semper tyrannis. Could there have been a fitter death for such a man"? Michael Davis, *The Image of Lincoln in the South* (Knoxville: Univ. of Tennessee Press, 1971), 99-100.

17. See, for example, *Little Rock Unconditional Union,* April 27, 1865.

18. For the political strength of former Whigs in the postwar South, see Alexander, "Persistent Whiggery in the Confederate South," 310-14.

19. Order Restoring Virginia, May 9, 1865, in Johnson, *JP,* 8:53; Lowe, *Republicans and Reconstruction in Virginia,* 26, 32-34; *New York Times,* June 23, 1865. In Texas, Lincoln's military governor, Andrew Jackson Hamilton, had failed during the war to reorganize a loyal government. On June 17, 1865, President Johnson appointed Hamilton provisional governor of the state.

20. Isaac Murphy and Others to Andrew Johnson, July 8, 1865, Johnson, *JP,* 8:373-74.

21. Andrew Johnson to Isaac Murphy, Oct. 30, 1865, in *The Papers of Andrew Johnson,* vol. 9, *September 1865-January 1866,* ed. Paul H. Bergeron (Knoxville: Univ. of Tennessee Press, 1991), 305; Sterling R. Cockrill to Andrew Johnson, March 26, 1865; Robert W. Johnson to Andrew Johnson, July 23, 1866, both in *The Papers of Andrew Johnson,* vol. 10, *February-July 1866* (Knoxville: Univ. of Tennessee Press, 1992), 309, 717-19.

22. Thomas B. Alexander, "Political Reconstruction in Tennessee," in Curry, *The Border States during Reconstruction,* 56-58; Francis C. Dunnington to Andrew Johnson, March 1, 1866, Sam Milligan to Johnson, March 29, 1866; R. Weakly Brown to Johnson, April 5, 1866, all in Johnson, *JP,* 10:201, 331, 356-57. One of the early targets of Brownlow radicals was U.S. District Judge Connally F. Trigg, a conservative Unionist appointed by Lincoln. Trigg's refusal to hear criminal and civil suits against East Tennessee Confederates aroused the ire of the radicals and contributed to the division over proscription. Connally F. Trigg to Oliver P. Temple, April 27, 1865, Oliver P. Temple Papers, Manuscript Division, Library of Congress.

23. Cox, *Lincoln and Black Freedom,* 134-35.

24. Lowery, "Wells," 1034. Historians have assumed that Johnson ordered Canby's removal. See Cox, *Lincoln and Black Freedom,* 138, and Tunnell, *Crucible of Reconstruction,* 96. Though Canby's action must have met Johnson's approval, no conclusive evidence has been found directly linking Banks's removal to the president. In his biography of Banks, Fred Harvey Harrington writes that the general

was deprived of his Louisiana command but remained in the army. Harrington, *Banks,* 168.

25. McCrary, *Lincoln and Reconstruction,* 315.

26. Indeed, until late summer Banks supported Johnson. Nathaniel P. Banks to Andrew Johnson, Sept. 8, 1865, Johnson, *JP,* 9:43-44; Nathaniel P. Banks to Mary, July 26, 1865, Banks Papers. Johnson's proclamation establishing provisional governments excluded the four states organized during the war.

27. J. Madison Wells to Andrew Johnson, July 3, 1865, Johnson, *JP,* 8:342.

28. Carl Schurz to Andrew Johnson, Sept. 4, 1865, in *Advice after Appomattox: Letters to Andrew Johnson, 1865-1866,* ed. Brooks D. Simpson, et al. (Knoxville: Univ. of Tennessee Press, 1987), 123-24; Johnson to J. Madison Wells, Sept. 18, 1865, Johnson, *JP,* 9:98 and n.

29. J. Madison Wells to Andrew Johnson, Sept. 23, 1865, ibid., 125-26 and n.

30. J. Madison Wells to Andrew Johnson, Oct. 6, 1865, ibid., 198-99 and n.; McCrary, *Lincoln and Reconstruction,* 334-36; *Appleton's Annual Cyclopedia, 1865,* 512-13. None of the parties participating in the election supported black suffrage. The enfranchisement of blacks was now a sine qua non for the Durant radicals and some members of the Banks-Hahn faction who did not participate in the election.

31. The alienation of the Conservative Union party, or the Banks-Hahn faction, which had staunchly supported Lincoln's reconstruction plan, was complete when the new legislature replaced Hahn and R. King Cutler as senators-elect.

32. Joe Gray Taylor, *Louisiana Reconstructed, 1863-1877* (Baton Rouge: Louisiana State Univ. Press, 1974), 82-83, 104; Tunnell, *Crucible of Reconstruction,* 106; Albert Voorhies and Andrew S. Herron to Andrew Johnson, July 28, 1866, Johnson, *JP,* 10:750, 752n.

33. Stampp, *Era of Reconstruction,* 215.

34. First Inaugural Address—Final Text, March 4, 1861, Basler, *CWL,* 4:271.

Bibliography

Manuscript Collections

Arkansas Historical Commission, Little Rock
C.C. Bliss Papers

Manuscript Department, Duke University Library, Durham, North Carolina
Campbell Family Papers
Oliver Coolidge Papers

Manuscript Division, Library of Congress, Washington, D.C.
Nathaniel P. Banks Papers
Blair Family Papers
Salmon P. Chase Papers
Henry L. Dawes Papers
Andrew Johnson Papers (microfilm)
Abraham Lincoln Papers (microfilm)
Thaddeus Stevens Papers
Oliver P. Temple Papers
Lyman Trumbull Papers
John C. Underwood Papers

Massachusetts Historical Society, Boston
Robert C. Winthrop Papers (microfilm)

National Archives, Washington, D.C.
Smith-Brady Special Commission Report, Records Group 94

North Carolina Division of Archives and History, Raleigh
Rufus L. Patterson Papers
Letterbook of Governor Zebulon B. Vance

The Historical Society of Pennsylvania, Philadelphia
Salmon P. Chase Papers

Southern Historical Collection, University of North Carolina, Chapel Hill
Edwin Ruffin Beckwith Papers
Thomas Bragg Diary
Joseph Fowler Papers
Nimrod Porter Books, 1819-71

Department of Special Collections, University Archives, Stanford University Libraries, Palo Alto, California
Frederick Steele Papers

Eugene C. Barker Texas History Center, University of Texas, Austin
Andrew Jackson Hamilton Papers

Virginia State Library, Richmond
Governor Francis H. Pierpont Letterbook, 1861-64
Papers of Francis H. Pierpont and the Restored Government of Virginia

Printed Federal and Confederate Documents

Congressional Globe, 1861-65.
Journal of the Congress of the Confederate States of America, 1861-1865. 6 vols. Washington, D.C.: GPO, 1904-5.
Official Records of the Union and Confederate Navies in the War of the Rebellion. Series I. 27 vols. Washington, D.C.: GPO, 1894-1917.
Testimony Taken by the Joint Select Committee to Inquire into the Condition of Affairs in the Late Insurrectionary States. Georgia. Vol. 1. Washington, D.C.: GPO, 1872.
U.S. Congress. *House Report No. 9,* 39th Cong., 1st sess.
———. *House Report No. 10,* 38th Cong., 2d sess.
———. *House Report No. 70,* 37the Cong., 2d sess.
———. "Protest from Charles Henry Foster in Relation to the Election of Jennings Pigott to Congress from the Second District of North Carolina." *House Miscellaneous Document No. 14,* 37th Cong., 3d sess.
———. *Senate Miscellaneous Document No. 2,* 38th Cong., 2d sess.
———. *Senate Miscellaneous Document No. 9,* 38th Cong., 2d sess.
———. *Senate Report No. 127,* 38 Cong., 2 sess.
———. "Report of the Adjutant General of the State of Arkansas, for the period of the late rebellion, and to November 1, 1866." *Senate Miscellaneous Documents No. 53,* 39th Cong., 2d sess.
U.S. *Supreme Court Reports,* John R. Bigelow v. Douglas F. Forrest, 9 Wallace (1870).

The War of the Rebellion: A Compilation of the Official Records of the Union and
    Confederate Armies. 73 vols., 128 parts. Washington, D.C.: GPO, 1880-
    1901. Cited as OR.

Printed State Documents

Arkansas. Journal of the Convention of Delegates of the People of Arkansas, Assembled
    at the Capitol, January 4, 1864; Also, Journals of the House of Representa-
    tives of the Sessions 1864, 1864-65, and 1865. Little Rock: Price and
    Barton, 1870.
———. Journal of the Senate of Arkansas, Sessions of 1864, 1864-65 and 1865.
    Little Rock: Price and Barton, 1870.
Louisiana. Journal of the House of Representatives of the State of Louisiana [1864-
    65]. New Orleans: W.R. Fish, 1865.
New York. Journal of the Senate of the State of New York: At Their Eighty-Seventh
    Session, Begun and Held at the Capitol, in the City of Albany, on the Fifth
    Day of January, 1864. Albany: Comstock & Cassidy, 1864.
Tennessee. Senate Journal of the First Session of the General Assembly of the State
    of Tennessee, Which Convened at Nashville, Monday, April 3 [1865].
    Nashville: S.C. Mercer, 1865.
Virginia. Constitution of the State of Virginia, and the Ordinances Adopted by the
    Convention Which Assembled at Alexandria on the 13th Day of February,
    1864. Alexandria: D. Turner, 1864.
———. Journal of the Constitutional Convention Which Convened at Alexandria on
    the 13th of February, 1864. Alexandria: D. Turner, 1864.
———. Journal of the House of Delegates, of the Commonwealth of Virginia, Extra
    Session, Held in the City of Wheeling, on Thursday, December the 4th, 1862.
    Wheeling: A.S. Trowbridge, 1862.
———. Journal of the House of Delegates of the State of Virginia, for the Extra Ses-
    sion, 1861. Wheeling: Daily Press Book and Job Office, 1861.

Newspapers

Alexandria Gazette, 1862-65.
Baltimore American and Commercial Advertiser, 1863-65.
Boston Daily Advertiser, 1863-64.
Boston Liberator, 1864-65.
Chattanooga Daily Gazette, 1864.
Chicago Tribune, 1863-65.
Knoxville Brownlow's Weekly Whig, 1861.
Knoxville Whig & Rebel Ventilator, 1864.
Little Rock National Democrat, 1863-65.
Little Rock Unconditional Union, 1864-65.
Louisville Daily Journal, 1863-65.
Lynchburg Virginian, 1863.

Nashville Daily Press, 1863-65.
Nashville Daily Union, 1863-65.
National Antislavery Standard, 1863-65.
New Bern Daily Progress, 1862.
New Bern North Carolina Times, 1864.
New Bern Semi-Weekly Progress, 1863.
New Orleans Bee, 1864.
New Orleans Daily True Delta, 1864.
New Orleans Picayune, 1864.
New Orleans Tribune, 1864-65.
New York Herald, 1865.
New York Principia, 1864.
New York Times, 1862-65.
New York Tribune, 1862-65.
New York World, 1862, 1864.
Raleigh North Carolina Weekly Standard, 1863
Richmond Sentinel, 1863.
St. Louis Missouri Republican, 1863-64.
Savannah Daily Republican, 1865.
Washington Constitutional Union, 1863-64.
Washington Daily Chronicle, 1862-65.
Washington Daily National Republican, 1864.
Washington National Intelligencer, 1862-64.
Washington Sunday Chronicle, 1863.

Contemporary Sources

Appleton's Annual Cyclopedia and Register of Important Events. 15 vols. New York: Appleton, 1861-75.

Banks, Nathaniel P. *The Reconstruction of States: Letter of Major-General Banks to Senator Lane.* New York: Harper & Brothers, 1865.

Basler, Roy P., ed. *The Collected Works of Abraham Lincoln.* 8 vols. and 2 supplements. New Brunswick, N.J.: Rutgers Univ. Press, 1953-55. Cited as Basler, *CWL.*

Beale, Howard K., ed. "The Diary of Edward Bates, 1859-1866." In *Annual Report of the American Historical Association for the Year 1930.* Vol. 4. Washington, D.C., 1930.

Berlin, Ira, et al., eds. *The Destruction of Slavery.* Series 1, vol. 1 of *Freedom: A Documentary History of Emancipation, 1861-1867: Selected from the Holdings of the National Archives of the United States.* Cambridge: Cambridge Univ. Press, 1985.

Bishop, Albert W. *Loyalty on the Frontier, or Sketches of Union Men of the South-West; With Incidents and Adventures in Rebellion on the Border.* St. Louis: R.P. Studley, 1863.

Blaine, James G. *Twenty Years of Congress: From Lincoln to Garfield with a Review of the Events Which Led to the Political Revolution of 1860.* 2 vols. Norwich, Conn.: Henry Bill, 1884-86.

Bokum, Herman. *The Testimony of a Refugee from East Tennessee.* Philadelphia, 1863.

Brownlow, William G. *Sketches of the Rise, Progress, and Decline of Secession; with a Narrative of Personal Adventures among the Rebels.* Philadelphia: George W. Childs, 1862.

Butler, Benjamin F. *Private and Official Correspondence of Gen. Benjamin F. Butler during the Period of the Civil War.* 5 vols. Norwood, Mass.: Plimpton Press, 1917.

Calendar of Virginia State Papers and Other Manuscripts, 1836-1869. 11 vols. Richmond: Virginia State Library, 1893.

Chambrun, Adolphe de. *Impressions of Lincoln and the Civil War: A Foreigner's Account.* Trans. Aldebert de Chambrun. New York: Random House, 1952.

Chase, Salmon P. Diary and Correspondence of Salmon P. Chase. *American Historical Association, Annual Report for the Year 1902.* Vol. 2. Washington, D.C., 1903.

Clemens, Jeremiah. *Letter from the Hon. Jere. Clemens.* Philadelphia: Union League of America, 1864.

Colyer, Vincent. *Report of the Services Rendered by the Freed People to the United States Army, in North Carolina, in the Spring of 1862, After the Battle of Newbern.* New York: Vincent Colyer, 1864.

Commager, Henry Steele, ed. *Documents of American History.* 8th ed. New York: Appleton-Century-Crofts, 1968.

Cox, Samuel S. *Three Decades of Federal Legislation, 1855 to 1885.* Freeport, N.Y.: Books for Libraries Press, 1970.

Crabtree, Beth G., and James W. Patton, eds. *"Journal of a Secesh Lady": The Diary of Catherine Ann Devereux Edmondston, 1860-1866.* Raleigh: North Carolina Division of Archives and History, 1979.

Cutler, R. King. *Address of Hon. R. King Cutler, United States Senator of Louisiana [1865].* In Henry Clay Warmoth Pamphlets, Davis Library, Univ. of North Carolina, Chapel Hill, vol. 2.

Davis, Henry Winter. *Letter of Thomas J. Durant to Hon. Henry Winter Davis.* New Orleans: H.P. Lathrop, 1864.

Dennett, Tyler, ed. *Lincoln and the Civil War in the Diaries and Letters of John Hay.* New York: Dodd, Mead, 1939.

Dickinson, Daniel S. *Speeches, Correspondence, etc., of the late Daniel S. Dickinson of New York.* 2 vols. New York: G.P. Putman & Sons, 1867.

Donald, David, ed. *Inside Lincoln's Cabinet: The Civil War Diaries of Salmon P. Chase.* New York: Longmans, Green, 1954.

Freidel, Frank, ed. *Union Pamphlets of the Civil War, 1861-1865.* 2 vols. Cambridge: Belknap Press of Harvard Univ. Press, 1967.

Gantt, E.W. *Address of Brig. Gen. E.W. Gantt, C.S.A., First Published October 7, 1863, at Little Rock, Arkansas.* New York, 1863.

Gilmore, James R. *Down in Tennessee, and Back by Way of Richmond.* New York: Carleton, 1864.

Gordon, George. *War Diary of Events in the War of the Great Rebellion, 1863-1865.* Boston: James G. Osgood, 1882.

Hahn, Michael. *Inaugural Address of Michael Hahn, Governor of the State of Louisiana, Delivered at New Orleans, March 4, 1864.* In Henry Clay Warmoth Pamphlets, Davis Library, University of North Carolina, Chapel Hill. Vol. 2.

————. *Resignation of Governor Hahn: His Farewell Message.* New Orleans: William H. Moore, 1865.

Haines, Z.T. *Letters from the Forty-Fourth Regiment M.V.M.: A Record of the Experience of a Nine-Months' Regiment in the Department of North Carolina in 1862-3, By "Corporal."* Boston: Herald Job Office, 1863.

Hamilton, A.J. *Letter of Gen. A.J. Hamilton of Texas, to the President of the United States.* New York: Loyal Publication Society, 1863.

————. *Speech of Gen. A.J. Hamilton, of Texas, at the War Meeting at Faneuil Hall, Saturday Evening, April 18, 1863.* Boston: T.R. Marvin & Son, 1863.

————. *Speech of Hon. Andrew Jackson Hamilton, of Texas, Late Representative of Texas, in the 36th Congress, on the Condition of the South under Rebel Rule, and the Necessity of Early Relief to the Union Men of Western Texas.* 1862.

Hughes, Sarah F., ed. *Letters and Recollections of John Murray Forbes.* 2 vols. Boston: Houghton, Mifflin, 1899.

Humphreys, D.C. *Address to the People of Alabama, by D.C. Humphreys,* 1864.

Hyman, Harold M., ed. *The Radical Republicans and Reconstruction, 1861-1870.* Indianapolis: Bobbs-Merrill, 1967.

Johnson, Andrew. *The Papers of Andrew Johnson.* Various editors. 12 vols. to date. Knoxville: Univ. of Tennessee Press, 1967-. Cited as Johnson, *JP.*

Julian, George W. "George W. Julian's Journal—Assassination of Lincoln." *Indiana Magazine of History* 11 (Dec. 1915): 324-37.

————. *Political Recollections, 1840 to 1872.* Chicago: Jansen, McClurg, 1884.

Lamon, Ward Hill. *Recollections of Abraham Lincoln, 1847-1865.* Chicago: A.C. McClurg, 1895.

Lewis, Virgil A., ed. *How West Virginia Was Made: Proceedings of the First Convention of the People of Northwestern Virginia at Wheeling, May 13, 14, and 15, 1861, and the Journal of the Second Convention of the People of Northwestern Virginia at Wheeling.* Charleston: State of West Virginia, 1909.

McPherson, Edward. *Political History of the United States of America, during the Great Rebellion.* 2d. ed. Washington, D.C.: Philp & Solomons, 1865.

Parton, James. *General Butler in New Orleans.* New York: Mason Brothers, 1864.

Pease, Theodore C., and James G. Randall, eds. *The Diary of Orville Hickman Browning.* 2 vols. Springfield: Illinois State Historical Library, 1925.

Pierce, Edward L. *Memoir and Letters of Charles Sumner.* 4 vols. Boston: Roberts Brothers, 1878-94.

Pierpont, Francis H. *Calendar of Francis Harrison Pierpont Letters and Papers in West Virginia Depositories.* Charleston: West Virginia Historical Records Survey, Works Progress Administration, 1940.

————. *Letter of Governor Peirpoint, to His Excellency the President and the Honorable Congress of the United States, on the Subject of Abuse of Military Power in the Command of General Butler in Virginia and North Carolina.* Washington, D.C.: McGill & Witherow, 1864.

————. *Reorganization of Civil Government: Speech of Governor Peirpoint, Delivered at Mechanics' Hall in the City of Norfolk on Thursday Evening, February 16th, 1865.* Norfolk? 1865.

Political Position of Thomas J. Durant. A Letter from Hon. A. P. Dostie, to Hon. Henry L. Dawes. New Orleans: Office of the True Delta, 1865.

Raymond, Henry J. *The Administration and the War: Remarks of Mr. H.J. Raymond of New York, at Wilmington, Delaware, November 6, 1863.* 1863?

Reese, George H., ed. *Proceedings of the Virginia State Convention of 1861, February 13-May 1.* 4 vols. Richmond: Virginia State Library, 1965.

Report of the Committee Who Visited Washington on the Affairs of Western Texas. New York: National War Committee of the Citizens of New York, 1862.

Rice, Allen Thorndike, ed. *Reminiscences of Abraham Lincoln by Distinguished Men of His Time.* New York: North American Review, 1888.

Sherman, William Tecumseh. *Memoirs of William T. Sherman,* rev. ed. 2 vols. New York: D. Appleton, 1913.

————. *Memoirs of Gen. W.T. Sherman, Written by Himself.* New York: Charles L. Webster, 1891.

Simon, John Y., ed. *The Papers of Ulysses S. Grant.* Vols. 10 and 14. Carbondale and Edwardsville: Southern Illinois Univ. Press, 1982, 1985.

Simpson, Brooks D., et al. *Advice after Appomattox: Letters to Andrew Johnson, 1865-1866.* Knoxville: Univ. of Tennessee Press, 1987.

Siviter, Anna P. *Recollections of War and Peace, 1861-1868.* Edited by Charles H. Ambler. New York: G.P. Putnam's Sons, 1938.

Stanly, Edward. *Letter from Hon. Edward Stanly, Military Governor of North Carolina, to Colonel Henry A. Gilliam, refuting certain charges and insinuations made by Hon. George E. Badger, in behalf of the Southern Confederacy.* New Bern, N.C., 1862.

————. *A Military Governor among Abolitionists: A Letter from Edward Stanly, to Charles Sumner.* New York, 1865.

Stephens, Alexander H. *A Constitutional View of the Late War between the States; Its Causes, Character, Conduct and Results.* 2 vols. Philadelphia: National Publishing Co., 1870.

Strong, George Templeton. *The Diary of George Templeton Strong.* 4 vols. New York: Macmillan, 1952.

[Sumner, Charles.] "Our Domestic Relations: Or, How to Treat the Rebel States." *Atlantic Monthly* 12 (Oct. 1863): 507-29.

————. *Works of Charles Sumner.* 15 vols. Boston: Lee and Shepard, 1875-83.

Thorpe, Francis N., ed. *The Federal and State Constitutions, Colonial Charters, and Other Organic Laws of the States, Territories, and Colonies Now or Heretofore Forming the United States of America.* 7 vols. Washington, D.C.: GPO, 1909.

Tilley, Nannie M., ed. *Federals on the Frontier: The Diary of Benjamin F. McIntyre, 1862-1864.* Austin: Univ. of Texas Press, 1963.

Weitzel, Godfrey. *Richmond Occupied.* Edited and introduced by Louis H. Manarin. Richmond: Civil War Centennial Committee, n.d.

Welles, Gideon. *Diary of Gideon Welles: Secretary of the Navy under Lincoln and Johnson.* Introduced by John T. Morse, Jr. 3 vols. Boston: Houghton Mifflin, 1911.

———. *Selected Essays by Gideon Welles: Civil War and Reconstruction.* Compiled by Albert Mordell. New York: Twayne, 1959.

Whiting, William. *The War Powers of the President and the Legislative Power of Congress in Relation to the Rebellion, Treason, and Slavery.* Boston: J.L. Shorey, 1862.

Secondary Accounts

Abbott, Richard H. *The Republican Party and the South, 1855-1877.* Chapel Hill: Univ. of North Carolina Press, 1986.

Alexander, Thomas B. "Persistent Whiggery in the Confederate South, 1860-1877." *Journal of Southern History* 27 (Aug. 1961): 305-29.

———. *Political Reconstruction in Tennessee.* Nashville: Vanderbilt Univ. Press, 1950.

———. *Thomas A.R. Nelson of East Tennessee.* Nashville: Tennessee Historical Commission, 1956.

Allardice, Bruce S. *More Generals in Gray.* Baton Rouge and London: Louisiana State Univ. Press, 1995.

Ambler, Charles H. *Francis H. Pierpont: Union Governor of Virginia and Father of West Virginia.* Chapel Hill: Univ. of North Carolina Press, 1937.

Ames, Susie M. "Federal Policy toward the Eastern Shore of Virginia in 1861." *Virginia Magazine of History and Biography* 69 (Oct. 1961): 432-59.

Appleton's Cyclopaedia of American Biography. 7 vols. New York: D. Appleton, 1887-1901.

Arnold, Isaac N. *The History of Abraham Lincoln and the Overthrow of Slavery.* Chicago: Clarke & Co., 1866.

Baxter, Maurice G. *Orville H. Browning: Lincoln's Friend and Critic.* Bloomington: Indiana Univ. Press, 1957.

Belz, Herman. *Emancipation and Equal Rights: Politics and Constitutionalism in the Civil War Era.* New York: W.W. Norton, 1978.

———. "The Etheridge Conspiracy of 1863: A Projected Conservative Coup." *Journal of Southern History* 36 (Nov. 1970): 549-67.

———. "The Freedman's Bureau Act of 1865 and the Principle of No Discrimination according to Color." *Civil War History* 21 (Sept. 1975): 197-217.

———. "Origins of Negro Suffrage during the Civil War." *Southern Studies* 17 (Summer 1978): 115-30.

———. *Reconstructing the Union: Theory and Policy during the Civil War.* Ithaca: Cornell Univ. Press, 1969.

Benedict, Michael Les. *A Compromise of Principle: Congressional Republicans and Reconstruction, 1863-1869.* New York: W.W. Norton, 1974.

Biographical Directory of the American Congress, 1774-1971. Washington, D.C.: GPO, 1971.

Blue, Frederick J. *Salmon P. Chase: A Life in Politics.* Kent, Ohio: Kent State Univ. Press, 1987.

Boritt, Gabor S. *Lincoln and the Economics of the American Dream.* Memphis: Memphis State Univ. Press, 1978.

Boritt, Gabor S., ed. *Lincoln the War President: The Gettysburg Lectures.* New York and Oxford: Oxford Univ. Press, 1992.

Bowen, David W. *Andrew Johnson and the Negro.* Knoxville: Univ. of Tennessee Press, 1989.

Brooks, Noah. *Washington in Lincoln's Time.* New York: Century, 1895.

Brown, Norman D. *Edward Stanly: Whiggery's Tar Heel "Conqueror."* University: Univ. of Alabama Press, 1974.

Bryan, Charles Faulkner. "The Civil War in East Tennessee: A Social, Political, and Economic Study." Ph.D. diss., University of Tennessee, 1978.

Bryan, T. Conn. *Confederate Georgia.* Athens: Univ. of Georgia Press, 1953.

Campbell, Stanley W. *The Slave Catchers: Enforcement of the Fugitive Slave Law, 1850-1860.* Chapel Hill: Univ. of North Carolina Press, 1968.

Capers, Gerald M. *Occupied City: New Orleans under the Federals, 1862-1865.* Lexington: Univ. Press of Kentucky, 1965.

Carman, Harry J., and Reinhard H. Luthin. *Lincoln and the Patronage.* New York: Columbia Univ. Press, 1943.

Cimprich, John. *Slavery's End in Tennessee, 1861-1865.* University: Univ. of Alabama Press, 1985.

Coulter, E. Merton. *The Civil War and Readjustment in Kentucky.* Chapel Hill: Univ. of North Carolina Press, 1926.

———. *William G. Brownlow: Fighting Parson of the Southern Highlands.* Chapel Hill: Univ. of North Carolina Press, 1937.

Cox, LaWanda. "From Emancipation to Segregation: National Policy and Southern Blacks." *Interpreting Southern History: Historiographical Essays in Honor of Sanford W. Higginbotham,* ed. John B. Boles and Evelyn Thomas. Baton Rouge: Louisiana State Univ. Press, 1987.

———. *Lincoln and Black Freedom: A Study in Presidential Leadership.* Columbia: Univ. of South Carolina Press, 1981.

Crofts, Daniel W. *Reluctant Confederates: Upper South Unionists in the Secession Crisis.* Chapel Hill: Univ. of North Carolina Press, 1989.

Current, Richard N. *The Lincoln Nobody Knows.* New York: Hill and Wang, 1963.
————. *Lincoln's Loyalists: Union Soldiers from the Confederacy.* Boston: Northeastern Univ. Press, 1992.

Curry, Richard O. *A House Divided: A Study of State Politics and Copperhead Movement in West Virginia.* Pittsburgh: Univ. of Pittsburgh Press, 1964.

Curry, Richard O., ed. *Radicalism, Racism, and Party Realignment: The Border States during Reconstruction.* Baltimore: Johns Hopkins Univ. Press, 1969.

Davis, Michael. *The Image of Lincoln in the South.* Knoxville: Univ. of Tennessee Press, 1971.

Dawson, Joseph G., III. *Army Generals and Reconstruction: Louisiana, 1862-1877.* Baton Rouge: Louisiana State Univ. Press, 1982.

Degler, Carl N. *The Other South: Southern Dissenters in the Nineteenth Century.* New York: Harper & Row, 1974.

Donald, David. *Charles Sumner and the Rights of Man.* New York: Alfred A. Knopf, 1970.
————. *Lincoln.* New York: Simon & Schuster, 1995.

Dorris, Jonathan T. *Pardon and Amnesty under Lincoln and Johnson: The Restoration of the Confederates to Their Rights and Privileges, 1861-1898.* Chapel Hill: Univ. of North Carolina Press, 1953.

Dougan, Michael B. *Confederate Arkansas: The People and Policies of a Frontier State in Wartime.* University: Univ. of Alabama Press, 1976.

Durham, Walter T. *Nashville, the Occupied City: The First Seventeen Months— February 16, 1862, to June 30, 1863.* Nashville: Tennessee Historical Society, 1985.

Durrill, Wayne K. *War of Another Kind: A Southern Community in the Great Rebellion.* New York and Oxford: Oxford Univ. Press, 1990.

Fehrenbacher, Don E. "The Making of a Myth: Lincoln and the Vice-Presidential Nomination of 1864." *Civil War History* 41 (Dec. 1995): 273-90.
————. *Prelude to Greatness: Lincoln in the 1850s.* Stanford: Stanford Univ. Press, 1962.

Fellman, Michael. *Inside War: The Guerrilla Conflict in Missouri during the American Civil War.* New York and Oxford: Oxford Univ. Press, 1989.

Fessenden, Francis. *Life of William Pitt Fessenden.* 2 vols. Boston: Houghton, Mifflin, 1907.

Fleming, Walter Lynwood. *Civil War and Reconstruction in Alabama.* New York: Columbia Univ. Press, 1905.
————. "The Peace Movement in Alabama during the Civil War." *South Atlantic Quarterly* 2 (1903): 114-24, 246-60.

Foner, Eric. *Reconstruction: America's Unfinished Revolution, 1863-1877.* New York: Harper & Row, 1988.

Foner, Philip S. *The Civil War, 1861-1865.* Vol. 3 of *The Life and Writings of Frederick Douglass.* New York: International, 1952.

Foote, Shelby. *The Civil War, a Narrative: Red River to Appomattox.* New York: Random House, 1974.

Hahn, Steven. *The Roots of Southern Populism: Yeoman Farmers and the Transformation of the Georgia Upcountry.* New York and Oxford: Oxford Univ. Press, 1983.

Hall, Clifton R. *Andrew Johnson, Military Governor of Tennessee.* Princeton: Princeton Univ. Press, 1916.

Hanchett, William. *The Lincoln Murder Conspiracies.* Urbana: Univ. of Illinois Press, 1983.

Harrington, Fred Harvey. *Fighting Politician: Major General N.P. Banks.* 1948. Westport, Conn.: Greenwood Press, 1970.

Harris, William C. "Andrew Johnson's 'First Swing around the Circle': His Northern Campaign of 1863." *Civil War History* 35 (June 1989): 153-71.

———. "Conservative Unionists and the Presidential Election of 1864." *Civil War History* 38 (Dec. 1992): 298-318.

———. "The East Tennessee Relief Movement of 1864-1865." *Tennessee Historical Quarterly* 48 (Summer 1989): 86-96.

———. "East Tennessee's Civil War Refugees and the Impact of the War on Civilians." *Journal of East Tennessee History* 64 (1992): 3-19.

———. "Lincoln and Wartime Reconstruction in North Carolina." *North Carolina Historical Review* 53 (April 1986): 149-68.

———. "The Southern Unionist Critique of the Civil War." *Civil War History* 31 (March 1985): 39-56.

———. *William Woods Holden: Firebrand of North Carolina Politics.* Baton Rouge: Louisiana State Univ. Press, 1987.

Harrison, Lowell. *The Civil War in Kentucky.* Lexington: Univ. Press of Kentucky, 1975.

Hesseltine, William B. *Lincoln's Plan of Reconstruction.* Tuscaloosa: Confederate, 1960.

———. *Lincoln and the War Governors.* Gloucester, Mass.: Peter Smith, 1972.

Hooper, Ernest Walter. "Memphis, Tennessee: Federal Occupation and Reconstruction, 1862-1870." Ph.D. diss., Univ. of North Carolina, Chapel Hill, 1957.

Humes, Thomas W. *The Loyal Mountaineers of Tennessee.* Knoxville: Ogden Brothers, 1888.

Hyman, Harold M. *A More Perfect Union: The Impact of the Civil War and Reconstruction on the Constitution.* New York: Alfred A. Knopf, 1973.

Johns, John E. *Florida during the Civil War.* Gainesville: Univ. of Florida Press, 1963.

Johnson, Allen, and Dumas Malone, eds. *Dictionary of American Biography.* 20 vols., plus supplements. New York: Charles Scribner's Sons, 1928-.

Johnson, Ludwell H. *The Red River Campaign: Politics and Cotton in the Civil War.* Baltimore: Johns Hopkins Univ. Press, 1958.

Kerby, Robert L. *Kirby Smith's Confederacy: The Trans-Mississippi South, 1863-1865.* New York: Columbia Univ. Press, 1972.

Klingberg, Frank W. *The Southern Claims Commission.* Berkeley and Los Angeles: Univ. of California Press, 1955.

Long, David E. *The Jewel of Liberty: Abraham Lincoln's Re-Election and the End of Slavery.* Mechanicsburg, Pa.: Stackpole Books, 1994.

Lowe, Richard G. "Another Look at Reconstruction in Virginia." *Civil War History* 32 (March 1986): 56-76.

————. *Republicans and Reconstruction in Virginia, 1856-70.* Charlottesville: Univ. of Virginia Press, 1991.

Lowrey, Walter M. "The Political Career of James Madison Wells." *Louisiana Historical Quarterly* 31 (Oct. 1948): 995-1117.

McCrary, Peyton. *Abraham Lincoln and Reconstruction: The Louisiana Experiment.* Princeton: Princeton Univ. Press, 1978.

McFeely, William S. *Frederick Douglass.* New York: W.W. Norton, 1991.

McGregor, James C. *The Disruption of Virginia.* New York: Macmillan, 1922.

McMillan, Malcolm C. *The Disintegration of a Confederate State: Three Governors and Alabama's Wartime Home Front, 1861-1865.* Macon, Ga.: Mercer Univ. Press, 1986.

McPherson, James M. *Abraham Lincoln and the Second American Revolution.* New York: Oxford Univ. Press, 1991.

————. *Battle Cry of Freedom: The Civil War Era.* New York and Oxford: Oxford Univ. Press, 1988.

————. *The Struggle for Equality: Abolitionists and the Negro in the Civil War and Reconstruction.* Princeton: Princeton Univ. Press, 1964.

Maness, Lonnie E. "Emerson Etheridge and the Union." *Tennessee Historical Quarterly* 48 (Summer 1989): 97-110.

Marszalek, John F. *Sherman: A Soldier's Passion for Order.* New York: The Free Press, 1993.

Marten, James. *Texas Divided: Loyalty and Dissent in the Lone Star State, 1856-1874.* Lexington: Univ. Press of Kentucky, 1988.

Maslowski, Peter. *Treason Must Be Made Odious: Military Occupation and Wartime Reconstruction in Nashville, Tennessee, 1862-65.* Millwood, N.Y.: KTO Press, 1978.

Miers, Earl Schenck, ed. *Lincoln Day by Day: A Chronology, 1809-1865.* 3 vols. Washington, D.C.: Sesquicentennial Commission, 1960.

Mobley, Joe A. *James City: A Black Community in North Carolina, 1863-1900.* Raleigh: North Carolina Division of Archives and History, 1981.

Neely, Mark E., Jr. *The Abraham Lincoln Encyclopedia.* New York: McGraw-Hill, 1982.

————. *The Fate of Liberty: Abraham Lincoln and Civil Liberties.* New York and Oxford: Oxford Univ. Press, 1991.

————. "The Lincoln Theme since Randall's Call: The Promises and Perils of Professionalism." *Papers of the Abraham Lincoln Association* 1 (1979): 10-70.

Nevins, Allan. *War for the Union: The Organized War, 1863-1864.* New York: Charles Scribner's Sons, 1971.

Nicolay, John G., and John Hay. *Abraham Lincoln: A History.* 10 vols. New York: Century, 1890.

Nieman, Donald G. "Andrew Johnson, the Freedmen's Bureau, and the Problem of Equal Rights." *Journal of Southern History* 44 (Aug. 1978): 399-420.

Oates, Stephen B. *Abraham Lincoln: The Man Behind the Myths.* New York: Harper & Row, 1984.

———. *With Malice toward None: The Life of Abraham Lincoln.* New York: Harper & Row, 1977.

O'Connor, Thomas H. "Lincoln and the Cotton Trade." *Civil War History* 7 (March 1961): 20-35.

Paludan, Phillip S. *"A People's Contest": The Union and the Civil War, 1861-1865.* New York: Harper & Row, 1988.

———. *The Presidency of Abraham Lincoln.* Lawrence: Univ. of Kansas Press, 1994.

Parks, Joseph H. "Memphis under Military Rule, 1862 to 1865." *East Tennessee Historical Society Publications* 14 (1942): 31-59.

Parrish, William E. *Turbulent Partnership: Missouri and the Union, 1861-1865.* Columbia: Univ. of Missouri Press, 1963.

Patton, James W. *Unionism and Reconstruction in Tennessee, 1860-1869.* Chapel Hill: Univ. of North Carolina Press, 1934.

Peabody, Charles A. "The United States Provisional Court for the State of Louisiana, 1862-1865." *Annual Report of the American Historical Association for the Year 1892.* Washington, D.C.: GPO, 1893.

Pearson, Henry G. *Life of John A. Andrew.* 2 vols. Boston: Houghton, Mifflin, 1904.

Potter, David M. *The Impending Crisis, 1848-1861.* Completed and edited by Don E. Fehrenbacher. New York: Harper & Row, 1976.

Quarles, Benjamin. *The Negro in the Civil War.* 2d ed. Boston: Little, Brown, 1969.

Queener, Vernon M. "The Origins of the Republican Party in East Tennessee." *East Tennessee Historical Society Publications* 13 (1941): 66-90.

Randall, James G. *Lincoln and the South.* Baton Rouge: Louisiana State Univ. Press, 1946.

Randall, James G., and Richard N. Current. *Lincoln the President: Last Full Measure.* New York: Dodd, Mead, 1955.

Schouler, William. *A History of Massachusetts in the Civil War.* Boston: E.P. Dutton, 1868.

Schuckers, Jacob W. *Life and Public Services of Salmon Portland Chase.* New York: D. Appleton, 1874.

Searcher, Victor. *Lincoln Today: An Introduction to Modern Lincolniana.* New York: Thomas Yoseloff, 1969.

Shofner, Jerrell H. *Nor Is It Over Yet: Florida in the Era of Reconstruction, 1863-1877.* Gainesville: Univ. Presses of Florida, 1974.

Simpson, Brooks D. *Let Us Have Peace: Ulysses S. Grant and the Politics of War and Reconstruction, 1861-1868.* Chapel Hill: Univ. of North Carolina Press, 1991.

Smith, William Ernest. *The Francis Preston Blair Family in Politics.* 2 vols. New York: Macmillan, 1933.

Smyrl, Frank H. "Texans in the Union Army, 1861-1865." *Southwestern Historical Quarterly* 65 (Oct. 1961): 234-50.

Stampp, Kenneth M. *The Era of Reconstruction, 1865-1877.* New York: Alfred A. Knopf, 1965.

Staples, Thomas S. *Reconstruction in Arkansas, 1862-1874.* New York: Columbia University, 1923.

Syrett, John. "The Confiscation Acts: Efforts at Reconstruction during the Civil War." Ph.D. diss., Univ. of Wisconsin, 1971.

Taylor, Joe Gray. *Louisiana Reconstructed, 1863-1877.* Baton Rouge: Louisiana State Univ. Press, 1974.

Temple, Oliver P. *East Tennessee and the Civil War.* 1899. Freeport, N.Y.: Books for Libraries Press, 1971.

———. *Notable Men of Tennessee, From 1833 to 1875: Their Times and Their Contemporaries.* New York: Cosmopolitan Press, 1912.

Thomas, Benjamin P., and Harold M. Hyman. *Stanton: The Life and Times of Lincoln's Secretary of War.* New York: Alfred A. Knopf, 1962.

Thomas, Emory M. *The Confederate Nation, 1861-1865.* New York: Harper & Row, 1979.

Thornton, J. Mills, III. *Politics and Power in a Slave Society: Alabama, 1800-1860.* Baton Rouge: Louisiana State Univ. Press, 1978.

Trefoussee, Hans L. *Andrew Johnson: A Biography.* New York: W.W. Norton, 1989.

———. *The Radical Republicans: Lincoln's Vanguard for Racial Justice.* New York: Alfred A. Knopf, 1969.

Tregle, Joseph G., Jr. "Thomas J. Durant, Utopian Socialism, and the Failure of Presidential Reconstruction in Louisiana." *Journal of Southern History* 45 (Nov. 1979): 485-512.

Tunnell, Ted. *Crucible of Reconstruction: War, Radicalism and Race in Louisiana, 1862-1877.* Baton Rouge: Louisiana State Univ. Press, 1984.

Voegeli, V. Jacque. *Free but Not Equal: The Midwest and the Negro during the Civil War.* Chicago: Univ. of Chicago Press, 1967.

Waller, John L. *Colossal Hamilton of Texas: A Biography of Andrew Jackson Hamilton.* El Paso: Texas Western Press, 1968.

Warner, Ezra J. *Generals in Blue: Lives of the Union Commanders.* Baton Rouge: Louisiana State Univ. Press, 1964.

Warren, Louis Austin. *Lincoln's Parentage and Childhood.* New York and London: Century, 1926.

Williams, Gary Lee. "James and Joshua Speed: Lincoln's Kentucky Friends." Ph.D. diss., Duke University, 1971.

Woods, James M. *Rebellion and Realignment: Arkansas's Road to Secession.* Fayetteville: Univ. of Arkansas Press, 1987.

Index

Note: Page numbers appearing in italic type refer to pages that contain photographs.